4/24

THE
KINGDOM,
THE POWER,
AND THE GLORY

Also by Tim Alberta

*American Carnage: On the Front Lines of the Republican
Civil War and the Rise of President Trump*

THE
KINGDOM,
THE POWER,
AND THE GLORY

American Evangelicals in an
Age of Extremism

TIM ALBERTA

HARPER
An Imprint of HarperCollinsPublishers

HarperCollins books may be purchased for educational, business, or sales promotional use. For information, please email the Special Markets Department at SPsales@harper collins.com.

FIRST EDITION

Library of Congress Cataloging-in-Publication Data has been applied for.

ISBN 978-0-06-322688-3

24 25 26 27 28 LBC 11 10 9 8 7

IN LOVING MEMORY OF "POP"

REVEREND RICHARD J. ALBERTA

A SINNER, LIKE HIS SONS

And the devil, taking Him up onto a high mountain, showed unto Him all the kingdoms of the world in a moment of time.

And the devil said unto Him, "All this power will I give Thee, and the glory of them; for this has been delivered unto me, and to whomsoever I will, I give it. If Thou therefore wilt worship me, all shall be Thine."

And Jesus answered and said unto him, "Get thee behind Me, Satan! For it is written: 'Thou shalt worship the Lord thy God, and Him only shalt thou serve.'"

—LUKE 4:5–8 (KJ21)

CONTENTS

x　　　　　　　　　　*Contents*

THE
KINGDOM,
THE POWER,
AND THE GLORY

PROLOGUE

It was July 29, 2019—the worst day of my life, though I didn't know that quite yet.

The traffic in downtown Washington, D.C., was inching along. The mid-Atlantic humidity was sweating through the windows of my chauffeured car. I was running late and fighting to stay awake. For two weeks I'd been sprinting between television and radio studios up and down the East Coast, promoting my new book on the collapse of the post–George W. Bush Republican Party and the ascent of Donald Trump. Now I had one final interview for the day. My publicist had offered to cancel—it wasn't that important, she said—but I didn't want to. It *was* that important. When the car pulled over on M Street Northwest, I hustled inside the stone-pillared building of the Christian Broadcasting Network.

All in a blur, the producers took my cell phone, mic'd me up, and shoved me onto the set with news anchor John Jessup. Camera rolling, Jessup skipped past the small talk. He was keen to know, given his audience, what I had learned about the president's alliance with America's white evangelicals. Despite being a lecherous, impenitent scoundrel—the 2016 campaign marked by his mocking of a disabled man, his xenophobic slander of immigrants, his casual calls to violence against political opponents—Trump had won a historic 81 percent of those white evangelical voters. But, as I'd written in the book, that statistic was just a surface-level indicator of the foundational shifts taking place inside the Church. A relationship that was once nakedly transactional—Christians trading their support, sans enthusiasm, in return for specific

policies—had morphed into something else entirely. Trump was no longer "the lesser of two evils," a grin-and-bear-it alternative to four years
of President Hillary Clinton and three pro-choice Supreme Court justices. Polling showed that born-again Christian conservatives, once the
president's softest backers, were now his most unflinching advocates.
Jessup had the same question as millions of other Americans: *Why?*

As a believer in Jesus Christ—and as the son of an evangelical minister, raised in a conservative church in a conservative community—I
had long struggled with how to answer this question. It would have been
easy to say something like: "Well, John, most evangelicals are craven
hypocrites who adhere only to selective biblical teachings, wield their
faith as a weapon of cultural warfare, and only pretend to care about
righteousness when it suits their political interests. So, it's no surprise
they would ally themselves with the likes of Donald Trump!"

But that wouldn't be fair. It wouldn't be accurate. The truth is, I knew
lots of Christians who to varying degrees supported the president, and
there was no summarily describing their diverse attitudes, motivations,
and behaviors. They were best understood as points plotted across a vast
spectrum. At one end were the Christians who maintained their dignity
while voting for Trump—people who were clear-eyed in understanding
that backing a candidate, pragmatically and prudentially, need not lead
to unconditionally promoting, empowering, and apologizing for that
candidate. At the opposite end were the Christians who willfully jetti-
soned their credibility while voting for Trump—people who embraced
the charge of being reactionary hypocrites, still fuming about Bill Clinton's character as they jumped at the chance to go slumming with a
playboy turned president. Most of the Christians I knew fell somewhere
in the middle. They had all to some extent been seduced by the cult of
Trumpism: convinced of the false choices that accompanied his rise,
drained of certain convictions in the name of others, infected with a
relativism that rendered once-firm standards suddenly quite malleable.
Yet to composite all of these people into a caricature was misleading.
Something more profound was taking place. Something was happening in the country—something was happening in the Church—that we
had never seen before. I had attempted, ever so delicately, to make these
points in my book. Now, on the TV set, I was doing a similar dance.

Jessup seemed to sense my reticence. Pivoting from the book, he asked me about a recent flare-up in the evangelical world. In response to the Trump administration's policy of forcibly separating migrant families at the U.S.-Mexico border, Russell Moore, a prominent leader with the Southern Baptist Convention, tweeted, "Those created in the image of God should be treated with dignity and compassion, especially those seeking refuge from violence back home." At this, Jerry Falwell Jr.—son and namesake of the Moral Majority founder, and then-president of Liberty University, one of the world's largest Christian colleges—took great offense. "Who are you @drmoore?" he replied. "Have you ever made a payroll? Have you ever built an organization of any type from scratch? What gives you authority to speak on any issue?"

This being Twitter and all, I decided to chime in. "There are Russell Moore Christians and Jerry Falwell Jr. Christians," I wrote, summarizing the back-and-forth. "Choose wisely, brothers and sisters."

Now Jessup was reading my tweet on-air. "Do you really see evangelicals divided into two camps?" the anchor asked.

I stumbled a bit. Conceding that it might be an "oversimplification," I warned still of a "fundamental disconnect" between Christians who view issues through the eyes of Jesus versus Christians who process everything through a partisan political filter.

It was painful. As the interview wound down, I knew I'd botched an opportunity to state plainly my qualms about the American Church. Truth be told, I *did* see evangelicals divided into two camps—one side faithful to an eternal covenant, the other side seduced by earthly idols of nation and influence and exaltation—but I was too scared to say so. My own Christian walk had been so badly flawed. And besides, I'm no theologian; Jessup was asking for my journalistic analysis, not my biblical exegesis. Better to leave the heavy lifting to the professionals.

Walking off the set, I wondered if my dad might catch that clip. Surely somebody at our home church would see it and pass it along. I grabbed my phone, then stopped to chat with Jessup and a few of his colleagues. As we said our farewells, I looked down at the phone, which had been silenced. There were multiple missed calls from my wife and oldest brother. Dad had collapsed from a heart attack. There was nothing the surgeons could do. He was gone.

*   *   *

THE LAST TIME I SAW HIM WAS NINE DAYS EARLIER. THE CEO OF *POLITICO*, my employer at the time, had thrown a book party at his Washington manor, and Mom and Dad weren't going to miss that. They jumped in their Chevy and drove out from my childhood home in southeast Michigan. When he sauntered into the event, my old man looked out of place—a rumpled Midwestern minister, baggy shirt stuffed into his stained khakis, rubbing elbows with Beltway power brokers in their customized cuff links—but before long he was the star of the show, holding court with diplomats and Fortune 500 lobbyists, making them howl with irreverent one-liners. It was like a Rodney Dangerfield flick come to life. At one point, catching sight of my agape stare, he peeked over, gave an exaggerated wink, then delivered a punch line for his captive audience.

It was the high point of my career. The book was getting lots of buzz; already I was being urged to write a sequel. Dad was proud—very proud, he assured me—but he was also uneasy. For months, with the book launch drawing closer, he had been urging me to reconsider the focus of my reporting career. Politics, he kept saying, was a "sordid, nasty business," a waste of my time and God-given talents. Now, in the middle of the book party, he was taking me by the shoulder, asking a congressman to excuse us for just a moment. Dad put his arm around me and leaned in.

"You see all these people?" he asked.

"Yeah." I nodded, grinning at the validation.

"Most of them won't care about you in a week," he said.

The record scratched. My moment of rapture was interrupted. I cocked my head sideways and smirked at him. Neither of us said anything. I was bothered. The longer we stood there in silence, the more bothered I became. Not because he was wrong. But because he was right.

"Remember," Dad said, smiling. "On this earth, all glory is fleeting."

Now, as I raced to Reagan National Airport and boarded the first available flight to Detroit, his words echoed throughout my entire body. There was nothing contrived about Dad's final admonition to me. That is what he believed; that is who he was.

Once a successful New York financier, Richard J. Alberta had become a born-again Christian in 1977. Despite having a nice house, beautiful wife, and healthy firstborn son, he felt a rumbling emptiness. He couldn't sleep. He developed a debilitating anxiety. Religion hardly seemed like the solution; Dad came from a broken and unbelieving home. He had decided, halfway through his undergraduate studies at Rutgers University, that he was an atheist. And yet, one weekend while visiting family in the Hudson Valley, my dad agreed to attend church with his niece, Lynn. He became a new person that day. His angst was quieted. His doubts were overwhelmed. Taking communion for the first time at Goodwill Church in Montgomery, New York, he prayed to acknowledge Jesus as the son of God and accept Him as his personal savior.

Dad became unrecognizable to those who knew him. He rose early, hours before work, to read the Bible, filling a yellow legal pad with verses and annotations. He sat silently for hours in prayer. My mom thought he'd lost his mind. A budding young journalist who worked under Howard Cosell at ABC Radio in New York, Mom was suspicious of all this Jesus talk. But her maiden name—Pastor—was proof of God's sense of humor. Soon she accepted Christ, too. When Dad felt he was being called to abandon his finance career and enter the ministry, he met with Pastor Stewart Pohlman at Goodwill. As they prayed in Pastor Stew's office, Dad says he physically felt the spirit of the Lord swirling around him, filling up the room. He was not given to phony supernaturalism—in fact, Dad might've been the most intellectually sober, reason-based Christian I've ever known—but that day, he felt certain, the Lord anointed him. Soon he and Mom were selling every material item they owned, forsaking their high-salaried jobs in New York and moving to Massachusetts so he could study at Gordon-Conwell Theological Seminary.

For the next few decades, they toiled in small churches here and there, living off food stamps and the generosity of fellow believers. By the time I arrived in 1986, Dad was Pastor Stew's associate at Goodwill. We lived in the church parsonage; my nursery was the library, where towers of leather-wrapped tomes had been collected by the church's pastors dating back to the mid-eighteenth century. A few years later we moved to Michigan, and Dad eventually put down roots at a recent start-up, Cornerstone Church, in the Detroit suburb of Brighton. It was part of a minor denomination called the Evangelical Presbyterian Church (EPC) and it was there, for the next twenty-six years, that he served as senior pastor.

Cornerstone was our home. Because Mom also worked on staff, leading the women's ministry, I was quite literally raised inside the church: playing hide-and-seek in storage areas, doing homework in the office wing, bringing high school dates to Bible study, even working as the church janitor during a year of community college. I hung around the church so much that I decided to leave my mark: At nine years old, I used a pocket knife to etch my initials into the brickwork of the narthex.

Cornerstone wasn't a perfect church. The older I got, the more skeptical I'd grown of certain individuals and attitudes and activities there. But it was *my* church. The last time I'd been there, eighteen months earlier, I'd spoken to a packed sanctuary at Dad's retirement ceremony, armed with good-natured needling and PG-13 anecdotes. Now I would need to give a very different speech.

Arriving at home, I met Mom in the entryway. She buckled into my arms. The high school sweethearts were a few months from celebrating their fiftieth wedding anniversary. We held each other in that entryway for a long time. Finally, I suggested she get some rest. Keeping Mom steady as we climbed the staircase, I could still smell Dad's aftershave.

When we reached the master bedroom, I noticed the door across the hall was swung open. It was Dad's study. I reached in and flicked the light switch. There, on a coffee table in front of the small sofa, was a Bible and yellow legal pad. We walked over and sat on the sofa. The pen he'd used hours earlier rested atop the legal pad. There were scribbled notes and observations. But at the very top of the page, in his most careful penmanship, Dad had written one verse: "Do not cast me away when I am old; do not forsake me when my strength is gone." Mom and I looked up at one another. In his final hours on earth, my father, who was seventy-one years old, had been meditating on Psalm 71.

I tucked her into bed. We said a prayer. Then I turned off the lights and walked down the hall, opening the door to my childhood bedroom. Unfolding my laptop, I tried to get started on a eulogy. But the words would not come. I shut the laptop, lay down, and wept.

* * *

STANDING IN THE BACK OF THE SANCTUARY, MY THREE OLDER BROTH-
ers and I formed a receiving line. Cornerstone had been a small church
when we arrived as kids. Not anymore. Brighton, once a sleepy town
situated at the intersection of two expressways, had become a prized
location for commuters to Detroit and Ann Arbor. Meanwhile, Dad,
with his baseball allegories and Greek linguistics lessons, had gained
a reputation for his eloquence in the pulpit. By the time I moved away
in 2008, Cornerstone had blossomed from a few hundred members to a
few thousand.

Now the crowds swarmed around us, filling the sanctuary and spilling out into the narthex, where tables displayed flowers and golf clubs
and photos of Dad. I was numb. My brothers, too. None of us had slept
much that week. So the first time someone made a glancing reference to
Rush Limbaugh, it did not compute. But then another person brought
him up. And then another. That's when I connected the dots. Apparently, the king of conservative talk radio had been name-checking me
on his program recently—"A guy named Tim Alberta"—and describing
the unflattering revelations in my book about President Trump. Nothing in that moment could have mattered to me less. I smiled, shrugged,
and thanked them for coming to the visitation.

They kept on coming. More than I could count. People from the
church—people I'd known my entire life—were greeting me, not primarily with condolences or encouragement or mourning, but with
commentary about Rush Limbaugh and Donald Trump. Some of it was
playful, guys remarking how I was the same mischief-maker they'd
known since kindergarten. But some of it *wasn't* playful. Some of it was
angry; some of it was cold and confrontational. One man questioned
whether I was truly a Christian. Another asked if I was still on "the right
side." All while Dad was in a box a hundred feet away.

It got to the point where I had to take a walk. A righteous anger was
beginning to pierce the fog of melancholy. It felt like a bad dream inside
of a bad dream. Here, in our house of worship, people were taunting me
about politics as I tried to mourn my father. I was in the company of
certain friends that day who would not claim to know Jesus, yet they

shrouded me in peace and comfort. Some of these card-carrying evangelical Christians? Not so much. They didn't see a hurting son; they saw a vulnerable adversary.

That night, while fine-tuning the eulogy I would give the following afternoon, I still felt the sting. My wife perceived as much. The unflappable one in the family, she encouraged me to be careful with my words and cautioned against mentioning the day's unpleasantness. I took half of her advice.

In front of an overflow crowd on August 2, 2019, I paid tribute to the man who taught me everything—how to throw a baseball, how to be a gentleman, how to trust and love the Lord. Reciting my favorite verse, from Paul's second letter to the early church in Corinth, Greece, I told of Dad's instruction to keep our eyes fixed on what we could not see. Reading from his favorite poem, about a man named Richard Cory, I told of Dad's warning that we could amass great wealth and still be poor.

Then I recounted all the people who'd approached me a day earlier, wanting to discuss the Trump wars on AM talk radio. I spoke of the need for discipleship and spiritual formation. I proposed that their time in the car would be better spent listening to Dad's old sermons. If they needed help finding biblical listening for their daily commute, I suggested with some sarcasm, the pastors here on staff could help. "Why are you listening to *Rush Limbaugh*?" I asked my father's congregation. "Garbage in, garbage out."

There was nervous laughter in the sanctuary. Some people were visibly agitated. Others looked away, pretending not to hear. My dad's successor, a young pastor named Chris Winans, wore a shell-shocked expression. No matter. I had said my piece. It was finished. Or so I thought.

A few hours later, after we had buried Dad, my brothers and I slumped down onto the couches in our parents' living room. We opened some beers and turned on a baseball game. Behind us, in the kitchen, a small platoon of church ladies worked to prepare a meal for the family. *Here*, I thought, *is the love of Christ*. Watching them hustle about, comforting Mom and catering to her sons, I found myself regretting the Rush Limbaugh remark. Most of the folks at our church were humble, kindhearted Christians like these ladies. Maybe I'd blown things out of proportion.

Just then, one of them walked over and handed me an envelope. It was left at the church, she said. My name was scrawled across it. I opened the envelope. Inside was a full-page-long, handwritten screed. It was from a longtime Cornerstone elder, someone my dad called a friend, a man who mentored me in the youth group and had known me for most of my life.

He had composed this note, on the occasion of my father's death, to express just how disappointed he was in me. I was part of an evil plot, the man wrote, to undermine God's ordained leader of the United States. My criticisms of President Trump were tantamount to treason—against both God and country—and I should be ashamed of myself.

However, he assured me, there was still hope. Jesus forgives and so does he. If I could use my journalism skills to investigate the "deep state," he wrote, uncovering the shadowy cabal that was sabotaging Trump's presidency, then I would be restored. He said he was praying for me.

I felt sick. Silently, I passed the letter to my wife. She scanned it without expression. Then, in a violent spasm, she flung the piece of paper into the air and with a shriek that made the church ladies jump out of their cardigans, cried out: "What the hell is wrong with these people?"

IN SEARCH OF ANSWERS TO THAT QUESTION, I TOOK DAD'S ADVICE AND pivoted away from political journalism. There would be no sequel to the Trump book. Moving my young family back to Michigan a few months after the funeral, I knew there was another project that demanded my attention. Dad had implored me to apply my talents to subjects of more eternal significance, and I could think of nothing more eternally significant than the crack-up of the American evangelical Church.

This would not be an examination of Christianity writ large. Whatever the problems plaguing the Catholic Church, the Orthodox Church, the Black Church, the rainbow-flag-flying progressive Church—and there are many—these are distinctive and diverging faith traditions. What I could offer was a window into *my* faith tradition. It happens to be the tradition that is the most polarizing and the least understood; the tradition that is more politically relevant and domestically disruptive than all the others combined: evangelicalism.

To a certain extent, definitional overlap does exist. Some Catholics self-identify as evangelical given the social connotations. Some non-white Christians count themselves as evangelicals due to denominational background or theological disposition (though research shows that Black Christians are far likelier to identify as "born again" than evangelical). A look at the broader Christian Church would be incomplete without investigating and contextualizing these convergences. Yet a look at the broader Christian Church would not yield a satisfying explanation of the turmoil within its commanding faction of conservative white protestants. However imperfect the designation, for brevity's sake, these are the *evangelicals* whom I set out to chronicle following my father's death.

Derived from the Greek *euangelion*, which means "good news" or "gospel," the English word *evangelical* was typically used to distinguish reformed Protestants, with their revivalist aims, from the staid customs of Catholicism. (Indeed, Martin Luther invoked the Latin translation of the term when breaking from the Roman Catholic Church in the sixteenth century.) During the first so-called Great Awakening in colonial America, clergymen shared a conviction to *evangelize* the masses—believing and unbelieving alike—with a purifying fervor. By the early nineteenth century, evangelicalism had become "by far the dominant expression of Christianity in the overwhelmingly Protestant United States," according to the Institute for the Study of American Evangelicals at Wheaton College.

Even as evangelicalism exploded, its definition remained somewhat ambiguous. In his book *Understanding Fundamentalism and Evangelicalism*, historian George Marsden observed that in the decades following World War II an evangelical was "anyone who likes Billy Graham." When Graham himself was asked to define the term, he responded: "Actually, that's a question I'd like to ask somebody, too." In 1989, a British scholar named David Bebbington posited that evangelicals were distinct because of four principal characteristics: Biblicism (treating scripture as the essential word of God); Crucicentrism (stressing that Jesus's death makes atonement for mankind possible); Conversionism (believing that sinners must be born again and continually transformed into Christlikeness); and Activism (sharing the gospel as an outward sign of that inward transformation). This framework—now commonly called the "Bebbington quadrilateral"—was widely embraced, including by the National Association of Evangelicals. But it also drew its share of criticisms. Efforts to formulate a more effective definition have failed time and again. To the present day there remains no real consensus around what it means to be an "evangelical."

There was a time when this etymological confusion proved a strength, prompting a growing number of Protestants to set aside organizational rivalries and join beneath a common decentralized banner. Yet such ambiguity was ripe for exploitation. Powerful people began to sense that if doctrinal differences were so easily set aside, then perhaps there was something else—not just something spiritual, but something *cultural*—that united these evangelicals. And indeed there was. By the 1980s, with the rise of the Moral Majority, a religious marker was transforming into a partisan movement. "Evangelical" soon became synonymous with "conservative Christian," and eventually with "white conservative Republican."

This is the ecosystem in which I was raised: the son of a white conservative Republican pastor in a white conservative Republican church in a white conservative Republican town. My dad, a serious theologian who held advanced degrees from top seminaries, bristled at this reductive analysis of his religious tribe. He would frequently state from the pulpit what *he* believed an evangelical to be: someone who believes the Bible is the inspired word of God and who takes seriously the charge to proclaim it to the world.

From a young age, I realized that not all Christians were like my dad. Other adults who went to our church—my teachers, baseball coaches, friends' parents—didn't speak about God the way that he did. Theirs was a more casual Christianity, a hobby more than a lifestyle, something that could be picked up and put down and slotted into schedules. Their pastor realized as much. Pushing his people ever harder to engage with questions of canonical authority and trinitarian precepts and Calvinist doctrine, Dad tried his best to run a serious church. There were no spiritual shortcuts at Cornerstone. Every Sunday of my life had begun with the congregation reciting, in one voice, the ancient Church creeds, the lyrical doxology, and the scripture passage from that week's sermon. Then, before Dad began preaching, we would stand and pray with the words Jesus taught His disciples:

> *Our Father, who art in Heaven, hallowed be thy name*
> *Thy kingdom come, thy will be done, on Earth as it is in Heaven*
> *Give us this day our daily bread, and forgive us our debts, as we forgive*
>   *our debtors*
> *And lead us not into temptation, but deliver us from evil*
> *For thine is the kingdom, the power, and the glory, forever*
> *Amen*

That penultimate verse—the kingdom, the power, and the glory— has haunted me since childhood. Its magnificence can be appreciated only in the context of the possessive pronoun *Thine*. (This is inspired by the King James Version; henceforth, in these pages, scripture will be presented in the New International Version.) That word, *Thine,* implies something more than mere ownership; it connotes exclusivity. Everything that Satan offered Jesus in the wilderness—to give Him power over all the kingdoms of the world and the glory that comes with it— Jesus rejected. Why? Because the only authentic version of those things belongs to God. What the devil tempted Jesus with two thousand years ago, and what he tempts us with today, are cheap counterfeits.

God has His own kingdom; no nation in this world can compare.

God has His own power; no amount of political, cultural, or social influence can compare.

God has His own glory; no exaltation of earthly beings can compare.

These are nonnegotiable to the Christian faith. One of the Bible's dominant narrative themes—uniting Old Testament and New Testament, prophets and disciples, prayers and epistles—is the admonition to resist idolatry at all costs. Jesus frames the decision in explicitly binary terms: We can serve and worship God or we can serve and worship the gods of this world. Too many American evangelicals have tried to do both. And the consequences for the Church have been devastating.

Christians are always falling short of God's standard. I have been an offender of the worst sort. If not for grace—His unlimited, unconditional grace—I would be condemned in my sins, doomed to permanent separation from my Creator. But grace is precisely the gift I have received, and, along with me, countless millions of Christians around the world. Perfection is not our mandate. Sanctification, the process by which sinners become more and more like Christ, is what God demands of us. And what that process requires, most fundamentally, is the rejection of one's worldly identity.

"Whoever wants to be my disciple must deny themselves and take up their cross and follow me," Jesus says in the Book of Matthew. "For whoever wants to save their life will lose it, but whoever loses their life for me will find it."

The crisis of American evangelicalism comes down to an obsession with that worldly identity. Instead of fixing our eyes on the unseen, "since what is seen is temporary, but what is unseen is eternal," as Paul writes in Second Corinthians, we have become fixated on the here and now. Instead of seeing ourselves as exiles in a metaphorical Babylon, the way Peter describes the first-century Christians living in Rome, we have embraced our imperial citizenship. Instead of fleeing the temptation to rule all the world, like Jesus did, we have made deals with the devil.

Why? Or as my wife might ask: What the hell is wrong with us?

In search of answers, I would spend much of the next four years embedded inside the modern evangelical movement. I toured half-empty sanctuaries and standing-room-only auditoriums; I shadowed big-city televangelists and small-town preachers and everyday congregants. I reported from inside hundreds of churches, Christian colleges, religious advocacy organizations, denominational nonprofits, and assorted independent ministries. Each of these experiences offered a unique insight into the deterioration of American Christianity.

But the farther I traveled from home, the clearer it became: The best explanation for what afflicts *the* Church was evident at *my* church.

PART I

THE
KINGDOM

CHAPTER ONE

BRIGHTON, MICHIGAN

My kingdom is not of this world.

—JOHN 18:36

Chris Winans was in trouble.

It was a frigid afternoon in February 2021, and Winans, the senior pastor of Cornerstone Evangelical Presbyterian Church, sat down across from me in a booth at the Brighton Bar and Grill. It's a comfortable little haunt on Main Street in my hometown, backing up to a wooden playground and a mill pond. But Winans didn't look comfortable. He looked panicked, even a bit paranoid, glancing around him as we began to speak. Soon, I would understand why.

Dad had spent years looking for an heir apparent. Several associate pastors had come and gone. Cornerstone was his life's work—he had led the church throughout virtually its entire history—so there would be no settling in his search for a successor. The uncertainty wore him down. Dad worried he might never find the right guy. And then one day, while attending a denominational meeting, he met a young associate pastor from Goodwill EPC—the very church where he'd been saved, and where he'd worked his first job out of seminary. The pastor's name was Chris Winans. Dad hired him away from Goodwill to lead a young adults ministry at Cornerstone, and from the moment Winans arrived, I could tell he was the one.

Barely thirty years old, Winans looked to be exactly what Cornerstone needed in its next generation of leadership. He was a brilliant student of the scriptures. He spoke with precision and clarity from the pulpit. He had a humble, easygoing way about him, operating without the outsize ego that often accompanies first-rate preaching. Everything about this young pastor—the boyish sweep of brown hair, his delightful young family—seemed to be straight out of central casting.

There was just one problem: Chris Winans was not a conservative Republican. He didn't like guns. He cared more about funding poverty programs than cutting tax rates. He had no appetite for the unrepentant antics of President Donald Trump. Of course, none of this would seem heretical to Christians in other parts of the world; given his staunch pro-life position, Winans would in most places be considered an archetype of spiritual and intellectual consistency. But in the American evangelical tradition, and at a church like Cornerstone, the whiff of liberalism made him suspect.

Brighton, Michigan, is a bubble within a bubble. The surrounding county, Livingston, is the most reliably Republican-voting jurisdiction in the state. For the last three decades, anyone looking to escape the high crime of Detroit and the high costs of its contiguous counties headed west to Livingston, and, if they could afford it, to the quiet little burg of Brighton. The town is deeply conservative, deceptively wealthy, and almost exclusively white. Its biggest church, Cornerstone, became a microcosm of the surrounding area. There was no meaningful diversity inside the church—ethnically, culturally, or politically—until Winans came to town.

Dad knew the guy was different. A trained musician, Winans liked to play piano instead of sports, and had no taste for hunting or fishing. Frankly, Dad thought that was a bonus. Winans wasn't supposed to simply placate Cornerstone's aging base of wealthy, white congregants. The new pastor's charge was to evangelize, to cast a vision and expand the mission field, to challenge those inside the church and carry the gospel to those outside it. Dad didn't think there was undue risk. He felt confident that his hand-chosen successor's gifts in the pulpit, and his manifest love of Jesus, would be more than sufficient to smooth over any bumps in the transition.

He was wrong. Almost immediately after Winans moved into the role of senior pastor, at the beginning of 2018, the knives came out. Any errant remark he made about politics or culture, any slight of Trump or the Republican Party—real or perceived—invited a torrent of criticism. Longtime members would demand a meeting with Dad, who had stayed on in a support role, and unload on Winans. Dad would ask if there was any substantive criticism of the theology; almost invariably, the answer was no. A month into the job, when Winans remarked in a sermon that Christians ought to be protective of God's creation—arguing for congregants to take seriously the threats to the planet—the dam nearly burst. People came to Dad by the dozens, outraged, demanding that Winans be reined in. Dad told them all to get lost. If anyone had a beef with the senior pastor, he said, they needed to take it up with the senior pastor. (Dad did so himself, buying Winans lunch at Chili's and suggesting he tone down the tree hugging.)

It was a tumultuous first year on the job, but Winans survived it. He tightened the screws and checked his ideological impulses, realizing that his good intentions had gotten the better of him. The people at Cornerstone were in a period of adjustment. He needed to respect that—and he needed to adjust, too. As long as Dad was in his corner, Winans knew he would be okay.

And then Dad died.

Eighteen months later, as we sat together picking at hot sandwiches, I was starting to understand the dismay I'd seen on his face at the funeral. Winans told me that he was barely hanging on at Cornerstone. The church had become unruly; his job had become unbearable. It wasn't long after Dad died—making Winans the unquestioned leader of the church—that the COVID-19 pandemic arrived. In the vortex of fear and uncertainty, Michigan's Democratic governor, Gretchen Whitmer, issued sweeping shutdown orders that implicated houses of worship. Churches everywhere had to choose: Obey the government and close for a period of time, or violate the orders and remain open. Winans felt it was a no-brainer. Whitmer wasn't ordering Christians to do something sinful or immoral or unholy. Scripture says to respect governing authorities, so that's what Cornerstone would do.

The decision didn't go over well. Some in his congregation swore that the virus was a hoax cooked up by globalist elites who wanted to control the population; others merely believed that church was too important—too "essential," in the parlance of the times—to be shuttered for any reason, ever. What these groups shared was a prophetic certainty, promulgated by the evangelical movement for decades, that godless Democrats would one day launch a frontal assault on Christianity in America. This belief wasn't limited to Pentecostals and their so-called charismatic spiritual practices, or to fringe fundamentalists, or to Dominionists, the nascent hard-liners who seek to merge church and state under biblical law. No, this was accepted dogma for conservative Christians of *every* tribe and affiliation. And it was only a matter of time, they knew, until secularists weaponized the government to eradicate the Almighty from public life.

In the spring of 2020, that prophecy was being fulfilled—and weak, spineless pastors like Chris Winans were letting it happen.

When Cornerstone reopened after several weeks of online Sunday worship, a chunk of the congregation was missing. The numbers dwindled further in the months ahead. As debates over shutdowns gave way to disagreements over masking and social distancing, more and more people left the church, believing their new pastor was being too deferential to government health guidelines.

Winans was reeling—and the ground beneath him was about to get a whole lot shakier. In May 2020, an unarmed Black man named George Floyd was murdered in Minneapolis by a policeman who knelt on his neck for almost nine minutes as he gasped, "I can't breathe." The incident sparked a summer of unrest: Protests for racial justice and scattered outbreaks of violent rioting prompted millions of Americans to pick sides, writing social media posts and putting up yard signs that invariably alienated neighbors, family members, and fellow churchgoers.

Turbocharging the chaos was Trump's campaign for reelection. The sitting president of the United States was adamant that Democrats were plotting to rig the contest against him, and he made clear that the ramifications of this reached beyond electoral politics. Trump had campaigned in 2016 on a promise that "Christianity will have power" if he won the White House; now he warned that his opponent in the 2020 election, former vice president Joe Biden, was going to "hurt God" and target Christians for their religious beliefs. Embracing dark rhetoric and violent conspiracy theories, the president seized upon notions of America's prophesied apocalypse, enlisting leading evangelicals to help frame a cosmic spiritual clash between the God-fearing Republicans who supported Trump and the secular leftists who viewed the forty-fifth president as the last obstacle standing between them and a conquest of America's Judeo-Christian ethos.

The consequences were real and devastating. People at Cornerstone began confronting their pastor, demanding that he speak out against government mandates and Black Lives Matter and Joe Biden. When Winans declined, more people left. The mood soured noticeably after Trump's defeat in November 2020. A crusade to overturn the election result, led by a group of outspoken Christians—including Trump lawyer Jenna Ellis, who was later censured by a judge after admitting to spreading numerous lies about election fraud, and author Eric Metaxas, who told fellow believers that martyrdom might be required to keep Trump in office—roiled the Cornerstone congregation. A popular church leader was fired after it was discovered that she had been proselytizing for QAnon, the far-right online religion that depicts Trump as a messianic figure battling a satanic cabal of elites who cannibalize children for sustenance. When the church dismissed her, without announcing why, the departures came in droves. Some of those abandoning Cornerstone were not core congregants. But plenty of them were. They were people who served in leadership roles, people Winans counted as confidants and personal friends.

By the time Trump supporters invaded the U.S. Capitol on January 6, 2021, in an attempt to thwart the transition of power, Winans believed he'd lost control of his church. "It's an exodus," he told me a few weeks later, sitting inside Brighton Bar and Grill.

The pastor had felt despair—and a certain liability—watching the attack unfold on television. Christian imagery was ubiquitous at the scene in Washington: rioters forming prayer circles, singing hymns, carrying Bibles and crosses. The perversion of America's prevailing religion would forever be associated with this tragedy; as one of the legislative ringleaders, Missouri senator Josh Hawley, explained in a speech some time after the blood had been scrubbed from the Capitol steps, "We are a revolutionary nation precisely because we are the heirs of the revolution of the Bible."

It all could have been prevented, Winans thought, if pastors like him had been more forceful in pushing back on the craziness that had penetrated the Church. He wrote a scorched-earth sermon to give the following Sunday, calling out the forces responsible for corrupting Cornerstone with lies and schemes and subversive political agendas. But Winans never delivered it. The church was falling apart, and he feared such a sermon could destroy any chance at healing.

I told Winans something I didn't believe. "It will be okay," I said. "Hang in there."

Winans asked me to keep something between us: He was thinking about leaving Cornerstone. The "psychological onslaught," he said, had become too much. Recently, he'd developed a form of anxiety disorder and had to retreat into a dark room between services to collect himself. After talking with his father, a physician, Winans met with several trusted elders, shared his illness, and asked them to stick close on Sunday mornings so they could catch him if he were to faint and fall over.

I thought about Dad and how heartbroken he would be. Then I started to wonder if Dad didn't have some level of culpability in all of this. Clearly, long before COVID-19 or George Floyd or Donald Trump, something had gone wrong at Cornerstone. I had always shrugged off the crude, hysterical, sky-is-falling Facebook posts I would see from people at the church. I had found it amusing, if not particularly alarming, that some longtime Cornerstone members were obsessed with trolling me on Twitter. Now I couldn't help but think these were warnings—bright red blinking lights—that should have been taken seriously. My dad never had a social media account. Did he have any idea just how lost some of his sheep really were?

I had never told Winans about the confrontations at my dad's viewing, or the letter I received after taking Rush Limbaugh's name in vain at the funeral. Now I was leaning across the table, unloading every detail. He narrowed his eyes and folded his hands and gave a pained exhale, mouthing that he was sorry. He could not even manage the words.

We both kept quiet for a little while. And then I asked him something I'd thought about every day for the previous eighteen months—a sanitized version of my wife's outburst in the family room.

"What's wrong with American evangelicals?"

Winans thought a moment.

"*America*," he replied. "Too many of them worship America."

HAVING SPENT THE PREVIOUS DECADE COVERING THE REPUBLICAN Party, in Congress and on the campaign trail, I could hear a Bible verse coming before it formed in the candidate's throat.

They would use scripture to make the case for capitalism (Proverbs 13:4: "A sluggard's appetite is never filled, but the desires of the diligent are fully satisfied") and to legislate against abortion (Psalm 139:13: "For you created my inmost being; you knit me together in my mother's womb") and to mobilize the faithful for the culture wars (Isaiah 5:20: "Woe to those who call evil good and good evil").

All these examples, and the great majority of what voters would hear from GOP politicians, came from the Old Testament. That never struck me as a coincidence. Jesus, in His three years of teaching, talked mostly about helping the poor, humbling oneself, and having no earthly ambition but to gain eternal life. Suffice it to say, the beatitudes from the Sermon on the Mount ("Blessed are the meek . . . Blessed are the merciful . . . Blessed are the peacemakers") were never conducive to a stump speech. This isn't to suggest that Old Testament passages are somehow backward or illegitimate; many of these writings, timeless in their wisdom, have shaped my own views of the world. I just always found it strange that these Christians relied so infrequently on the words of *Christ*.

It was during Trump's takeover of the Republican Party, and his four years in office, that this reliance on Old Testament language became troubling.

There was justifiable alarm among many Christians when Trump clinched the GOP presidential nomination. The immorality in his personal life aside, Trump had spent his campaign inciting hatred against his critics, hurling vicious ad hominem insults at his opponents, boasting of his never having asked God's forgiveness, and generally behaving in ways that were antithetical to the example of Christ. If Trump possessed any of what Paul dubbed "the fruit of the spirit" (love, joy, peace, patience, kindness, goodness, faithfulness, gentleness, and self-control), it wasn't hanging low enough to be picked. Trump's evangelical allies—the handful of high-profile pastors and figureheads who'd supported his campaign from its inception—knew this needed to be addressed if the evangelical community was going to rally around the GOP nominee. For decades, the religious right had imposed exacting moral litmus tests on public officials, taking particular glee in tormenting the forty-second president, Bill Clinton, whose duplicity and womanizing allegedly made him unfit for office. Godly character, they had told us, was a requirement when it came to running the country. Ignoring the sins of Trump was not a sustainable approach.

Instead, they deployed a novel strategy: Evangelical leaders *embraced* Trump's shortcomings. At a meeting of more than five hundred prominent Christian conservatives in June 2016 at the Marriott Marquis hotel in New York City, Trump was introduced by the likes of Franklin Graham (son of famed evangelist Billy Graham) and Mike Huckabee (a Baptist preacher turned populist Arkansas governor turned Fox News host turned Trinity Broadcasting Network host) as the latest in a long tradition of flawed men who were being used by God to advance His purposes. The blueprint was obvious enough: Because the scriptures were filled with examples of great leaders who had grave personal failings, Trump could be considered an imperfect instrument of God's perfect design for America. Talking with attendees at the Marriott that day, I heard unceasing comparisons to David, to Solomon, and to King Cyrus, the Persian leader who protected the Israelite people despite not personally worshipping their Lord.

It was a clever way to cover all bases: Whether or not Trump *believed* that Jesus of Nazareth was God incarnate, the spotless lamb who was sacrificed for the sins of the world then raised from the dead three days later—and really, who could know what was on the candidate's heart?—he was an agent of the Almighty, born for such a time as this, ordained to fight on behalf of God's people and their shining city on a hill.

The danger of this rhetoric, deployed by people who knew better, is that it dovetailed with the most pernicious theological and political intuitions of those who did not. The notion of America declining as a nation due to diminished religiosity was nothing new; Church leaders had spent a half century warning that to ban prayer in public schools and to legalize abortion and to normalize drugs and pornography and unwedded sex was to invite God's wrath, or at the very least, His indifference. But now the signs of his judgment were proliferating. There was the shame of Clinton's carnal exploits in the Oval Office. The Islamist terror attacks of September 11, 2001. And, of course, the rise of President Barack Obama, a man whom millions of evangelicals believed to be a secret Kenyan at best or a sleeper-cell Muslim extremist at worst. (Franklin Graham managed to both question Obama's birthplace and speculate on his devotion to Islam.)

By the time Trump declared his candidacy in the summer of 2015, descending an escalator that would be the envy of Aaron's golden calf, the twin narratives of *America at the abyss* and *Christianity in the crosshairs* were ubiquitous within evangelicalism. Trump instinctually understood this. Surrounding himself with faith leaders who split their time between church pulpits and Fox News greenrooms, Trump set about catering to the panicked masses of American Christendom. He pledged to appoint "pro-life" Supreme Court justices. He promised to overturn an obscure statute, "the Johnson Amendment," that he claimed would allow the government to silence conservative pastors and shut down conservative churches. He vowed to move the U.S. embassy in Israel to Jerusalem, a prospect packed with spiritual and geopolitical implications Trump almost certainly did not grasp, even if he was keen on the electoral upside. Perhaps most consequentially, he chose Mike Pence, the governor of Indiana, as his running mate.

Once a failed politician who repented after running a dirty campaign for Congress, Pence rehabilitated his image by hosting a successful talk-radio show in Indiana. He was elected to Congress in 2000 and wasted no time distinguishing himself as a small-government absolutist who could not stomach the excesses of his own party. Despite being known as an ideological crusader on Capitol Hill, Pence was always better understood as a born-again evangelical. He believed that God had a plan for him, a plan for America, and a plan for Israel, and saw his unlikely partnership with Trump as a way of advancing all three. Pence made no apology for mixing faith and politics, though he was always quick to prioritize. "I'm a Christian, a conservative, and a Republican," he would say at the beginning of every speech. "In that order."

As Pence headlined rallies around the country in late 2016, I was interested less in his opening line—which I'd heard a thousand times—and more in his sign-off. After slamming the Clintons (so much for positive campaigning) and extolling the "broad shoulders" of Trump, pleading with people to get out and vote, Pence would remind his audience what was at stake in the coming election. He would claim that their beloved nation was slipping away. Then, in a solemn tone, he would tell them it wasn't too late. "If my people, who are called by my name, will humble themselves and pray and seek my face and turn from their wicked ways," Pence would say, quoting God's voice in the Second Book of Chronicles, "then I will hear from heaven, and I will forgive their sin and will heal their land." The crowd would roar in response.

It was a risky application of scripture. God is speaking in that passage to Solomon, the king of Israel, after the dedication of the temple in Jerusalem. This is a specific word of forewarning, issued at a uniquely sacred moment, from God to the ruler of His covenant nation. For Pence to appropriate this language and apply it in the context of an American political campaign dozens of centuries later meant one of two things: Either the Republican nominee for vice president didn't know his Bible history; or he did, and he believed that God's relationship with Israel was somehow parallel to God's relationship with the United States.

Pence knew his Bible history.

"A LOT OF PEOPLE BELIEVE THERE WAS A RELIGIOUS CONCEPTION OF this country. A *biblical* conception of this country," Pastor Winans told me. "And that's the source of a lot of our problems."

Two things can be true. First, most of America's founding fathers believed in some deity, and many were devout Christians, drawing their revolutionary inspiration from the scriptures. Second, the founders wanted nothing to do with theocracy. Many of their families had fled religious persecution in Europe; they knew the threat posed by what George Washington, several weeks into his presidency in 1789, described in a letter to the United Baptist Churches of Virginia as "the horrors of spiritual tyranny." Washington was hardly alone: From skeptics like Benjamin Franklin to committed Christians like John Jay, the founders shared John Adams's view that America was conceived not "under the influence of Heaven" or in conversation with the Creator, but rather by using "reason and the senses."

That is not the biblical story of Israel.

"*God* established Israel through the means of a covenant with Him," Winans explained, unpacking the Old Testament narrative. "This was God's chosen nation, created for God's chosen people, living by God's chosen laws."

After the chosen people repeatedly strayed from those chosen laws—instead honoring the codes, customs, and gods of other nations—God allowed the destruction of ancient Israel. Through hundreds of years of exile and oppression, the Jewish people yearned for a return to this covenant relationship. It was Jesus of Nazareth, a carpenter's son raised in the Roman-occupied province of Galilee, who came to deliver the news: The old kingdom was gone for good. In its place, He promised something even better—a kingdom not of this world, and not just for Jews, but for everyone who accepts Jesus as their personal mediator between God and mankind.

The significance of this development cannot be overstated. We are taught in the Book of Hebrews that God, by providing Jesus as the new covenant, "has made the first one obsolete." In his letter to the Philippians, Paul, an exemplary Jew—"circumcised on the eighth day, of the people of Israel, of the tribe of Benjamin, a Hebrew of Hebrews"—describes this identity, once so precious to him, as "garbage" compared to what Jesus now offers.

That offering—of grace, salvation, citizenship in an eternal kingdom—ought to be enough to quell the temporal desires of those who identify as Christians. But it often isn't, Winans said, and for the same reason that God's covenant wasn't enough for the ancient Israelites thousands of years earlier. "God's people have always been tempted to be like the rest of the nations. It was true back then, and it's true now," Winans told me. "There's a pretty consistent pattern in scripture of what that looks like: I want to be in power, I want to have influence, I want to be prosperous,

I want to have security. And even if God gives me some of those things, I'll try to achieve even more through worldly means."

For much of American history, white Christians had *all* of those things. Given that reality—and given the miraculous nature of America's defeat of Great Britain, its rise to superpower status, and its legacy of spreading freedom and democracy (and yes, Christianity) across the globe—it's easy to see why so many evangelicals believe that our country is divinely blessed. The problem is, blessings often become indistinguishable from entitlements. Once we become convinced that God has blessed something, that something can become an object of jealousy, obsession—even worship.

"At its root, we're talking about idolatry. America has become an idol to some of these people," Winans said. "If you believe that God is in covenant with America, then you believe—and I've heard lots of people say this explicitly—that we're a new Israel. You believe the sorts of promises made to Israel are applicable to this country; you view America as a covenant that needs to be protected. You have to fight for America as if salvation itself hangs in the balance. At that point, you understand yourself as an *American* first and most fundamentally. And that is a terrible misunderstanding of who we're called to be."

This can happen anywhere, Winans explained, but the conditions in America are especially ripe for national idolatry. "The freedoms in our Bill of Rights, we like to call them 'God-given.' Now, think about what that means in the context of gun control," he said. "If someone's trying to take away something God has given you, well, shoot, that's pretty upsetting! But is there a *God*-given right to bear arms? Or is it a *cultural* right? If I went to the U.K., or most other places in the world, they would say it's a cultural right. In America, many Christians believe it's a God-given right. So, you can see how, even in that one small example, we start running into problems."

A small example, perhaps, but one with cascading implications. The Second Amendment is among the most sacred of our national texts, a governing maxim regarded as infallible by the American right. I wondered aloud how many Christians could recite that language verbatim, compared with how many could do the same with one of *God's* laws, say, the Second Commandment, which forbids worship of idols.

"The Second Amendment," Winans said, shaking his head, "by a landslide."

Winans was quick to clarify something. "I have affection for America. I'm glad I live here. But my citizenship is not here. It cannot be here," he said. "We're clinging to something in America that is a sad parody of what Jesus has already won. We have a kingdom awaiting us, but we're trying to appropriate a part of this world and call it a kingdom."

Winans pointed out the window. "God told us, this place is not our promised land," he said. "But they're trying to make it a promised land."

To be clear, plenty of nations are mentioned in the Bible. The United States is not one of them. Most American evangelicals are sophisticated enough to realize that, to avoid talk of a "new Israel," to reject the idea of this country as something consecrated in the eyes of God. But many of those same people have nonetheless allowed their national identity to shape their faith identity instead of the other way around. To some extent, I watched it happen with my own father.

Once a fine young athlete, Dad came down with tuberculosis at sixteen years old. It hospitalized him for four months; at one point doctors thought it would kill him. He eventually recovered, and with the Vietnam War breaking out, he joined the Marine Corps. Dad was the son of a poor Sicilian immigrant who had no formal education but somehow built a thriving restaurant business. Their family was patriotic, and Dad saw fighting for Old Glory as a sacred obligation. But it wasn't meant to be. At the Officer Candidate School in Quantico, Virginia, he fell behind in the physical work. His lungs were not healthy; he could not keep up. Receiving an honorable discharge, Dad went home saddled with a certain shame. In the ensuing years, he learned that dozens of those second lieutenants he'd trained alongside at Quantico—as well as a bunch of guys he'd grown up with—were killed in action. It burdened him for the rest of his life.

This experience, and his disgust with the hippies and the drug culture and the war protesters, turned Dad into a law-and-order conservative. Then he became a born-again Christian. Marinating in the language of social conservatism during his time in seminary—this was the heyday of the Moral Majority—he emerged a full-spectrum Republican. Dad was unapologetic about his beliefs, though he was careful about partisan preaching. His biggest political concern was abortion; his mother, trapped in a broken and emotionally abusive marriage, had attempted to end *his* pregnancy in 1947. (She had a sudden change of heart at the clinic and walked out, a riddle he would always attribute to holy intercession.) But he also waded into the culture wars: gay marriage, education curriculum, morality in public life.

Throughout my childhood, Dad always talked about politics through the lens of ethics. He believed that integrity was a prerequisite for political leadership. He was so relieved when Bill Clinton's second term ended that he and Mom hosted a small viewing party in our living room for George W. Bush's 2000 inauguration to celebrate the return of morality to the White House. Over time, however, his emphasis shifted. One Sunday in early 2010, when I was home visiting, he showed the congregation an ominous video in which Christian leaders warned about the menace of Obamacare. I told him afterward that it felt inappropriate for a worship service; he disagreed. We would butt heads more regularly in the years that followed. It was always loving, always respectful. Yet clearly our philosophical paths were diverging—a reality that became unavoidable during the presidency of Donald Trump.

Dad would have preferred any of the other Republicans who ran in 2016. He knew that Trump was a narcissist and a liar; he knew that he was not a moral man. Ultimately Dad felt he had no choice but to support the Republican ticket, given his concern for the unborn and the Supreme Court majority that hung in the balance. I understood that decision. What I couldn't understand was how, over the next couple of years, he became an apologist for Trump's antics, dismissing criticisms of the president's conduct as little more than an attempt to marginalize his supporters. Dad really did believe this; he believed that the constant attacks on Trump's character were ipso facto an attack on the character of people like himself, which I think, at some subconscious level, created a permission structure for him to ignore the shows of depravity. For my part—as a Trump critic, as a member of the media, and, most importantly, as a Christian—all I could do was tell Dad the truth. "Look, you're the one who taught me to know right from wrong," I would say. "Don't be mad at me for acting on it."

To his credit, Dad was not some lazy, knee-jerk partisan. He was vocal about certain issues—gun violence, poverty, immigration, the trappings of wealth—that did not play to his constituency at Cornerstone. To his even greater credit, whenever he turned political, especially around election time, he was quick to emphasize the proper Christian perspective. "God doesn't bite his fingernails over any of this," he would say. "Neither should you."

Dad's kryptonite as a Christian—and I think he knew it, though he never admitted it to me—was his intense love of country. He did not think America was a new Israel, but he did believe that God had blessed the country uniquely and felt that anyone who fought to preserve those blessings was doing the Lord's work. This made for an unfortunate scene in 2007, when a young man from Cornerstone, a Marine named Mark Kidd, died during a fourth tour of duty in Iraq. Public opinion had swung sharply against the war and Democrats were demanding that the George W. Bush administration bring the troops home. My dad was devastated by Kidd's death. They had corresponded regularly while he was overseas and always met for prayer in between his deployments. His grief as a pastor gave way to his grievance as a Republican supporter of the war: He made it known to local Democratic politicians that they weren't welcome at the Marine's funeral.

"I am ashamed, personally, of leaders who say they support the troops but not the commander in chief," Dad thundered from his pulpit at Cornerstone, earning a raucous standing ovation. "Do they not see that discourages the warriors and encourages the terrorists?"

It touched off a firestorm in our community. Most of the church members were all for Dad's remarks, but even in a conservative town like Brighton, plenty of people felt uneasy about turning a fallen Marine's church memorial into a partisan political rally. Patriotism in the pulpit is one thing; lots of sanctuaries fly an American flag on the rostrum. This was something else. This was taking the weight and the gravity and the eternal certainty of God and lending it to an ephemeral and questionable cause. This was rebuking people for failing to unconditionally follow a president of the United States when the only authority we're meant to unconditionally follow—particularly in a setting of stained-glass windows—is Christ Himself.

I know Dad regretted it. But he couldn't help himself. His own personal story—and his broader view of the United States as a godly nation, a source of hope in a despondent world—was impossible to divorce from his pastoral ministry. Every time a member of the military came to church dressed in uniform, Dad would recognize them by name, ask them to stand up, and lead the church in a rapturous round of applause.

This was one of the first things Winans changed as senior pastor. He would meet the military personnel after the service, shaking their hands and individually thanking them for their service. But he refused to stage a corporate ovation in the sanctuary. This wasn't because he was some bohemian antiwar activist; in fact, his wife had served in the U.S. Army. Winans simply felt it was inappropriate.

"I don't want to dishonor anyone. I think nations have the right to self-defense. I respect the sacrifices these people make in the military," Winans told me. "But they would come in wearing their dress blues and get this wild standing ovation. And you contrast that to whenever we would host missionaries: They would stand up for recognition, and we give them a golf clap."

Winans paused, measuring his words. "Again, I don't want to dishonor anyone. But we give standing ovations inside the church, with the flag flying, to the person who's been designated to go to war for America. And then we give a golf clap to the missionary. We give a golf clap to the ambassador we're sending out, who represents the kingdom we're supposed to have our citizenship in. And you have to wonder: Why? What's going on inside our hearts?"

I asked Winans to answer his own question.

"Think about Jesus's disciples," he said. "They debated, in front of Him, 'Who is going to sit at your left and who's going to sit at your right?' They believed they were about to assume power. They thought that when Jesus became king, they were going to get to run things in His kingdom. But Jesus had to keep telling them—over and over—that His kingdom was not here."

The disciples didn't get it. Even as Jesus stunned His would-be executioner, the Roman governor Pontius Pilate, with words that changed history—"My kingdom is not of this world"—they were crushed and inconsolable, believing the prophecy of a promised ruler had died along with Him. It wasn't until Jesus reappeared to them, describing how the prophecy was in fact now fulfilled, that the disciples realized what *real* power looks like.

"Once they finally understood, after Jesus was crucified and raised from the dead and ascended into heaven, it changed their faith," Winans said. "And here's the thing. The word *faith* is not just about belief; faith is about allegiance. When you declare faith in Jesus, you transfer your allegiance. In the first-century Roman context, that's what they did: They transferred their allegiance away from Caesar, and the gods of Rome, and certain laws of the Jewish leaders, and pledged allegiance to Jesus."

SURRENDERING EARTHLY POWER CAME AT A COST FOR THE DISCIPLES: Most of them were murdered for following Jesus.

Winans faced real difficulties, but not martyrdom. As 2021 went on, we continued our conversation about Cornerstone and the American Church. He learned to cope with the emotional and physical stress, taking long walks around the church softball field, praying the Psalms, and asking for the Lord's protection. He decided to stay on the job, at least a little while longer, not wanting to walk away from a problem that God was calling him to help solve. Still, he told me, the effort he had undertaken—convincing people to transfer their allegiance away from America, and toward Jesus—was coming at a cost.

Lots of his congregants had already left Cornerstone, and more were trickling out each week. Many were relocating to one particular congregation down the road, a revival-minded church that was pandering to the whims of the moment, led by a pastor who was preaching a blood-and-soil Christian nationalism that merged two kingdoms into one.

"The Church is supposed to challenge us," Winans told me. "But a lot of these folks don't want to be challenged. They *definitely* don't want to be challenged where their idols are. If you tell them what they don't want to hear, they're gone. They'll find another church. They'll find a pastor who tells them what they want to hear."

None of this is new. In his second letter to Timothy, the apostle Paul, recognizing that his death was near, offered his pupil some parting wisdom about the fickle nature of a religious audience. "For the time will come when people will not put up with sound doctrine," he wrote. "Instead, to suit their own desires, they will gather around them a great number of teachers to say what their itching ears want to hear."

In a strange way, Winans said, he found encouragement knowing that so many churches were enduring the same stress as Cornerstone. He shared stories of denominational meetings, of conversations with close friends in the ministry, in which pastors of every age, experience level, and ideological makeup confessed to being on the verge of quitting. The whole of the American evangelical movement, he said, was in turmoil.

I pressed for details. I wondered if there was one church horror story that stood out from the rest.

Winans fought a smirk. Then he asked me: "Have you ever been back to Goodwill?"

CHAPTER TWO

MONTGOMERY, NEW YORK

Get behind me, Satan!

—MARK 8:33

I did not know John Torres, but he knew me.

"Still can't believe you called out Rush Limbaugh like that," Torres, the senior pastor of Goodwill Evangelical Presbyterian Church, said as he shook my hand.

Until Pastor Chris Winans brought up Goodwill, and told me the story of his embattled mentor, I had never heard Torres's name. Now, as we stood chatting in the hallway of his church, outside a room where an addiction-recovery meeting had just kicked off, it was like we'd known each other for years. Technically, we had. Torres didn't just recognize me from attending the funeral. He had been Goodwill's music director when my dad was the church's associate pastor. He had held me when I was a baby.

Torres, who wore a crew cut and a permanent waggish grin, had been raised in a nonreligious home. Studying music under a famed composer at the University of Connecticut, he felt adrift, lost interest, and dropped out of school. It was the out-of-left-field conversion to Christianity that reignited Torres's passion for music. He joined a Christian band, toured the Northeast, and pursued a career as an evangelical musician. When that failed—he would've had better odds chasing a conventional dream, like playing center field for the New York Yankees—Torres responded to an ad in the paper: "keyboard player, local church."

Meeting with Stewart Pohlman, the senior pastor of Goodwill, Torres felt an uncanny connection with the place. The two men hit it off. Pohlman—whom everyone in the area, congregants and nonchurchgoers alike, knew as "Pastor Stew"—hired Torres on the spot. Before long, Torres took over as choir director. But Pastor Stew had a bigger promotion in mind. He told Torres that God had made something apparent to him: The young man was meant to go into the ministry. He should think about applying to seminary and preparing for life as a preacher.

Torres was flabbergasted. A relatively new believer, he scarcely felt at ease *attending* church. Joining the Goodwill staff had been nerve-racking enough; now the senior pastor was telling him that God wanted him to preach? It made no sense, Torres thought. He had long hair and didn't own a suit (and caught lots of grief about both from Dick Alberta, the associate pastor). Surely this was a mistake.

It wasn't. Under the patient tutelage of Pastor Stew and my father, Torres began to recognize the talent, the potential, the plan for his life. He returned to a local college to finish his undergraduate studies, then went straight to Alliance Theological Seminary in Nyack, New York. He stayed on staff at Goodwill and hustled between side jobs to pay for school: tuning pianos, cleaning horse stalls, doing housework for church families. He later joined the Air National Guard, eventually obtaining the rank of lieutenant colonel, and to this day serves as chaplain at the nearby Air Force base in Newburgh.

When he wasn't studying at seminary, he was drilling with Dad and Pastor Stew. The two pastors and the eager apprentice discussed and debated every theological, historical, cultural, and political topic imaginable. Disagreement was common—and enjoyable. Each of them had come from unique backgrounds; each of them had unique views of the Church and the country and the world. Uniformity of belief was necessary in but one sense: Jesus Christ had died for their sins and was resurrected for their justification before God.

"Pastor Stew was a Democrat. The three of us, we would talk about it all the time. Your dad didn't care, just like Stew didn't care that your dad was a Republican," Torres told me. "That's the church I knew. Sure, most people who attend an evangelical church tend to be Republican. Occasionally politics would become an issue, but it was rare. Today, politics is changing the definition of what a *Christian* is. We're setting the Bible aside and using a different standard."

As we talked, Torres gave me the tour of Goodwill. Eventually we walked out of the church, across a vast parking lot, and approached a small chapel. This was the original sanctuary, he explained to me, the place where Goodwill members had gathered for centuries until the magnificent new worship center was erected in 2010. This was where my dad had accepted Christ and later began his preaching career. My mom called it "holy ground" for our family.

Walking inside, I felt transported in time. The lights were dim and the air was dusty. Thirteen rows of upholstered wooden pews were divided in half, a distressed blue carpet providing an aisle toward the one-step stage at front. There a communion table, draped in purple cloth, was flanked by a white piano and a simple, wheat-stained pine pulpit. At back was a small riser, another communion table, several chairs, and a cross affixed to the wall. Arching above the rostrum were woodblock letters, spelling out the message delivered by a heavenly host on the first Christmas night: "Glory to God in the highest and on earth GOODWILL toward men."

On the back walls of the sanctuary hung intricate, pearl-colored tablets. They commemorated some of Goodwill's former pastors, dating as far back as the mid-eighteenth century. The church had nearly been destroyed—from within and from without—on numerous different occasions. One pastor, Rev. Andrew King, had led Goodwill during the years of the American Revolution. Others had preached before, during, and after the Civil War.

"You think those guys had some division to deal with?" Torres joked. The smile soon vanished. He stood, eyes fastened on one of the plaques, talking as much to me as to himself. "I've always wondered," he said, "how long can a church survive?"

THE TROUBLE AT GOODWILL HAD STARTED WHEN BARACK OBAMA WAS elected president in 2008.

Torres sensed an uneasiness in his conservative, predominantly white congregation. He wasn't thrilled with Obama's victory himself: Once a Democrat, Torres had drifted rightward in recent years, due primarily to the issue of abortion. It was a sermon my dad preached in the late 1980s, Torres said, that left him wholly convicted on the issue. What persuaded him even more was seeing the work Dad put into the pro-life cause. Despite having no money and four young children of their own, he and my mom gave all that they had to women in need, whatever stage of motherhood they were in. In 1984, they established the first crisis pregnancy center in Orange County, New York. As Torres spoke, his eyes welled with tears. He and his wife adopted their two daughters through a related Christian ministry.

Those two daughters happened to be Black. Whatever his disagreements with Obama on policy matters, Torres said, he recognized the historic significance of the man's ascent to the presidency. He and his wife, Shannon, cried on election night, overjoyed that their daughters would have the first family as role models.

Their elation was not shared in the church. Many of his members were hostile, even hateful, toward the incoming president, and he sensed that race had much to do with it. Torres never talked politics on Sunday mornings. But when Rufus Smith, a highly respected Black pastor who was leading an EPC megachurch in Houston, wrote a letter to his white counterparts explaining the meaning of Obama's victory to Black Christians, Torres decided to make an exception.

"He basically said, 'I know you might not have voted for Barack Obama, but there's something about little Black girls running through the hallways of the White House, calling it home, that has a profound spiritual effect on us. And I just want to communicate that to my brothers in the clergy.' It was a beautiful letter. So I read it to the church," Torres said. "We're charged to pray for those in authority over us, whether we agree with them or not. I felt it was important to share with our people that, for our Black brothers and sisters, we had arrived somewhere special as a nation."

The backlash was sudden and severe. A chorus of Goodwill members rebuked Torres for reading the letter. Several left the church altogether. Chastened and thoroughly disheartened, Torres decided to revert to his old rules: no politics in church. He would stick to scripture. Apparently that's what his people wanted.

He began to realize, however, that this wasn't necessarily the case. During Obama's eight years in office, Torres observed more and more partisan hubbub inside the church. Some of it was harmless enough. But some of it was unhealthy and even unsafe: the murmurs of Obama as a Muslim Manchurian candidate, appointed by Satan himself, on a mission to destroy America and American Christianity. Torres couldn't decide whether to confront this talk. It was clearly untrue, the by-product of too many nights spent marinating in hateful right-wing media. But Torres didn't want to turn his church into a cable news set, and he worried that engaging this nonsense would only create more of a distraction. He resolved to just keep pushing Jesus, in higher and higher doses, hoping to rebalance perspectives and restore some normalcy.

It didn't work. Torres knew, when Trump charged the political scene in the summer of 2015, that things were going to get worse. The candidate was serving up a cocktail of discontent—one part cultural displacement, one part religious persecution, one part nationalist fervor—that would prove irresistible to certain people he pastored, people who were scandalized by shifting public norms and by the prospect of Christians losing their status in a secularizing America.

Nevertheless, Torres stayed the course. He preached the gospel and blocked out the noise. Even after Trump won, and people came to him—some wanting the pastor to mirror their joy, a few hoping he would share their concerns, most merely curious for his thoughts on the president—Torres didn't bite. He refused to let Trump set the agenda inside his church. Yes, he was disturbed by the man's behavior. But if he commented on one controversy, Torres feared, he would be expected to comment on *every* controversy. He prayed for an end to the insanity. He prayed for an end to the fear and hatred and discord. What he received was a pandemic.

Torres struggled with the idea of shutting down Goodwill. This was a time when people needed his church the most—not just the members, but members of the community, people who relied on Goodwill for help of every sort. Torres worried about people catching COVID-19 at his church. But he also worried about a different sickness, one that could spread just as rapidly, one that preyed on hurting people who would be sealed off in their homes with nothing to do but surf the internet and swim in bad information.

The pastor tried to make lemonade. He held marathon Zoom meetings with anxious church members and worked hard to make the Sunday livestream energetic and uplifting. He staged drive-through worship services in the Goodwill parking lot, "hoping we could have a time of great revival amidst all the conflict." All the while, tensions mounted. Some people were furious with him for submitting to the edict of the state's Democratic governor, broadcasting their wrath on Facebook. Torres had never looked at the social media accounts of his members. Now he found himself open-mouthed, stunned and sickened by what he was seeing. It wasn't just anger over COVID protocols; it was sheer derangement. People were trafficking in conspiracies over everything from the global elites who'd planned the pandemic to the global elites who sacrificed children and drank their blood for sustenance. (Often, they were one and the same.)

Having been exposed to this digital idiocy, Torres might have avoided the topic of George Floyd's murder. Nothing good was going to come from commenting on the racial-justice demonstrations breaking out across the country. He was better off playing it safe, keeping consistent in his approach, not antagonizing anyone. But Torres couldn't help himself. The same feeling that had inspired him to read the letter after Obama's election—a nagging sense that racism dwelled someplace deep inside the heart of the evangelical Church—compelled him to speak out again.

"We take a long view of human nature. Christianity is about changing the way we look at ourselves and look at other people. If you have any kind of racist ideas, as a Christian, you can confront those sins, repent, and become more like Christ," Torres explained to me. "Think about the British slave trader who wrote 'Amazing Grace.' You know—*I once was lost, but now am found; was blind but now I see.*"

Torres decided to shoot a video of himself interviewing Smith, the Black megachurch pastor, who was his EPC colleague and friend. They talked about the scourge of slavery, about America's history of racial oppression, about the biblical mandate for Christians to lead the way toward reconciliation. "If we're gonna be a church—if we're gonna be a church in America—then this is an issue that's *ours*," Torres said on the video. It was published on the church's website and Facebook page.

"That day," the pastor told me, "I became an apostate."

The pushback was private at first. Individual church members began calling Torres, texting him, emailing him, asking for a meeting. The conversations took on a familiar rhythm. The member would ask Torres if he knew about Floyd's personal history; if he knew that Floyd was a drug addict and a convicted criminal. Then, after Torres would respond that it was irrelevant—that sinning and falling short of the glory of God, as all men do, is no defense for murder by the state—the member would interrogate Torres. Did he think America was a racist country? Why wasn't he standing up for law enforcement? Would he denounce the rioting and looting on the news? Finally, the member would suggest an apology: Torres should confess his error to the church body and ask for forgiveness.

Torres began to suspect that the effort was synchronized. Sure enough, a group of disgruntled church members soon joined together in formal rebellion. They recruited congregants to the cause and adopted aggressive new tactics. One of them secretly audiotaped a meeting with Torres—to the great satisfaction of the cabal—in which the pastor shared that he'd been reading a book, *Stamped from the Beginning: The Definitive History of Racist Ideas in America*, by Ibram X. Kendi, an academic and civil rights activist. This was a smoking gun. The cabal went to Goodwill's board of elders and alleged that Torres was a Marxist who was teaching Critical Race Theory. They demanded he be fired. Rebuffed by the elders, the cabal wrote a letter to the EPC denomination repeating the claims and seeking Torres's removal from the church.

Their letter found a stack of similar missives at the denominational headquarters. As it turned out, Torres wasn't the only pastor in the crosshairs of his congregation.

"I went to this meeting with pastors of large churches in the EPC. And everyone's telling the same story. Everyone's got some of their members saying: 'He's woke. He's teaching Critical Race Theory. He's a liberal, a socialist, a Marxist,'" Torres said. "It was actually pretty funny. Because we're all realizing, these words don't mean anything anymore. They're just smears."

The humor didn't last. Enraged by the elders' refusal to fire Torres, the cabal resorted to guerrilla methods. For months, they waged an innuendo campaign aimed at undermining his authority. They openly antagonized him, using church networks to organize a trip to Washington, D.C., for the January 6 protest against the election result. They printed fliers itemizing the pastor's alleged transgressions and passed them around Goodwill. Finally, two members accosted Torres one Sunday morning, in full view of the congregation, shouting and pointing in his face and calling for him to repent. One instigator screamed that Torres was sowing racial hatred in the church. "My older daughter is standing right there, listening to this. And she's like, 'Hello! Do you see me?'" Torres recalled.

The whole church was shaken by the incident. Torres now believed there was a credible threat of violence. His wife feared for the safety of their family. After consulting with his elders, Torres addressed an email to one of the men, requesting that he stay off the church property for good. In response, the man created a photoshopped image of Goodwill going up in flames. *Literally*—the church on fire. He posted the image on social media and blasted it around via email.

Torres felt defeated. This extremism represented nowhere near a majority of the church; the cabal numbered no more than twenty, a fraction of the hundreds of people who attended services every week. But these troublemakers were not a bunch of fringe, Easter-and-Christmas-Eve churchgoers. One of them worked on his staff. Another taught confirmation classes. Several were close friends—people he'd spent years praying with, laughing with, hanging around with. They had even gone on a trip together to the Holy Land. Now some of them were turning his church into a war zone. Torres was spiraling. For the first time, he began to question God.

"Those questions came up," Torres said, voice trembling, eyes closed, recalling his dialogue with the Lord. "What's going on? What did I miss? I felt like I was tracking with you, but apparently I'm not. You called me into this vocation, but now it seems like I'm not any good."

Torres thought about quitting. In fact, the idea of walking away from Goodwill consumed him. The church was bleeding attendance—civil war tends to thin out a congregation—and he feared an outright collapse. Torres did not want to be responsible for destroying a three-centuries-old institution. Perhaps there was a different pastor, he thought, a *better* pastor, who could salvage the situation.

The elder board wouldn't hear of it. Seeing the pastor's fragility, the elders arranged for him to take a four-month sabbatical. Torres reluctantly agreed. For the first three months, he did nothing but shuffle around his home, "stewing in my own failure." Finally, his wife convinced him to get out of town. He spent the final month of sabbatical in Key West, Florida, reading and praying and wondering if he could still lead Goodwill.

He was shocked, upon returning, to receive a protagonist's welcome from the church body. The congregation was noticeably smaller, but also noticeably healthier. A procession of members approached Torres, hugged him, said they'd been praying for him. Some of them apologized. They hadn't been a part of the cabal, Torres explained, but they hadn't pushed back on it, either. Maybe they were sympathetic to some of the complaints against him; maybe they simply didn't want to get involved. Either way, they hadn't backed up their pastor. It took him having an emotional breakdown, and nearly quitting the church, for them to extend their support.

Torres could have been upset. Instead, he was relieved.

"Here's the thing. I always figured it was five percent that was crazy—no more than that," Torres said. "We have a lot of strong Christians here. Some of them like Trump; some of them might be worked up about CRT or whatever else. But they would never do that crazy stuff."

Back in the pulpit at Goodwill, Torres still felt a quiet anxiety. He needed to protect the church—and himself—from any more suffering. He didn't regret speaking up after George Floyd's murder, but he saw how even the perception of choosing political sides had fractured Goodwill. The only certainty was that there would be more uncertainty: elections, wars, acts of God. Torres knew that he needed to set the eyes of his flock on Jesus. What he didn't know was how to keep them there.

* * *

THE SUNLIGHT FLOODED GOODWILL'S SANCTUARY. THIS SPACE WAS THE centerpiece of an ambitious building project that the church undertook in stabler times. Large high-definition screens lined either side of a blue-carpeted, multilevel stage. The cream-colored walls were accented by custom chestnut woodworking; everything from the towering ceiling arches to the miniature silhouetted steeple behind the lectern to the modest cross inside it was of a matching tone. Six sections of tan chairs fanned out across the cavernous auditorium, plus additional seating in the overhead gallery, gave Goodwill a capacity of one thousand or more.

But most of the chairs were empty. A few minutes before the start of the eleven o'clock service, there were maybe one hundred people—a generous estimate—seated in the sanctuary. Torres had warned me that some of his members were still watching online, still reluctant to come back for in-person worship. That was believable only to a point; it was March 2022 and the COVID-19 vaccines were widely available. However large Torres's online-viewing contingent, it was apparent that his church had been gutted by the infighting of recent years.

As I found my seat, an older gentleman approached. He introduced himself as Perry Songer, an elder at the church. He told me he'd been a member since 1980—and that he, too, had held me as a newborn in the church nursery. Torres had told him that I was visiting, but Songer, a stout older man with whisps of white hair thrown across his forehead, still seemed fuzzy on the why. I recounted my conversations with Torres.

"Yeah, all the stuff about woke theory and whatnot." Songer nodded, chewing on the side of his lip. Then he shrugged. "I'm still not sure what that means. But people sure are mad about it."

The title of Torres's sermon was "The One We Didn't Plan On." His reading came from the Book of Mark, chapter eight. The story picks up with Jesus, having just performed a series of spectacular miracles, asking His disciples what the people believed Him to be. When they replied that most thought Him to be a prophet, Jesus challenged the disciples: "But what about you? Who do you say I am?" Then Peter answered: "You are the Messiah."

This was a critical moment in the life of Jesus, the first time any of

His disciples dared to speak out loud that He was Israel's prophesied savior. Immediately, Jesus warned them not to reveal His identity to the masses, because the time was not right. Then He began to explain to the disciples His purpose on earth. He would be rejected by the Jewish leaders, killed by the authorities, and resurrected on the third day.

The disciples, understandably, were in disbelief. This group of misfits had put their lives on pause to travel with an eccentric young rabbi who worked miracles. Now they had finally figured out who He was—the long-anticipated Messiah—and He replied by informing them that He would soon be killed. Peter, the scripture says, took Jesus aside "and began to rebuke him." Peter told Jesus that He was wrong; that He would not, could not, suffer such a cruel fate.

When Torres reached this part of the reading, his voice hissed to emphasize Jesus's reaction.

"But turning and seeing his disciples, he rebuked Peter and said, 'Get behind me, Satan!'" Torres said. "'For you are not setting your mind on the things of God, but on the things of man.'"

The context here is paramount. For some seven hundred years, the Jewish people had been awaiting the king that God had promised them before the fall of Israel. This ruler would come from the line of David and restore security and prosperity to the chosen people. Because of the prophetic description in the ancient texts—a "Prince of Peace" who would conquer all of God's enemies—the Jews were expecting a strongman, an indomitable potentate whose political power and military might could not be rivaled.

When the disciples realized that their personal rabbi was, in fact, this future ruler of Israel, their self-image no doubt began to swell. Their imaginations began to run wild. Soon Jesus of Nazareth was going to sit on a throne, scepter in hand, and they would sit alongside Him. They would be the king's key lieutenants, highest counselors, and most influential proxies, the Mike Pences and Jared Kushners of Jerusalem.

For that thought bubble to suddenly burst—for Jesus to tell them that, actually, He would soon be tortured and executed—must have felt to the twelve disciples like a celestial sucker punch. Jesus didn't care. His entire ministry rested on the commitment to build a kingdom and the caveat that it would not be found here.

Remarkably, He chastises Peter—the disciple closest to Him, "the rock" upon whom Jesus vowed to build the Church—with identical language that He used with the devil during His temptation in the wilderness. ("Get behind me, Satan!" Jesus said, after the devil had offered Him dominion over all the nations.) Peter was pursuing victory in the world; Jesus was promising victory *over* the world.

If Peter could be singled out as "Satan" for putting an earthly kingdom ahead of an eternal kingdom, Torres warned, we're all fair game.

"It seems harsh, doesn't it? 'Get behind me, Satan!'" Torres said, wincing as he repeated the quote. "Jesus is saying this to Peter, but He's speaking to the belief system inside of Peter. And that belief system is inside all of us."

Indeed, the "things of man" Peter worried about twenty centuries ago are the same things that preoccupy us today: wealth, prestige, control. All of this, Torres said, competes with Jesus for our hearts. Everything to which we attach significance in this life—family, country, politics, bodily health, even the clothes we wear and the food we eat—can become a substitute religion.

"Whatever is tempting you to go astray, to sin, you can go full-bore, like Jesus did, and call it 'Satan.' Tell it to get behind you. You can say that to your temptation, say that to your sin," Torres told his congregation. "Because you know what 'get behind me' means? It means, 'I'm not following you.' It means I'm going to follow Christ."

The preacher's admonition was straightforward: By setting their minds on the things of man, Christians are telling Jesus to get behind *them*.

THERE WAS ONE THING THAT BOTHERED ME ABOUT THE SERVICE. THE night before, Torres had told me about a dilemma he and his staff were facing. With Russia's invasion of Ukraine underway, church leaders planned a special offering on Sunday morning to raise funds to send to missionaries doing humanitarian work on the ground there. An older Ukrainian woman attended Goodwill and still had family there; she agreed to tape a video message that could be played for the congregation. But during the taping, after telling of the suffering in her country and asking for Christians to pray for Ukraine, the woman began tearing into Russian president Vladimir Putin. She called him a war criminal who was slaughtering innocent civilians.

Putin *is* a war criminal. He *was* slaughtering innocents. Torres knew this and so did his staff. But they worried about diverting attention away from the plea for prayers and humanitarian aid—and antagonizing some of Goodwill's congregants in the process. "The thing is, we know there are some people here who would say, 'No, no—Putin's the good guy, [Ukrainian president Volodymyr] Zelenskyy is the bad guy. That's what Tucker Carlson told us,'" Torres said, referring to the outlandishly dishonest media personality who was then still the top attraction at Fox News. "Now, we could try to fight that battle, but I'm not sure that's our job. Because at that point, maybe it distracts from all the other great stuff she says on the video, and people who might have been willing to donate, they aren't willing to donate. And ultimately, maybe we're just hurting the cause."

The next morning, when Torres played the video ahead of the special offering for Ukraine, the woman's rant against Putin was edited out. Sensing my disappointment as we talked after the service, Torres invited me back to his home for a longer dialogue.

Joining us was Martin Sanders, a close friend of the pastor's and a longtime player in the evangelical movement. Sanders had spent decades speaking and teaching around the world, and was now the director of the Doctor of Ministry program at Alliance Theological Seminary in New York. Sanders was also a cigar aficionado. Pulling out three oversize stogies, he suggested we move the conversation to Torres's front porch. He, too, was interested in what his friend had to say.

"These are people I'm called to pastor," Torres explained to us. "I've got to work with them, meet them where they are. I've got to be careful about not playing the game by their terms. I really think that once I start down that road, opening the door to any sort of political disagreement, they win. Because now we're on ideological turf; we're not on theological turf."

Torres conceded that he might've been too cautious in this case. He said the church leadership might, in certain instances, determine that something extrabiblical was so urgent—so relevant and so clearly consistent with Christ's teachings—that it warranted discussion in the church. Still, he said, the past few years had taught him to err on the side of theology. "If you start playing by the rules of another game, then suddenly you're playing that other game. If you bring a football onto the baseball diamond and start throwing it around, are you still playing baseball?" Torres said. "I don't know. I don't think so."

Sanders nodded along in agreement. The past few years had been painful for him, too. Sanders had come to Goodwill nearly twenty years ago at the urging of his wife, Dianna, who loved Torres's preaching and thought it would be a good fit for their family. Her husband and Torres became fast friends. When Dianna died of cancer in 2014, Sanders sought refuge in traveling and teaching, which took him away from Goodwill as things were going south for Torres. Sanders told me he was relieved—if not a bit surprised—that his friend survived the ordeal.

"This has been a long time coming for the American Church, and John dealt with the worst of it," Sanders said, blowing smoke into the blustery spring breeze. "But this stuff is everywhere. *Everywhere*."

Sanders, who does consulting work for pastors and churches all over the country, offered a captivating illustration. Recently, his childhood church in small-town Ohio had commissioned a project on the future of their mission; Sanders advised them to put down in writing the five key principles of a solid, Bible-believing church. At that very same time, Torres had been asked to counsel an all-Latino congregation in the South Bronx. He gave them an identical assignment.

"Here's what I found interesting," Sanders said. "The two churches had none of the same five key principles—not even close. The church in Ohio, they left no room for anything that was different from their experience: white, conservative, midwestern, *American*. They had totally lost sight of people who aren't like them. And I said, 'What you've done is you've baptized your worldview and called it Christian.'"

Sanders—an older white evangelical himself—said it's hardly coincidental that most of the churches in chaos are old, white, and evangelical. These are the congregations, he said, that have spent decades marinating in rhetoric of "Armageddon for the Church, enemies coming for us." Having come to faith in the mid-1970s, Sanders told us he has noticed a substantial shift in perception as to where the threat to

Christianity originates. Whereas it was once feared that sinister geopolitical forces would target America as a means to extinguishing its holy light to the world, the narrative began to shift as the Moral Majority gained clout in the 1980s. Leading voices on the religious right argued that Christ's kingdom could be advanced only if American believers were willing to fight for it. By the time the Iron Curtain fell, and the United States was left standing as the world's sole superpower, it was clear to evangelicals that the only enemy left to defeat was the one within.

"For a lot of these people, if you've got a philosophy or a worldview to oppose, that became the mission of the Church," Sanders said.

"The scary thing now," Torres interjected, "is that the enemy is *inside* the Church."

"Right. And they'll say it's because the stakes have gotten so high," Sanders said. "That's what you saw on January 6. That's why, if you're an evangelical, you think it was okay to club the cops or break the windows. And it wasn't Nancy Pelosi they were after; it was Mike Pence. A fellow believer. This is the biggest change I've observed in the last few years. The enemies aren't those outside of the Church; it's people in your church who don't think exactly the way you do."

Just the other day, Sanders told us, a friend who pastors a large congregation in Cleveland called him to vent. A longtime member of the church had asked for a meeting and broken some difficult news. "I'm afraid we have to leave the church after all these decades," the man said, "because you're not interpreting the Bible in light of the Constitution."

Torres let out a groan. "I'm telling you, I thought I had seen it all—sex scandals, embezzlement, disagreements over every kind of church doctrine. But we never dealt with that stuff before," he said. "Usually the people who had strong points of view, they were focused on the mission of the church and what the church believed. But that's become secondary."

I asked Sanders if he had a theory as to why American Christianity had become so uniquely dysfunctional.

"When I spent some years living in Canada, I became friends with a renowned Canadian sociologist," Sanders said. "He would always say—he wrote books on this—that 'Americans always want to be number one. They always go for the gold. Canada shoots for bronze, settles for fourth, then talks about how well they represented themselves.'"

Sanders shrugged. "Americans always think they deserve to win. And so, naturally, the Church has become about winning, too."

He stopped and jabbed a cautionary finger toward the sky.

"Now, let me tell you the good side of that," Sanders said. "I talk with church leaders regularly, and what they've said to me is, 'Some of the people in our churches who have lost the plot—or, in some cases, downright lost their minds—they're the ones giving the most time to the homeless shelter down the street. They're the ones coming here on the weekends to cook meals for hungry people.' And so, you have this contradiction within the American Church."

I turned to Torres. This is why, I concluded, he didn't want to turn the Ukrainian fundraising effort into a dispute over Vladimir Putin.

"Exactly," he said. "They might have been watching Tucker Carlson all week. But they're still going to write a check on Sunday morning. That's the best of the American Christian psyche—even if it's also the worst of the American Christian psyche."

"These are good people," Sanders insisted. "They have the Father's heart. They want to be like Jesus. But they've lost their way a little bit. We need to bring them back."

So, how could Torres bring them back? How could he make them forget about winning and focus on following Jesus?

"The whole idea of a Messiah coming was that he was going to arrive and there wouldn't be a living Roman anywhere. It was going to be a bloodbath. All the Romans were gonna be dead," Torres replied. "And yet Jesus had a very different program. His kingdom is so different from what we envision as a kingdom. We think in terms of beating the other side, of winning the argument. The problem is, if you win the argument, you've won nothing."

Jesus could have chosen to win the argument. He could have come down from the cross, as the jeering onlookers dared Him to do, proving that He really *was* the son of God; He could have confronted Caiaphas, the Jewish high priest, after the resurrection, proving that He really *did* rebuild the temple in three days. But He didn't. Jesus chose to submit Himself to a brutal, dehumanizing death. Once resurrected, He chose to appear to His believers, instructing them to take a message of salvation to all the nations, emulating His example of lowliness and servanthood and self-sacrificial love.

Torres took a final puff of his cigar.

"All the winning in this world doesn't make a difference. If you beat your opponent—if you crush them in some political argument—what do you have to show for it? A better country?" the pastor asked, shaking his head. "You think so, but you don't."

CHAPTER THREE

～∞✕∞～

LYNCHBURG, VIRGINIA

Then give back to Caesar what is Caesar's, and to God what is God's.

—LUKE 20:25

A month after he graduated from high school, Doug Olson stood at the top of Liberty Mountain, looking out over his future home.

Olson had become "born again" when he was eleven years old. Accepting Jesus Christ as his savior during a summer church program in his native Lewistown, Pennsylvania, he eagerly embarked on a new life as God's adopted son. Olson analyzed the scriptures with intensity, skipping typical children's activities to study alongside the adults inside his church. Even as his congregation split over denominational differences—the Conservative Baptist Association was not, for many in Lewistown, conservative enough—Olson was a unifying figure. Everyone knew the young man would do great things for the Lord.

When it came time to choose a college, Olson narrowed his options to three Christian schools. His first two choices were Lancaster Bible College, an easy drive from his home in Central Pennsylvania, and Biola University in Southern California, a premier training ground for missionaries and evangelists. The third option: Lynchburg Baptist College in Virginia.

There was no obvious reason to enroll there. The school had been founded just a few years earlier, in 1971; Olson had never even heard of Lynchburg until his father, who had visited for a conference, came home raving about the work God was doing there. Olson grew more intrigued as he studied up on the school and its leader. Over the past twenty years, Jerry Falwell had taken a start-up congregation of three dozen people and turned it into one of the South's biggest mega-churches. If Falwell could replicate that model with Lynchburg Baptist College—which was now being renamed Liberty Baptist College—Olson figured he'd be getting in on the ground floor of something special.

When Olson committed to the school, his father planned a celebratory trip for the entire family to Lynchburg. It was the summer of 1976 and Falwell had been advertising—on his radio and TV programs—a blockbuster event on July Fourth to commemorate the nation's bicentennial. Olson didn't know quite what to expect as the family sedan snaked through the hills and hollers east of Appalachia. When they finally arrived at Liberty Mountain, the sight was like nothing the eighteen-year-old Olson had ever imagined.

More than twenty-five thousand people swarmed the open pastureland, a sea of humanity robed in red, white, and blue. Flags and banners and festoons were draped across a great platform stage. Its centerpiece was a full-scale replica of the Liberty Bell, shiny and sturdy as Philadelphia's original, the fruit of an ambitious fundraising campaign. Olson could hardly fathom all the heart-stirring sights and sounds. And then the program commenced.

Welcoming the masses to Liberty Mountain, the gospel choir of Thomas Road Baptist Church sang praise to the Lord (and this, His sweet Land of Liberty). B. R. Lakin, the famed fundamentalist preacher and mentor to Falwell, declared that another Great Awakening could be at hand. When it was his time to speak, however, Falwell warned the crowds that nothing was promised to them. America was under assault from secular liberal elites and godless government bureaucrats, and Christians needed to start fighting back. "The nation was intended to be a Christian nation by our founding fathers," Falwell thundered. "This idea of 'religion and politics don't mix' was invented by the devil to keep Christians from running their own country!"

Falwell offered a reading from the Second Book of Chronicles: "If my people, which are called by my name, shall humble themselves, and pray, and seek my face, and turn from their wicked ways, then will I hear from heaven, and forgive their sin, and will heal their land." When the program ended, fireworks spewed forth from the mountaintop, illuminating the flags and church steeples that dotted the landscape below.

Everything Falwell was selling, Olson bought. "I fell in love," he recalled decades later, "with the idea of Liberty."

That enthusiasm was soon curbed. When the Olsons returned to Lynchburg after Labor Day, excited to move their oldest son into his new home, they were dismayed to find themselves at a boarded-up hotel in a tough part of downtown. The condemned building was all that Liberty could offer its newest students. Olson flopped a mattress onto the floor and unloaded boxes of his clothing and books, assuring his parents that he would be fine. They drove off with tears in their eyes—not tears of joy, but tears of concern and bewilderment. The July Fourth celebration was suddenly a distant memory; this seedy neighborhood in downtown Lynchburg bore no resemblance to that bucolic scene on Liberty Mountain. Their son had signed up to be part of something he didn't fully understand.

Olson had reason to worry, too. He could not have known that Falwell would soon emerge as one of the most consequential figures of the late twentieth century; that his synthesizing of Christianity and conservatism would roil America's political landscape and radicalize its Protestant subculture; that his small school in Lynchburg, Virginia, would eventually develop into a multibillion-dollar behemoth and, become the embodiment of both the great promise and wasted potential of the evangelical Church.

None of this was conceivable to the college freshman sleeping in that condemned hotel. Studying his surroundings, Olson simply wanted to know: Did Falwell have a vision?

BORN INTO A FRONTIER FAMILY OF BOOTLEGGERS, ALCOHOLICS, AND atheists, Jerry Laymon Falwell was hardly the prototype for a preacher.

As a child, Falwell hated those occasions when his mother forced him to attend church. When his father died of cirrhosis of the liver—Jerry was just fifteen years old—he stopped going altogether. His mother, the lone devout Christian in the extended clan, prayed daily for her son's salvation. Then, one Sunday morning in 1952, three years after his father's death, Falwell joined a group of friends at Park Avenue Baptist Church. He responded to the altar call and prayed to receive Jesus. In the context of the times, Falwell's decision seemed typical. Church attendance was soaring in the postwar era; Billy Graham, the brilliant young evangelist, was drawing stadium-sized crowds for his revivals around the country. The only remarkable thing about Falwell's story was that, in an age of spiritual dramatics, his own conversion was utterly dull. "There was no vision. No blinding light. No miracle," he wrote in his autobiography. "I didn't even feel particularly emotional."

Once interested in engineering, Falwell abruptly switched vocational lanes. He enrolled at a Missouri Bible college and began training under a pair of fundamentalist—and segregationist—preachers. In the absence of outward religious fervor, the best explanation for Falwell's career turn was his attraction to the nature of ministry work. He was a people person, an extrovert who loved to schmooze and argue and persuade. He was also a born salesman. Despite his youthful aversion to churchgoing, Falwell constantly overheard the radio programs echoing around his mother's house, such as Charles Fuller's *Old-Fashioned Revival Hour*, and found himself fascinated by the market dynamics at play. In 1956, Falwell started his very own congregation in Lynchburg, calling it Thomas Road Baptist Church, and began airing his own local radio show. Within months, he had broken into an experimental new medium for his profession, television, airing his Sunday sermons on WLVA, Lynchburg's ABC affiliate.

In a town crammed with churches—Lynchburg was thought to have more than a hundred at the time—Falwell's media savvy proved a differentiator. His congregation swelled from thirty-five at the first service to more than eight hundred one year later. Physical expansion followed: Thomas Road commenced a building campaign that never truly ended, growing from a 1,500-square-foot facility into the nearly 900,000-square-foot colossus that spans multiple blocks in Lynchburg today. Television was the rocket fuel: Not long after the founding of Thomas Road, Falwell had expanded his telecast into four states plus Washington, D.C., and was reaching hundreds of thousands of viewers each Sunday. By the mid-1970s, Falwell's *Old-Time Gospel Hour* was shown on more stations throughout the United States than any single telecast.

Falwell was not flashy in the pulpit, nor was he especially eloquent. Substantively, his sermons emphasized what he called "the fundamentals of the faith"—the virgin birth, the resurrection of Christ, the inerrancy of scripture—and mostly avoided extrabiblical commentary. In keeping with the fundamentalist doctrine of his independent Baptist tradition, Falwell preached "separatism," the idea that followers of Christ are distinct, set apart, called to a citizenship in heaven that takes precedence over earthly identities. He frowned upon civic activism and expressly denounced political entanglements. In 1965, at the climax of the civil rights movement, Falwell delivered a sermon scolding his colleague, Rev. Martin Luther King Jr., for sullying their profession. The goal of the Church, Falwell decreed, is "not reformation but transformation," a fact that certain clergy would do well to recognize. "As a God-called preacher, I find that there is no time left after I give the proper time and attention to winning people to Christ," Falwell said. "Preachers are not called to be politicians, but to be soul winners."

He cited Jesus's own words as evidence. "'Render therefore unto Caesar the things which are Caesar's, and unto God the things that are God's,'" Falwell said, reading his vintage translation from the New Testament. "In other words," Falwell continued, "He said, 'Pay your taxes, forget politics, and serve Me with all your heart.'"

Falwell and his congregants could afford to forget politics: He had launched his ministry during an idyllic age for the white American Christian. Wars had been fought and won. Incomes and education levels were taking off. Opportunity—in the form of jobs, housing, transportation—abounded. Social progress did not yet imperil the nation's Christian values; the most immediate cultural threat came in the form of a onetime gospel singer who now gyrated his hips on stage.

In truth, Falwell had never been apolitical. Back in 1958—just his second year of pastoring—Falwell denounced the *Brown v. Board of Education* Supreme Court decision of 1954, saying "the devil himself" was pushing integration and that "the true Negro" did not want it. ("What will integration of the races do to us?" Falwell asked his all-white congregation. "It will destroy our race eventually.") As the years went on,

Falwell was selective—but hardly silent—with his partisan punditry. He aligned himself with Senator Joe McCarthy, alerting his flock to the risks of communist infiltration. He chastised King for having "left-wing associations." Although he would later retract his comments about segregation and race—calling it "false prophecy" and welcoming Black families to his church—Falwell's trajectory was bending inexorably toward the flag-waving figurehead he would become. By the mid-1970s, there was no use in trying to separate politics and theology. In fact, Falwell realized, combining the two might be the way to save both the country and his upstart college.

Given the astonishing success of his ministry—the church, the broadcasting enterprise, the flourishing private K–12 academy he oversaw at Thomas Road—Falwell had felt confident about his foray into higher education. That confidence soon proved misplaced. It became apparent, shortly after Falwell opened Lynchburg Baptist College in 1971, that this entrepreneurial endeavor was quite unlike his others. No plates were being passed; no donations were being dialed in. The school, whose primary source of revenue was meager tuition payments, rapidly accumulated debt. It owned property—including a piece of Candler's Mountain, which Falwell envisioned as the site of a future campus—but had no funds to build. This forced its students to live and learn in dilapidated, long-abandoned buildings, which in turn made it harder to recruit new students. Within a few years of its founding, the school was in danger of collapse.

There were other reasons Falwell had such a hard time luring young people to central Virginia. He was a fundamentalist, an adherent to the independent Baptist code, which outlawed, among other things, movies, dancing, drinking, smoking, and one-on-one dating. For all the success Falwell had in reaching older, traditionalist Christians with his TV show, he was now dealing with a very different demographic. Fundamentalism was outmoded to many younger believers. Inspired by the likes of Billy Graham, they gravitated toward a broader, more modern Christianity less about rules and more about relationships; it was joyful and civic-minded and proudly pro-American. For the first time, significant numbers of young adults who had been raised in diverging traditions—Pentecostals with their emphasis on charismatic expression, fundamentalists with their old-fashioned rituals, Southern Baptists with their cultural etiquette, mainline Protestants with their social awareness—were amalgamating under a shared, if loosely defined, label: "evangelicals."

In this moment, Falwell saw opportunity. He had limited the college's reach by stressing its fundamentalist roots and regional identity. In 1975, with the bicentennial approaching, Falwell considered a change. Inspired by the shrewdness of a friend, Arthur DeMoss, a multimillionaire businessman who'd founded the National Liberty Corporation—a life insurance giant that used a Valley Forge, Pennsylvania, mailing address, even though it was headquartered in Philadelphia—Falwell undertook a makeover of the school's image. Lynchburg Baptist College became Liberty Baptist College (it would later be shortened to Liberty University). The school's colors changed from green and gold to red, white, and blue. With Olympiad undertones—1976 was a triumphant year for Old Glory on the world stage, punctuated by a young decathlete named Bruce Jenner breaking the world record—Falwell stressed the school's motto, "Training Champions for Christ." He began touring the country with a choir. Performing at rallies and concerts in starspangled attire, the roaming ensemble raised millions of dollars from *Old-Time Gospel Hour* devotees to fill the school's budget shortfalls. It was a promising blueprint. The next year—an election year—Falwell turned the choir routine into a traveling church service. He called it the "I Love America" tour and took it to 112 locations nationwide.

"That's when things started to turn around," recalled Jerry Falwell Jr., who as a teenager would accompany his father on these road trips. "Nobody wanted to send their kids to *Lynchburg*. The school needed a national appeal, and that patriotic angle sold a lot of people."

To understand the long-unfolding crisis at Liberty—an institution known today less for charity and Christian disciple-making than for corruption and Republican kingmaking—is to understand that, in the half a century since its rebranding, the university has struggled to execute on the supposed double meaning of its name. Patriotism divorced from piety is futile, after all; those who win the world but lose their souls are champions of nothing. In the heart of campus, through the main doors of DeMoss Hall—a regal brick building featuring tall white columns—students are greeted with a wall-length inscription from Second Corinthians: "... where the Spirit of the Lord is, there is Liberty."

But according to Falwell Jr.—his father's namesake, and also his successor as university president—there was no double meaning intended.

"It had nothing to do with theology. It was a marketing thing. My dad was appealing to a sense of patriotism that was big in Christianity at that time," he told me.

The younger Falwell added: "'Champions for Christ' was just a tagline. It wasn't a vision for the university."

WHEN *NEWSWEEK* CALLED 1976 "THE YEAR OF THE EVANGELICAL," IT WAS both an observation of the present and a remark on the past.

Historians and religious scholars had long understood the American story in the context of its "Great Awakenings." The first broke out in the British American colonies during the 1730s. With echoes of the Protestant Reformation—which had destabilized the aristocratic Roman Catholic Church two centuries earlier—frontier preachers democratized the revival process, calling for a renewed focus on holiness and individual salvation. The second awakening, in the 1790s, offered similar revivals but with far greater breadth, its emphasis on converting the unchurched, spawning myriad new Christian organizations and associations that became central to the young nation's civic life. The third awakening—generally thought to be the least impactful, at least theologically speaking—stressed missionary work and moral activism in the latter half of the nineteenth century. It gave rise to the Prohibition movement and the so-called Social Gospel, which presented Christianity as a cure to poverty and other societal ills.

In the early twentieth century, however, American religiosity went into recession. Clashes with modernity became recurring and problematic, never more so than in 1925, when, after Tennessee banned the teaching of evolution in schools, the American Civil Liberties Union recruited a young science teacher, John Scopes, to be indicted for violating the law. The ensuing trial was a media phenomenon. Former secretary of state William Jennings Bryan, a fundamentalist Christian and three-time presidential candidate who had retired from politics to focus on defeating the scourge of Darwinism, led the prosecution's case. In a surprise move, Clarence Darrow, Scopes's renowned lawyer, called Bryan himself to testify. Bryan's wobbly performance on the stand—his loose understanding of science, paired with a fringe interpretation of the biblical account of earth's creation—produced a moment that was re-created in newspapers, radio broadcasts, and telegraph reports that permeated the country. Bryan won the conviction of Scopes—though it was later overturned, as was Tennessee's law—but lost badly in the court of public opinion. "The Scopes Trial" became shorthand, iconographic of the twentieth century's embrace, even worship, of technology and science.

By the time Liberty University opened in 1971, fundamentalism was enjoying a resurgence. This was partly thanks to mass communication media that brought Falwell and his comrades into the living rooms, kitchens, garages, and automobiles of tens of millions of Americans. But it was also because the very nature of fundamentalism was changing. Preachers who once prescribed total detachment from worldly affairs were now trafficking in jeremiads of civilizational collapse, winning huge audiences of older, conservative Christians who feared that the American apocalypse was nigh. Education had become a national flashpoint. The Supreme Court's 1962 ruling in *Engel v. Vitale*, which banned prayer in public schools, inflamed the intensifying fights over curriculum relating to evolution, history, and human sexuality. Falwell began floating his belief that public schools should be abolished entirely. Detecting a secular plot to brainwash the next generation, fundamentalists yanked their kids out of local K–12 programs and launched alternative Christian academies at a frenetic clip, foreshadowing the antipathy toward public education that evangelicals have come to practice at a massive scale today.

For Falwell, however, this change wasn't happening fast enough. He had concluded—rightly, based on the research—that most fundamentalist Christians remained uninterested in politics. Many were not even registered to vote and those who were showed no reliable appetite for engagement. Falwell hoped to bring his tribe along. But he couldn't ignore the potential that existed elsewhere. In 1976, the pollster George Gallup found that one in three Americans identified as born-again

Christians, and that an even larger share of the electorate agreed that the Bible should be interpreted literally. Falwell sensed that a fourth great awakening could be at hand, but only if he broadened his existing tent. If Christians were going to reclaim America—and if he was going to save his school—he would need to cast a wider vision.

So in the year of the bicentennial, Falwell initiated a public relations blitz aimed at capitalizing on love of country and exploiting fears of secularism. To raise his (and his fledgling school's) profile, Falwell picked a surprising target: Jimmy Carter. The Democratic candidate for president was a Sunday School teacher, a devout Southern Baptist from Georgia who identified as "born again" at a time when few politicians of either party did so. Falwell didn't merely throw his support behind the Republican, Gerald Ford; he set out to destroy the Democratic nominee. Specifically, Falwell railed against Carter for giving an interview to *Playboy* magazine in which the politician admitted to having "looked on a lot of women with lust," and "committed adultery in my heart many times," describing it as beneath the dignity of a candidate for the nation's highest office.

In reality, the source of Falwell's antagonism was standard partisanship. Long before the "Southern Strategy" transformed the political loyalties of white conservatives in places like Lynchburg, Falwell had been a staunch Republican, believing the party's business-friendly dogma and law-and-order policies more than offset the elite cultural sensibility that alienated so many southerners. ("I thought Goldwater was too liberal!" he wrote in one of his books.) Given how the country had turned on Republicans after Watergate, Falwell was destined to be disappointed in 1976. Carter won the election, but with the culture wars beginning to rage, Falwell sensed an opening to turn Democratic rule into a referendum on American morality.

DOUG OLSON DIDN'T SEE IT AT FIRST. HE HADN'T EVEN VOTED IN 1976; the energy on campus centered on Christ and carrying out the mission as His disciples. The freshman had thrown himself into classes and church and volunteering in the community, activities that made Lynchburg feel like home.

Despite the initial shock of his new environment —lodging at a condemned hotel, walking to class through a gauntlet of beggars and drunks and drug addicts—Olson had taken to life at Liberty. His classmates were "on fire for the Lord." His professors were brilliant and godly. He especially liked the school's president, Falwell—or "Doc," as the students dubbed him. (Falwell did not have any advanced degree, though he was conferred several honorary doctorates.) Olson saw in Falwell what even his fiercest critics would concede: a heart for people. Thomas Road was extravagantly generous with its resources. The church purchased a large farmhouse to rehabilitate alcoholics; ran camps for underprivileged kids; sponsored adoption and foster-parenting programs; ministered to Lynchburg's homeless population; and raised money for missionaries who served in impoverished nations abroad. The students saw in their school president—and, for most of them, their pastor— a man whose sole focus was living out his faith.

At eighteen, Olson lacked the guile to discern Falwell's endgame for Liberty. The patriotic relabeling had been perfectly timed and expertly executed. Carter's victory in 1976 uncorked a pent-up sense of panic on the American right, and Falwell knew that his school—more than any church or tent revival or television show—stood to benefit. With enrollment pushing fifteen hundred that fall, a tenfold increase from a few years earlier, Liberty was starting to imitate the explosive growth of Thomas Road. But Falwell didn't need another church. He needed an institution *parallel* to the church, a cultural stronghold that could train conservative warriors to wage a frontal strike on the forces of secularism. The Catholics of the University of Notre Dame were too dignified to battle the left; the Mormons of Brigham Young University were too genial. To rescue the nation from Sodom-and-Gomorrah-style destruction, Falwell decided, Protestant Christians would need to lead the charge.

On January 21, 1977, yellow school buses transported several thousand people to the top of Liberty Mountain. Friday morning chapel was typically held inside the Thomas Road sanctuary, but this was a momentous occasion. The students and faculty of Liberty University had come to hear from their founder about a vision.

"I want us here today to ask the Lord to do something special for us on what we believe to be a sacred spot of ground," Falwell told the crowd. "We are asking God to build us a college."

Sweeping his finger across the frozen landscape, Falwell asked everyone to imagine these hundreds of barren acres being transformed into buildings—laboratories, dorms, lecture halls. God had placed it on his heart, Falwell explained, to turn this small school into a world-class university. He was not shy about his ultimate aims. The school would promote Christian values, certainly; but even more so, it would grow big enough and strong enough to reverse the leftward currents in academia that were running downstream into the rest of American life.

Standing in six inches of snow, with icy winds lashing through the open pasture all around them, the students and professors joined hands in prayer. They sang a song, "I Want That Mountain," written by one of Jerry Jr.'s friends. They climbed onto the buses and continued singing on their ride down, stirred by Falwell's fantasy and deeply skeptical that it would ever become reality.

"I'll never forget the day Doc claimed that mountain for God," Olson told me, recalling his delight at hearing Falwell articulate this grand plan. "I'll also never forget thinking, *never gonna happen.*"

The supernatural, against-all-odds framing of the Liberty Mountain conquest—David slaying Goliath, Jesus feeding the five thousand, pick your biblical wonder—would soon become central to the school's self-mythologizing narrative. Yet in many ways, the episode was straightforward. Liberty had owned the property for years. Now, thanks to increasing enrollment and an infusion of donations, both of which owed directly to Falwell's "I Love America" tour, the university had dug out of its financial hole. If Falwell was waiting for a sign from above, it came quickly: Construction on the new campus began less than two months after the January prayer summit.

The ensuing years were an exhilarating time at Liberty. New structures sprang up everywhere. Prospective students and their parents swarmed the embryonic campus. Journalists descended on Lynchburg to marvel at the spectacle. Millions of viewers watched a televised special, *The Miracle of Liberty Mountain*, sparking yet another surge in enrollment and long-distance donations. Falwell kept cultivating his celebrity in the political world, joining fights against gambling and gay rights (among other issues) while chastising Carter, with language increasingly strident, for ushering in America's decline. Falwell had spent decades building his brand as a down-home preacher from Virginia. Now he was recognized as a political player. And he was just getting started.

In June 1979, Falwell took a brief leave from his revamped "I Love America" tour—it was now playing at state capitol buildings from coast to coast, earning huge crowds and enormous revenues—to meet with a group of prominent conservative activists. Among them were Howard Phillips, a free-market advocacy wonk and Jewish convert to evangelicalism, and Richard Viguerie, a campaign strategist who had perfected direct-mail technology as a means of mobilizing Christian voters. The organizer was Paul Weyrich, a Catholic journalist turned political insider who in 1973 had cofounded the Heritage Foundation, which would become Washington's leading conservative think tank. Each of these men had effectively abandoned the Republican Party in the aftermath of Watergate, hoping that a descendant of purer ideology would supplant the GOP. But that romanticism now gave way to reality. Carter's presidency was proving injurious to the right—to the whole country, they would argue—and conservatives were desperate to defeat him in 1980. Republicans could not retake the presidency with their existing coalition. They needed to engage an untapped segment of voters. They needed to galvanize fundamentalist Christians. They needed Falwell.

It was an easy sell. Falwell had long awaited the chance to lead conservatives into combat—and not just *Christian* conservatives. Francis Schaeffer, a bohemian theologian who rose to prominence in the 1970s, had revolutionized the ways in which people like Falwell thought about cultural conflict. Even before they became personal friends, Schaeffer had sold Falwell on the need to partner with "co-belligerents," people of different beliefs but shared objectives. The implications, political and spiritual, were profound. Whereas Falwell had once treated theology as the imperative—prioritizing saving the individual soul, believing that America's redemption was downstream from mass conversion—he was now operating in reverse, setting aside religious differences and working with non-Christians toward a supposed national salvation. In this sense, Falwell was a mirror image of Billy Graham, who in the early stages of his career had stressed patriotism and courted political power, only to later back away from both.

Falwell's loathing of President Carter was white-hot. In particular, he claimed that the government's decision to deny tax-exempt status to a Christian college, Bob Jones University, on the basis of its racially discriminatory practices set a precedent for secular politicians to shut down churches. Deploying ever-more-apocalyptic rhetoric, Falwell pleaded with Christians to resist. He believed that America was, as he would proclaim in 1980, "floundering to the brink of death." He also believed himself uniquely situated to the challenge: Over the past few years, Falwell had watched kindred spirits such as James Dobson (Focus on the Family), Beverly LaHaye (Concerned Women for America), and Donald Wildmon (American Family Association) launch faith-based organizations that reached much of the evangelical world but missed his fellow fundamentalists. There was a certain asymmetry at work: Evangelicals could not seem to engage their fundamentalist brethren, but Falwell, having invested considerable resources in expanding his school and telecast empire, was learning how to engage evangelicals. Weyrich and his associates realized as much. These men had come to Lynchburg wanting Falwell to be more than just a missing cog in their new political machine. They wanted him to be its leader.

When the discussion turned to tactics—they would target Protestants, Catholics, Mormons, Jews, even conservative atheists, an evolution of the co-belligerent construct—Weyrich told Falwell there was a "moral majority" of Americans on their side. Falwell glanced over at his staff.

"That's the name of our organization," he said.

FALWELL AND HIS NEWFOUND ALLIES HAD A NAME. WHAT THEY DIDN'T have was a rationale—at least, not a rationale for justifying this God-ordained incursion into the blood sport of presidential politics.

These men were political animals. Much of their disdain for Carter and his Democratic Party owed to essential partisan disagreements: taxation, spending, regulation, foreign policy, labor disputes, and the like. Yet these matters were of no obvious *moral* urgency. And Falwell's crew couldn't build a viable public-facing effort—in the twilight of the 1970s—around some of their pet causes, such as fighting the Equal Rights Amendment and supporting religious schools that discriminated against Blacks. They needed an issue set that would satisfy the lowest common denominator of their socially conservative constituency. And so Falwell would launch the Moral Majority with a focus on pornography, homosexuality, drug use, rising divorce rates, secularism in public schools, and, above all, abortion.

That the pro-life cause has become synonymous with Falwell, his Moral Majority, and its successor movements is evidence of careful storytelling and masterful salesmanship. But it does not stand up to factual scrutiny.

In the decades preceding the landmark *Roe v. Wade* decision that legalized abortion in 1973, abortion was considered a "Catholic issue." In 1968, *Christianity Today*, the flagship evangelical publication founded by Graham, convened a symposium of some two dozen theologians who ultimately could not agree whether abortion is sinful. In 1971, the Southern Baptist Convention passed a resolution affirming the procedure under a generous range of circumstances. (W. A. Criswell, the SBC ex-president and legendary pastor of First Baptist Church in Dallas, one of America's leading megachurches, approved: "I have always felt that it was only after a child was born and had a life separate from its mother that it became an individual person.") In 1973, Barry Garrett, the D.C. bureau chief for Baptist Press, reacted to the *Roe* decision by writing that the Supreme Court had "advanced the cause of religious liberty, human equality and justice."

Falwell was no stranger to opining on court rulings. Yet the first time he mentioned abortion from the pulpit was 1978—five years after the *Roe* decision. Ed Dobson (no relation to James), one of Falwell's closest friends and an original dean at Lynchburg Baptist College, sat at his side during that fateful 1979 meeting with Weyrich. Years later, commenting on the notion that *Roe v. Wade* had ignited the religious right, Dobson said, "I sat in the non-smoke-filled back room with the Moral Majority, and I frankly do not remember abortion being mentioned as a reason why we ought to do something."

This is not to discount genuine changes of heart and conscience. In retrospect, given the dramatic jump in abortion rates following *Roe*, advances in medical technology that gave the public a window into the procedure, and the attention lavished on the subject by influential Christians, the overnight groundswell of opposition makes sense. Falwell's own whirlwind fixation on abortion tracks with a 1979 film series, *Whatever Happened to the Human Race?*, created by Schaeffer and the pediatric surgeon (and future surgeon general of the United States) C. Everett Koop. At screenings around the country, Schaeffer argued that the casual devaluing of life portended catastrophic consequences for America, a message that surely resonated with Falwell and his like-minded religious patriots.

Even so, the political context cannot be ignored. In the 1978 midterm elections, Republicans scored multiple major upsets over Carter's Democratic Party; three of those victories were heavily attributable to grassroots pro-life activism. This was astonishing to Weyrich, who, as a staunch Catholic and anti-abortion conservative, had long lamented the GOP's unwillingness to organize around the abortion issue. Randall Balmer, a Dartmouth professor who is perhaps the preeminent historian of the Moral Majority, has described the 1978 elections as a turning point. He discovered one telling correspondence between Weyrich and Robert Billings, who would become the Moral Majority's first executive director. The triumph of pro-lifers in 1978, Billings wrote to Weyrich, would "pull together many of our 'fringe' Christian friends."

Indeed it did. In 1980, Falwell assembled a new coalition of voters—fundamentalists, evangelicals, Southern Baptists, Pentecostals, and all manner of vagrant Christians, plus, thanks to the emphasis on abortion, Catholics—around the message that traditional values were being extinguished by Carter and his godless government. The Republican presidential primary was the first chance for Falwell's group to flex its muscle. Whereas the GOP establishment's preference, George H. W. Bush, kept a strategic distance from the religious right, Ronald Reagan made his courtship of these newly mobilized Christian voters a tactical linchpin of his campaign, specifically engaging on the abortion issue in ways Bush would not dare. After a photo finish in Iowa—Bush carried the state by some two thousand votes—Reagan went to South Carolina.

His biggest rally came at Bob Jones University, the school that had been punished by the Internal Revenue Service for refusing to admit Blacks. (It had recently changed policies, though the school still banned interracial dating and marriage.) Reagan trounced Bush in South Carolina. Emboldened, Falwell redeployed resources and personnel to upcoming primary states and even hit the ground to stump for Reagan himself. It was all too much for Bush to overcome. When Reagan clinched the nomination, he rewarded Falwell by naming Robert Billings as his faith-based liaison for the general election.

A new standard had been set in Republican politics. That which had animated the party for much of its modern history—an educated, moneyed, socially moderate, culturally coastal sensibility—was suddenly and unceremoniously out of style. Moving forward, passing muster in the GOP would require talking as much about abortion as economics. It would mean campaigning more from the pulpits of southern churches and less inside the parlors of northeastern country clubs. It would involve the concession that base voters no longer took their orders from a party boss or precinct captain, but rather, from a Baptist preacher in Virginia.

The Moral Majority had taken over the Republican Party. But Falwell wanted more. He wanted America.

Carter was always going to struggle to win a second term. His presidency had been defined by dreadful inflation, an energy crisis, and an embarrassing hostage situation in Iran. Adding insult to ineptitude, the president had survived a bruising primary challenge from Senator Ted Kennedy, who depicted him as aloof and overmatched. All these obstacles might have been surmountable if not for the added problem posed by the religious right.

Working closely with the Reagan campaign, Falwell's organization helped build out a sophisticated, hyperlocal organizing system that targeted churchgoers, and more specifically, the millions of evangelicals who had backed Carter in 1976. Converting any small number of these voters could make the math unworkable for the incumbent; according to some estimates, Falwell and his allies converted one in four of them. That September, Falwell graced the cover of *Newsweek* with a one-word headline, "VOTE," the letter *T* fashioned into a crucifix framing a photo of him mid-sermon. By the time Reagan came to Lynchburg for a speech in October, the election was a wrap. Not that Falwell was taking any chances: Having already spent millions of dollars pummeling the president on radio stations nationwide, he poured an additional $10 million that fall into ads portraying Carter, as he himself would later recall, as "a traitor to the South and no longer a Christian."

Reagan crushed Carter in November, winning 489 electoral votes to the incumbent's 49. The morning after Election Day, when Falwell arrived on campus, the Liberty band serenaded him with "Hail to the Chief." Less than a decade removed from founding a small Christian college in Lynchburg, Virginia, this country preacher was one of the most powerful men in America.

The benefits were immeasurable. Membership at Thomas Road shot past twenty thousand early in Reagan's first term. Falwell sold millions of dollars' worth of books and tapes, never mind the passive income collected from his endorsed roster of authors, preachers, radio hosts, and evangelists. He continually raked in contributions from *Old-Time Gospel Hour* viewers via a cutting-edge mailing list which now exceeded 7 million names and addresses. He bought a private plane and embarked on a circuit of revivals, political rallies, and church pulpits—often, the locations were one and the same—while appearing on national news programs such as *Nightline* and *Larry King Live*. In 1985, almost five years to the day after the *Newsweek* splash, *Time* magazine featured Falwell on its cover with a headline, "Thunder on the Right."

Amid this circus, some of Falwell's students grew uneasy. For most of its first decade in existence, Liberty had adhered to those old-school separationist instincts. Even as the school's president entertained bigger and more worldly ambitions—even as he began packaging the cross with the flag, often quite literally—there had been no apparent overhaul of the teaching or campus culture. Yet that was beginning to change. The enrollment spike following Reagan's election brought a wave of politically crazed young conservatives to campus. This influx demanded a hiring spree, and some of the folks Falwell brought in, particularly for administrative positions, were partisan cronies he'd met through his burgeoning Republican network. Falwell was becoming borderline fanatical in his own right. His Wednesday morning chapels—students met for chapel three times each week, but he was now traveling almost every Monday and Friday—became Republican pep rallies, with fleeting references to God drowned out by legislative updates and news bulletins and tales from his Moral Majority travelogue.

"We were getting a lot of political commentary during Falwell's weekly chapel message, and that started to feel uncomfortable. He was wearing all these different hats—Thomas Road, Liberty, Moral Majority—and he really didn't compartmentalize," recalled Mark DeMoss, who enrolled in the fall of 1980, one year after his father—Falwell's friend Arthur DeMoss, a major donor to Liberty—died of a heart attack.

"I think the students liked it at first. It was kind of exciting," DeMoss added. "Our school's president was out there mixing it up with liberal politicians and telling us all about it. But I think, after a while, it became a bit much."

This problem—to the point about compartmentalizing—wasn't unique to Liberty. Falwell's political celebrity won him new Republican friends, but it would soon cost him a chunk of his original TV viewership, namely those older fundamentalists who still distrusted the mixing of religion and politics. Around that time, he encountered similar troubles at Thomas Road. Congregants began leaving the church in bunches over their concerns about a lack of spiritual feeding. This didn't make much of a dent—Lynchburg was a Liberty-fueled boomtown, with fresh recruits walking into Thomas Road every week—and yet, for the broader Church, the defections foretold of the divisions to come.

"We just got tired of the God-and-country stuff. It started to feel like the heart of everything we were doing, both at the school and at church," Olson recalled. "On Sunday mornings we'd be looking at each other—my wife, my friends—just rolling our eyes, like, 'Oh boy, Doc's at it again.' We had to find another church. And listen, I loved Doc. But we needed something more than just *America, America, America* all the time."

The Moral Majority had seemed harmless enough at first, Olson told me. "But then I watched it grow into this monster."

Olson had come to call Lynchburg home. He arrived at Liberty with plans to major in biblical studies, perhaps with an eye toward preaching himself. Later he gravitated toward an interest in building management, and proved so effective that as a student he worked his way up from custodian at Thomas Road to chief of operations for Liberty's maintenance plant. During that time, he met and married a Liberty girl—and not just any Liberty girl, but a Lynchburg native, a product of Thomas Road's private K–12 academy whose family had deep ties to Falwell's empire.

Once a stranger to Falwell's world, Olson had reached the inner sanctum. He did not always like what he saw. He admired Falwell personally, especially his heart for the lowly and broken. Still, Olson felt a nagging angst at his surroundings. Some of Liberty's higher-ups had earned reputations for being less than Christlike in their treatment of people. His own brother-in-law, who worked for *The Old-Time Gospel Hour*, had become deeply disillusioned with the ways in which Falwell milked audiences for money. Indeed, the prodigious amount of cash being spent across these various enterprises, and the methods of replenishing those outgoing funds, disturbed many in Falwell's orbit. Perhaps most upsetting for Olson was the revelation that his favorite professor, a man he loved, a mentor who had guided his Christian walk, was having an extramarital affair.

"That really shook me up, spiritually," Olson recalled. "And I remember, my mother finally had to sit me down one day. And she asked me, 'Are you serving God? Or are you following a man?'"

Olson realized that she wasn't talking about the professor.

When he landed a lucrative job offer that required moving to Florida, Olson didn't hesitate. Eager to build a new life, he and his wife packed up their newborn son, Nick, and said goodbye to her family in Lynchburg. They had always expected to raise Nick there; they dreamed of him attending Liberty, starting his own family in Lynchburg, serving the Lord, and carrying out that vision Falwell had shared on the mountaintop.

Doug Olson still carried that dream. Despite what he knew, he still believed in Liberty. He still believed in Falwell's vision—at least, the unspoiled version. Human legacies are inherently complex in the eyes of a Christian. Olson knew that Falwell loved God; he also knew that Falwell was a sinner who, like all sinners, was prone to wander. Olson had seen too much good in Falwell and too much good in Liberty to let the bad color his remembrances. He moved the family to Florida, and then back to his home in central Pennsylvania, evicting the bad from his mind. He raised Nick to love Jesus, to romanticize Lynchburg, to know the amazing story of how God had blessed Liberty University. Maybe, one day, he would carry out that vision after all.

IN MAY 2007, THIRTY YEARS AFTER HE ASKED GOD TO BUILD A COLLEGE on Liberty Mountain, Jerry Falwell Sr. died of a heart attack inside his office on campus. He was seventy-three.

The latter years of Falwell's life had been forgettable. He still preached to a large congregation and reached a sizable audience with his TV and radio programs. Yet his influence was dwindling. Ever since he disbanded the Moral Majority in 1989—sensing, rightly, that he'd lost sight of his responsibilities as a pastor—Falwell had been eclipsed by a new generation of Christian culture warriors. He launched the "God Save America" campaign in 1996, and a new radio program, *Listen America*, in 1998, but neither one did much to move the needle. Republican leaders would still make the pilgrimage to Lynchburg, but it was proving more an obligatory photo op than a kissing of the ring. Falwell didn't take well to the diminished role.

Clinging to relevance in increasingly transparent and pitiful fashion, Falwell had, by the turn of the century, reduced himself to a caricature, more a punch line than a provocateur. He reacted to actress Ellen DeGeneres's coming out by calling her "Ellen Degenerate." He ranted about Tinky Winky, an animated purple creature on the toddler-aged TV show *Teletubbies* who was supposedly homosexual despite a lack of reproductive organs. He predicted that the Antichrist would be arriving soon and added: "of course he'll be Jewish." He said the September 11, 2001, terror attacks that killed three thousand people were "probably deserved" because of how America had turned away from God, and blamed "the pagans, and the abortionists, and the feminists, and the gays and the lesbians"—as well as the ACLU—for inviting such devastation on the country.

Less visible, but every bit as problematic, was his mismanagement of Liberty University.

Back in 1988, the school had nearly gone belly-up. Enrollment and donations had plateaued since the Reagan spike of the early 1980s, but

Falwell had kept on building, kept on spending, pushing Liberty deeper into a hole without any apparent plan to climb out. All told, Falwell had "racked up more than $100 million in debt" to keep the university afloat, according to a 2020 *Politico* investigation, and could not pay it back. Falwell's finances were hurting across the board: Revenues from *The Old-Time Gospel Hour* had been falling for several years, and the 1987 sex scandal involving televangelists Jim and Tammy Faye Bakker prompted untold millions of Christian viewers to close their checkbooks for good.

Help arrived in the form of Jerry Falwell Jr. A recent graduate of the University of Virginia Law School, the younger Falwell aspired to a career in commercial real estate. He had never shown interest in the family business; Jonathan, his younger brother, was the preacher, and Jerry Jr. had no great affection for Liberty. His undergraduate years there had been often torturous; smuggling beers onto the campus was hard enough for kids who didn't share a name with the founder and president. Jerry Jr. considered himself a Christian—he studied some theology during his college years and came away convinced of Jesus's deity—but had no patience for the "rules and rituals" of fundamentalism. First at the Thomas Road academy, and then at Liberty, the younger Falwell chafed at these man-made restrictions on the life he wanted to lead.

It was out of duty, and devotion to his father, that Jerry Jr. stepped into the quagmire at Liberty. He had always been close to his dad. As he later recalled to the journalist Gabriel Sherman, both were pranksters, troublemakers, rule-breakers. Jerry Jr. always found it strange that his father chose the fundamentalist lifestyle—especially given Jerry Sr.'s concession to him, on many an occasion, that their Baptist rules had no bearing on anyone's salvation—yet he loved him unconditionally. Now there *was* a condition on their relationship: If Jerry Sr. wanted his son's help, he would need to let go. That's what he did. The medicine was bitter: construction halted, programs axed, employees laid off, property sold, assets liquidated, loans rewritten. The school that Falwell had expanded was swiftly right-sized; the television show that made him famous was abruptly canceled.

These emergency measures worked. After several years of fiscal fasting, Liberty emerged lean and viable. For the remainder of his life, Falwell would credit his son with rescuing the school. "He is more responsible, humanly speaking, for the miraculous financial survival of this ministry than any other single person," Falwell wrote in his autobiography.

After his death in 2007, Falwell's domain was divided in two. Jonathan took over as senior pastor of Thomas Road, while Jerry Jr. was named president of Liberty University. Their sister, Jeannie, a doctor, would play no part in the family business. But there was a fourth sibling to consider: Mark DeMoss. After his own father's untimely death, DeMoss became like an adopted son to Falwell. He even lived with the family for a time, and after graduating went to work for Falwell as his chief of staff. For the ensuing seven years, DeMoss was at Falwell's side during every meeting, every trip, every decision. When DeMoss left to start a public-relations firm, Liberty became his first client. Falwell had buried DeMoss's father and his younger brother; he was the first person at the hospital when DeMoss's oldest two children were born. Shortly before he died, Falwell asked that DeMoss—who by then had built a powerful PR firm—take over as chairman of the school's Executive Committee, the second-most-important position at Liberty. Little did he know he had placed his adopted son on a collision course with his firstborn.

"Jerry Jr. went to great lengths to let the world know he was 'not a preacher, pastor, or spiritual leader,' but that he was a UVA-trained lawyer and businessman," DeMoss said, looking back on what transpired between them. "Those comments were always a concern to me, and should have been to the entire board."

It's true that the school's new president had never portrayed himself as a pious man. If anything, he went out of his way to inform people—perhaps even *warn* them—that he was not a religious role model. That nobody seemed to mind only reinforced his own view of what Liberty was meant to be. Jerry Jr. had studied his father's every move during the university's formative years. He was convinced that, aside from preaching and practicing those "fundamentals of the faith," the school should be organized and run like any other enterprise. The welcome he received felt like validation of this view.

To Jerry Jr., it was his résumé—never mind the name—that made him a celebrated selection. Everyone knew what he'd done to resuscitate Liberty. And, in the coming years, he would help usher in a new era of prosperity. Thanks to an early investment in online education and some aggressive bets on real estate development, the school's finances took off. Liberty had listed $259 million in assets at the time of Falwell's death; by 2012, just five years later, that number had quadrupled.

Unlike his larger-than-life father, Jerry Jr. was awkward and introverted, shy and always slow to speak. He kept quiet about his faith, and even quieter about his politics. No matter. Enrollment was rising. New buildings were going up. The endowment was bulging. Liberty was back on the map—and Jerry Falwell Jr. was in charge.

NARRATIVES SURROUNDING THE SHAKESPEAREAN DEMISE OF FALWELL often hinge on his relationship with Donald J. Trump: the candidate's speech to Liberty in early 2016, Falwell's endorsement of his campaign, and their intertwined arcs in the years thereafter.

And yet to fully appreciate the correspondence between Trump's rise and Falwell's fall is to remember the future president's *first* visit to Liberty.

In the fall of 2012, some six weeks before Election Day, Trump arrived on the Liberty campus to surprising fanfare. He had come to address the thrice-weekly Convocation—Liberty was now too large for those quaint old chapel services—and although attendance was mandatory for students, the campus auditorium overflowed with other guests: faculty, staff, family members, citizens of Lynchburg and beyond. In a press release, Falwell called Trump "the most popular Convocation speaker in our history." An exaggeration, perhaps, but not by much.

Trump had been in the public eye for decades: the brash New York billionaire who stamped his name on skyscrapers, paraded mistresses through the tabloids, and ultimately scored a hit reality television show. More recently, he had become a mascot for right-wing Republicanism. Having fronted the noxious crusade to expose then-president Barack Obama as illegitimate—Trump bragged about bankrolling an investigation in Hawaii, and speculated that Obama wasn't just foreign-born, but was a foreign-born *Muslim*—the future president enjoyed a cult following among a segment of the conservative base. Trump had passed on a run for the White House in 2012, then shamed the eventual GOP nominee, Mitt Romney, into appearing onstage with him to accept his endorsement. Now, with Romney headed toward a defeat at the hands of Obama, Trump had come to Liberty to lay the groundwork for a future campaign.

"I see the way Liberty University has been run. I've seen where you came from, and how it was a struggle, and how it is right now. Our country has the same potential, if we ever wanted to do something about it," Trump said, referencing Liberty's financial turnaround, but not its underlying spiritual mission. Disparaging the weak leadership at the highest levels of American government—and the soft, turn-the-other-cheek mentality that this particular audience was wont to possess—Trump offered two words of advice to the ten thousand students inside the Liberty auditorium: "Get even."

For his part, Falwell lauded Trump as "one of the greatest visionaries of our time" and "one of the most influential political leaders in the United States." In front of his students, the university president saluted Trump for having "single-handedly forced President Obama to release his birth certificate," and then awarded him an honorary doctorate.

Politics at Liberty was nothing new. But there was an edge to this event, a raw antagonism that felt unique. Falwell had grown more comfortable in his skin as the school's leader; that skin was combative, conservative, *Trumpian.* A few years into Falwell's tenure, and soon after Obama took office, Liberty stripped its College Democrats club of official recognition, denying it the use of university funds. Not long after that ordeal, Liberty blocked campus networks from accessing the website of Lynchburg's newspaper, the *News & Advocate,* after it reported on the school's reliance on federal financial aid. Eventually Falwell seized editorial control of Liberty's student-run newspaper, the *Champion,* regularly censoring criticisms of his own views and favored political figures. In December 2015, the month before Trump made his triumphant return to Convocation, Falwell shocked the student body with his remarks about a recent shooting carried out by a Muslim couple in California. "If more good people had concealed-carry permits, then we could end those Muslims before they walked in," said the university president.

Long before then—and long before Trump's second speech at Liberty, during which he famously butchered a biblical pronunciation—Falwell had made up his mind: He would endorse Trump for president in 2016. Falwell believed the two men were born of shared DNA. They both were businessmen. They both liked to play hardball. They both had a distrust of authority and a proud disregard for etiquette. To Falwell, the partnership made all the sense in the world.

Not to Mark DeMoss.

When Falwell announced his endorsement in January 2016, days before the Iowa caucuses, the Liberty community was stunned. Crushing on Trump at Convocation was odd enough; hitching the school's reputation and the Falwell name to his presidential ambitions was inexplicable. Trump had campaigned in ways that would make Barabbas blush: calling Mexican immigrants rapists; insulting the looks of his opponents and spreading malicious lies about their family members; encouraging violence at his campaign rallies; openly flirting with white nationalists and proposing a ban on Muslims entering the country. Most foreign and grating to the ears of the faithful, Trump had boasted that he'd never needed to ask for God's forgiveness. With a dozen other candidates in the race, several of whom were decent, Bible-believing Christians, DeMoss could not fathom why Falwell was using his influence to put Trump over the top.

DeMoss kept silent at first. But as the weeks went by, with tensions on the campus mounting and Trump's victories piling up, he felt obligated to say something. In an interview with the *Washington Post* on Super Tuesday, as primary voters went to the polls in Virginia and numerous other states, DeMoss let it rip. "Donald Trump is the only candidate who has dealt almost exclusively in the politics of personal insult," he said. "The bullying tactics of personal insult have no defense—and certainly not for anyone who claims to be a follower of Christ. That's what's disturbing to so many people. It's not [the] Christ-like behavior that Liberty has spent 40 years promoting with its students."

Pointing to a particularly grotesque recent episode—Trump's refusal to disavow the endorsement of former Ku Klux Klan leader David Duke—DeMoss told the *Post*: "I think a lot of what we've seen from

Donald Trump will prove to be difficult to explain by evangelicals who have backed him."

DeMoss knew what kind of enemy he was making. Catering to the old guard of trustees and administrators who shared his father's far-right politics, Falwell had in recent years consolidated power at the school, silencing dissenters and eliminating adversaries with a systematic, menacing efficiency. DeMoss harbored no illusions about winning a power struggle with his childhood friend. But he did believe, given his decades of service to Liberty and his position as Executive Committee chairman, that he had the stature to speak freely in ways others did not.

Hours after the *Post* published his comments, DeMoss received an email from Falwell with no subject line. The body was one sentence: "Mark, I'm very disappointed in you."

DeMoss dialed up Falwell immediately. The conversation was courteous enough; DeMoss said he hadn't meant to hurt Falwell personally, and Falwell, playing it cool, expressed concern that DeMoss may have jeopardized the school's tax-exempt status with his political remarks. (Years later, DeMoss still laughs when recounting this part of the call.) After they hung up, DeMoss emailed him, offering to fly to Lynchburg to talk more in person. Falwell replied that it wasn't necessary; a board of trustees meeting was already scheduled for the following month, in April. They could discuss everything then.

In the weeks that followed, sympathetic trustees reached out to DeMoss, telling him that Falwell was lobbying behind the scenes for his ouster. Then DeMoss received an email from Jerry Prevo. A strident fundamentalist preacher who built Alaska's largest Baptist megachurch, Prevo was a longtime Republican operator and one of Falwell Sr.'s key allies at the Moral Majority. He now chaired the Liberty board of trustees. Prevo got straight to the point: DeMoss may have violated the board's confidentiality policy, he wrote, and some of his colleagues might ask him to resign.

This was nonsense. The board had never discussed an endorsement; there was nothing for DeMoss to violate. Still, he had been around Liberty long enough to see this for what it was. Typing up his resignation letter, DeMoss flew to Lynchburg for the April meeting. When he arrived at the boardroom the night before the full meeting—Executive

Committee members always meet separately in advance—something was comically amiss. Typically, the school's president sits at the head of the table, with the Executive Committee chairman seated to his right and the board chairman seated to his left. Surveying the thirty-some placards arranged around the sprawling, magnificent wooden table, DeMoss saw that he was no longer situated to Falwell's right. Instead, his placard was ten chairs away. He walked over and sat down there.

"And Jerry, kind of awkwardly, he says, 'Mark, I don't know who put your name card over there. Come on and sit up here,'" DeMoss recalled. "And I said, 'No, no, that's fine. I'll sit here.'"

DeMoss grimaced. "They had already decided," he told me.

Recusing himself from the Executive Committee meeting as soon as he had called it to order, DeMoss returned to his hotel room. Two hours later, his phone rang. It was Liberty's general counsel, David Corry. "And he says, 'Mr. DeMoss, the committee has deliberated, and they've asked me to tell you they'd like for you to resign from the Executive Committee,'" DeMoss recalled. "And then he said, 'And they would like for you to tell the board tomorrow that the reason you're resigning from the Executive Committee is because you wanted a change of committee assignments.'"

DeMoss told me: "I said, 'David, I may resign tomorrow, but if I do, I won't give the reason that you just asked me to give. Because it's not the truth. And you know it.'"

Within a few days, DeMoss had resigned from both the Executive Committee and the board of trustees. The news jolted the extended Liberty family and particularly chilled those on campus—students, faculty, and administrators alike—who found themselves in disagreement with Falwell's vision for the school. If he could to this to Mark DeMoss, he could do it to anyone. There was no such thing as checks and balances. It was less a presidency than it was an autocracy. Falwell was untouchable.

EVEN BEFORE HE BECAME ENSNARED IN A LOVE TRIANGLE WITH HIS wife and a Miami pool boy, Falwell seemed intent on testing the limits of his invincibility.

In June, after Trump had clinched the Republican nomination for president, Falwell traveled to New York City to introduce him to a meeting of some five hundred evangelical influencers. No longer a mere supporter, Falwell embraced the role of pitchman. He joined the likes of Franklin Graham in vouching for Trump's character and integrity, helping the man who'd once joked on Howard Stern's radio show about sleeping with his own daughter to forge an alliance with America's leading Christian conservatives.

Later that day, at the top of Trump Tower, Falwell was euphoric. Recalling his father's unlikely alliance with Reagan and how it reshaped American politics, Falwell exchanged hugs and high-fives and toasts, celebrating the ways in which history was repeating itself. Indeed, some of the parallels were striking. But certain things had changed. When they took a photograph to document the occasion, Trump stood in the middle, flanked by Falwell and his wife, Becki. Thumbs went up. The camera flashed. Falwell tweeted the photo to his sixty thousand followers. There was just one hiccup: Lurking over Becki Falwell's left shoulder, framed in gold, was a cover of *Playboy*, graced by a bow-tied Trump and a smiling brunette covered only by his tuxedo jacket. Forty years after his father had singled out the magazine as a symbol of civilizational decay, Falwell posed in front of it, beaming shoulder to shoulder with a man who had appeared in a soft-core porno flick (and who, one-upping the adultery Jimmy Carter confessed to committing in his heart, engaged in the real thing, including with a *Playboy* model and an adult-film actress).

For Falwell to be embarrassed by the photo would have required a capacity for embarrassment. The ensuing years would suggest that no such capacity exists. With Trump performing the part of strongman in the White House, Falwell doubled down on his own tyrannical instincts. He continued to crack down on the student newspaper to the point where its former editor felt compelled to publish an exposé in the *Post*. He enraged the student body by defending Trump's abhorrent response to the white nationalist march in nearby Charlottesville, Virginia, saying he was "proud" of the president for being "bold" and "truthful." He turned the school into a satellite location for the Conservative Political Action Conference, disseminating ad hominem insults and deranged conspiracy theories throughout campus. He accelerated a pattern of overt self-dealing, as documented by journalist and Liberty alumnus Brandon Ambrosino, channeling tuition funds into projects that benefited friends and family. He eliminated programs (in the case of Philosophy, an entire department) with a supposedly liberal bent, and funneled more money into political projects. He launched a campus think tank in partnership with Charlie Kirk, the firebrand activist and president of Turning Point USA, calling it "The Falkirk Center for Faith and Liberty." He denied tenure to faculty—forcing professors to work on one-year contracts, the surest way to keep people in line—and required anyone affiliated with the school to get his personal approval before speaking with the media. He ordered campus police to remove an evangelical pastor who'd visited Liberty to meet with students organizing a protest of Trump, and threatened the pastor with arrest if he returned.

The school was no stranger to totalitarian rule; administrators had long used its ultra-strict and preposterously detailed honor code, "The Liberty Way," to control the student body. (Dancing, among other activities, remains banned on campus to this day.) What felt different about this crackdown was that it coincided with flagrant misconduct by the university president himself. Falwell's personal behavior had become a constant source of campus gossip. He was frequently witnessed slurring his words and smelling like alcohol. Word got around that he was fond of making jokes about his genitals. At one point, his weight ballooned noticeably; then, with the apparent help of hormone supplements, he cut up his figure, and began acting with an even more reckless aggression. In one incident captured on video—that Falwell himself inexplicably posted to Instagram—he hit a campus gym and asked two attractive female students to climb onto a bench-press bar that rested on his lap before proceeding to perform a series of pelvic thrusts, the intended sexual nature of the act registering on the girls' faces.

How did Falwell get away with this behavior? The question seemed answered easily enough: Liberty was thriving by every outward metric, with assets listed at $2.6 billion in 2017, an increase of 900 percent from when he had taken over a decade earlier. (That number would soon surpass $3 billion, tangible evidence, in the interpretation of so many people affiliated with the school, of God's favor being shown.) Falwell was rightly seen as a developer extraordinaire—the Donald Trump of Lynchburg, if you will—having poured billions of dollars into constructing a modern, state-of-the-art campus that now stretched across seven thousand acres. Enrollment continued to shatter year-over-year records: Well over 100,000 students now matriculated through Liberty every four years, more than half of whom participated via the exceedingly profitable online-learning program. Perhaps most impressive for the school's visibility, Liberty was competing in more NCAA Division I athletic programs than ever before. In 2018 it joined the FBS, the premier echelon of college football, and began playing nationally televised games against top programs such as Auburn, Virginia Tech, and Ole Miss. (In 2020, Liberty enjoyed a fairytale ten-win season, finishing as the No. 17–ranked team in the Associated Press poll.)

Yet there existed another explanation for Falwell's survival, something just as obvious if perhaps less observable. The reason nobody confronted him—some combination of donors, administrators, trustees, Executive Committee members—is that many of them were just as complicit in the school's broken culture. In my conversations with Falwell, this was the one thing that rang true: His father, short on money and desperate to turn his faltering school around, had cut corners by hiring people who "got stuff done" but weren't necessarily good managers—or good Christians. The older Falwell never bothered to upgrade the university's personnel; even as Liberty grew into a juggernaut, it was still run by the same cast of third-string operators who couldn't get hired at most community colleges.

"I should have fired everybody in the top leadership the day I walked in—from vice presidents on down—and hired everyone new," Falwell told me. "You see, my dad didn't have the money back then to hire people who were honest *and* competent. So, he typically had to choose, one or the other. And those are the people who were still around when the school became prosperous."

Falwell seemed to get along just fine with these folks while he was still president. Everyone at Liberty was flying high, especially in the Trump years, the success breeding a sense of indomitability. Yet all the while, Falwell was self-destructing. In the spring of 2020, with the COVID-19 pandemic raging, the school's president tweeted an image of a face mask illustrated with the purported image of Virginia's Democratic governor,

Ralph Northam, wearing blackface. Falwell apologized in response to an outcry from students, but the social media mishaps continued. A few months later, in the summer of 2020, while touring Key West on a Liberty donor's yacht, Falwell published a photo of himself—dark drink in hand, pants unzipped, with his hand around the bare midriff of a young pregnant woman—on Instagram. Given the intensifying scrutiny of the school, the board had no choice but to place him on leave.

Falwell wasn't meant to be sidelined for long. But then, a few weeks into the leave, he and his wife, Becki, issued a bizarre statement to a blogger at the *Washington Examiner* explaining that Becki had carried on an affair with a family friend. This was an obvious attempt at pre-emptive damage control—and a bad one at that. The next day, Reuters published a stunning report detailing the account of Giancarlo Granda, a young man whom the Falwells befriended while patronizing the Miami hotel where he worked. The upshot: As Becki became romantically involved with Granda—Jerry, he claimed, approved of this arrangement and occasionally supervised—the Falwells made him a part of their entourage, taking him on trips, bringing him to their son's wedding, and inviting him to meet Trump during his visit to Liberty. To this day, Falwell insists that the details of Granda's story are wrong and says that his wife carried on the affair without his knowledge or consent. But the evidence strongly suggests otherwise.

When Granda went public, Liberty officials were gift-wrapped a scapegoat. They painted Falwell as a rogue and pushed him out. It was Crisis Management 101: make the embattled leader into a fall guy, get rid of him, and hope the scrutiny goes away, too.

The scrutiny didn't go away. When Falwell resigned in the summer of 2020, and Jerry Prevo took his place as interim president, the Liberty community exhaled as one. Students and professors prayed for an overhaul of the institution. The things Falwell had gotten right—the physical buildings, the balance sheets, the bells and whistles that drew tens of thousands of young people to campus—could be united, finally, with the Christian ethos that had once animated Liberty. In this period of transition, optimism overflowed. Reform seemed to be within reach.

But it wasn't. The new Liberty was, in some ways, more broken than the old Liberty.

Early in his presidency, Prevo told Scott Lamb, Liberty's then–chief communications officer, in a recorded phone call that electing Republicans to office was one of the university's "main goals." (This fit a pattern, under Prevo, of Liberty boosting Republican causes; Lamb would later publicly accuse the school of violating its 501(c)(3) status.) Around that time, the new president began a mini-purge. He axed the campus pastor, David Nasser, who was known to be a Falwell Jr. loyalist. Prevo also ousted the man who'd succeeded him as board of trustees chairman: Allen McFarland. A well-liked pastor, and one of the few Black leaders in Liberty's history, McFarland had made enemies, he told the journalist Julie Roys, by saying things like, "We're raising champions for Christ, not champions for the Republican Party. We're raising champions for Christ, not champions for Donald Trump." Prevo replaced McFarland with Tim Lee, a double-amputee Vietnam veteran and outspoken MAGA enthusiast.

Efforts at rehabilitation were mostly symbolic. After students took the extraordinary step of rebelling against the Falkirk Center—drafting a petition that read, "Associating any politician or political movement with Christianity bastardizes the Gospel of Jesus Christ"—Liberty changed the name. But the relabeled think tank ("The Standing for Freedom Center") would prove every bit as pugnacious and extrabiblical as its predecessor.

The post-Falwell low point came in July 2021 when twelve women came forward to sue the university, alleging that it had violated federal Title IX law by discouraging the reporting of rape and sexual violence on campus. More plaintiffs soon came forward. Everyone associated with Liberty could tell, right away, that it was trouble. The school's ban on certain behaviors—drinking, partying, premarital sexual contact—made reporting abuse all but impossible, given the associated violations of the honor code. Liberty settled with some of the accusers in 2022, but multiple plaintiffs refused, casting a new sort of pall over the school. The Clery Act requires universities to assist students in contacting law enforcement about alleged sexual assaults; it also requires universities to report certain crime statistics. If Liberty was in violation, the consequences could be ruinous. By the fall of 2022, the feds were circling Lynchburg.

* * *

ON A SUNNY MORNING IN THE SPRING OF 2023, THE LIBERTY CAMPUS had a utopian feel. Students laughed and shouted while scurrying between buildings. The baseball team ran drills on its flawlessly manicured diamond. Bulldozers hummed and construction workers heaved, one new facility going up quicker than the last. It was, in so many ways, a manifestation of the vision Jerry Falwell Sr. had shared atop Liberty Mountain.

Inside a nearby coffee shop, however—not far from that place where "Doc" Falwell had stood—one Liberty professor sat in anguish. All was not well, he told me, burying his head in his hands. What I saw outside was a parody of that vision, a cheap facsimile that brought glory to men instead of to Christ. And he would know. The Liberty story was *his* story; the school was in his blood. His parents met there. His father had helped claim that mountain for God back in 1976. All he ever wanted, the professor told me, was to serve God at Liberty University.

His name was Nick Olson.

He had moved back to Lynchburg at eighteen years old and never really left. After earning his bachelor's degree, and then a master's degree, Olson accepted a teaching job in the English Department in 2013. He started a family and bought a home. He served his church and loved his students and tried to tune out the rest. Olson wasn't naïve. His dad had sheltered him, downplaying the dark side of Liberty. But he'd seen it as a student. He'd seen it as a professor. There was an ugliness that lurked in the subconscious of the school, a spiteful alter ego to the Christlike character that was meant to permeate the institution.

Olson tried to ignore it, negotiate with it, make peace with it. But he couldn't. Like his own father some three decades earlier, Olson could not unsee the corruption of that vision.

When we first met, I wondered aloud: *Had* the vision of Jerry Falwell Sr. been corrupted? Or was Liberty today reaping precisely what the school's founder had sown a half century earlier?

Olson seemed thrown, even a bit offended, by the question. I couldn't blame him. Here was an outsider, someone he barely knew, chipping away at the assumptions that had formed the foundation of his life. The longer we spoke, however, the more introspective he became. "I think I'm probably doing the thing we've always done here: telling myself a story," Olson said. "The stories Liberty tells itself about the founding are only half-true. Those stories omit some uncomfortable truths. I don't think that's uncommon. But for the biggest Christian school in the world? It's unacceptable. It's hypocritical."

He shook his head. "It cannot go on like this."

Sitting in the corner of the coffee shop, speaking at a cautious pitch, Olson agonized over whether he should go on the record with these assessments. There was no obvious upside: He would lose his job, his trajectory toward a choice faculty position, and potentially, all future opportunities in academia. He would probably have to move, uprooting his wife and two young sons. Perhaps most painful, he would upset some friends and family members, people who love Liberty unconditionally and don't want to confront its sins.

Olson worried about all of this. Still, he told me, he worried even more about something else.

"I have to wonder if my unwillingness to challenge the family business of Liberty is because of my own family. I want to protect my wife and kids, provide for them, keep them comfortable," Olson said. "But in prioritizing those things—in keeping quiet to protect the family, so to speak—am I doing the very thing Liberty has done all along?"

This comparison—Liberty as a mafia, the Falwells as ruthless dons—was so provocative that Olson looked surprised with himself for having invited it. Still, there was no questioning the earnestness of his analysis. The young professor, in this most determinative moment, was more interested in removing planks than in finding specks.

"When Jesus said that a man should leave his father and mother, it wasn't just about getting married and starting a new family," Olson told me. "It was an instruction, I think, to challenge the things you're taught in your upbringing—*with the things you're taught in your upbringing*."

He ran both hands through his curly black hair. "That's the hardest part of this," Olson said. "These things we inherit, when it comes to faith and family, we don't want to question them."

I could relate. And so, too, I told Olson, could many of the Christians I'd met in my journeys. Despite our different labels and traditions, we were crumbling under the weight of a shared spiritual legacy. We were saddled with a heritage that felt unsustainable; we were handed down an identity that no longer fit.

What past generations of the American Church had given us—"These things we inherit"—were hard to stomach, and yet somehow even harder to shed.

CHAPTER FOUR

ATLANTA, GEORGIA

*But seek first his kingdom and his righteousness,
and all these things will be given to you as well.*

—MATTHEW 6:33

"A pastor asked me the other day, 'What percentage of churches would you say are grappling with these issues?'" Russell Moore told me. "And I said, 'One hundred percent. All of them. I don't know of a single church that's not affected by this.'"

Moore would know. A preacher's grandson raised in Biloxi, Mississippi, he spent his life steeped in ecclesiastical subculture. For as long as he can remember, Moore identified primarily not as an American, or as a southerner, or even as a Christian, but as a member of America's largest Protestant denomination: the Southern Baptist Convention. He learned and lived by the rules, written and unwritten. He never missed Sunday morning service or Wednesday night fellowship. He worked as a youth pastor at an SBC church, earned his master's and doctoral degrees at SBC seminaries, taught theology to the next generation of SBC clergy, edited a journal of SBC news and opinion. He became a denominational prodigy. Ascending to one of evangelicalism's highest peaks—president of the SBC's Ethics and Religious Liberty Commission—at just forty-one years old, Moore ranked among the world's best-known and best-connected Southern Baptists.

As we talked in the upstairs lounge of a downtown Atlanta hotel one fall evening in 2021, Moore remarked on how strange it felt to say this aloud: He was a *former* Southern Baptist.

Moore had quit the denomination a few months earlier. The only surprise was that he lasted as long as he did. Years of low-intensity conflict within the SBC had given way to vicious internecine fighting, and Moore was at the center of it. Because of his push for an open-aired reckoning on racial tensions in the denomination and for probes into the church-sanctioned concealment of sexual abuse—never mind his vocal denunciations of Donald Trump—Moore had gone from wunderkind to whipping boy. Since Trump's election, far-right forces inside the Southern Baptist Convention had monitored him closely, believing that he was on a mission to overthrow the conservative order that had governed the denomination for decades. It made no real difference that Moore was himself, by any measure, a conservative: pro-life, anti–gay marriage, a champion for religious freedom, an undeviating voice for traditional values. Nor did it matter that Moore was a model witness for Christ, someone who lived his faith and practiced every bit of what he preached. He was on the wrong side of the culture wars that were consuming the church. And for that, Moore said, he was subjected to "psychological warfare" that became so paralyzing he ultimately had no choice but to raise a white flag.

When I'd spoken with Moore back in May, on his final day as a member of the Southern Baptist Convention, he sounded like a man whose cell door had just swung open. "Free at last," he said, laughing. For the first time in decades, Moore said, he wouldn't need to attend the summer's annual SBC conference, which was expected to devolve into a bare-knuckle brawl over proposals to investigate and report instances of sexual assault. Moore didn't want any part of it. He had a pile of speaking invitations on his desk; pastors in every corner of the country wanted him to come visit their churches. Moore was looking forward to a reprieve from the SBC spectacle. He was excited to move past the madness and put the gospel first again.

So much for that.

As we talked in Atlanta, he couldn't help but chuckle. Most of those invitations he'd received turned out to be from pastors in crisis; they were hoping that Moore, the punching bag of the Southern Baptists, could teach them how to duck a haymaker. Moore knew that the clashes within American evangelicalism weren't unique to the SBC. Still, he was startled by the scale of the devastation. No matter the type of church he would visit—affiliated or independent, rural or suburban, auditorium or roadside chapel—it was coming apart.

"I can't even count how many conversations I've had with pastors who've said, 'I'm crushed. I'm broken. I don't know what to do,'" Moore said. "And they've all lived through the exact same story: it's COVID, it's CRT, it's Trump. These pastors are a shell of their former selves. The stress has made the job impossible. They're either watching people leave, worrying about the next person who's going to leave, or wondering who's going to come after them for something they said last Sunday and threaten to leave."

When it comes to political extremism infiltrating churches, Moore acknowledged that sometimes the pastor is responsible. ("Crazy as a church growth strategy," he mused.) But he insists this isn't typical. In most cases, Moore said, the tension is coming from the bottom up. Members complain about a sermon or a social media post from the church account; angry emails to the leadership prompt an emergency meeting among elders and the pastor; the complaint goes ignored, which enrages the aggrieved members, or it earns an apology, emboldening those members while irritating a different clique. A church can only endure one or two such cycles before the scent of insurgency becomes overpowering.

"At that point, the pastor is in trouble. Because a lot of them—most of them—are afraid of their own congregants," Moore said. "It's not because they're cowards, it's just the way the system is set up. This exists regardless of the specific type of church polity. Wherever people can vote with their feet, you're going to have pastors feeling paralyzed, unsure of whether they'll lose more people by keeping quiet or by taking their own people on. And the problem is, most of these pastors don't feel like they've built up the capital with their congregation to take them on. So they shy away from the fight, which tends to perpetuate the problems."

Moore felt a responsibility—and an urgency—to help fortify these pastors in crisis. He had spent the last several years building out an informal network of fellow travelers, clergymen and church leaders who had come under attack and were desperate for support. Now he was traveling to different churches every week, sometimes three or four of them, a one-man fire engine racing between blazes. He had come to Atlanta, in fact, to check in on a former seminary protégé who was leading a pop-up church in the city.

All that Moore was doing—the four-leg flight itineraries and run-on Zoom meetings and late nights typing prayerful emails to people he didn't know—was aimed at solving a problem. He was so consumed with that problem, I realized, that there was little time left to consider its cause.

For most of his life, Moore had belonged to a tribe that considered itself special, superior, singularly blessed. Moore wasn't just any old Christian; he was a *Southern Baptist*. Not anymore. He had ditched that identity—an identity that once meant everything to him, an identity that was central to his worldview and sense of self—because it had become a barrier to his true identity. I had to ask: What took so long?

WHEN MOORE WAS TWELVE YEARS OLD, HE PRAYED TO ACCEPT JESUS and promised himself there would be no half measures. He could not understand how some people—people like his father—called themselves Christians but did not radiate their religious convictions in public. Gary Moore was a Southern Baptist, a member of their congregation at Woolmarket Baptist Church. But he scarcely attended Sunday services. The younger Moore silently judged his father, doubting the deepness of his faith, vowing he would never be that sort of listless follower of Christ.

Committing himself to intense theological study—day after day of his adolescence was spent in the classrooms at Woolmarket Baptist, memorizing entire books from his King James Bible—Moore began to sense a call to the ministry. Preaching was in Moore's blood: His grandfather was the pastor of their Southern Baptist congregation in Biloxi. But there was one obstacle Moore couldn't get beyond: the Church itself. As a teenager in the 1980s, he watched as the fervor of the religious right spread through his church community like a cancer, exposing moral opportunism and political hypocrisy and racial animus. Some of the people he'd once revered as mature believers were revealed to be spiritually empty. Their gods were not his God.

Suddenly Moore began to understand the quiet faith of his father. Having grown up as the pastor's son in Jim Crow–era Mississippi, Gary Moore had seen things inside the church that haunted him. The story of the Southern Baptist Convention, after all, was inseparable from America's original sin. Formed in 1845 by slave-owning whites who were alarmed at abolitionist efforts within the national Baptist Church, the SBC became an avatar of religious justification for the trafficking and ownership of human beings. Losing the Civil War did little to reform the Southern Baptist worldview: For most of the century that followed Robert E. Lee's surrender to Ulysses S. Grant at the Appomattox Court House, SBC churches were intentionally and proudly segregated. Gary Moore did not make a show of rebelling against his father or the Southern Baptist Convention. He simply kept a distance. Now his oldest son—once on fire for the Lord, newly agonizing over the authenticity of the Christian witness—wanted some distance, too.

Russell enrolled at the University of Southern Mississippi in the late 1980s and studied history and political science. Developing a fascination with government, he eventually got hired by his hometown congressman, Gene Taylor, a pro-life Democrat. Moore found the work fascinating but decidedly unfulfilling. The more he thought, the more he prayed, the more certain he felt that his teenage instinct had been correct. Moore resigned from Taylor's office and moved to New Orleans for seminary. It was the hardest conversation he ever had with his father. "I'm only going to say this once. From this minute out, I'll support you no matter what," Gary Moore told his son. "But I wish you wouldn't do this. I think you're going to get hurt."

Moore halted at this point in the story. Collecting himself, he noted that we were approaching the one-year anniversary of his father's death. "He was right," Moore whispered.

The hurt wouldn't arrive for some time. In fact, Moore's early foray into institutional Christianity was charmed. Racing through degree programs, blowing away peers and professors alike, he distinguished himself as a sort of spiritual phenom. He was viewed as the future of the Southern Baptist Convention, a generational talent who could speak both with biblical authority and cultural relatability. When Moore was just thirty years old, rumor rippled through denomination that

Richard Land, then the president of the Ethics and Religious Liberty Commission—the SBC's public-facing policy institute—was leaving for a post in academia. Moore was informed that he would be tapped as Land's replacement.

It didn't come to pass. Land remained ERLC president for another eleven years. Up until that point, Moore had been riding a hot hand inside the SBC, never bothering to stop and question much of what he saw. He was brilliant and precocious and more than a bit naïve. The disappointment of not replacing Land soon gave way to relief: As he studied the history of the job, the man he would be replacing, and the internal politics that shaped Land's own career, Moore reached some uncomfortable conclusions about the deep waters in which he was now swimming.

"All those questions that my fifteen-year-old self had, they came rushing back, and I still wasn't mature enough to answer them," Moore recalled. "I am so thankful to God that I didn't get that job at the time. Because I was not ready for the things I would have been exposed to, the decisions I would have had to make. I'm fearful that I would've ended up an atheist. I think it might have destroyed me."

The Ethics and Religious Liberty Commission was, at that point, on its third historical act. It had begun as the Committee on Temperance— the SEAL Team Six of the Southern Baptists' war against alcohol— and was later rebranded as the Christian Life Commission. In 1960, a Texas theologian named Foy Valentine was elected to lead the organization. Valentine had written a doctoral dissertation on the SBC's racist practices of the early twentieth century; his mandate was to help usher in a new, integrated era of Southern Baptist life. Valentine succeeded not only in engineering a reversal of the SBC's mistreatment of Black people but also in liberalizing the denomination more broadly. The pendulum swung with sudden speed: Whereas the SBC had since its founding been regarded as deeply conservative, by the early 1970s it had earned a reputation for being socially progressive. Leading SBC seminaries took heterodox (and to some, heretical) positions on issues such as abortion, homosexuality, and women serving in leadership. The SBC's elected polity, from Valentine on down, pushed an apolitical vision, and a liberal theology, that aligned with mainline Protestantism. "Southern Baptists are not evangelicals," Valentine told *Newsweek* in 1976, not long before Carter was elected president. "That's a Yankee word."

It wasn't long, however, until the pendulum swung back, this time even faster than before. The cultural fault lines exploited by the Moral Majority during Carter's presidency suggested that Valentine was out of step with his denomination. While he loathed the upstart evangelical movement, what with its shameless incursion into politics, it became apparent that his Southern Baptist brethren did not. In 1979, a group of archconservatives inside the SBC, including Land, Paige Patterson, and Adrian Rogers, staged a coup that disposed of much of the denominational leadership. Supporters called it the "conservative resurgence," while critics dubbed it the "fundamentalist takeover." Whatever the label, it was a watershed in American Christianity. Southern Baptists were rebranding themselves as theologically pure, embracing the concept of "biblical inerrancy" and taking hard-line, literalist positions on anything pertaining to the intersection of scripture and culture. Rogers became the denomination's president, and together with his allies set about purging the Southern Baptist Convention of liberal voices, from seminaries to churches to its national leadership. Valentine refused to cede his perch atop the ERLC. By the time he was pushed out, in 1986, the trajectory of the denomination was inexorable: Most Southern Baptists now identified as evangelicals, and most evangelicals had voted for Ronald Reagan twice. They were Republicans, and there was no looking back.

Land, who formally took over the ERLC in 1988, might have done more than anyone to marry conservative theology with conservative political ideology. He made partisan affiliation a spiritual metric for millions of Southern Baptists, unapologetically allying himself with Jerry Falwell Sr. and his Moral Majority. Under Land's leadership, the ERLC—and the SBC as a whole—became an overpowering electoral force. He led a chorus of evangelicals calling for Bill Clinton's resignation and lent religious legitimacy to George W. Bush's invasion of Iraq, all while helping to mobilize an unprecedented mass of conservative Christians to vote for the Republican Party.

One of Land's truly good, nonpartisan deeds was to continue Valentine's effort to eradicate racism within the SBC. It was ironic, then, that his professional demise was due to racial controversy. In 2012, after a white neighborhood-watch volunteer in Florida named George Zimmerman killed an unarmed Black teenager named Trayvon Martin, Land said on his radio show that Democrats would use the tragedy to "gin up the Black vote for an African-American president." Facing an outcry, Land dug in, arguing that Zimmerman had been justified in shooting Martin, who was "statistically more likely to do you harm than a white man."

A subsequent apology could not save him. Land was forced out of the post and replaced by Russell Moore.

MOORE ENTERED THE OFFICE A MAN CONFLICTED. ON ALMOST EVERY issue he was a traditionalist; he had long believed that on balance the conservative resurgence was a positive development for the Southern Baptist Convention. Yet Moore had grown deeply uncomfortable with the intrusion of electoral politics into the eschatological mission of the Church. He remembered, some years earlier, how after he'd finished preaching in Evansville, Indiana, a married couple had approached him. They asked Moore if he had ever considered preaching on judges. He told them that, yes, actually, he had preached from the Book of Judges on many occasions. "No, we mean *judges*," the man said. He explained that George W. Bush's judicial nominees were under attack from the left and needed support from the Church.

Before the 1980s, Moore said, "there were two ways of evangelizing. You could focus on end-times prophecy, which a lot of people did; or you could talk about marriage and parenting, using practical advice, talking about how the Church could help your family," Moore said. "But by the nineties, being a real Christian meant voting Republican. And suddenly, the easiest way to reach people, by far, was through political identification."

Studying Land's partisan maneuverings as his young heir apparent, Moore was struck by how self-defeating it all was. Clinton emerged from his scandals more popular than ever thanks to the public's disdain for his holier-than-thou tormenters, many of whom were revealed to have their own inconveniently similar flaws. Bush's presidency imploded thanks to failing wars and a neglected economy. Barack Obama won in a landslide despite being the most liberal presidential nominee in a generation. Evangelicals had mortgaged the future of the Church on extrabiblical causes, Moore thought to himself, and all they had to show for it was smaller numbers and a diminished witness. In 1991, according to the Pew Research Center, 90 percent of Americans identified as Christians, while just 5 percent called themselves religiously unaffiliated. Thirty years later, as Moore and I spoke in Atlanta, the collapse was staggering: 63 percent of Americans identified as Christians and 29 percent called themselves unaffiliated.

"People saw that Christianity was a means to an end, and they realized they could get to that end without Christianity," Moore said. "We were no longer distinctive. The focus was on values and worldview and identity in ways that obscured the distinctiveness of the message itself."

Moore thought he could do things differently. He would not hesitate to promote that which was ethically nonnegotiable or biblically obvious; sometimes, politics could not be avoided. But he made it known, upon assuming the presidency of the Ethics and Religious Liberty Commission, that he would not risk the reputation of the gospel for passing partisan gain. There was no ambiguity in his message. Moore told everyone—from the entry-level staffers at the ERLC to the Executive Committee members of the Southern Baptist Convention—that he did not care about winning and losing elections. He cared about advancing the kingdom of Christ.

It was sort of funny, Moore confessed, that he—the political science major, the recovering congressional hack—was the one warning about the idolatry of politics and country. In reality, Moore loved the game of politics more than most, and he considered himself quite patriotic. "But Jesus looks at those valid natural affections and warns us that they cannot be the most important thing," he told me. "What the New Testament emphasizes is that once those affections are secondary, then you're able to better love them because they *don't* come first."

Moore wasn't fazed by the recoil from SBC lifers who'd fought on the front lines of the culture wars. He figured that time was on his side: While partisan cheerleading was catnip to the over-fifty crowd in SBC churches, the young seminarians he'd been teaching wanted nothing to do with it. They were as conservative as he was—in some cases, downright fundamentalist in their worldviews—but they felt politics had no place in the Church. This generational turnover was his great source of optimism. For all the trials Moore faced in his new role, confronting the corruption of Christianity and the dilution of the gospel, he knew that better days were ahead.

In the fall of 2015, Moore met with "The Outliers," a group of friends and fellow high-profile believers: Tim Keller, the founding pastor of Redeemer Presbyterian Church in New York City; Pete Wehner, the former head of strategic initiatives in the George W. Bush White House; Francis Collins, the director of the National Institutes of Health; and David Brooks, the *New York Times* columnist. When their conversation turned to the mud-wrestling match that was the GOP presidential primary, and the evangelical voters who were flocking toward the most spiritually unserious candidates, Moore offered his optimistic take. Yes, he said, there were Christians who seemed intent on undermining their witness. But they were dying off. Their kids and their grandkids—the future of the electorate, the future of evangelicalism—were about to take over.

There was a pause. "Yeah," Brooks said. "But you'd better watch out for the death spasms."

Moore was puzzled. Brooks, who was raised Jewish but harbored a nagging interest in Jesus, was typically the one asking *him* for insights into Christianity.

"Anytime you have a group that feels as though it's headed toward generational demise, it lashes out," Brooks told Moore. "It puts up a fight. It refuses to give up what's theirs."

Moore thought about that remark every single day over the coming year. He had been worried about Trump's candidacy from the jump, believing that his hateful rhetoric was unbecoming of anyone who called themselves a Christian (which Trump did, though he declined to cite a favorite passage from scripture, saying he found the entire Bible "very special"). Where some evangelical leaders saw an elaborate publicity ploy, Moore saw Trump's campaign as a broken man's ultimate quest for significance. Such a narcissistic pursuit could not be shrugged off. The higher his poll numbers climbed, the larger his circle of evangelical allies grew, the more concerned Moore became. By January 18, 2016, it was apparent that Trump could win the Republican nomination. Iowa voters would soon kick off the nominating process, and Trump, trying to close the deal with evangelical voters, came to Liberty University. Taking the stage to address ten thousand students at Convocation, the candidate was welcomed by Liberty's president. "By their fruits ye shall know them," Jerry Falwell Jr. declared. "Donald's Trump's life has borne fruit."

Moore couldn't hold back.

"Absolutely unbelievable," he tweeted in response to Falwell Jr.

Moore knew there was no climbing down from that comment. And so, having spent the past six months holding back, he let it rip.

"Winning at politics while losing the gospel is not a win," he added, sending evangelical Twitter into a frenzy. "Trading in the gospel of Jesus Christ for political power is not liberty but slavery."

The event had been an indignity for Trump. Quoting a Bible verse that Tony Perkins, president of the Family Research Council, had suggested to him in an exchange prior to the event, the candidate pronounced Paul's epistle as "Two Corinthians" instead of "Second Corinthians," a linguistic distinction understood by anyone approximating a churchgoer. The laughter and ridicule were embarrassing enough for Trump; the news of Perkins endorsing Ted Cruz, just a few days later, sent him into a spiral. He began to speculate that there was a conspiracy among powerful evangelicals to deny him the GOP nomination. When Cruz's allies began using the "Two Corinthians" line to attack him in the final days before the Iowa caucuses, Trump told one Iowa Republican official: "You know, these so-called Christians hanging around with Ted are some real pieces of shit." (In private over the coming years, he would use even more colorful language to describe the evangelical community.)

Moore was on Trump's radar, but there was no immediate threat. Unlike Perkins and others, the ERLC president was not supporting a rival candidate. Trump waited until after the nomination was clinched, in early May, to strike back, tweeting that Moore was "truly a terrible representative of Evangelicals" and calling him "a nasty guy with no heart!" Moore's phone lit up with texts and emails. Pastor friends warned him to be careful; SBC officials suggested it was time for him to stand down. But Moore was just getting started. He couldn't fathom how evangelicals—*especially* Southern Baptists—were making peace with Trump's candidacy. It was the SBC that in 1998 responded to Bill Clinton's affair with White House intern Monica Lewinsky by passing a resolution that famously stated: "Tolerance of serious wrong by leaders sears the conscience of the culture, spawns unrestrained immorality and lawlessness in the society, and surely results in God's judgment."

Moore believed those words when they were first written, and he believed them still. All throughout the summer of 2016, he prosecuted the case against not just Trump but those evangelical supporters who were "willing to redefine the gospel" to rationalize the candidate's behavior. In June, he told CBS that Trump represented "the very kind of moral and cultural decadence that conservatives have been saying for a long time is the problem." That same week, when hundreds of evangelicals came to New York for the Trump summit, Moore joked that the attendees were drinking "Kool-Aid."

Southern Baptist worshippers could, at that time, live with criticisms of Trump himself. But the notion that *they* were in the wrong by promoting his candidacy—according to a denominational leader whose salary was paid by their collection plates—was unforgivable. Moore had become a marked man inside the SBC. If he noticed, he didn't seem to care. In October, when the *Washington Post* published an old audio recording of Trump boasting that he had pressured a married woman to sleep with him, and that he could get away with sexual assault because of his celebrity status, Moore waited to see if any of Trump's evangelical backers would jump ship. None of them did. In fact, they all circled the wagons. "What a disgrace. What a scandal to the gospel of Jesus Christ and to the integrity of our witness," Moore tweeted. A day later, he added: "The political Religious Right Establishment wonders why the evangelical next generation rejects their way. Today illustrates why."

When Trump won the election a month later, it was open season on Moore. He went underground in the weeks after the election, believing that a cooling-off period would be healthy for all parties. But some Southern Baptists weren't interested in cooling off. In December, while watching a *Star Wars* film at the theater with his kids, Moore received word that one of the denomination's largest churches was threatening to cut off funds to the SBC. In the months that followed, more than one hundred other churches followed suit. Pastors called for Moore to apologize; when he offered only a tepid modulation of his past remarks, and a plea for unity moving forward, they called for his head.

Moore had powerful enemies. Some of them resided on the SBC's Executive Committee. But he also had job security: It was the ERLC's board of trustees who chose the presidency. They were allies of Moore. He wasn't going anywhere—yet.

At the SBC's annual meeting in 2017, all eyes were on Moore. The most polarizing figure in a denomination of some 14 million members, he was relieved, if a bit surprised, to encounter so many sympathetic people. They encouraged him, prayed with him, passed him notes of support. But not everyone was on Moore's side. A large group of pastors, members of a far-right faction called the Conservative Baptist Network, spent the meeting spreading word that Moore was on his way out. They knew it wasn't true, but the gamesmanship had begun. In between sessions, one of the antagonistic pastors grabbed Moore. "We can't get rid of you," the man warned him. "But we can make you think twice before you say something."

For the next four years, the SBC Executive Committee stalked Moore with sham investigations that aimed to destabilize his reputation and make Southern Baptists hesitant to ally with him. These probes focused on Moore's censuring of Trump—increasingly, the shiniest of objects in SBC circles—and concluded that the ERLC president had caused "a significant distraction" that cost the denomination seven figures' worth of giving. But Moore knew what the real distraction was. He had scarcely uttered a word about Trump, positive or negative, after the presidential election of 2016. There was bigger game to hunt. A renaissance of nationalist and neo-Confederate sentiment was discernible inside the SBC; meanwhile, the #MeToo movement, which had emboldened women to come forth with allegations of sexual abuse, was pounding on the denomination's door. Moore knew that to shine a light on either of these epidemics, much less to challenge his SBC brethren over them both, was to invite even fiercer scrutiny than what he'd endured in 2016. But he didn't believe there was a choice. God had called him to this position to pursue truth, to hold the Church accountable, to defend the honor of the witness.

Moore gave everything he had to these twin causes. He traveled far and wide pleading with Southern Baptists to confront the original sin of their country and their denomination. He met with sexual abuse survivors, investigated cover-ups, and warned churches of the dangers many of them did not want to see. Every step of the way, Moore was shadowed by investigations aimed at undermining his credibility. The campaign of innuendo and intimidation was unrelenting.

One afternoon in February 2021, Samuel Moore, Russell's fifteen-year-old son, confronted his mother, demanding to know if his father was having an affair. Why else, the son asked, would there be such intense scrutiny of him?

When his wife shared the conversation, Moore didn't know whether to laugh or cry. He decided to ask his son to accompany him to the upcoming SBC Executive Committee meeting, where the charges against him would be laid out. Samuel agreed. Together they sat in a room for hours, listening to committee members list their allegations against the president of the Ethics and Religious Liberty Commission. They described him as divisive, spiteful, un-Christlike, even conspiratorial, seizing upon issues that were tangential to the life of the Southern Baptist Convention and weaponizing them for purposes of personal gain at the expense of denominational unity.

As they walked out of the meeting, Moore asked his son what he was thinking.

"There's something I still don't understand," Samuel replied. "Why do we want to be a part of this?"

MOORE HAD GRAPPLED WITH THIS QUESTION FOR YEARS.

He would fantasize about walking away from the whole awful mess. How liberating it would be, he thought, to shed the baggage of *Southern Baptist* and simply be a *Christian*. But it never felt plausible. Like it or not, he was a Southern Baptist. It was more than a denomination; it was a lifestyle. All that Moore knew—his jargon and inside jokes, his teetotaling and love of sweet tea—was shaped by the SBC. Even as denominational leaders made his life miserable, so many SBC members had loved on him. They were like his family. He couldn't abandon them.

"God gave me the opportunity to lead people to Christ and to baptize them in Southern Baptist churches, to help people through their marriage crises in Southern Baptist churches, to help welcome orphaned children into families in Southern Baptist churches, to do evangelism and Bible teaching in prisons and homeless shelters, through Southern Baptist churches," Moore wrote in a letter to ERLC trustees in early 2020, as the SBC Executive Committee ramped up its latest investigation of his alleged wrongdoing. "I love the Southern Baptist Convention, and am a faithful son of the Southern Baptist Convention."

At a certain point, however, Moore had to think of his *actual* family. They had been bullied right alongside him, facing "constant threats from white nationalists and white supremacists, including within our convention," Moore wrote in his letter. As he agonized over what to do, his wife, Maria, began to lose patience.

"This is getting absurd," Maria told him early in 2021. "Do whatever you want. But just know, if you're still a Southern Baptist a month from now, you're going to be in an interfaith marriage." This was no empty threat. Maria left the SBC and began searching for a new church near their home in Nashville, Tennessee.

Moore felt convicted of a certain posturing. Many Christians he respected, longtime friends, had already left the SBC. Another prominent evangelical, Beth Moore (no relation), had recently shocked the denomination by announcing her own departure. Every single day, he had been taking calls from pastors—most of them young or Black or both—who were thinking of deserting the SBC. Moore had urged them to stay. He had promised that if they stuck around, and secured a seat at the table, they could effect change from the inside. "After a while," Moore told me, "I stopped believing my own rhetoric."

There was but one reason for Moore to stick around: The Southern Baptist Convention was all he'd ever known. It was his identity. And that, he began to realize, was the entire problem.

"You know, I think about Walker Percy, when he was asked to explain why he was a Roman Catholic," Moore said of the noted American writer. "He said, 'The reason I am a Catholic is that I believe what the Catholic Church proposes is true.' And I just got to the point where—"

Moore stopped himself, struggling to find the right words.

"I believed, and still believe, what the Southern Baptist Convention claims *about Jesus* is true," Moore said. "But what the Southern Baptist Convention claims about itself? I couldn't believe that anymore."

I asked Moore which claim he struggled with the most.

A long pause. "Adrian Rogers would always say, 'The hope of the world is America. The hope of America is the Church. The hope of the Church is evangelical revival. And the hope of evangelical revival is the Southern Baptist Convention.' So, pretty quickly, you've gotten to a place where you believe the SBC is the hope of the world," Moore said. "I just don't think that's true anymore. And, as I look back, I'm realizing that maybe I never did."

Moore couldn't help but wonder if his loyalty to the Southern Baptist Convention had eclipsed an even higher loyalty. He had spent so much time warning about idolizing country, but never appreciated how the exaltation of another earthly institution was doing similar harm.

"Richard Land, my predecessor at the ERLC, used to say, 'We want the 1950s without the racism and the sexism.' His point was, there was a time when things were mostly the way they ought to be, and there's a path back to that time," Moore told me. "In that sense, Christians could point to these single events—Supreme Court rulings, or the sexual revolution, or whatever—as the moment America fell. Which assumes we were blessed until something went wrong. But that ignores that America has always been fallen. Because humanity has always been fallen."

He thought a moment. "There's a tendency in fallen human beings to take secondary identities that are important and make them ultimate. In Galatians 3, Paul warns explicitly against doing that," Moore said. "From my earliest memories, my identity was as a Southern Baptist. But that could never fulfill me like the identity of the gospel."

THE NEXT MORNING, WE WORSHIPPED THE LORD INSIDE A LOCAL DIS-tillery.

Jason Dees had been one of Moore's brightest seminary students. In December 2016, he organized a start-up, Christ Covenant Church, in his living room; by the following summer he had formally launched the church. For the next several years he and his fast-growing congregation rented spaces around Atlanta to host their weekly services. Despite being itinerant, the church attracted more and more people, and by the summer of 2021 they had secured a plot of land to build the Christ Covenant campus. With construction underway, the church was meeting on Sundays in the event hall of American Spirit Works. The day Moore quit the Southern Baptist Convention, his brother had joked that now he could finally enjoy a glass of whiskey. Little did Moore know that a few months later, he'd be preaching in front of barrels of the stuff.

Every chair was occupied. Every person was singing—not just mouthing the words, but belting out the lyrics. The congregation was as eclectic as any I'd seen: college-aged guys with unkempt beards and flannel shirts sat next to older gentlemen in jackets and ties. The hipster-vibe band onstage, complete with a Rastafarian-looking guitarist, played traditional hymns. "Come Thou fount of every blessing / Tune my heart to sing Thy grace / Streams of mercy never ceasing / Call for songs of loudest praise."

I was struck by the self-evident health of the fledgling church. And then I found out *why* it was so healthy. Several of Dees's staff members had come from toxic environments, prominent churches that had been ripped apart over the past few years. So too had many of the folks seated in the stackable chairs around me. There was an unspoken understanding at Christ Covenant: Nobody was here for a cable news panel. They were coming to church to be discipled, not demagogued. Scripture was going to dictate their interpretation of the world, not the other way around.

And so, on this Sunday morning, Christ Covenant dedicated its service to adoption. Testimonials were given, promotional videos were played, special funds were raised. Speakers stressed that not everyone had the capacity to adopt—but everyone had the capacity to do something. They could babysit for adoptive families; they could support pregnant women in need; they could do something as simple as teach single moms how to maintain the tire pressure in their vehicles.

Moore's sermon was titled "The Orphan in the City," and he read from the eighth chapter of Romans: "For those who are led by the Spirit of God are the children of God. The Spirit you received does not make you slaves, so that you live in fear again; rather, the Spirit you received brought about your adoption to sonship. And by him we cry, 'Abba, Father.' The Spirit himself testifies with our spirit that we are God's children. Now if we are children, then we are heirs—heirs of God and co-heirs with Christ, if indeed we share in his sufferings in order that we may also share in his glory."

Moore explained that the semantics of this biblical cry—"Abba! Father!"—are evidence of our intimate relationship to God. It is used to capture the most joyous of circumstances, such as rebirth in His eternal family. It can also convey anguish, such as when Jesus sweated blood in the garden of Gethsemane, praying to His Father that the cup might pass to another.

Then Moore told a story I had never heard.

When he and his wife first met their youngest son, inside an orphanage in Russia, the child would not speak. It wasn't until they took him outside the building, to bring him to his new home in America, that the child turned and started shouting. He was terrified to leave, the orphanage being all he had ever known.

Christians are not born into God's family, Moore explained. They are adopted into His family. God calls the spiritually stray to come to Him as a son or daughter. This is a gift of immeasurable generosity: The orphan, who had nothing, receives an inheritance of eternal life. And yet the orphan reaches back and cries out, terrified of leaving behind the life they knew.

"What you can do for the orphan," Moore said, "is realize that you were once an orphan yourself."

CHAPTER FIVE

DALLAS, TEXAS

If the world hates you, keep in mind that it hated me first.

—JOHN 15:18

Robert Jeffress was backpedaling.

It was the spring of 2021. A few months had passed since the storming of the Capitol Building, a despicable and deadly event inspired by the president whom Jeffress had supported unfailingly for the previous five years. From his perch as senior pastor of First Baptist Dallas, an influential megachurch that ranked among the largest affiliates of the Southern Baptist Convention, Jeffress had distinguished himself as evangelicalism's most prominent and unapologetic defender of Donald Trump. He preached the service for the incoming president and vice president at historic St. John's Church, across the street from the White House, on Inauguration Day 2017. He said it was "immoral" for Democrats to oppose Trump's construction of a wall on the southern border, citing Old Testament precedent. He warned of a "Civil War–like fracture" if Trump was removed from office following his first impeachment. He even commissioned the First Baptist Dallas music director to write a hymn, "Make America Great Again," which the church choir performed for the president in Washington.

Jeffress was not one to back down from controversy. Whether in accusing Barack Obama of paving the way for the Antichrist, or ripping Mitt Romney and his Mormon "cult," or calling anti-Trump evangelicals "spineless cowards," Jeffress showed no appetite for uncertainty.

But now, his tone was different. He sounded pensive, reflective, maybe even contrite. Unsolicited, he retraced his own journey, wondering aloud what had caused him to become so preoccupied with politics in the first place, questioning whether it had gotten the better of him.

"I had always believed, as far as the relationship between evangelicals and social change, that our main job was to witness and share the gospel. This idea of trying to stop the current of evil that's flooding into our culture—there's just not much we can do about that," Jeffress told me. "But over the last twenty years or so, I began rethinking that. Yes, our primary job is to witness. But as part of Jesus's mandate to be salt in this world, we also need to push back against evil, to restrain evil so that this world might last a little longer, so that we have more opportunities to share the gospel."

This epiphany was provoked by a scale of evil that churches had not dealt with before, Jeffress explained. We were not merely discussing a coarsening of the culture; we were confronting a secular onslaught that would bring a Christian society to its knees. It was something he could not in good conscience ignore.

"I think that's what changed. I came to the conclusion that it was a unique point in time," Jeffress said. "I wanted to be actively involved not only in getting people into the next world, but in pushing back against evil in this world."

Ironically, pushing back required allying himself with secular forces. That meant becoming a regular on-air contributor to Fox News, the right-wing panic factory. It meant trading his church pulpit for a campaign podium, sharing the stage with crooks and grifters who were selling lies for political profit. Most conspicuously, it meant endorsing, promoting, and protecting Trump.

The first lesson Jeffress learned about Trump is that he prefers people to be either hot or cold. Loyal backers and loyal haters alike have utility to the man; the people he cannot stand are lukewarm, with him one day and against him the next, their assessments subject to some pesky moral standard. If Jeffress was going to stick close to Trump, influence Trump, earn the respect and trust of Trump, he had to stay hot. So that's what he did. Whether it was laughing off the hush money Trump paid a porn star to keep quiet during the 2016 campaign, or excusing the administrative policy of separating babies from their mothers at the Mexican border, or overlooking the lethal stolen-election rhetoric in the aftermath of Trump's defeat in 2020, Jeffress never allowed one beam of daylight between himself and the forty-fifth president.

It paid off, at least in the short term. Attendance at First Baptist Dallas boomed during Trump's four years. Money poured into the church. Jeffress's salary jumped. Fox News gave him more and more airtime. His phone book bulged with A-list Republicans. He became a regular at the White House. Yet all the while, Jeffress was laying his spiritual authority on the line, his service to Jesus Christ largely indistinguishable from his servitude to Donald Trump.

Now, as he reflected on this in the wake of January 6, the pastor allowed that some damage may have been done.

"I've wrestled with it. I mean, I've wrestled with it *personally*, because I realize there were people who were turned off by my association with President Trump," Jeffress told me. "I had that internal conversation with myself—and I guess with God, too—about, you know, when do you cross the line? When does the mission get compromised? And so, it was a real struggle."

I asked Jeffress if, looking back, that line was crossed.

"I think it *can* be," he said. The pastor thought a moment. Then he added: "I think perhaps it even was, these last few years."

This was an astonishing confession. In the brief time since Trump had departed the White House, I'd encountered small pockets of compunction in the evangelical world. The people I spoke to were like hungover frat brothers the morning after a kegger—not necessarily apologizing for their behavior the night before, but acknowledging somewhat sheepishly that things had gotten out of hand. But none of these people had been close to Trump like Jeffress was. If *he* was regretful, if *he* was reconsidering his political priorities, maybe there was a broader phenomenon of repentance at hand inside American evangelicalism.

Or maybe not. I thought about the "current of evil" he'd declared war on all those years earlier. Jeffress believed the threat to American

Christianity at the turn of the century was too menacing to ignore. How could he possibly retreat from the battlefield now?

HE WAS NINETEEN YEARS OLD, A FRESHMAN AT BAYLOR UNIVERSITY, when God spoke to him. "You may ask, 'Was it audible?' It was louder than that," Jeffress recalled in August 2007, according to local newspaper accounts, during his debut in the pulpit at First Baptist Dallas. "God told me, 'One day, you will be pastor at First Baptist Church of Dallas.'"

Jeffress had never shared that story before—not with his college roommates, not with his wife, not even with the search committee that had spent a year sorting through a hundred candidates to lead the Dallas megachurch. Nor had Jeffress ever doubted, even for a moment, that it would come to pass. On that Sunday morning, standing before thousands of his congregants, the new pastor of First Baptist Dallas saw that the Lord's plan for his life had been realized.

The church had always been his home. When Jeffress was five years old, he made a confession of faith and promptly met with Rev. W. A. Criswell, the famed pastor, to formalize his commitment. Criswell took the child seriously—so seriously, in fact, that he began suggesting to Jeffress at a young age that someday he would lead the church. This was heady stuff, even for someone with the outsize self-assurance of Jeffress. First Baptist Dallas was established in 1868; Criswell had succeeded a legend, George Truett, who had pastored the church from 1897 until his death in 1944. Truett was the prototype celebrity preacher of the early twentieth century. He spoke in storied venues nationwide, served as president of the Southern Baptist Convention, and built First Baptist Dallas into a behemoth, overseeing a tenfold increase in membership. Criswell kept that momentum going. He was a megachurch visionary, the rare clergyman who thought church should be more than sermons and songs. He built a recreational commons, designed a tiered Bible education program, and launched numerous initiatives aimed at integrating the church into the surrounding community, making it a home for seekers and seasoned believers alike. He was also a celebrated theologian; at one point, Billy Graham counted Criswell as his own personal pastor.

Criswell's reputation was stained, however, by his retrograde views on race. In February 1956, a few months after Jeffress was born, Criswell delivered a speech to the South Carolina Baptist evangelism conference that inveighed against "this thing of integration." He called forced desegregation "idiocy" and "foolishness" and "a denial of all that we believe in." Contrasting the pious, traditional Baptists of the South against those self-righteous evangelicals up north, Criswell said: "Let them integrate. Let them sit up there in their dirty shirts and make all their fine speeches. But they are all a bunch of infidels, dying from the neck up."

This was no slip of the tongue: Criswell accepted an invitation from the South Carolina legislature to give the exact same speech one day later. He was promoted by Dixiecrats like Strom Thurmond and quoted approvingly by racist groups such as the White Citizens' Council. Known for his frequent appeals to a Genesis passage that purportedly cursed Noah's son, Ham, and doomed all African descendants to a life of subservience, Criswell openly preached the politics of white supremacy.

Like any effective leader, Criswell had the savvy to adapt to changing times. In 1968, with progressives pushing for reform in the Southern Baptist Convention, a stunning three-quarters of "messengers," or church delegates at the annual meeting, adopted a denominational statement condemning racism. It happened to be the year Criswell—who led the largest Southern Baptist church in America—was seeking the presidency of the SBC. Criswell endorsed that statement, won the election, and explained to reporters that his "heart" had changed. The following week, he preached a sermon to First Baptist Dallas titled "The Church of the Open Door." It was a call to his congregation to welcome Black believers, to move beyond the conflation of politics and theology, to embrace a common citizenship in the body of Christ.

This was the church, the cultural and theological biome, in which Robert Jeffress was raised. He was baptized there, studied there, got married there, worked there as a youth pastor. Everything he witnessed—the programmatic planning and capital-raising campaigns, the hard-line stances and timely backpedaling—informed his view of megachurch ministry. Criswell was more than a mentor to Jeffress; he was an icon of the evangelical movement. Still, Jeffress must have struggled with the pastor's inconsistencies. Criswell supervised the denominational shift pertaining to race, which became the catalyst for a broader leftward drift in the SBC, which then, a decade later, invited the fundamentalist backlash that Criswell helped to spearhead. It all made for a dizzying epitaph: Criswell was closely associated with both the progressive takeover of the late 1960s *and* the conservative resurgence of the late 1970s, a legacy so convoluted it couldn't help but overshadow his preaching, evangelizing, and church building.

Jeffress wanted to avoid such complications. He started small, pastoring a rural church in Eastland, Texas, for seven years before jumping to a larger congregation in nearby Wichita Falls. For the first fifteen years of his ministry, Jeffress preached the Bible and nothing but the Bible. There was no mention of any newspaper headlines, no discussion of legislation or elections. Jeffress was content. And then, one day in the spring of 1998, a church member asked to meet with him. She showed the pastor two books she'd just discovered at the local public library: *Daddy's Roommate* and *Heather Has Two Mommies*.

Jeffress promptly called the library himself, asking that the books be removed from circulation. The head librarian refused. That Sunday morning, Jeffress stood in front of his congregation and held the books up high, declaring that they would never—ever—be returned. (The pastor still has both of them; he wrote a check to cover the requisite library fees.) All in an instant, Wichita Falls was transformed into a war zone. Media outlets from across the state—and eventually, from across the nation—flooded into the town as secular groups and gay rights activists squared off against Jeffress and his evangelical allies. When the city council pursued a compromise that would relocate the books to an adults-only section of the library, the ACLU sued the city in federal court and won. The city council declined to appeal. Feeling betrayed, Jeffress turned his congregation loose on the local elected officials who had backed down from a fight for the moral fiber of their community. In one sermon, the local newspaper reported, Jeffress urged his members to "vote out the infidels who would deny God and His word."

The phrasing could not have been coincidental. Criswell, his teacher, had called the northern Christians who fought segregation "infidels." Four decades later, Jeffress was affixing that label to the politicians in his town—many of whom surely identified as Christians—who refused to join his crusade against a pair of library books.

There was no turning back for Jeffress. He had tried formerly to insulate his preaching from the chaos outside the church walls. He had wanted to avoid the distraction and division that came with commenting on extrabiblical issues. But now, he felt, the decision had been made for him. Christian values were under attack in America. There was no choice but to fight back.

By the time Jeffress took over First Baptist Dallas, he'd gone from fighting back to picking fights. Christians had been playing defense in the culture wars for a half century and were continually losing ground. It was time to go on offense. This was how the new pastor at one of America's most illustrious churches began to make a name for himself—not for his fluency in the pulpit, or his outreach initiatives, or his social welfare programs, but for his strike-first mentality. He attacked the Catholic Church. He attacked the gay community. He attacked Oprah Winfrey.

Most Americans still didn't know the name Robert Jeffress. And then he started attacking Mitt Romney.

THE YEAR JEFFRESS TOOK OVER FIRST BAPTIST DALLAS, 2007, IS THE same year he began publicly decrying Mormonism as a "cult." There was no real mystery to the timing: The Republican presidential contest was heating up, and Romney, a Mormon, was one of the betting favorites. Everyone from Rush Limbaugh to Laura Ingraham to Sean Hannity was gushing over the former Massachusetts governor, pushing him as a conservative alternative to the churlish, orthodox-defying Arizona senator John McCain.

Alarmed at their lack of discernment, Jeffress felt the need to push back on his fellow right-wingers who were throwing their support behind someone who wasn't really a Christian. Surely, Jeffress thought, if everyday evangelical voters were educated about the teachings of the Church of Jesus Christ of Latter-day Saints, they would rise up in opposition to Romney's candidacy.

And so, from the pulpit and any other public stage he could find, Jeffress repeatedly belittled Mormonism and bludgeoned Romney, insinuating that there was something dangerous about his beliefs. He could gain only so much traction. YouTube was in its infancy. Fox News had yet to discover him. Romney did eventually lose the nomination to Mc-Cain, though it was unclear what role if any Mormonism played in the defeat. On the right there was such loathing of McCain—not to mention of the emerging Democratic nominee, that dark-skinned senator with the exotic name—that the attacks on Romney's religion were soon forgotten.

But not by Romney himself. The candidate could not get over what Jeffress had said and done. He was baffled at how a megachurch minister—not some soapbox cleric, but the pastor of *First Baptist Dallas*—could spew such venom without consequence. Romney's team was equally alarmed. Building off a strong showing in 2008, they began laying the groundwork for another campaign in 2012. Romney would be the favorite to win the GOP nomination, his allies realized, but only if they neutralized these attacks on his faith. The decision was made to engage with Jeffress directly. One of Romney's evangelical backers, attorney Jay Sekulow, agreed to debate Jeffress at a forum in Washington, D.C. The topic: "How 'Christian' Does a Presidential Candidate Need to Be?"

Jeffress used the occasion to do more than simply bash Mormonism. He issued a broader challenge to the consistency of his fellow evangelicals. He blasted "the hypocrisy" of church leaders who "for the last eight years of the Bush administration have been telling us how important it is to have an evangelical Christian in office who reads his Bible every day, and now suddenly these same leaders are telling us that a candidate's faith really isn't that important."

Jeffress added: "My fear is such a sudden U-turn is going to give people a case of voter whiplash. I think people have to decide, and Christian leaders have to decide once and for all, whether a candidate's faith is really important."

The Dallas pastor had walked into the event a relative unknown; he walked out one of the most prominent evangelicals in the country. Political reporters in Washington put him on speed dial; Romney's rivals for the 2012 nomination began reaching out, wooing him, urging him to turn up the attacks on the GOP front-runner. Jeffress savored every moment of this star turn. In the fall of 2011, at the Values Voter Summit in Washington, I watched the pastor hold court with a mob of reporters for nearly an hour in a crowded hotel hallway. Jeffress had just endorsed Texas governor Rick Perry for the Republican nomination, and he wanted every journalist present to quote his conclusions about why evangelicals could not trust Romney.

"I just do not believe that we as conservative Christians can expect him to stand strong for the issues that are important to us," Jeffress told reporters. "I really am not nearly as concerned about a candidate's fiscal policy or immigration policy as I am about where they stand on biblical issues."

Five years later—almost to the day—Jeffress taped an interview with National Public Radio. The *Access Hollywood* tape had just dropped. Trump's character was under assault and his campaign was on life support. Prominent evangelicals, such as Russell Moore, were openly questioning how anyone who had demanded a values-based, biblical litmus test for political leaders could now be advocating for Trump. The NPR host asked Jeffress for his response.

"I don't want some meek and mild leader or somebody who's going to turn the other cheek," Jeffress told the host. "I want the meanest, toughest SOB I can find to protect this nation."

For a man who'd once complained about giving voters "whiplash," this was a U-turn taken at Formula 1 speed. How could Jeffress possibly reconcile these statements?

One answer is starstruck opportunism. Their relationship began when Trump spotted Jeffress on Fox News and, impressed by his skill on television, summoned the pastor to New York City for a meeting. They hit it off—a couple of born charmers, two guys who can disarm just about anybody behind closed doors—and that was that. Jeffress soon joined Trump's evangelical advisory board and started stumping with him, vouching for the candidate in front of Christian audiences. He told Texas voters, in the thick of a hot primary, "I can tell you from personal experience, if Donald Trump is elected president of the United States, we who are evangelical Christians are going to have a true friend in the White House." Jeffress's political clout had been rising for years, but no politician had ever lavished attention on him, brought him into the inner circle, had him speak to rallies of tens of thousands of people, the way Trump had. Whatever the offenses of the candidate—and there were too many to count—Jeffress wasn't about to give that up. Not when Trump still had a fighting chance to be president. Not when *he*, Robert Jeffress, who confessed his faith at age five, still had a fighting chance to be the spiritual consigliere to the leader of the free world.

There was another explanation for Jeffress's inconsistency—something less satisfying than political opportunism, but far more powerful.

Jeffress had spoken of his pastoral career as two distinct eras: There was the period before he got involved with politics, and there was the period after he got involved with politics. The more we talked, however, I began to sense that there was a third period. He had been able to define, almost down to the date, the point at which he recognized that our culture was being inundated with evil, and his concomitant conviction to fight that evil with good. But there was another inflection point—a fuzzier inflection point—that seemed even starker, even more relevant to Jeffress and his decision-making. It had happened only recently. It had come about subconsciously at first, in response to the culture war defeats, and then more and more consciously in response to the feeble state of conservatism and the feckless state of the Republican Party. It had happened so organically that he could not precisely account for it: Jeffress no longer cared about fighting evil with good. He just wanted to fight evil—period.

He wasn't the only one. Back in 2011, around the time Jeffress was insisting that a candidate must share the values of a Christian voter, the Public Religion Research Institute commissioned a fascinating survey. It asked Americans of all faith backgrounds to answer the question: Could a politician who behaved immorally in their personal life still perform their public duties with integrity? Only 30 percent of white evangelicals said yes, the lowest of any group surveyed. This trend line was steady since the days of Bill Clinton's impeachment: Conservative Christians still believed character was a prerequisite for public office.

In October 2016—the very week, in fact, that Jeffress sneered at the notion of turning the other cheek—the Public Religion Research Institute released a new survey that asked the same exact question. This time, incredibly, 72 percent of white evangelicals responded that, yes, a politician who behaved immorally in their personal life could still perform their public duties with integrity. Five years earlier, white evangelicals had registered the lowest rate of support for that idea; now they were registering the highest.

Something had changed, and it wasn't just the party affiliation of the scoundrel in question. To be sure, plenty of those evangelicals had always cared more about power than principle and were predisposed to ignoring the sins of their own tribe. But there was something deeper at work. What I'd personally encountered during those five years wasn't just an increased appetite for power; it was a sudden onset of dread. They had spent Obama's presidency marinating in a message of end-times agitation. Something they loved was soon to be lost. Time was running out to reclaim it. The old rules no longer applied. Desperate times called for desperate—even disgraceful—measures.

Inside Jeffress's office at First Baptist Dallas, I pressed him on whether he had seen this same phenomenon. He acknowledged that he had. When I asked him to explain it—to make sense of how millions of evangelicals, himself included, had so casually discarded the code that guided their political engagement for a generation—Jeffress offered two words. They were the same words I'd heard Trump speak to evangelical audiences during his presidency. Words that Jeffress, no doubt, had whispered into the president's ear.

"Under siege."

THE CAMPUS OF FIRST BAPTIST DALLAS FEELS MORE LIKE A CONVENtion center than a church. There are parking garages and escalators, a coffee shop and bookstore and ATM machine, floor-to-ceiling windows and floodlit fountains that spray a hundred feet high. After checking in at the security desk—the friendly guards don't allow backpacks but do validate parking—I caught a glimpse of the control room. It would be the envy of CNN. Through the dark-tinted windows I could see dozens of high-definition monitors being operated by a team of tech professionals. This struck me as an unnecessary investment. Then I stepped into the worship center.

A concave screen, rivaling the tract of the jumbotron at nearby Cowboys Stadium, wrapped around the sprawling main stage. It displayed lyrics so that we might keep up with the eleven singers with coordinated outfits, men in blue suits alternating with women in teal blouses, and the choir arrayed on the five rows of risers to the rear. I counted 119 of them in total, clad in black robes, accented in purple and gold, overlooking an orchestra pit that housed three dozen musicians. As they played—trumpets, violins, tuba, saxophone, guitars, drums—a real-time highlight montage of the singers and musicians rolled above us.

The cameras circled Jeffress as he strode onto the stage. No introduction necessary; his name was shown on the screen's lower third, along with his Twitter handle. The pastor skillfully located his mark on the stage, smiled, and announced that he was beginning a ten-part series: "What Every Christian Should Know." His tie knot was immaculate. His cadence was impeccable. Jeffress struck every syllable with precision, made every aside with purpose. The sermon was tightly packaged and expertly delivered. I could see why three thousand people had packed into the hall around me; why many thousands more were watching via livestream around the world; why this was arguably America's most successful megachurch.

It didn't used to be. Despite the church's fabled history, Jeffress said it was "dying, deteriorating" when he arrived in 2007. Attendance had been falling for years. The physical structures were unsalvageable. A dramatic renovation was required. Jeffress decided to embark on what he describes as "the largest church building program in history." He announced a $135 million capital campaign that would blow up—literally—six blocks of downtown Dallas. And he didn't stop there. All told, Jeffress said, the church had spent $250 million on renovations since he arrived.

The makeover helped to reestablish First Baptist Dallas as a titan in the evangelical world. Attendance, membership, and giving all spiked. There was more to this resurgence, however, than the dazzling new campus. It was Jeffress himself who made the church irresistibly relevant. When he took the big job, the pastor had pitched himself as a visionary in the mold of his hero and predecessor, Criswell. His industry-rattling ambition forced leaders from every denomination to study him and demanded coverage from Christian and secular journalists alike. The success became self-perpetuating. With all eyes on Jeffress, he negotiated a lucrative multimedia contract that made him one of America's most broadcasted ministers.

The man knew how to draw a crowd—and how to keep it. Whether from the pulpit or the television set or the radio booth, Jeffress was a continuous manufacturer of controversy. It could be political one day and theological the next; the substance wasn't necessarily the point. That long-ago library fight in Wichita Falls had taught him the awesome power of publicity: Despite losing the actual dispute, and coming under widespread criticism in the process, Jeffress had grown his church and burnished his celebrity. He built on that model at First Dallas Baptist. Every bit of opposition he generated was an opportunity. Every rebuke he elicited had its own reward.

This was great for First Baptist Dallas. But was it good for the witness of Jesus Christ?

It seemed fair to wonder whether the qualities that attracted certain people to Jeffress—the pugilism and unceasing provocation—were repelling many others from Christianity at large. After all, Americans were shedding the label of "Christian" at a record clip, and they were doing so just as public perception of the Church was plummeting to all-time lows. In 1975, more than two-thirds of Americans expressed "a great deal or quite a lot of confidence in the Church," according to Gallup, and as of 1985 it was "the most revered institution" in American life. Toward the end of Trump's presidency, just 36 percent of Americans had confidence in the Church. Pollsters made no distinction between Catholics and Protestants, and no doubt the epidemic of priests trading white collars for orange jumpsuits contributed to the plunge in public confidence in organized Christianity. Still, evangelicals had done more than their share of damage. Given Jeffress's long-running feud with the LDS Church, I couldn't help but think of the perception gap illustrated by a satirical Babylon Bee headline: "Evangelical Mistaken for Mormon After Treating Everyone with Kindness, Respect."

As we settled into his office, a spectacular sixth-floor suite with panoramic views of downtown Dallas, I asked Jeffress why so many Americans had turned against evangelicals like him.

"I don't think it's Donald Trump or the Republican Party or Christian nationalism that's keeping people from accepting the gospel. They just provide a convenient excuse," Jeffress told me. "I think at the end of the day, it's all about a person's personal relationship with God. He can come up with all kind of intellectual reasons for not accepting the gospel—'look at this hypocrite over here' and so forth—but I think deep down, there's a personal reason he doesn't come to faith in Christ. The reason a lot of seekers never find God is the same reason that a thief never seems to find a policeman: They're not looking."

The pastor chuckled. "I'm not gonna take responsibility for somebody going to hell. If they go to hell, it's because they've rejected God's invitation of forgiveness."

Might Jeffress at least entertain other explanations? Was there no truth to the idea that evangelicals had taken their eye off the ball? Could he not see how the fixation on this world had created a barrier to entry for those seeking knowledge about the next? Jeffress shook his head. Most of the work he does, he insisted, has nothing to do with societal skirmishes or upcoming elections or anything else found outside the Bible. He said the caricature of him doesn't align with reality.

Glancing to my right, his left, I took note of the irony. The corner of Jeffress's office was a shrine—his secretary used that specific word to describe it—to President Donald J. Trump. There was an eight-foot-tall poster memorializing the "Celebrate Freedom" concert in D.C. (the one where the choir sang "Make America Great Again"). There were boxes of Trump cuff links and a golden Trump commemorative coin. There were dozens—*dozens*—of framed photos of Jeffress and Trump: praying over him, talking with him, shaking hands with him, giving thumbs-up with him, walking alongside him, speaking in front of him, standing dutifully behind him. (There were also a few photos of Jeffress with Mike Pence, and one, seemingly misplaced, of him with right-wing pundit Ann Coulter.) In the sweep of my reporting on the former president and his many sycophants, I had never seen such a temple to Trumpism. Anything that carried the man's distinctive Sharpie signature was framed: news articles, White House proclamations, email correspondences, even printed-out tweets.

A year earlier, when we spoke following Trump's departure from office, Jeffress had hinted at feeling some remorse for the depth of his political involvement. It didn't last. By the end of 2021—not long after the former president boasted that "nobody has done more for Christianity or for evangelicals or for religion itself than I have"—Jeffress was hosting Trump in his pulpit at the First Baptist Dallas celebration of Christmas service. The program cover that day suggested a certain competition: Half the page depicted a twinkling Nativity scene, while the other half proclaimed the star-spangled arrival of Trump.

"There's a lot of clouds hanging over our country right now. Very dark clouds," the former president had somberly announced at the service. Instead of pivoting to declare the good news of great joy (you know, about the baby in the manger), Trump concluded: "But we will come back bigger and better and stronger than ever before." The worship center filled with cheers.

When I asked about the concern he'd once voiced to me—that some Christians had crossed the line in conflating politics and faith—Jeffress said he agreed. Some of Trump's evangelical followers, he said, were "acting like nutcases" when they stormed the Capitol and spread conspiracy theories about vaccines. He called it a case of misplaced priorities.

"They think they're following in his footsteps—they don't mean Jesus, they mean Donald Trump," Jeffress clarified, chuckling. "But Trump, I could tell you for sure, he took the vaccine. I hear these people who think it's the mark of the Antichrist, and I say, 'Well, Trump's the one who developed it, so what does that make him?'"

Jeffress insisted, however, that this represented a fringe of Trump's evangelical base. Most conservative Christians were like him: supportive of Republican policies, opposed to Democratic policies, eager for a restoration of traditional values as defined by the right. They sense "an overlap between constitutional freedoms and biblical responsibilities" and vote accordingly. Being alarmed about the state of the country—feeling "under siege" by a secular government and a hostile culture, as Jeffress repeatedly phrased it—does not make someone an extremist.

Broadly speaking, of course, this is true. But a few zealots can define an entire movement—and given the sudden scale of this persecution sentiment inside the evangelical Church, it was only a matter of time.

In early 2017, a month into Trump's presidency, the Public Religion Research Institute asked a sample of Americans which religious group they thought faced more discrimination in the United States, Muslims or Christians. The general public was twice as likely to pick Muslims in response; non-religious respondents were three times as likely. Both white Catholics and white mainline Protestants agreed, in overwhelming fashion, that Muslims face more discrimination in the United States than Christians. Only one group of respondents dissented from this view: white evangelicals.

Jeffress was inviting an obvious question: Once a person becomes convinced that they are under siege—that enemies are coming for them and want to destroy their way of life—what is to stop that person from becoming radicalized? I wondered if Jeffress felt any responsibility to dial back the rhetoric. Instead, he doubled down.

"When I addressed the National Religious Broadcasters [a few months ago], the title of my message was 'When Persecution Comes.' I talked about how the same persecution that our brothers and sisters in Christ are experiencing around the world is coming to the shores of America," Jeffress said. "I talked about the first instance of persecution, in the Book of Acts, and how persecution was always incremental. It started with verbal admonishments, then light scouring, then imprisonment, and then beheading."

Jeffress continued, "It happened in Nazi Germany. They didn't put six million Jews in the crematorium immediately. The Germans would never have put up with that initially. It was a slow process of marginalization, isolation, and then the 'final solution.' And I think you're seeing that happen in America. I believe there's evidence that the Biden administration has weaponized the Internal Revenue Service to come after churches."

The "evidence" Jeffress cited in making this leap—bureaucratic regulations clearing the way for concentration camps—was nonexistent. When pushed, he mentioned a single court case that was ultimately decided in favor of religious liberty. "You sound like a hysterical maniac if you say the government's coming after us," Jeffress said with a shrug. "But I believe they are."

There were reasonable concerns, following the 2015 *Obergefell v.*

Hodges ruling that legalized same-sex marriage, that churches and religious nonprofits might be punished for acting in accordance with their traditional beliefs. But no such punishment ever materialized. In fact, according to David French, a conservative Christian attorney who spent decades arguing religious liberty cases in front of federal courts, "the record for religious freedom since *Obergefell* is extraordinary." The judicial branch, French wrote in The Dispatch, had "expanded the autonomy of religious organizations to hire and fire employees . . . protected churches time and again from discriminatory regulations . . . [and] expanded the ability of religious institutions to receive state funds."

This hasn't stopped evangelicals from subscribing to a narrative of mass marginalization. In 2022, an essay published in *First Things* magazine lamented that American society has gradually turned against Christianity over the past fifty years. The author, Aaron Renn, described three distinct eras: the "Positive World," predating 1994, in which Christianity was embraced; the "Neutral World," from 1994 to 2014, in which Christianity was tolerated; and the "Negative World," from 2014 to present, in which Christianity is rejected. The essay, a viral sensation among evangelicals, made some compelling arguments. Yet its thesis evinced three essential blind spots. First, only those American Christians who are white and Protestant can recall such a halcyon age; neither the Catholic student whose school was targeted by the government nor the Black worshiper whose church was firebombed by Klansmen saw "positive" treatment because of their religion. Second, Jesus says that Christians should have no reasonable expectation of being treated well by the world around them; in this sense anything less than brutal, unceasing oppression should be considered downright utopian. Third, given that context, describing the modern era as "negative" betrays a certain blinkered privilege on the part of American Christians. Even if society is more antagonistic toward the Church today than at any time in U.S. history, our status remains the envy of Christians the world over. Believers aren't getting rounded up and imprisoned here. Churches aren't being monitored or censored. Pastors aren't being coerced to do the bidding of the state.

This is why Russell Moore, while leading the Ethics and Religious Liberty Commission, was so vexed by Trump's scaremongering around "the Johnson Amendment." There were genuine threats to religious expression in America, Moore said, but a government crackdown on churches wasn't among them. Assuming pastors played by the rules that govern all nonprofits—namely, no endorsing political candidates from the pulpit—there would be no trouble.

As it happens, some pastors have openly flouted this regulation for years, all but begging the IRS to come after them. The government has done exactly nothing in response. Jeffress knows this better than most. Numerous high-profile churches in Texas, including several in the Dallas area, are notorious for their brazen defiance of the Johnson Amendment. (The *Texas Tribune* has reported on this extensively.) Not only was the Biden administration not coming after churches; the Biden administration was actively looking the other way as churches broke the law.

In the end, it was revealing that Jeffress felt the need to fabricate these threats to the Church. Far more revealing, however, was that he saw the persecution of Christians as sufficient to justify behavior that is antithetical to what Christ taught.

There are two promises that attend faith in Jesus. The first is of eternal life in heaven. The second is of discrimination, cruelty, abuse, and possible martyrdom on earth.

"If the world hates you, keep in mind that it hated me first," Jesus told His disciples, according to the Book of John. "If you belonged to the world, it would love you as its own. As it is, you do not belong to the world, but I have chosen you out of the world. That is why the world hates you. Remember what I told you: 'A servant is not greater than his master.' If they persecuted me, they will persecute you also."

In his Sermon on the Mount, Jesus went out of His way to explain that believers should welcome this maltreatment. "Blessed are those who are persecuted because of righteousness," He said, "for theirs is the kingdom of heaven."

Christians volunteered to live in a negative world. Christians *signed up* to be under siege. The notion that some conjectural bullying of the American Church is a defense for the indefensible—while Christians worldwide are being harassed and hunted and even killed for their faith—would be comical if it weren't so calamitous.

Jeffress did concede one point. "I've said before, 'You'd better be sure that if you're suffering, you're suffering for righteousness and not for your own stupidity,'" the pastor told me, citing examples of congregants who've claimed to be oppressed by vaccine policies or mask mandates or proposed gun laws. "I do think some of what we've categorized as Christian suffering is not suffering for righteousness. We're supposed to be suffering for doing God's will and what His word prescribes to do, not because government goes against my preferences."

This is the paradox of Robert Jeffress. One moment he was grumbling that some of his church members had gotten the wrong idea about "this synthesizing of the Constitution and the Bible." In the next, he was recommending that I return to First Baptist Dallas a couple of Sundays later. It would be a special occasion—the church's annual celebration of "Freedom Sunday"—featuring country musician Lee Greenwood singing his soppy ballad, "God Bless the USA." Jeffress handed me a promotional flier. There was a photo of the keynote speaker, Kelvin Cochran, and the caption: "Former Atlanta Fire Chief Fired for Christian Beliefs."

Jeffress smirked as I studied the handout.

"The people who talk about how wonderful persecution is," he said, "are those who've never experienced it."

CHAPTER SIX

WHEATON, ILLINOIS

You have heard that it was said, "Love your neighbor
and hate your enemy." But I tell you, love your
enemies and pray for those who persecute you.

—MATTHEW 5:43–44

Something happened fifteen years ago, Professor John Dickson explained to a packed auditorium on the campus of Wheaton College, that "changed the way I view Christianity."

He was back home, in his native Australia, participating in a nationally televised program that aimed to settle a debate: "Are we better off without religion?" Each side of the conversation featured a small team of scholars making their case. Dickson, a celebrated theologian, author, and expert on the apostolic age of the early Church, argued that society benefits from Christian influence.

Before the debate began, an entrance poll was taken to quantify the sentiments of a sample group. A majority of respondents came in rejecting the idea that any religion—especially Christianity—somehow made for a better society. That same group was then surveyed in an exit poll after the arguments concluded; the numbers did not budge. Dickson wasn't necessarily surprised by the results. What *did* surprise him was the rationale being presented by his opponents for opposing Christianity, and how thoroughly it resonated with the broader public.

"Whereas it used to be quite popular for people to say the problem with Christianity is that it's too self-righteous," Dickson concluded, "it was now far more common for people to say, 'Actually, the problem with Christianity is that it's wicked.'"

Having spent decades scrutinizing the shifting impressions of religion worldwide, Dickson said, here was a "crystallized thought" to explain the rising hostility toward his own faith. The more he studied the social science, the more obvious it became. It required no leap of logic to connect the public's deteriorating opinion of the Church—in Australia, in America, and elsewhere—to other corresponding metrics, such as falling Sunday attendance, declining denominational membership, and fewer people identifying as Christians.

Just recently, Dickson informed the crowd at Wheaton College, Australia had officially become a "post-Christian nation." To great media fanfare, the Australian Bureau of Statistics released figures in June 2022 showing, for the first time, that fewer than 50 percent of Aussies identified as followers of Jesus. This was the culmination of a decades-long trajectory that had bowed severely downward in recent years: from 61 percent in 2011, to 52 percent in 2016, to 44 percent in 2022.

And then Dickson dropped the bomb.

"Within ten years, Christians will be a minority *in America*," the professor announced. The numbers were straightforward: America's share of self-identified Christians was shrinking at roughly the same rate as Australia's. In 2007, 78 percent of Americans identified with Christianity; by 2021, it was down to 63 percent.

"We're ten years ahead of you," the professor said, extending his arms with a good-natured grin. "Greetings from the future, my friends."

Wheaton College is a keystone of the American evangelical movement, widely recognized as one of the world's most important Christian institutions. Founded in 1860 by an abolitionist named Jonathan Blanchard, the school was pioneering in its education of both women and Black students, even serving as a stop on the Underground Railroad. Over the next century and a half, Wheaton grew to become a doctrinal and academic giant, producing influential figures such as John Piper, Michael Gerson, and Billy Graham.

Like some of its counterparts—Liberty University, Bob Jones University, Oral Roberts University, and a whole host of Southern Baptist schools—Wheaton is conservative in its values and teachings. The school prohibits the use of alcohol and tobacco, as well as "homosexual behavior," and embraces a strict reformed Protestantism. What sets Wheaton apart is its distinctive approach to the culture. Unlike so many other right-wing Christian colleges, Wheaton has long been known for its relatively placid disposition when it comes to politics and current events. The school isn't exactly a pushover; it successfully sued the Obama administration in federal court over a mandate to provide contraceptive coverage to employees, claiming a major victory for the religious liberty cause. But this sort of activism isn't where Wheaton makes its mark. The school's charge, etched into gray slate at the entrance to its campus, is FOR CHRIST AND HIS KINGDOM.

All this helps to explain why the college has in recent years become a clique without a tribe: too theologically conservative for many liberal Christians, too attitudinally passive for many conservative Christians. These days, to the extent Wheaton belonged to anyone, it was to the quiet, committed, politically homeless church leaders who had traveled to Illinois this October afternoon. They were Black and white, man and woman, from congregations big and small, packed into this cramped, dusky auditorium, all on a common mission to save American evangelicalism from itself.

Convening the school's annual "Amplify" conference, Wheaton president Philip Ryken did not delay in acknowledging the peril of the moment. The American Church, he said, was fracturing in real time, right in front of us. And for one reason: fear.

"Some of us are afraid of suffering harm from a white-majority culture. Or, for some of us, becoming a racial minority in a nonwhite culture. Or, for some of us, becoming a religious minority in a post-Christian culture," Ryken said. "We all have our fears. There are things happening in the culture, and also happening in the Church, that only exacerbate them."

And yet, Ryken declared, the people in this auditorium should be unified by a message of hope. He read from Paul's first letter to the Corinthians: "For what I received I passed on to you as of first importance: that Christ died for our sins according to the Scriptures, that he was buried, that he was raised on the third day according to the Scriptures, and that he appeared to [Peter], and then to the Twelve."

Paul's words are a reminder, Ryken said, that Christians "have a great love that will cast out our fear." That great love should embolden us to share the gospel *especially* when met with bitterness. It should embolden us to realize that Jesus's sacrifice "is so much more important than all the other worldly things." It should embolden us to recall "how fearless the apostles were" and to emulate them—not just their courage, but their kindness and gentleness and humility.

"All of the things tearing us apart are rectified when we understand this message," Ryken said. "Not just as something that defines who people are when they receive it, but also defines who we are when we give it."

I could see why Dickson, the Aussie theologian, was being featured so prominently at the Amplify program.

With Christians soon to be a minority in the United States, the question shouldn't be how best to fight back and reclaim their lost status. Rather, Dickson said, the question should be how Christians might "lose well"—carrying themselves in ways that reflect the hope and confidence and great love found in the gospel.

At present, Dickson said, the American Church is suffering from "bully syndrome." Too many Christians are swaggering around and picking on marginalized people and generally acting like jerks because they're angry and apprehensive. "Every teacher will tell you, the bully on the playground is usually the most insecure boy. It's a compensation mechanism. If the boy were truly confident, he wouldn't need to throw his weight around," Dickson said. "It's the same with the Church. The bully Church is the insecure Church."

He asked the crowd to remember how Paul was unjustly jailed in the ancient Macedonian city of Philippi. "What was his response? To sing hymns!" Dickson shouted, eliciting hoots from the audience. "Of course he would! We're in prison; let's sing!"

Some years later, Paul was jailed again, this time in Rome. Paul's followers were worried for his life, Dickson said, and the apostle responded most curiously in his letter to the people in that city of Philippi. "Now I want you to know, brothers and sisters, that what has happened to me has actually served to advance the gospel. As a result, it has become clear throughout the whole palace guard and to everyone else that I am in chains for Christ," Paul wrote. "And because of my chains, most of the brothers and sisters have become confident in the Lord and dare all the more to proclaim the gospel without fear."

Dickson stopped to underscore the point.

"What must have felt like a loss at many levels—social status, freedom—was actually a *win* for Paul," the professor said. "He was the master of being a cheerful loser. Probably because he knew that it's a win for the gospel."

Dickson shared his own stories of losing. He'd been taunted and scorned in the elite circles of Australian cultural life. He'd had a book banned by the public school system. And of course, he'd been defeated in that nationally televised debate all those years ago.

But something happened after that debate, Dickson told us. One of his opponents, an observant Jewish professor, was so intrigued by Dickson's arguments that she asked him to come speak to her class. And then she asked him back again and again. Finally, after a number of speeches, she asked Dickson to come teach a full, four-credit course on "The Life of Jesus and the Gospels." He wound up teaching for ten years at Sydney University, one of the country's leading secular institutions, and reached countless young people with the message of Christ.

"Sometimes, friends, losses turn out to be wins in disguise," Dickson said in a soft voice.

He paused. "After all, we're the death and resurrection people."

THE UNOFFICIAL THEMES OF WHEATON'S EVENT WERE MARTYRDOM and persecution, and the juxtapositions felt downright jarring. There was the authentic martyrdom that established the early Church and the artificial martyrdom of the Church today; there was the actual persecution of Christ's followers in Rome and the embellished persecution of his followers in America.

Like almost every other speaker at the conference, Charlie Dates, a dynamic Black preacher from the south side of Chicago, invoked the example of the apostle Paul. But Dates took a unique tack. He built his sermon around the glory of Rome, the city of Paul's citizenship.

"When one thinks of Rome, one thinks of the undisputed power of Claudius and Nero. The twin towers of opposition to any idea promoting any authority other than Rome. One thinks of the foothills and the giant legions; that imperial capital, waiting to seize lesser military powers around the world. It was a powerful, prideful city," Dates bellowed in his striking baritone. "The intelligentsia of the day lived and breathed in Rome. Rome was the world's capital. So much to be proud about in Rome, as the economic and political and influential supercenter of the then-known world."

Paul—born as Saul—was a product of this glorious empire. An "intellectual powerhouse," Saul "attended the universities in Tarsus, sat at the feet of one of the most prolific rabbis of the then-known world," Dates said. The young man observed the religious customs of his Jewish people, but he was nationally Roman. Saul earned respect in both worlds, so much so that the Pharisees—the Jewish religious elite—authorized him to oversee the persecution of Christians.

But then something happened. After supervising the murder of an outspoken Christian named Stephen, and setting off to Damascus to round up more heretics like him, Saul was suddenly blinded. "Saul, Saul, why do you persecute me?" came a voice from heaven.

"Who are you, Lord?" Saul asked.

"I am Jesus, whom you are persecuting."

The New Testament records few moments more consequential than this one. Soon, Saul's sight is restored. His name is changed to Paul. And he begins traveling throughout the Roman Empire—visiting the same places, according to the Book of Acts, where he had been "breathing out murderous threats against the Lord's disciples"—spreading the very message he'd formerly been oppressing.

Sometime later, in his letter to the early church in Rome, Paul wrote something that Dates described as "the most absurd" sentence in the Bible. "For I am not ashamed of the gospel," Paul wrote, "because it is the power of God that brings salvation to everyone who believes."

It was absurd, Dates said, because Paul had every reason to feel ashamed.

"What kind of man with this pedigree would claim saving power in a man called Jesus?" Dates asked us. "No self-respecting Pharisee would look at a man hanging on a tree and consider him to be the savior of the world. No judge of popularity trying to win the masses would affiliate himself or herself with such an unpopular message."

History would agree. The emperor Nero, who infamously scapegoated Christians for the burning of Rome, set the precedent for centuries of imperial persecution. He murdered the followers of Jesus en masse: beheadings, crucifixions, death by lion, and other public displays of savagery. It was during Nero's reign that Paul traversed the empire, preaching that a carpenter's son from rural Galilee had established a kingdom that surpassed anything Rome could ever hope to be.

Paul paid the price for renouncing his allegiance to the rulers of this world. After years of being beaten, tortured, imprisoned, and placed under house arrest, he was executed by the state of Rome.

And he wasn't the only one.

Consider the case of Peter, the right-hand disciple of Jesus. In his first epistle, Peter writes from Rome to the Christians in Asia Minor—modern-day Turkey—who were suffering for their faith. He beseeches them to rejoice in their torment. Peter teaches them that suffering brings us closer to Jesus; that to suffer is to be cleansed by a refining "fire" that rids Christians of the impulses, attitudes, and identities they once possessed.

Laurel Bunker, another pastor at the Wheaton conference, pointed out the most crucial component of Peter's letter. After comforting these early Christians, Peter admonishes them not to allow this persecution to change the way they witness to the world. Specifically, he tells them to show goodness to the very people who are persecuting them.

Bunker read from First Peter, chapter three: "Finally, all of you, be like-minded, be sympathetic, love one another, be compassionate and humble. Do not repay evil with evil or insult with insult. On the contrary, repay evil with blessing, because to this you were called so that you may inherit a blessing."

She noted how Peter, in his letter, stopped to recite a Psalm: "Whoever would love life and see good days must keep their tongue from evil and their lips from deceitful speech. They must turn from evil and do good; they must seek peace and pursue it. For the eyes of the Lord are on the righteous and his ears are attentive to their prayer, but the face of the Lord is against those who do evil."

After speaking the word *evil*, Bunker looked up from her Bible. Then she gazed upward.

"My God," she said. "If the evil comes from us, what shall we do?"

Bunker's message dovetailed with Dickson's earlier theory about the world's vanishing confidence in the Church. The public hasn't turned against Christians because they act better than the rest of the world, she said. The public has turned against Christians because they act *worse* than the rest of the world. Bunker argued that much of this bad behavior can be traced back to the Christian victimhood complex, which causes some believers to lash out against enemies real and imagined. Such behavior defies the words of Peter, and the very instruction of Jesus, who famously stated: "You have heard that it was said, 'Love your neighbor and hate your enemy.' But I tell you, love your enemies and pray for those who persecute you."

Bunker admitted to being the worst offender.

"The reality is, I have messed up. I've taken the bait of social media with family. My husband and I are surrounded by family members who are not saved," Bunker said. "We've been excluded. We've been ostracized. We've been talked about. It hurts. It's hard. It's frustrating. Sometimes you want to lose your mind."

She recounted a particularly tense Facebook argument with her brother. After she'd typed out a long, spiteful message, Bunker said, her husband stepped into the room. He asked her to delete it and get off the computer. "As I sat there and cried, God said to me, through His Holy Spirit, 'You're not angry because he rejected me. You're angry because he rejected you,'" Bunker recalled. "And I was embarrassed. Because it was true."

Bunker noted that God doesn't simply treat sinners with grace; He commands *us* to do the same. Showing grace, she said, is easy when you're winning. It's much harder when you're losing. Paraphrasing the

Protestant reformer Martin Luther—"One plus God is a majority"—Bunker argued that promoting unconditional grace is the defining challenge of evangelicalism today.

"We've got to remember there is nothing too hard for God," she said. "If you're sitting here, in your right mind, you're a walking miracle. You weren't too hard for God—with your messed-up, jacked-up self. So listen, make a little room for a child of God. Make a little room for a misfit. Make a little room for that single mother. . . . Make a little room for that kid who is mentally burdened with their sexuality. Because here's the reality: We can be mad all we want, at the quote-unquote liberal agenda, but unless the people of the gospel have a better way, we have nothing to talk about."

The next generation of would-be believers, Bunker warned, is watching us. "They want to know if we love Jesus first"—more than money, more than social status, more than a political party, more than a country.

"The work of the kingdom can't be hit-and-run evangelism," she said. If Christians want to win souls for Jesus, they can start by showing grace to those who don't deserve it; by showing kindness to the culture; by seeing in everyone, especially our enemies, "the image and likeness of God." None of this can be accomplished with a mentality of fear, Bunker said. She pleaded with her audience to overcome it.

"Jesus knows something about being in an opposing place with opposing forces. He used twelve weirdos to turn the world upside down. I think He can certainly use a few of you weirdos here," the pastor said. The room filled with laughter. But she was serious.

"The Black kids of the city of Chicago; the gay kid who struggles with suicidal ideation; the single mothers; the prostitutes; the broken of society. The only way they will know is if we *go*," Bunker preached. "They are not going to come to us. They don't care about our steeples. They want to know, is my life redeemable? Does my life have purpose?"

Bunker finished where she started, by reading from the Book of First Peter. It was a call to action from a future martyr—Peter, like his friend Paul, would be executed in Rome during the reign of Nero—who pleaded with believers to keep their perspective.

"But even if you should suffer for what is right, you are blessed," Peter wrote. "Do not fear their threats; do not be frightened."

Bunker bowed her head to pray.

AT CERTAIN POINTS IN HISTORY, FRACTURES IN SOCIETY HAVE MADE the Church stronger.

Ed Stetzer, the executive director of the Billy Graham Center at Wheaton, asked us to think back to the 1960s and early 1970s. There was "division all around us": the assassinations of President John F. Kennedy and his brother Robert F. Kennedy and the Reverend Martin Luther King Jr.; the Kent State shooting and deadly rioting in cities nationwide; the Watergate break-in and needless bloodshed of Vietnam; the drug-culture explosion and pornography epidemic and *Roe v. Wade* ruling. "And then 1976 was called 'the year of the evangelical,'" Stetzer said, shrugging, as if to say, *go figure.*

Today is a different story. The fractures in society, Stetzer told us, are making the Church weaker. Everyone around me nodded in agreement.

"The Church of Jesus Christ has been distracted and divided in a way that I have never seen in my whole lifetime. And for most of us, it's been some of the hardest years we've led," Stetzer said. "We've got to show again who we really are. There are things that need to get discipled out of this movement that's called evangelicalism, and new things that need to get discipled in."

Stetzer focused on what needed to be purged from evangelicalism—starting with the nastiness. The love of a merciful God "is not what we're known for," he said, but it could be again if Christians would check themselves. Without naming names, Stetzer was speaking to an obvious truth. This idea, promoted by the likes of Robert Jeffress, that the Church's unpopularity has nothing to do with its ugly behavior, simply does not pass the smell test.

"Here's the reality. The last few years, I and many others have expressed concern that people of God seem to be radiating something other than the gospel in too many places in too many ways," Stetzer said. Multiple people shouted "Hallelujah!" in unison. Nodding, Stetzer continued: "I believe we've got to call God's people back to radiating the beauty of the gospel."

The subtext of Stetzer's remarks was clear enough. It was time for evangelicals to stop talking about Christianity and start practicing Christianity. Key to that practice is discipling. In Christian vernacular, *discipling* means more than the dictionary.com definition ("to convert into a disciple"). It is an aggressive, active verb. It refers to instruction—specifically, the teaching of challenging and problematic truths.

Bunker wasn't wrong when she called Jesus's disciples "twelve weirdos." They were an eclectic and unqualified bunch. There were fishermen and small-time merchants, a tax collector and a political activist. While following Jesus on His three-year journey of ministry, the disciples were repeatedly, and often comically, oblivious to His teachings. Jesus loved them, but He did not infantilize them. Time and again, when His disciples got something wrong—or even when they simply showed human weakness—Jesus rebuked them. He chided them for being faithless. He censured them for their vanity and bigotry and prejudice. He criticized them for not grasping His instruction.

This is what discipling looks like. And this, Vincent Bacote told me, is what's absent inside much of the American evangelical Church.

"If you ask me what's the biggest problem with evangelicalism, I'd say it's a catechesis problem. It's a formation problem, a discipleship problem. These are people who are supposed to have a knowledge of the Bible, but many of them don't," said Bacote, a renowned theologian on the Wheaton faculty. "The genius of evangelicalism is the breadth of it. The hazard is the lack of depth. A lot of these people are just not going deep enough."

By remaining shallow in the scriptures, Bacote said, too many American Christians have avoided a necessary showdown between their own base cultural proclivities and God's perfect standard. When Christians are discipled primarily by society, inevitably they look to scripture for affirmation of their habits and behaviors and political views. "But if the Bible is the word of God, then God ought to be interrogating those things. That's why Jesus came: to fix your vertical relationship with God," Bacote said. "He wants your whole life. He wants to transform who you are."

We were sitting in Bacote's fifth-floor office. The shelves appeared liable to collapse under the weight of his tomes. Bacote, an author himself, and a longtime professor of theology, is also the director of the Center for Applied Christian Ethics. This is Wheaton's de facto arm of civic and cultural engagement. Fittingly, the books surrounding us ranged from religion to warfare, elections to history, music to sports.

Reflecting on the sum total of his scholarship, Bacote said he felt confident sharing two basic observations about evangelicalism in the United States. The first is that too many American Christians are woefully under-discipled. The second—a by-product of the first—is that too many American Christians think of themselves as *American* Christians.

"Who's preaching to them about idolatry? I mean, really, in evangelical churches, how many sermons are people hearing about idolatry of any kind, much less national idolatry?" Bacote asked, turning his palms upward, as if begging me to provide examples. "If people generally aren't preaching about idolatry in the first place, it's no surprise that this particular species of idolatry just hides in plain sight."

The positive we can take from this, Bacote noted, is that some Christians "are now showing us what they've always been thinking." Indeed, the tumult of this era has brought forth from the shadows some of the blood-and-soil compulsions of the American evangelical. What Bacote wants to do—what he wants his students, who are mostly current and prospective pastors, to do—is challenge these people the way that Jesus challenged His disciples.

"They need help to understand that you can care for your country without worshipping your country," Bacote said. "They also need help to understand that you can care for your country *and* seek good for your neighbors. Just because other people are getting something, doesn't mean you're losing something."

These answers aren't difficult to find, Bacote told me. Christians just need to start looking.

"The ongoing opportunity for evangelicalism is to live up to the language that's right there in the Bible," he said, "which is love your neighbor as yourselves."

Jesus stressed two commandments as more important than the rest. Bacote had just named the second one. The answer to our problem of national idolatry, he told me, comes from a discipleship that stresses the first—and greatest—commandment: "Love the Lord your God with all your heart and with all your soul and with all your mind and with all your strength."

STROLLING THROUGH CAMPUS, A SHARP WIND SCATTERING THE LEAVES of scarlet and fiery orange, Professor John Dickson told me he'd arrived at Wheaton just three weeks earlier. There had been many opportunities over the years to teach full-time in the United States, he said, but he'd never wanted to leave his native Australia. His children were there. His friends were there. His church was there. It would require something extraordinary—nothing less than a provocation from the Almighty—to uproot him.

So, I asked Dickson, what was it that finally brought him to America?

"*This*," he said, gesturing around us, as if to synopsize the themes of the Amplify conference. "The division, the anxiety, the fear about losing power and status. It's entirely why I'm here."

A questionable choice at best. Dickson had a good thing going in Australia. Sure, the trend lines of secularization might have been troubling, but at least the remnant of the Church itself was reasonably healthy. There was no civil war in Australian Christendom; the fights that had so divided the American evangelical movement over the past decade were largely nonexistent in Dickson's country.

He didn't disagree. Dickson cautioned, however, that American Christianity doesn't exist in a vacuum.

"Evangelicals in Britain and Europe and Australia are very different from evangelicals here. And I've noticed, in the last ten years, lots of Australians who used to be happy going by *evangelical*, because they meant British evangelical—that gentle Anglicanism of William Wilberforce, socially engaged, happy to be in public, keen to see people evangelized with the Bible—they don't want to go by *evangelical* anymore."

Why not?

"Because there's not this politically zealous evangelicalism in Australia and Britain. It's just never been that way," Dickson said. "But we keep on hearing about American evangelicalism in our media reports.

And what happens in America matters. These days, even in Australia, if someone asks if you're an 'evangelical,' they don't mean: Are you mild-mannered, intellectually incisive, Bible expounding, pastorally warm? No, they mean: Are you right-wing?"

These were the international symptoms of America's illness. Over the last few years, I had engaged in similar conversations with Christians around the United States. There was one particular anecdote, still stuck in my mind, that I shared with Dickson. During a visit to Aldersgate United Methodist Church in Greenville, South Carolina, I had convened an amateur focus group with the pastor and two dozen of his elders. Their denomination was on the verge of a split over social issues, namely the question of ordaining gay ministers and marrying gay couples, and their individual church was also approaching a fracture. The pastor had welcomed me to Aldersgate in hopes of bringing some long-simmering tensions to the surface and seeing if the church might be salvaged. Early on, as the folks assembled dug into Styrofoam bowls of vanilla ice cream, I asked how many people in the room identified as "evangelical." Half of them raised a hand. For the next two hours, every disagreement that surfaced—about partisan affiliation, media consumption, current events—was split between the half who identified as "evangelical" and the half who didn't. The term no longer conveyed much about biblical beliefs. It was mostly a proxy for cultural belonging.

"That really is not the case in England or Australia," Dickson replied. "Australians inherited British evangelicalism, so we've just stayed in that mold. There have been individual Americans who influenced us; Billy Graham had a massive effect in Sydney in '59. And in the sixties, loads of people were converted. But they were converted into Anglican churches. So, the original evangelicalism has remained in both Britain and Australia, while America sort of went its own way."

As we sat down in the campus dining hall, surrounded by hundreds of flags representing the nations of the world, I couldn't help but think of the role reversal at work. American churches had for centuries trained, funded, and dispatched missionaries across the globe to preach the good news of Jesus. Now here was Dickson, picking at a plate of rice and chicken curry, describing America as his "mission field." There was nothing caustic or condescending in his tone. Yet he didn't shy away from the point: The people of this country needed some help.

Dickson told me that his calling here wasn't simply to equip pastors as they prepared for combat; it was to charge into the fray himself. Since coming to the States, he had already begun preaching Sunday services at a few different churches. He was pleased, if a bit surprised, to report that he'd been well received thus far.

"You know, people hear it differently from a different accent," Dickson said, grinning.

"Actually, it isn't just the accent," the professor decided, correcting himself and turning serious. "It's the fact that people don't peg me as either Republican or Democrat because I can't fit into those categories. They don't even know what our categories are. I mean, conservatives in Australia support universal health care. So do evangelicals. I come from a country where a levy of 1.5 percent of my salary runs the whole medical system for everyone. Hospitals are free, doctors are free. But that makes you a socialist here."

Now Dickson was laughing. "So, when I've been here in the past, I'll give talks on the history of medical welfare from antiquity to today, because, you know, it was the early Christians who started public hospitals in the fourth century. And Americans hear me doing this without ever thinking I'm some sneaky Obamacare supporter. They just think, 'Oh, he's Australian.'"

I laughed, too. Those were the good old days, I told Dickson, when American evangelicals squabbled over things like socialized medicine. At present the Church was imploding over the legitimacy of our elections system; the question of whether to confront racism in society; the etiquette of wearing masks during a lethal pandemic; the morality of vaccines; and the existence of a satanic cult of Democrats who cannibalize kids.

The American Church was no stranger to discord. But not since the Civil War had there been such intense polarization in the body of believers. One of the speakers at the conference had suggested that this period was even more precarious than the 1860s; that we were living through a five-hundred-year moment for Christianity. I asked Dickson if he believed that.

He began to slowly nod his head. "Yes. Yes, I do," Dickson replied. "But

I dare to think it's more likely to be a positive moment than a negative moment. Because I think of American evangelicalism as a giant that's fallen asleep in a bit of a fog. And if American evangelicals can pivot in this moment and work out the answers to those questions—What does it mean to lose well? What does it mean to be cheerfully confident without being brash and arrogant and manipulative and controlling?—I think it will bless America, and I think it will bless the world."

To awaken from its fog, Dickson told me, American evangelicalism must first rid itself of its persecution complex.

"My academic specialty is the first century to sixth century," he explained. "You know, Nietzsche accused the Christians of having a slave mentality. He thought that's what gave them their ethic of humility. But the data is exactly the opposite. The Christians of the first few centuries, especially, were *so* confident Jesus was Lord that they could be quite rude in mocking the gods and so on. They were confident and cheerful; even when they're locked up in prison, they're singing hymns, they're writing letters encouraging others."

This was not performative in nature; members of the early Church didn't behave this way to prove a point. Rather, these people who lived in such close proximity to the time of the eyewitnesses—and some were *themselves* eyewitnesses—acted out of a euphoria rooted in absolute certainty. They had zero doubts that Jesus, the rabbi who'd been publicly executed, was later seen alive, and were so giddy about spreading the news that they couldn't be bothered to care about their circumstances otherwise.

Dickson continued: "I think we need to bring some of that wisdom of the evangelizing of the pre-Christian world to bear on the re-evangelizing of the post-Christian world."

I must have gone cross-eyed at that last point. Sensing my confusion, Dickson leaned in.

"I've spent time with underground pastors in China and the amazing thing about them is how cheerful they are," he said. "I've been with pastors who have all been to prison—one of them three times. But they're not afraid, they're not paranoid. They are *genuinely* cheerful. Because they think, 'Well, if I go to prison, there will be more people for me to preach the gospel to.'"

It makes for an unflattering comparison, he told me, with the attitude of the American Church. Much of what drives evangelicals here is "fear that we're losing our country, fear that we're losing our power," Dickson said. "And it's so unhealthy. We should think of ourselves as eager dinner guests at someone else's banquet. We are happy to be there, happy to share our perspective. But we are always respectful, always humble, because this isn't our home."

Humility doesn't come easy to the American evangelical. The self-importance that accompanies citizenship in the world's mightiest nation is trouble enough, never mind when it's augmented by the certainty of exclusive membership in the afterlife. We are an immodest and excessively indulged people. We have grown so accustomed to our advantages—to our prosperity and our worldly position—that we feel entitled to them.

The way to vanquish that entitlement, Dickson said, is by doing the lowliest thing imaginable: studying the scriptures with PhD-type rigor and kindergarten-level vulnerability.

"There are Bible people, and there are non-Bible people. I'm just not sure how many American churches are filled with Bible people," Dickson said. "In America, there is so much focus on the illustration, on the modern application, compared to that boring, stiff British Anglicanism with its constant emphasis on the scripture itself."

He tapped two fingers on his Bible. "Maybe we could use something more boring."

CHAPTER SEVEN

BRIGHTON, MICHIGAN

When he lies, he speaks his native language,
for he is a liar and the father of lies.

—JOHN 8:44

"Before I turn to the word," the preacher announced, "I'm gonna do another diatribe."

"Go on!" one man yelled. "Amen!" shouted a woman several pews in front of me.

Sandwiched between forty minutes of praise music and forty minutes of preaching was the strangest ritual I had ever witnessed inside a house of worship. Pastor Bill Bolin called it his "diatribe." The congregants at FloodGate Church had taken to calling it something else: "Headline News."

A gregarious man in his mid-sixties, with thick jowls and a thinning wave of dyed hair, Bolin looked the part of a hippie turned hipster. His floral-patterned shirt was untucked from dark blue jeans. "About the vaccines . . ." Bolin began, the crowd hanging on his every syllable.

For the next fifteen minutes Bolin did not mention the forgiveness of sins, the resurrection of the body, or the life everlasting. Instead he spouted misinformation and conspiratorial nonsense, much of it related to the "radically dangerous" COVID-19 vaccines. "A local nurse who attends FloodGate, who is anonymous at this time—she reported to my wife the other day that at her hospital, they have two COVID patients that are hospitalized. *Two.*" Bolin paused dramatically. "They have *one hundred and three* vaccine-complication patients." The people around me gasped.

"How about this one?" Bolin said a few minutes later. He told of a doctor who claims to know that "between one and two hundred United States Congress members, plus many of their staffers and family members with COVID, were treated by a colleague of his over the past fifteen months . . . with . . ." Bolin stopped and puts a hand to his ear.

A chorus of people responded: "Ivermectin."

Bolin pretended not to hear. "What was that?" he said, leaning over the lectern.

This time, they shouted: "Ivermectin!" Bolin nodded.

This wasn't my first time at FloodGate. I wasn't too surprised by anything that Bolin was saying. Yet I was still struggling to make sense of this place.

Having grown up just down the road, the son of the senior pastor at the largest church in town, I knew the local evangelical scene like it was a second reporting beat. I knew which pastors were beefing; whose congregations were mired in scandal; which church softball teams had a deacon playing shortstop and which ones stacked their lineups with non-tithing ringers. But I had never heard of FloodGate. And neither had most of the people sitting around me—until recently.

For years, Bolin had preached to a crowd of about one hundred on a typical Sunday. Then came Easter of 2020, when Bolin announced that he would refuse to comply with Michigan's emergency COVID-19 shutdown orders and hold indoor worship services. When word got around Brighton—and around ultraconservative Livingston County—that one area pastor was defying the Democratic governor, FloodGate morphed from a church into a cause. Bolin became a small-time media celebrity. Local politicians and activists borrowed his pulpit to promote their causes, and, all the while, FloodGate's attendance soared. Longtime members from other area congregations defected in droves to the small roadside church. By Easter of 2021, FloodGate was hosting 1,500 attendees every Sunday.

This was how I came to know the name Bill Bolin. Having just recently moved back to Michigan, it seemed like every time I ran into a family friend during the early days of the pandemic they wanted to know if I'd heard about this upstart church called FloodGate. It was only a few miles away from Cornerstone, the church that raised me, and it was raiding members from there and every other local congregation. At first I rolled my eyes at what seemed like trivial gossip. Churches don't like losing congregants to other local churches—this tension has always existed. With that, I figured, came hard feelings and anxious chatter. It would pass.

But it didn't. People could not stop talking about FloodGate. The church was a phenomenon in my hometown, and when I finally attended services there, I could see why. Bolin was less a pastor than he was a performer. He had traded his pulpit for a soapbox, riffing like it was open-mic night at a campus coffeehouse. He openly preyed on the political and cultural insecurities of his congregants. And it worked. The hardest part of witnessing all this was to see people I knew—people I respected and cared about from around the community—falling for this spiritual farce. Rather than being challenged and transformed by the gospel, they were now coming to church to have their worst impulses confirmed. Bolin was offering a tawdry translation of the message of Jesus Christ, and people adored him for it.

On this particular Sunday in October 2021, the pastor riffed on everything from California forcing vaccines on schoolchildren to the IRS proposing more oversight of personal banking accounts. He promoted a new book that warned of a "war on Christianity" in America that will strip believers of their right to worship God (prompting the couple in front of me to make a one-click Amazon purchase). He shared that, after a recent conversation with a Fox News commentator, he could no longer rule out a second civil war. He suggested there was mounting evidence that the presidency was stolen from Donald Trump in 2020, concluding, "With the information that's coming out in Arizona and Georgia and other places, I think it's time for there to be a full audit of all fifty states to find out the level of cheating and the level of manipulation that actually took place." The churchgoers around me cheered.

At one point, Bolin looked up from his notes.

"We had a visitor this morning who said, 'You know, it's really refreshing to hear a pastor talk about issues like this,'" Bolin said. Basking in the ovation he'd just invited, the pastor added: "I'm okay talking about these things."

Bolin asked if he could keep going. The crowd answered with more applause.

THE FIRST TIME I WALKED INTO THE SANCTUARY AT FLOODGATE, I didn't see a cross. But I did see American flags—lots of them. There were flags on the screens behind the stage, flags on the literature being handed out. There was even a flag on the face mask of the single person I spotted wearing one. It was May 2021, and the church was hosting an event for Stand Up Michigan, a group that had formed to protest pandemic shutdowns, masking, and, most recently, vaccine mandates. This was the launch of the group's Livingston County chapter.

While covering presidential campaigns, I had attended political rallies at churches across Iowa, South Carolina, Texas, and elsewhere. But I'd never seen anything quite like this. The parking lot swarmed with vehicles covered in partisan slogans. The narthex was jammed with people scribbling on clipboards. (I thought this was preemptive COVID contact tracing; they were actually enlisting volunteers for all manner of right-wing causes.) Inside the sanctuary, attendees wore MAGA caps and Second Amendment–related shirts. I didn't see a single person carrying a Bible.

For the next three hours, the church became a coliseum. The executive director of Stand Up Michigan decried the "evil" Democrats in charge of the state; said there was "probably some truth" to QAnon's claims of ritualistic child sacrifice; and warned that Christians are "too nice," imploring her audience to "fight fire with fire." The chair of the county board of commissioners railed against Critical Race Theory and bragged about kneecapping a local official who voted to fund diversity training. A state senator tried to play to the base—joking that she'd asked God why He'd allowed Gretchen Whitmer to become governor—but then cowered when the base turned on her, with people standing and shouting to demand that she answer the question of whether Trump had won Michigan in 2020. Visibly shaken, she refused to answer.

I knew the senator; her name was Lana Theis. For many years she had attended Cornerstone. She considered my dad a spiritual mentor and told me tearfully, not long after his passing, how much she missed him. Theis had left the church a little while after he died, and I wasn't exactly floored to see her pop up at FloodGate. The senator was facing a far-right primary challenger and needed people like Bolin to vouch for her. Still, watching her get heckled by MAGA zealots, watching her refuse to say that Biden had won Michigan fairly—despite in fact knowing that he did, as she was coauthoring a Senate report stating as much—I couldn't suppress a feeling of absolute disgust. Here she was, in a place of worship, refusing to speak perhaps the most basic truth that could be expected of a politician. I was glad my dad wasn't there to see it.

Maybe I was being too hard on Theis—after all, she was a mere elected official. The real embarrassment was Bolin himself. Introduced at the beginning of the program as the "rock star" who disobeyed the government, the pastor seemed intent on showing just how uncouth one could be in the pulpit. Bolin began by suggesting that COVID-19 was "possibly being manipulated with the funding and blessing of Dr. Anthony Fauci, the man who put us in masks." When he heard scattered boos, Bolin egged on the crowd: "That's right, go ahead!" The sanctuary filled with vicious jeers. A minute later, the pastor was boasting about how far he'd taken his insults of Governor Whitmer. "Probably the most egregious thing I ever did," Bolin said, chuckling, "was I did do a Nazi salute and called her 'Whitler.'"

I scanned the sanctuary. Not a single person seemed to register any objection, or even surprise, at this pastor boasting that he'd done a Nazi salute from the pulpit. In my ensuing visits to FloodGate, and in long conversations with Bolin, I never ceased to be aghast at what I heard. It became clear that this type of extreme political expression was central to his church's identity—and to his own.

Raised in a broken home in Southern California, Bolin told me he was a "radical liberal" before he came to Christ. He began drinking and doing drugs when he was nine years old. At age twelve, he met a church-going man who attempted to convert Bolin to Christianity; the man subsequently tried to molest him. Bolin said this incident accelerated his pursuit of self-destruction. He dabbled in the occult, ran with a violent gang, and lived on the wrong side of the law. He once got "so high on

LSD" after sneaking into a Tom Petty concert that he jumped onstage and grabbed a guitar.

As he matured, he discovered an interest in progressive causes. He became infatuated with Robert F. Kennedy and Martin Luther King Jr., committing himself to the art of protesting: marches, sit-ins, hunger strikes. No longer drawn to witchcraft or gang activity, Bolin became a "proud hippie," immersing himself in politics and counterculture activism.

Then, when he was twenty years old, while packing for a cross-country hitchhiking trip, he discovered an old Bible. It was a long-forgotten gift from the man who'd tried to molest him. "I lifted it up—and remember, I'm a supernaturalist—and felt like my arm was on fire," Bolin told me. "And I heard a voice: 'Return to me, or you will die.'"

Bolin got a ride to Reno, Nevada, where he had a Christian cousin. He asked her if they could go to church together. "There was an altar call, and I went down and got baptized that same afternoon," Bolin said. "I've never been the same. It changed who I am."

That change included his politics. Setting out on his Christian journey—working as a substance abuse counselor, attending Bible college, pastoring in churches from California to Pennsylvania—Bolin found that many of his old stances were incompatible with his new faith. In particular, his views of abortion and religious freedom were turned upside down. One thing didn't change. "I have always been prone to protesting," Bolin told me. "Then and now."

From there it was a familiar trajectory: Bolin, a Moral Majority–era product of epistemologically homogeneous evangelical institutions, was quick to marry conservative theology to conservative ideology. Unlike many of the pastors his age I'd met, guys who eventually became disillusioned by the religious right's hypocrisy and ruthless approach to the culture, Bolin believed that evangelicals didn't go far enough. "Christians have languished with their participation in politics," he told me, "which is one of the reasons we're in this dire position as a nation."

As a young Christian, Bolin says the more he studied history—of the Church and of America—the more he came to appreciate how "pastors used to be the primary influencers in their communities in determining who we elected." He aimed to restore that tradition in his own ministry.

When Bolin arrived at FloodGate in 2010, the church—founded in 1972 and once upon a time called The Father's House—was mostly apolitical. "It was pro-life, but the more aggressive stance on politics did not exist," Bolin recalled. When he set about changing that, "people either adapted to it, or they left."

Bolin said his congregation always hovered around one hundred during his first decade at the church. He leaned into plenty of political controversies—including Trump's candidacy—but his membership stayed flat. Looking back, it's fair to wonder whether that's because he was on the wrong side of that particular issue. "Donald Trump was the last person I wanted elected president," Bolin told me, releasing a belly laugh. He thought Trump was a charlatan, a lifelong Democrat who was defrauding conservative voters. "And all the attacks, the crudeness of his speech—I found it to be rather repulsive," Bolin said.

What happened?

"He proved me wrong," Bolin replied. "He turned out to be the most pro-life president we've ever had. His influence on the courts will change the country for the next fifty years. Because of those two issues alone—the life issue, and the remaking of the judiciary—I admire the man."

I asked Bolin to help me unpack this emotional arc: from repulsion to admiration in the space of just a few years. He answered by pivoting away from his own erstwhile opposition to Trump, talking as though anyone who held the position he once did could not possibly have come by it honestly. "A lot of people say Christians shouldn't have been involved with supporting Donald Trump. Because of his ethics, or his multiple marriages, blah, blah, blah," he said. "My answer to that would be: At what point have we ever excluded people from politics because of their personal ethics?"

This is the juncture at which most evangelicals would pause, reflecting on their crusade against Bill Clinton in the 1990s. Bolin was part of it. But he rejects the comparison. Clinton, he argued, was a serial liar with a long history of being accused of sexual misconduct. Before I could pick my jaw up off the floor and ask how that differentiates Clinton from Trump, Bolin started rattling off fantastical, fever-dream allegations against not just Clinton, but against the current president, Joe Biden, too, describing the whole of the Democratic Party as sinister and predatory.

As the conversation wore on, Bolin sounded ashamed of having ever doubted Trump. He itemized all the former president's accomplishments and rolled his eyes at the "condescending" Christians who were still bothered by Trump's personal ethics. He defended the January 6 insurrection as "not a big deal." In fact, Bolin himself nearly traveled to Washington that day "because a lot of people from our church were going, and because I love Donald Trump."

And then the pastor said something that made it all click. Bolin believes Trump was not a Christian when he ran for president, "but became born again during his presidency, under the influence of Mike Pence and other Christians in his orbit."

If that was true, I asked Bolin, did it bother him that Trump did nothing to help the man who helped bring him to Christ when that man's life was endangered on January 6?

"Yes," he replied blushingly, before adding: "Maybe don't quote me on that."

The Trump conversion experience—having once been certain of his darkness, suddenly awakening to see his light—is not to be underestimated, especially when it touches people whose lives revolve around notions of transformation. And yet it reflects a phenomenon greater than Trump himself. Modern evangelicalism is defined by a certain fatalism about the nation's character. The result is not merely a willingness to forgive what is wrong; it can be a belief, bordering on a certainty, that what is wrong is actually right.

VERN HOFFNER WAS ONE OF MY DAD'S ELDERS. THE VETTING PROCESS AT Cornerstone was serious, and Vern was a serious guy. He earned a doctorate in management science, held top corporate positions at IBM and General Motors, and served as an elder at another large church before moving to Brighton and joining Cornerstone. He and his wife, Nancy, always struck me as reasonable folks. There was never any reason to scrutinize them—until I saw Vern and Nancy one morning, in the spring of 2021, at FloodGate.

It was hardly surprising at this point to see Cornerstone expats sitting in Bolin's pews. I knew that my home church was, in the words of

Pastor Chris Winans, suffering "an exodus" of members. Most people leaving Cornerstone were doing so because of specific objections that were peripheral to the mission of the church: Winans's cautious handling of COVID-19, his unwillingness to endorse Trump, his general aversion to nationalist ideals. Anyone listing these grievances found a natural home at FloodGate. I had assumed that these refugees were newer Christians, spiritually immature, people who didn't have a rich history of being discipled. Some of them were. But lots of them were seasoned believers. They were leaders in their former churches. They weren't leaving for a lack of discipling; they were leaving because they didn't *want* to be discipled. They were people like Vern Hoffner.

When I sat down with Vern and Nancy over coffee, they looked anxious. They confessed feeling a bit uncomfortable detailing their departure from Cornerstone to the son of the pastor they'd been loyal to for many years. I asked them what my dad's successor, Winans, had done to lose their loyalty. They exchanged glances.

"We don't follow people. We follow God," Nancy said. "But the more time you spend in a church, the more you learn it's a fallible place full of fallible people, people who will fail you."

Vern nodded his head. "Absolute power corrupts absolutely."

They were speaking in code. I asked the Hoffners to explain what, exactly, went wrong at the church they attended for twenty years.

"Cornerstone shut down," Nancy said. "I know COVID was a crisis, but when you have a crisis, why would you shut down the very place that's supposed to help people get through it? The pastor there made that decision. It was the wrong decision. And Bill Bolin chose the opposite."

Vern told me that COVID, and Winans's decision to shutter Cornerstone, should not be considered in a vacuum. Godless government bureaucrats have been scheming for years to silence conservative, Bible-preaching churches, he explained. The pandemic was just a dry run. Any pastor who folded in the face of this pressure, Vern said, wouldn't be able to protect their congregation when the real test came.

"The Church needs to stand up for itself. That's what Bill Bolin is doing," Vern said. "If what's happening right now keeps going, it could be like Nazi Germany—you better toe the party line, or else. We could have the same thing here."

I asked Vern to spell that out.

"The cancel culture, the kicking people off various platforms, our First Amendment rights, our Second Amendment rights. We are under attack right now. Christians are under attack because we're different," he replied. "Maybe it's not clear and present right now. But if this trend continues . . . pastors who talk about certain topics from the pulpit are going to wind up in jail."

Nancy grumbled that Democrats had done more to restrict Christians from worshipping during COVID-19 than they had done to prevent illegal immigrants from crossing the southern border.

"They're spreading all over the country, and they're carrying all kinds of diseases, and they're being moved under the cover of night," she said. "And look who's doing it: the Catholic Church."

She shook her head in disgust. I was struck by her tone—and by the fact that Nancy had been involved with supporting missionaries during her time at Cornerstone. Perhaps sensing how callous his wife sounded, Vern jumped in.

"We're compassionate. We want to help the people already here. We want to keep this country strong," he said. "Our compassion is focused on not taking us down a path to socialism."

The more we talked, the clearer it seemed that the Hoffners' problem with Cornerstone wasn't COVID-19 protocols. The language they used—about immigrants, about America, about Trump and Biden and the duty Christians have to engage in political combat—was precisely the sort of thinking that Winans was trying to disciple out of his congregants.

I recalled something Bolin had told me: Almost all his new members came bearing grievances against their former pastors, he said, but most of them had never considered leaving. It took a pandemic, and the closing of their churches, for them to sever ties. As I got to know more of the new arrivals at FloodGate, that story checked out.

Jeff and Deidre Myers started attending FloodGate in the summer of 2020. For years they had belonged to Oak Pointe Milford, another suburban Detroit church. Though they were frustrated that the preaching wasn't more overtly political, they were highly engaged: leading a marriage ministry, active with other homeschoolers. They were friends with the pastor, Paul Jenkinson, and his wife.

Then COVID hit. When the church closed, rumors flew about the board of elders holding contentious late-night meetings to debate pandemic protocols. The longer the church remained locked, the more people speculated on who was casting the deciding votes. Around that time, George Floyd was murdered. Oak Pointe Novi, the parent church, introduced a video series called *Conversations,* which featured interviews with Black pastors and social-justice activists.

"I thought I was going to vomit," Deidre told me, recalling her reaction to one episode. Jeff added: "It was the pastor's son"—who, he claimed, was a member of Antifa in Canada—"lecturing on white privilege and Critical Race Theory." (I could not confirm that the pastor's son was, in fact, affiliated with Antifa; several people who know the family laughed when I asked the question. That said, the episode in question was clearly over the top, brazenly injecting left-wing politics into a church that had been wary, appropriately so, about the incursion of right-wing politics.)

After an outcry, the pastor apologized for "the ruptures that have occurred," while the elders issued a separate statement denouncing Critical Race Theory. It wasn't enough. According to Jeff and Deidre, they were just two members in a stampede out of Oak Pointe.

Deidre had seen friends from other congregations, also displaced by shutdowns, posting on Facebook about FloodGate. The first service she attended—in which Pastor Bolin unapologetically advocated for people, like Jeff and Deidre, who felt cheated by their old churches—brought her to tears. Jeff was equally moved. They had found a new home.

When Jeff and Deidre met with Jenkinson to inform him that they were leaving the Milford church, tensions ran high. Their worst fears had already been confirmed: A friend on the elder board had told them that Jenkinson—their pastor, their friend—had argued to keep the church closed. Jeff and Deidre grilled Jenkinson on the church's refusal to engage with politics. When they asked the pastor why, despite being personally pro-life, he never preached on abortion, they got the response they'd dreaded. "He said, 'I'd lose half my congregation,'" Jeff recalled.

When I spoke with Jenkinson, he remembered the conversation somewhat differently. Jeff and Deidre, he told me, weren't just pushing him on abortion; they were challenging the pastor's policy of political neutrality from the pulpit, and accusing him of taking the easy way out of the debates fracturing his church.

"And I remember telling them, 'The harder thing to do is what I'm doing,'" the pastor said. "This is how you lose people. How you gain people is, you pick a tribe, raise the flag, and be really loud about it. That's how you gain a bunch of numbers. That is so easy to do. And it cheapens the gospel."

Whatever the specifics of their exchange, to Jeff and Deidre, Jenkinson's stance amounted to cowardice. "I realize these are hard conversations, but the reason we left Milford is they were never willing to have the conversation," Jeff said. "They were just trying to keep everybody happy. Paul is a conservative, but his conservatism has no teeth."

Tony DeFelice was another new arrival at FloodGate—and another Christian who got tired of his pastor lacking teeth. At his previous church, in the Democratic-leaning Detroit suburb of Plymouth, "They did not speak a single word about politics. Not on a single issue," he told me. "When we got to FloodGate, it confirmed for us what we'd been missing."

DeFelice, a building inspector, had been attending the Plymouth church for fourteen years when the pandemic began. He and his wife, Linda, had friends and family there; one of their daughters still works on the church staff. Tony and Linda had their share of complaints—the church was too moderate and "too seeker-friendly," catering more to newcomers than longtime Christians—but they had no plans to leave.

And then, in March 2020, everything fell apart.

"We didn't leave the church. The church left us," Tony told me. "COVID, the whole thing, is the biggest lie perpetrated on humanity that we're ever going to see in our lifetime. And they fell for it."

Tony and Linda told me that FloodGate's style, as well as Bolin's fiery messages on topics like vaccines and voter fraud, changed the way they view their responsibilities as Christians. "This is about good against evil. That's the world we live in. It's a spiritual battle, and we are right at the precipice of it," Tony said.

This was the gospel according to Bill Bolin. Just down the road, at Cornerstone, Chris Winans was preaching something very different.

"The Bible definitely portrays a spiritual battle that's ongoing. The problem is, a lot of Christians believe they're engaging in that battle by promoting a political platform, and they treat that political battle as if the kingdom of God is at stake," Winans told me. "But the kingdom of God isn't at stake. The Bible clearly tells us that our struggle is not against flesh and blood. What Christ accomplished on the cross is not threatened by Donald Trump losing an election."

I could see why Vern and Nancy chose to leave Cornerstone. People like the Hoffners—and the Myerses, and the DeFelices—were no longer interested in distinguishing between the political and the spiritual. With the country on the brink of defeat at the hands of secularists and liberals, churches could not afford to stay neutral. An attack on Trump, Tony DeFelice told me, was indeed an attack on Christianity. He believed the 2020 election was stolen as part of a "demonic" plot against Christian America. And he was confident that righteousness would prevail: States were going to begin decertifying the results of the last election, he insisted, and Trump would be returned to office before the conclusion of Biden's first term.

"The truth is coming out," Tony said.

When I pressed him on these beliefs—offering evidence that Biden won legitimately, and probing for the source of his conviction—Tony did not budge. He is as convinced that Trump won the 2020 election, he told me, as he is that Jesus rose from the dead two thousand years ago.

SITTING INSIDE A CRAMPED OFFICE AT THE BACK OF FLOODGATE, BILL Bolin was second-guessing himself.

It was the spring of 2022. In several conversations over the past year, we had talked at length about extremism in his church. There were people who were certain that Trump was still running the government; people convinced that Biden didn't actually live in the White House; people who swore by QAnon; people like Tony DeFelice who were willfully conflating their identities as Christians and Americans.

Bolin seemed, at some level, to be reckoning with his role in this. He told me he was worried about Christians getting their priorities mixed up. He said he never intended for his rants about Biden or the 2020 election—which are "nonessentials"—to be taken with the seriousness of his statements about Jesus, which are the "essentials" people should be coming to church for.

"I do make a separation between our religious perspective and our political perspective," Bolin told me. "I don't view political statements as being infallible."

That was putting it generously. In the time I spent listening to Bolin preach, sitting with him for interviews, and following his Facebook page, I recorded dozens of political statements that were either recklessly misleading or flat-out false. Whenever I would challenge him, asking for a source, Bolin would either cite "multiple articles" he had read or send me a link to a website like Headline USA or Conservative Fighters. Then he would concede that the claims were in dispute, and indicate that he didn't necessarily believe everything he said or posted.

This was a dangerous practice for anyone, let alone someone trusted as a teacher of truth. Jesus did not take lightly the question of veracity. Contrasting Himself with Satan—"the father of lies"—Jesus described Himself as truth incarnate, and told His disciples that "the truth will set you free." This should be a terrifying thought for any professing Christian: Spreading lies is not only antithetical to the example of Christ; it is doing the devil's work.

Bolin didn't seem burdened knowing that so many people were relying upon him to do the heavy lifting of discernment on their behalf. Many of the backwater websites and podcasts to which the pastor attributed his commentaries were the same ones cited to me by people from his church. FloodGate had become a circular food chain of misinformation. In a sense, Christians have always lived a different epistemological existence than nonbelievers. But this was something new. Something decidedly nonessential.

At one point, I showed Bolin a Facebook post he had written months earlier: "I'm still wondering how 154,000,000 votes were counted in a country where there are only 133,000,000 registered voters." This was posted to his page, I told him, well after the U.S. Census Bureau had published data showing that more than 168 million Americans were registered to vote in 2020. A quick Google search would have given Bolin the accurate numbers.

"Yeah, that's one I regret," he said, explaining that he subsequently learned that the numbers he'd posted were incorrect. (The post was still active. Bolin texted me the following day saying he'd deleted it.)

Didn't he worry that if people saw him getting the easy things wrong, they might suspect he's also getting the hard things wrong? Things like salvation and sanctification?

"I really don't. No. Not too much. I don't," Bolin said, shaking his head back and forth hurriedly. "Firebrand statements have been part of the pulpit, and part of politics, for as long as we've been a nation. And there is a long history of both sides exaggerating—like in a post like that."

Still, Bolin seemed rattled. He began telling me about a couple of Democrats who attend FloodGate and have rebuked him for his political rhetoric—but who have reassured him, Bolin says, "When it comes to the word, you're rock-solid."

Then he told me something unexpected: He was thinking of scaling back "Headline News" on Sunday mornings. Maybe he would just read news clips verbatim, he suggested, without adding commentary. Or maybe he would cut the political headlines in half, adding some "feel-good" news to balance the mood. The more he thought about it, Bolin said, he might just cut the segment altogether, posting those political musings on Facebook but keeping them out of worship.

"We're now going from pandemic to endemic. Our culture will change. There will no longer be this massive division over COVID," Bolin said. "The fervency is going to die down."

Except there would always be something new. Literally moments before he talked about the fervency dying down, Bolin previewed a shtick he was going to deliver on Sunday morning about Apple adding a "pregnant-man emoji" to the iPhone. There was no going back.

The dopamine rush supplied by dropping rhetorical bombs on left-wing targets—"owning the libs," as the young conservatives say—had become addictive to Bolin. Yet this approach is irreconcilable with the words of Paul, who told us, "If it is possible, as far as it depends on you, live at peace with everyone." Later, in that same letter to the Romans, he reminds Christians of Solomon's proverb: "If your enemy is hungry, give him food to eat; if he is thirsty, give him water to drink. In doing this, you will heap burning coals on his head, and the Lord will reward you." These words, written at the end of chapter twelve, happen to preface Paul's instruction to submit to governing authorities in chapter thirteen—the text cited by pastors who agreed to close their doors for a short time during COVID.

Bolin had diagnosed in some detail "the sorting" within evangelicalism—the scramble of Christians switching congregations, churches rising and falling, pastors adapting or heading for the exits. It occurred to me, as he reflected on the meteoric growth of his ministry, that Bolin had gotten himself into something from which there was no escape. The moment he stopped lighting fires from the pulpit at FloodGate, how many of its members—who were now accustomed to that sort of inferno, who came to FloodGate precisely because they wanted the heat—would go looking for it elsewhere?

Bolin wasn't going to take that risk. Just recently, he said, the church had sold the building we were sitting in—where the congregation had met since the 1970s—and purchased a sprawling complex down the road. Bolin said that FloodGate's revenue had multiplied sixfold since 2020. It was now charging ahead into an era of expansion, with ambitions of becoming southeast Michigan's next megachurch.

I HAD NEVER SEEN A SANCTUARY SO FULL ON A TUESDAY NIGHT.

The people packed into FloodGate weren't here for Bolin. No, they had come out by the hundreds, decked out in patriotic attire, to hear from a man who was introduced to them as "America's greatest living historian." They had come for David Barton.

It would be of little use to tell the folks around me that Barton wasn't a real historian. They wouldn't care that he had no formal training; that his lone academic credential was a bachelor's degree in religious education from Oral Roberts University; that he was a punch line in the community of letters. It wouldn't matter that Barton's 2012 book on Thomas Jefferson was recalled by Thomas Nelson, the world's largest Christian publisher, for its countless inaccuracies, or that a panel of ten conservative Christian academics who reviewed Barton's body of work in the aftermath of that affair ripped the entirety of his scholarship to shreds. It would not bother the congregants of FloodGate Church to learn that they were listening to a political hustler masquerading as a scholar, a man whose work was found by one of America's foremost conservative theologians to include "embarrassing factual errors, suspiciously selective quotes, and highly misleading claims."

All this would be irrelevant to the people around me because David Barton was one of them. He believed the separation of church and state was a myth. He believed America should be declared a Christian nation. He believed the time had come for evangelicals to reclaim their rightful place atop the nation's core governmental and cultural institutions. Hence the hero's welcome Barton received when he rolled into Flood-Gate with his "American Restoration Tour."

Throughout his decades of public life—working for the Republican Party, forming alliances with powerful politicians, becoming a darling of Fox News, launching a small propaganda empire, preaching at churches like First Baptist Dallas, carving out a niche as the American right's chosen peddler of nostalgic alternative facts—Barton had never been shy about his ultimate aims. He is an avowed Christian nationalist who favors theocratic rule; moreover, he is a so-called Dominionist, someone who believes Christians should control not only the government but also the media, the education system, and other cultural institutions. This is what the "American Restoration Tour" was all about: restoring a version of America that never existed.

There was a time when Barton, for all his trickery and misdirection, was genuinely compelling. But this performance had all the passion of a late-night encyclopedia infomercial. In a baggy dark suit and bright orange tie, clicker in hand, Barton droned through a slide show that patched together quotes and dates and bygone events to make his case that America is a good nation because it was founded as a godly nation. Inconvenient episodes such as slavery were relegated to a footnote. Barton assured us that America's misdeeds were relatively minor—"All races, all people, all nations, have had slavery and been slaves at some point themselves," he said nonchalantly—and that secular progressives were deliberately amplifying them to diminish that goodness and godliness of America.

Barton was so loose with his facts, so lazy with his analysis, that he made Bolin look meticulous by comparison. At one point, Barton told the story of a Black evangelist named Harry Hosier, who traveled the American frontier preaching to farmers in the early 1800s. Asserting that Indiana residents, "Hoosiers," had inherited their nickname from a Black Christian—a claim that is *not* factual—Barton marveled at the people who somehow believe that America has a problem with racism.

Inside this house of worship, Barton spent an hour and fifteen minutes exalting a curious version of the Christian ideal. He slammed gun restrictions and progressive income taxes, government health care and state-run education curriculum. At one point, while denouncing Critical Race Theory, he posted an ominous slide showing logos for the *New York Times*'s 1619 Project and Black Lives Matter framed around a Soviet hammer and sickle. Rounding out the collage were Antifa and anarchist symbols. The left, Barton said, was encouraging "rioting, rebellion, and radicalization" that threatened our blessed nation from within.

After citing that familiar verse from Second Chronicles—"If my people, who are called by my name, will humble themselves and pray and seek my face and turn from their wicked ways, then I will hear from heaven, and I will forgive their sin and will heal their land"—Barton closed with a quote from Charles Finney. The famed evangelist, Barton explained, had "led one hundred thousand people to Christ in one year" during the early nineteenth century. He was central to the Second Great Awakening and preached that revival would only come to people who were pursuing it. Part of that pursuit, Barton said, quoting Finney, was to realize that "politics are a part of religion" in America, "and Christians must do their duty to their country as a part of their duty to God."

Barton's final slide—at least, before he began hawking his books, which were available on his website and outside in the lobby area—featured a fuzzy shot of Finney against a black screen. In vivid white, Finney's words were proclaimed by Barton: "God will bless or curse this nation according to the course Christians take in politics." (This was in fact a paraphrasing of Finney's words, and not a direct quote, the sort of small detail to which most historians pay close attention.)

When Barton stepped down from the stage, nodding to acknowledge the standing ovation, Chad Connelly jogged up to take his place.

Connelly was Barton's partner, the other half of the American Restoration Tour. He was also an old acquaintance from my time spent covering campaigns in South Carolina, where he had chaired the state Republican Party. He had jumped to the Republican National Committee in 2013, accepting an appointment as the national party's first-ever director of faith engagement. After mobilizing evangelicals to vote for Trump in 2016, Connelly launched his own venture, a group called Faith Wins, which sought to replicate that model and turn out conservative Christians on behalf of GOP causes nationwide.

Faith Wins is a nonprofit—like Barton's organization, WallBuilders—and thus cannot explicitly endorse candidates or parties. But the American Restoration Tour made no secret of its partisan affiliations. Connelly, a husky, energetic southerner, had opened the event by declaring that people like them needed "to take this nation back for God." By the end of Barton's presentation, there wasn't much ambiguity about what the white, conservative Christians in the audience needed to do to take America back—or who they needed to take it back from.

As Connelly launched into his own homily, encouraging people to visit his website and join their movement, it struck me that the American Restoration Tour represented more than another grifting scheme. (Though it certainly *was* that: WallBuilders raised $5.5 million in 2021, while Faith Wins, a smaller organization, collected an impressive $800,000 in 2022.) This road show was a call-and-response for American evangelicals. It was a lesson in being under siege and a tutorial in going on the attack. Barton and Connelly had cooked up a slick, codependent rendering of the crisis facing Christians in this country. Theirs was an all-inclusive offering that packaged the problem with the solution.

Barton had convinced the people at FloodGate Church that their kingdom was being overrun. Now Connelly wanted to know: What were they going to do about it?

PART II

THE
POWER

CHAPTER EIGHT

COLUMBUS, OHIO

You are the salt of the earth. But if the salt loses its saltiness,
how can it be made salty again? It is no longer good for
anything, except to be thrown out and trampled underfoot.

—MATTHEW 5:13

Gary Click, the state representative from Ohio's 88th House District, explained how his recent Sunday sermon had emphasized the Buckeye State's biblical ethos: Ohio was the only state in the union with a motto ("With God All Things Are Possible") lifted directly from the scriptures.

Then Click, the senior pastor of Fremont Baptist Temple, reminded us that November 8, 2016, was "the day Christians changed America" by electing Donald Trump and restoring hope to a nation in decline.

Finally, Click, the candidate standing for reelection in the fall of 2022—six months away—said that despite being pitted against wicked progressives who want to "groom our kids" into sadistic sexual rites, evangelicals must remember they have a "secret weapon" on their side. I assumed he was referring to Jesus.

"Donald Trump appointed three very constitutional judges" to the U.S. Supreme Court, Click said, who were helping Christians to retake control of America.

At that point, he clarified: "This is not a campaign event."

You wouldn't know it. We were, after all, inside the atrium of the Ohio state capitol building, and Click had just run through a list of

Republican dignitaries who were on hand: numerous lawmakers, school board members, the state auditor, and two Ohio Supreme Court justices. Click highlighted some of the work he and like-minded Christian conservatives were doing to defeat the left. The people around me, a couple hundred of them, clapped and cheered. Then, detailing the tight margins of that 2016 election—"It was the Christian vote that made the difference"—Click introduced the Republican operative who had mobilized the masses of evangelicals to vote all across the country, tipping the election to Trump: Chad Connelly.

Theatrical music filled the atrium. Two massive screens flanking the stage showed Connelly striking a patriot's pose in front of Old Glory. "Faith Wins when people of faith vote their values!" he announced in his boisterous southern twang, eyes boring straight into the camera. The promotional video told of Connelly's exploits: Over the past few years, his organization had partnered with fifty thousand church leaders and registered more than one million Christians to vote. These reinforcements were desperately needed. Because, according to the montage of clergymen who vouched for Connelly's organization, America was flirting with annihilation.

"The battle for the soul of our nation has never been greater than it is today," said Pastor Josiah Kagin, from Kettering, Ohio.

"America's founding principles, that were built on biblical values, are under attack," said Pastor Jake Samples, from DeBary, Florida.

"This," said Byron Foxx, a televangelist from Virginia, "is our 1776 moment."

When Connelly stepped to the microphone, he laid the urgency on thick. This was the sixteenth state visited by the American Restoration Tour over the past three months; he and David Barton had spoken to hundreds of churches in that time and engaged with tens of thousands of Christian voters. Their goal for the election year 2022, Connelly said, was to double the one million voters they had registered over the previous few years. "We're losing the country. We're *losing* the country," he told the audience. "If Christians, who outnumber all the whiners and complainers and God-haters in America, if Christians would just be the salt and light that Jesus asked us to be, we wouldn't have this mess."

Connelly's call to action was straightforward. "We need to make sure everybody in our churches is registered to vote, and all of 'em are voting biblical values," he said. Hesitating, just as Click had done a little while earlier, Connelly added: "We don't tell 'em who to vote for. This isn't about party or politicians; it's about policies and principles that most closely align with our biblical worldview."

This whole roadshow was expressly designed to turn out voters to help the GOP win elections. And yet, Connelly swore to us, this was not about partisanship. He was not fighting to promote *Republican* values. He was fighting to promote *American* values. And that meant he was fighting to promote *Christian* values.

When it was Barton's turn, he built on this theme. America is special because of our ideas, he said. But those ideas hadn't come from men; they came from God through the mouths of Revolutionary-era preachers who laid the groundwork for the rebellion against Great Britain with their sermons and appeals to heaven. Citing the works of several long-since-forgotten clergymen, Barton made the case that every issue Americans face today, from war to welfare to health care to taxation, was preached about in sermons in early America. His point was that the Bible is not just a spiritual text, but a governing manual, one that explicitly informed our system of self-rule from the very beginning.

This was conventional wisdom in America for almost the first two centuries of its existence, Barton argued. Then came the 1960s. Prayer was banned from public schools. Social policies were designed to undermine the family unit. *Patriotism* became a dirty word. Christians responded to this cultural upheaval by "compartmentalizing our faith," he said, drawing lines between private religious conviction and public-facing civic engagement. To the extent Christians got involved, Barton claimed, it was in the big picture, voting in presidential elections and rallying around issues of national relevance. As a result, Democrats were left alone to radicalize communities with under-the-radar policy making—through libraries, school boards, city councils, and other hyperlocal entities.

Barton unpacked a scary—and, based on the available public polling, mostly inaccurate—collection of statistics. Three in ten Millennials identify as LGBTQ, he said, whereas less than 2 percent of their parents did. Half of Millennials prefer socialism over capitalism, whereas just 14 percent of their parents did. Only a third of Millennials believe in God, whereas 89 percent of their parents did.

"What's going on?" Barton asked.

He answered his question by quoting Jesus in Luke, chapter six: "Every student, when fully trained, will be like his teacher."

Barton shook his head in disgust. "Schools have become the enemy of the country," he said.

There was hope, however. Barton cited Republican Glenn Youngkin's surprising victory in the Virginia governor's race a year earlier. It was proof, he said, that evangelicals had finally gotten off the sidelines—with some help, of course, from his partner organization, Faith Wins. Barton claimed that Connelly's group worked with 312 churches in Virginia to identify 77,000 congregants who had never voted before. Barton built up to a dramatic reveal: "Youngkin won by *66,000 votes.*" The crowd buzzed with delight.

It was the same story, Barton said, in "heavily progressive" places around the country: St. Paul, Denver, Boise, and elsewhere. Flashing news headlines onto the screens touting Republican victories in local races—typically the candidates had run on a platform of opposing Critical Race Theory or COVID-19 restrictions—Barton concluded that a pattern was emerging. Wherever churches got involved, Republican candidates were winning key elections at the local level.

Unlike Click and Connelly, who had played dumb about the nakedly partisan aims of this event, Barton didn't bother speaking in code. It was a refreshing bit of honesty from the most dishonest man in the room. Barton, who once served as vice chairman of the Texas GOP—and who had quietly built a super PAC to aid Ted Cruz's presidential run in 2016— had long been known for hiding his political agenda behind a scholarly veneer. Not anymore. Time was running out. The fate of America was hanging in the balance, and now he was spoiling for a fight.

Right on cue, Barton returned to the theme of the American Revolution. Despite being massively outnumbered by the Redcoats, the colonial forces under George Washington were successful because they focused on winning small battles. It was local churches, sometimes led into combat by their pastors, that were instrumental in defeating the superior British forces. This was the model. It was time, Barton said, for Christians to leverage the organizational muscle of their congregations to defeat progressive causes in their neighborhoods and towns. Win enough of those individual battles, and the war for America's soul could yet be won.

The event wound down in predictable fashion. There was Charles Finney's contorted quote ("God will bless or curse this nation according to the course Christians take in politics"); Connelly's plea to scan the QR code and visit the Faith Wins website; and a slide promoting Barton's various books that were available at WallBuilders.com. (Click pulled out a signed copy of *The Founders' Bible* by Barton and recommended everyone buy it: "As you do your devotions in the morning, you get a little bit of history.")

With the attendees making a beeline toward Barton in search of selfies and autographs, I pulled Connelly aside. We had spoken a handful of times over the years, always in the context of South Carolina politics, and I wanted to reintroduce myself. He remembered me right away—and seemed nervous about why I was there. I told him about the reporting I'd done at churches and the concerns I had about how political extremism was infiltrating American evangelicalism.

Connelly frowned.

"Christians have a responsibility, before God, to get involved," he said. "How can you be salt and light if you're not engaged with politics? Churches have failed us. Pastors have failed us."

Before I could respond, Click rushed over. He looked frazzled. "Why aren't there any books to sell?" he asked Connelly. "All these people want to buy David's books."

Connelly winced. "I wasn't sure of the rules. I thought it might be inappropriate," he replied, motioning toward our stately surroundings.

Then Connelly perked up. "We'll be selling them at the church later today," he told Click. "Tell 'em to follow us there."

The American Restoration Tour had one more stop to make before leaving Ohio. I asked Connelly if I could follow them, too. I wanted to know more about these pastors who were failing us. Connelly agreed, and I aimed my minivan west, leaving the capital of Columbus for a little place called Vandalia.

*   *   *

PAT MURRAY, THE LEADER OF LIVING WORD CHURCH, WAS CONNELLY'S
kind of pastor.

Standing before many hundreds of his members inside a cavernous,
beige-and-white colored sanctuary, Murray asked that everyone "stand
to your feet and grab the hand of another American" so that he might
pray over the proceedings. Beseeching God to "save the nation," Murray spelled out the path to salvation: "For those who aren't registered to
vote, God, I pray in Jesus's name you would touch them right now."

The Americans inside the church were treated to something extra
on this Monday night. Connelly decided that after showing the Faith
Wins promotional video—and before introducing Barton—he would
share his own testimony. Hailing from small-town Prosperity, South
Carolina, Connelly had been raised to know the Lord, had tried to walk
faithfully in his ways, but found himself at a crossroads upon finding his
wife "in a pool of blood" after she'd committed suicide. Connelly said he
heard a voice from the devil: "You failed." He was inclined to agree. But
the people of his church wouldn't let him. They wrapped Connelly and
his two young sons in the love of Christ. They protected them, nurtured
their faith. Eventually a wise older friend from the church—a Democrat, believe it or not—introduced Connelly to a young widow with two
children of her own. "I got to watch faith work," he explained. "I got to
watch God work."

Transitioning from his own story to the ongoing struggle for America, Connelly said that God's work is never finished. The nation could
still be spared. But, he emphasized, the Lord needs our cooperation.

"We're losing the country, y'all. We're losing the country to people
who don't even understand what made it special," Connelly said. "Christians need to stand up. And to do that, they need the truth."

Connelly pointed to Barton: "This guy has got the truth."

As the two men switched places, and Barton launched into his slide
show homily, I wrestled with competing impressions of Connelly.
He was hard not to like. He was warm and self-deprecating, someone
who quoted scripture as naturally as he quipped redneck one-liners. It
seemed plausible that he wasn't just running a gospel-based grift; that

unlike Barton, he was a man of integrity and real conviction. But then why would anyone of integrity and real conviction tour the country with a known huckster like Barton? Connelly had to know how silly this operation looked from the outside. How did he justify the damage being done—not to his own reputation, necessarily, but to the witness of the gospel? The American Restoration Tour was turning pastors into pundits and church sanctuaries into Fox News sets. To what end?

As we sat down in the sleek designer coffee shop situated just outside the worship center—Living Word was the finest building development I saw in all of Vandalia—Connelly could sense my skepticism.

"Let's go. We'll do the King James Version. I've got it marked," he told me, pulling out his leather Bible and turning to Matthew, chapter five.

"Ye are the salt of the earth: but if the salt have lost his savour, wherewith shall it be salted? It is thenceforth good for nothing, but to be cast out, and to be trodden under foot of men," Connelly read. "Ye are the light of the world. A city that is set on an hill cannot be hid. Neither do men light a candle, and put it under a bushel, but on a candlestick; and it giveth light unto all that are in the house. Let your light so shine before men, that they may see your good works, and glorify your Father which is in heaven."

He put down the Bible and threw up his hands. "How do I be salt and light in a culture, except that I engage the culture?" Connelly asked.

This sounded familiar. Over the past few years, almost every evangelical I'd questioned about the commingling of politics and religion responded with some variation of "salt and light." The difficulty is, biblical scholars have never agreed on what, exactly, Jesus meant by this. Surely He was encouraging Christians to be distinct—to flavor this world, to shine in its darkness. But people like Connelly were taking it a step further. They supposed—and preached with absolute certainty—that we should be distinct by fighting for Christian values inside America's secular political arena. Yet plenty of other believers, including believers of a conservative disposition, feel quite confident that we should be distinct by *not* prioritizing America's secular political arena at all.

It's notable that Jesus references "salt" in three of the four gospels. In each account, Jesus warns about salt losing its saltiness, its taste, its character. Jesus talks about salt not as an additive, necessarily, but as something unique that should be guarded against contamination. In Matthew, He says salt without flavor is good only to be trampled beneath our feet along with other ordinary rocks; in Luke, He says it has lost its purpose entirely and should be disposed of.

Most Christians would agree that a healthy dose of civic participation—including political engagement—does not risk contaminating our distinct flavor. But how quickly the unique can become ordinary. Some people hear "We're losing the country" and decide to run for school board. Others hear it and travel to Washington, D.C., to disrupt the peaceful transition of power. Did Connelly worry, in the context of campaigning inside houses of worship, about a blurry line between engagement and idolatry?

He gave me a puzzled look. "America has been the shining city on the hill for the rest of the world. Just look at the long line of people coming here," Connelly said. "Our four percent of the world's population gives like eighty cents of total missionary dollars worldwide. So, there's a reason the enemy would try to take us down and divide us."

It wasn't clear if "the enemy" referred to Satan or to the secular progressives he'd been bashing during his American Restoration Tour; the Russians currently making war in Ukraine or the low-salt-diet adherents here in America; those who wouldn't buy the Barton books or those who thought it curious that it was just fine to sell them in a church but not in a governing edifice.

Before I could ask, a man interrupted us. He was a pastor from a nearby town. Connelly had never met him but quickly vaulted from his seat, shook the pastor's hand, and complimented his Georgia Bulldogs shirt. The pastor seemed conflicted. He was worried about the country, he said, but wasn't sure he felt comfortable handing over his church to political operators.

"We do talk about some of the big issues," the pastor told Connelly. "I just don't know—"

"Do you do voter registration?" Connelly cut him off.

The pastor shook his head. "We have not. We could, I suppose."

Connelly was in sale-closing mode. "Listen, hit that QR code," he said, pointing to a poster nearby. "Here's my card. Email me. I'll send you everything you need. We'll get you set up right."

The man nodded, still looking torn, and thanked Connelly. As he walked away, Connelly turned to me. "I have a hundred of those conversations a week," he said. "I don't think that pastor is going to take things too far. Do you?"

It was evident, I replied, that the pastor himself worried that he might. Not everyone thinks voter registration drives—or any sort of electioneering activity—are appropriate inside a temple of the Lord. This returned us to the concept of a slippery slope. The church that wades into politics with a voter registration drive might one day find its Sunday morning worship interrupted with "Headline News" like at FloodGate Church in Brighton, Michigan.

"I haven't been there," Connelly shrugged.

Yes, I replied, he *had* been there. It was at FloodGate, the previous fall, that I first encountered their American Restoration Tour. And it turned out, Connelly and Barton had just been back to FloodGate for an encore presentation the week before this Ohio trip.

Connelly shrugged again. "Look, I don't get to know all these pastors. I can't remember them," he said. "I can't remember the name of the church I was at this morning."

This wasn't a guilt-by-association exercise. The point, I suggested to Connelly, is that he'd spent the last forty minutes insisting that churches were not being radicalized by politics, swearing that he'd never seen any examples of what I was warning about. But it turned out he had twice recently visited a church that had plainly lost sight of its mission—and Connelly did not recognize it.

Connelly conceded that he's heard of churches fracturing. "But that's nothing new. I've had people leave our church over the color of the carpet. There's always been fighting in churches," he replied. "I'm genuinely struggling to think of some new issue that's dividing churches."

As we talked, it became obvious that Connelly lived deep inside a bubble. His home church, a Southern Baptist congregation in Prosperity, South Carolina, had only closed for two weeks during COVID-19. The congregation was monolithic: white, conservative, Republican, Trump-supporting. It would make sense that he hadn't experienced fault lines around elections or vaccines or racism. ("Obama created the race problem in America," he pronounced at one point, all but confirming the absence of any Black Christians in his Bible study.) I asked Connelly if he could try to understand how these divisions were surfacing in churches different from his own.

"If you keep your focus on Jesus Christ, it washes a lot of those things away, because He keeps preeminence in the Church," he replied. "If you take the spotlight off Jesus and put it on anything else, you're gonna have division."

Within moments of these words leaving Connelly's lips, a man walked out of the sanctuary and approached the coffee area. He was wearing a red Make America Great Again baseball cap. "So," I said to Connelly, "about taking the spotlight off Jesus . . ."

He gave me a politician's grin. "I wouldn't wear *any* hat to church."

PEOPLE HUSTLED OUT OF THE WORSHIP CENTER TOWARD THE POP-UP market where a team of older ladies awaited. Before them small towers of Barton's books had been erected. Within minutes of the event wrapping up, a line stretched all the way back to the coffee shop. I felt a certain queasiness at the scene: Connelly and Barton weren't comfortable selling these products inside a state capitol building, but they had no qualms about setting up money tables inside a church.

The people in line were a colorful sort. Some folks dressed casually for the weeknight gathering; others, mostly older folks, wore formal church attire. What stood out was how many people were dressed for a political rally: There were flag-draped jackets, artillery-themed shirts, camouflage hats, and, naturally, an assortment of MAGA gear.

"Bad news!" hollered one of the cashier ladies. "We've sold out of books!"

Groans came from the dozens of people still waiting in line.

"Here's the good news," she continued. "If you sign up to become a WallBuilders member, and join our email list tonight, we'll send you a link to get thirty percent off any of David's books!"

The people shouted their approval. One of them was Jim Wright. He wore a collared shirt that embossed the cursive script of the Declaration of Independence over a yellowed-but-resilient flag. He had a thick white beard and twinkling eyes that would allow him to pass for a slender

Santa Claus. He toted a copy of the 1599 Geneva Bible, Patriot's Edition, the cover of which showed Washington crossing the Delaware. Wright had hoped to purchase a complementing product—Barton's own *The Founders' Bible*, which literally wraps the good book in Old Glory—but they had just sold out. (The publication of patriotic-themed Bibles has long been a cottage industry on the right; Donald Trump Jr. would later that year begin to hawk copies of the *We the People Bible*, which he promised would uphold our "American Judeo-Christian values.")

Wright didn't want *The Founders' Bible* merely because Barton was his favorite author and historian. He wanted it, Wright explained, because the book wouldn't be available for much longer. The government was coming for books like this, and it was coming for people like him. Under President Joe Biden, Wright said, bureaucrats would soon mobilize to "curtail our rights and our free speech and freedom of religion."

I asked Wright where he'd gotten that impression. One place was the internet: He was an avid reader of websites like ZeroHedge, LouRockwell.com, TheNewAmerican.com, HumansBeFree.com, and the Citizen Free Press. (He also subscribed to the *David Knight Show* podcast, a spinoff from InfoWars that makes Alex Jones look decaffeinated by comparison.)

The other place was church. For many years, Wright and his wife were members of a nearby congregation, SouthBrook, that was "more liberal." (By this, Wright told me, he meant that the church did not engage in political campaigning.) His wife still attends SouthBrook. But Wright broke away a few years earlier, upset that its pastor was refusing to speak to the imminent threats facing Christianity in America. When he walked into Living Word Church—and heard the calls to action from Pastor Pat Murray—Wright knew that he'd found a home.

"The Bible says we don't wrestle against flesh and blood, but against the powers of the air. But those powers of the air are becoming more physical, more flesh and blood," Wright told me. "We're seeing it every day."

Asked for examples, Wright assured me that the 2020 election had been stolen from Trump; that a global cabal had seized control of both American political parties; that the COVID-19 virus had been manufactured to control the population; that vaccines made from aborted babies had killed millions of people by design; and that Christian elites were involved in all of it.

"Look at Francis Collins," Wright said, referring to the man who until recently had led the National Institutes of Health.

I replied that Collins was highly regarded in evangelical circles; that while his policies and decisions were certainly fair game to criticize, he was known to be a faithful brother in Christ.

"No, no, no," Wright said, shaking his head. "Follow the baby parts."

This was the type of anecdote that, if relayed to Connelly, would be met with eye-rolling. He would dismiss Wright as a crackpot who might be found on the periphery of any group. There would be some truth to this; people like Wright did not constitute a majority of American evangelicalism. Yet they were everywhere I went. Whether it was a big urban church or a small rural church, a mainstream event with respected headliners or a sideshow circus featuring professional grifters, I kept running into people like Jim Wright. At one point they had been typical Christians, people who shrugged off the noise of the world and focused on Jesus. But the world had since gotten to them. And when they came to gatherings like these—when they heard Barton and Connelly implore Christians to take their country back before it was too late—there was no telling exactly how they might interpret that message.

"I always thought we'd have a major event in my lifetime—an uprising, a revolution," Wright told me. "Some Christians say we should stay out of politics, that we don't have to worry about any of this because this isn't our home. But it is our home right now. And the persecution that's all around the world is coming for us."

Wright said the present offensive against Christianity—private citizens being coerced by the state, traditional thinkers being marginalized in academia and corporate America—is only the beginning. Things are going to get much worse. Christians are right, he said, to pursue partisan victories to keep this persecution at bay. But it's only a temporary solution. Escalation, he said, is inevitable.

"We're not looking for a fight. But we have a sword of truth," Wright told me, nodding to his Bible. "We're fighting a spiritual battle, and it could turn into a physical battle before long."

*   *   *

A FEW MONTHS LATER, I REJOINED THE AMERICAN RESTORATION TOUR back in Michigan, determined this time to avoid fringe characters. Connelly thought I'd been going around cherry-picking crazy Christians and using them to paint his entire movement in an unsavory light; in truth, I was desperate to meet some normal ones. At our next meeting, Connelly promised to bring along some pastor friends to add some balance to my reporting.

Seated in the sanctuary of Our Savior Evangelical Lutheran Church, I felt a tap on the shoulder. The man behind me looked familiar. It was Matthew Shepherd, an activist I'd seen at right-wing political rallies around Michigan. I had first met him at a tailgate outside a local Ford plant where then-president Trump was speaking to automakers. The scene was unforgettable: Shepherd stood in the bed of his orange paramilitary-style truck, adorned with American flags and Tea Party slogans, chanting against the Democratic governor for her COVID-19 policies.

Two years later, Shepherd and I were making small talk in the sanctuary of Our Savior. I asked what had brought him to the church.

"I'm a chaplain," he responded, "with the Great Commission."

Before I could indulge him—this was clearly not a real position with any actual organization—the American Restoration Tour was back underway. The pastor of the host church, a young man named Chris Thoma, opened by noting the privilege of sharing the stage with Barton and Connelly. It was Barton, he said, who had inspired him to enter the ministry, and he had recently gotten to know Connelly at an event in San Diego. I knew what Thoma was referring to: It was the first-ever "Pastors Summit" put on by Charlie Kirk—the activist who described Trump as "the most moral president on record"—and his organization, Turning Point USA. Connelly had gone all in. Partnering with Barton was bad enough. There was something especially foul about allying with Kirk, a serial liar and professional political arsonist, in a campaign to advance Christian virtue.

Connelly announced to the crowd that the footprint of Faith Wins was expanding every day. He and Barton had taken their American

Restoration Tour to twenty-three states during this election year and were closing in on their voter registration goals. This was being accomplished, he noted, with the help of pastors like Chris Thoma, who weren't "squishy" in their convictions.

Sensing an opportunity, Connelly decided to challenge everyone in the room. "Are you gonna be a squish, or someone who stands for truth?" he said. The sanctuary rumbled in response.

As Barton began his presentation, I slipped away to a parlor room at the back of the sanctuary. Connelly wanted me to meet three local pastors who stood for truth. Seated around a large, rectangular folding table were Connelly; Donald Eason, the pastor of Metro Church of Christ in Sterling Heights; Jeffrey Hall, the pastor of Community Faith Church in Holt; and Dominic Burkhard, who described himself as "a full-time missionary to the legislature in Lansing."

Connelly opened by summarizing for his friends the conversations we'd been having about political activism tearing churches apart. Clearly expecting that they would back him up, Connelly again announced that he'd seen no such thing in his tour of hundreds of churches around the country, and asked the pastors to weigh in.

"There's definitely some political divisions here in Michigan churches," said Hall.

Eason nodded. "Lots of political division."

"COVID definitely drew some lines," Hall continued. "I had people calling and emailing our church asking if we were open. They had come from churches that closed, and they wanted to know if we were taking a hard stance against the government. I never wanted to make a war with the government. We closed for about a month. I just wanted to honor God. But some people weren't looking for that."

I reminded Connelly of the story of FloodGate Church, which had made war with the government and increased its membership tenfold. The church's expansive new campus was miles down the road from where we were sitting. Connelly gave me that familiar far-off look.

"He's talking about Bill Bolin," Eason chimed in.

I asked Eason how he knew about FloodGate's pastor.

"Oh, I know about Bolin," Eason said with an uneasy smile. "We all know about Bolin."

Connelly still claimed not to know about Bolin. So the others filled him in—the refusal to comply during COVID, the cries of martyrdom, the attacks on Whitmer, the alliances with right-wing politicians and activists.

"Well, he'd be a unicorn in our crowd," Connelly said. "I don't know any other pastors like that."

But Connelly had just been in San Diego with Charlie Kirk and a small army of pastors *exactly* like that. It was true that much of the turmoil in churches was coming from the bottom up, with radicalized members rebelling against the insufficient political efforts of their pastors. But it was also true that a growing number of conservative pastors were doing just what Bolin had done at FloodGate. Meanwhile, it was the pastors who refused—the pastors who didn't want to host the American Restoration Tour in their sanctuaries—whom Connelly had deemed "squishes."

We had come full circle from our conversation at the Ohio capitol. Connelly told me then that pastors "failed us" by not getting their churches involved with politics. Now he was doubling down.

"Do you know what the research tells us is the biggest reason people leave church? They say it's not relevant. Why would they come, when the pastor isn't teaching me how to think through the issues?" Connelly said. "Christianity should permeate the culture, not be separated from it."

The way for Christianity to permeate the culture, he insisted, was by tackling these great debates of our time: abortion, homosexuality, transgenderism. I didn't bother questioning why Connelly always listed the same narrow set of topics; the answer was apparent. Talking about other clear-cut biblical issues—such as caring for the poor and welcoming the refugee and refusing the temptation of wealth—did not animate the conservative base ahead of an election. (Or, relatedly, manifest as moral imperatives nearly as often on Fox News.)

There were more pressing questions on my mind. Connelly's organization was called "Faith Wins," but what did that even mean? Could faith really win or lose something? It all just felt so trivial. If we believe that Jesus has defeated death, why are we consumed with winning a political campaign? Why should we care that we're losing power on this earth when God has the power to forgive sins and save souls? And why should we obsess over America when Jesus has gifted us citizenship in heaven?

Burkhard, the lobbyist-slash-missionary in Lansing, jumped in.

"People need to be saved *and* America needs to be saved. It's perfectly good to want both," he said. "There's nothing wrong with trying to save America. Somebody needs to try to do it. Somebody needs to try to save America."

Eason, seated to Burkhard's right, shook his head in disagreement. The more we'd been talking about this, he confessed, the more uneasy he felt. He believed, like Connelly did, that Christianity was in the cross-hairs of the American left. But he had just preached a sermon that was weighing on him. It was about the uniqueness of the early Christian Church. He had described for his congregation how Christians had gained influence—and won converts—by being countercultural, by rejecting the trends that preoccupied so much of the world around them. American evangelicals, Eason said, would do well to study that tradition.

"Our goal should be to save souls, not to save America. The reality is, we can't save America anyway, unless we're saving those souls first," he said to Burkhard. "We can fight for America all day long, but if we don't save the *people* here, it won't matter."

The great obstacle to saving souls, I suggested, wasn't drag queen performances or Critical Race Theory. It was the perception among the unbelieving masses—the very people these evangelicals were called to evangelize—that Christians care more about reclaiming lost social status than we do about loving our neighbor as ourselves. I relayed what Chris Winans, the pastor of my hometown church, had said about evangelicals: "Too many of them worship America."

Connelly looked incredulous. He turned to his pastor friends. "I don't see that happening," he told them. "You see any of that?"

"Oh, I see it," Hall said. "I know of a pastor who just recently stood up in his pulpit and told people that they're insane if they vote Democrat this fall."

Eason had similar stories to tell. I pointed out that Al Mohler, the president of Southern Baptist Theological Seminary, one of America's most prominent Christian conservatives, had recently said something similar. This was not an anomaly. Pastors and church officials and evangelical leaders were feeling the pressure to classify Jesus as a registered Republican—and they were feeling it from people like Chad Connelly.

Thoroughly flustered now, Connelly argued that if pastors didn't address current events head-on, the Christians in their care would resort to "secular sources" to form their political viewpoints. The way to ensure that Christians vote biblical values, he said, was for pastors to preach politics. This struck me as completely backward. If pastors were doing their job—going deep in the word, discipling their flocks, stressing scripture and prayer above social media and talk radio—their people wouldn't need to be infantilized with explicit partisan endorsements. Those Christians would know how to vote biblically, because they would know their Bible.

Connelly whipped his head back and forth. "I'd love to meet a pastor who thinks he's doing a good enough job discipling to where he doesn't need to engage with this stuff, because that pastor is deceived. He's badly deceived," he said. "I've told my Sunday School class: Don't tell anybody you're doing a good job telling people about Jesus, because we're losing the culture. If we were doing a good job telling people about Jesus, we wouldn't be losing the culture."

This fixation on winning and losing was revealing. In the sanctuary behind us, a body of Christians had just sat through an hourlong lecture that was designed to make them smarter and more powerful citizens. They were supposed to take the information Barton had given them, Connelly instructed, then charge into the trenches of America's political battlefield.

And yet, there was no instruction on *how* to fight. There was no perspective on the appropriate way to win. There was no lesson on what John Dickson described as "losing well." This was very much by design. Because losing, in the eyes of men like Connelly and Barton, was no longer an option."The stakes are too high," Connelly told me at one point, to cede any ground to the opposition.

Unsavory alliances would need to be forged. Sordid tactics would need to be embraced. The first step toward preserving Christian values, it seemed, was to do away with Christian values.

CHAPTER NINE

NASHVILLE, TENNESSEE

You brood of vipers, how can you who are evil say anything good? For the mouth speaks what the heart is full of. A good man brings good things out of the good stored up in him, and an evil man brings evil things out of the evil stored up in him.

—MATTHEW 12:34–35

At sixty-one years old, Ralph Reed's bronzed skin exposes nary a wrinkle. His perfectly parted swoop of hair remains brown and boyish. He carries himself with a lightness that is so inspiring as to be suspicious.

It was the third and final day of Road to Majority, the annual symposium organized by Reed's Faith and Freedom Coalition. The last forty-eight hours had been a chorus of wailing and gnashing of teeth: Dozens of politicians and evangelical leaders had taken to Reed's podium warning that it was open season on Christians in America, urging attendees (and anyone watching from home via Fox News' livestreaming service) to vote Republican in 2022 and end the secular occupation. November was five months away, they said, and if Democrats were left in charge of the country we might never get it back.

Yet here, presiding over this funeral for Christian America, was a man who wore a wedding-photo smile to match the designer pinstriped suit, purple tie and corresponding pocket square, polished rings on both hands, cuff links the size of half-dollars, stretching out his arms to remind everyone of the good news. "We know how the story ends!" Reed announced to the faithful on the first day of the conference. His words were a reminder, Reed told me later, that Christians should never be discouraged; that God is sovereign over the universe no matter our woes in America. I think he believed that. But I knew it wasn't the reason he was smiling.

For the past thirty years, no person has done more to organize, mobilize, and manipulate the political sensibilities of American Christians than Ralph Eugene Reed Jr. The son of a Navy man, he was born in Virginia, raised in Florida, and educated in Georgia. But Reed came of age in Washington, D.C., where early in Ronald Reagan's presidency he fell in with a company of influential young conservatives such as Grover Norquist and Jack Abramoff. Rising fast in the GOP ranks—and, by his own admission, hesitating at no dirty deed—Reed faced a decision after praying to accept Jesus in the mid-1980s. He could carry on with the blood sport of partisan politics or he could devote himself to something stabler and more civil, like academia. For a while, he split the difference, working on behalf of Republican causes while also working toward his PhD in American history. Reed was about to commit himself to scholarship for good—until a chance encounter with Pat Robertson.

It was 1989, and Robertson, the televangelist who had run unsuccessfully for president in 1988, cornered Reed at the inauguration of President George H. W. Bush. Robertson confided to Reed that he worried about spiritual backsliding in the GOP. He had never been a fan of Jerry Falwell—in fact, they had been rivals for decades—but he respected the influence Falwell had amassed with his Moral Majority. Now Falwell was shuttering that organization, Reagan's religious-right allies were spinning off into other pursuits, and Bush seemed likely to leave evangelicals out in the cold. Robertson sensed an opportunity to start a new enterprise, better funded and even more sophisticated than the Moral Majority, to harness the evangelical movement's momentum for a new decade of politics. Reed went home and wrote a memo detailing his vision for such an organization. Just like that—and with Reed, not Robertson, assuming command—the Christian Coalition was born.

Reed wasted no time turning the Christian Coalition into a behemoth. He tapped his D.C. Rolodex to forge strategic alliances on K Street and Capitol Hill, raising the sort of money that made party officials do double takes. He built voter-contact databases, befriended promi-nent ministers, and set up state and local chapters. All the while, Reed crafted a story that proved irresistible to donors and journalists and politicos of all spiritual persuasion. Even more than his Moral Major-ity progenitors, Reed understood the power of an underdog narrative. He sold the Christian Coalition as a real-time grassroots uprising. He wanted it known that evangelicals were no longer content playing the clubby old game of politics; they would create a new game altogether. From electing precinct captains to national party delegates, the Chris-tian Coalition was going to take over the Republican Party, and then it was going to take over the American electoral process, and Reed was the only person who knew how to achieve it. "I do guerrilla warfare," he told the Norfolk *Virginian-Pilot* in 1991. "I paint my face and travel at night. You don't know it's over until you're in a body bag."

The timing was just right. Even as evangelicals collected policy wins in the 1980s, there had been persistent grumbles of exploitation, of opportunism, of being used by a sneering party establishment that looked down on them. They had been pawns on the GOP chessboard. Not anymore. The Christian Coalition helped evangelicals become co-ordinated, empowered—and embittered. The Republican Party needed these voters, Reed would say, more than those voters needed the Re-publican Party. Using Bill Clinton's 1992 victory to demonstrate how the GOP was aimless and spiritually hollow, Reed argued that a party that believed in nothing could be saved only by true believers. By 1994, when Newt Gingrich engineered a GOP occupation of the House of Rep-resentatives for the first time in four decades, it was no longer moderate Republicans dictating terms to conservative evangelicals, but the other way around. Dozens and dozens of right-wing evangelicals were elected to Congress with a seeming mandate to restore limited government and Judeo-Christian values to America—and not necessarily in that order. The next year, *Time* magazine featured Reed on its cover with a head-line, "The Right Hand of God." He was thirty-three years old.

Sitting with him nearly three decades later, retracing the arc of his career, I could see why Reed was smiling. He really did know—in more ways than one—how the story would end. It looked something like this scene around us. Thousands of people singing hymns in between stump speeches. Roving spotlights and booming intro music. Packed ballrooms and standing ovations. One president kissing his ring and a multitude of would-be presidents lining up for their turn. Regardless of which party won or lost a given election, evangelicals were never returning to the periphery of American politics. The campaign for a Christian America had become central to their identity as believers. And the only thing more exhilarating than winning power, Reed knew, was the pursuit of reclaiming it.

"You see so many people here, walking around with smiles on their faces, hugging and embracing. There's such a spirit of joy, because everybody knows it's going to be all right," Reed told me. "Like I said, we know how the story ends."

Or maybe, I suggested to Reed, they were hugging and embracing because Republicans had the momentum in this election season—and November was looking like a potential GOP landslide.

He flashed that dazzling smile. "Yeah," Reed replied. "That could be."

THIS WASN'T MY FIRST ROAD TO MAJORITY EVENT. UNLIKE OTHER right-wing political carnivals, such as the Conservative Political Action Conference, Reed's gathering typically had a semblance of seriousness. "Faith" came before "Freedom" in his organization's title, after all. While Reed was always quick to point out that he was no preacher, and that this was no church service, the Road to Majority events were usually a few degrees removed from the raving, truculent mess of your standard Republican cattle call.

Not this year. From the very first speech, when an activist named Leo Terrell warned that "people on the left are trying to take our freedom... and keep us from worshipping," something was different. There was an openly apocalyptic tone to the proceedings. This wasn't about airing some policy differences or praying for a restoration of certain values. The purpose of this conference, it quickly became evident, was first to establish as fact that forces of darkness—namely Democrats and deep-state bureaucrats, corporate elites and Hollywood fiends—were targeting Christianity in America, and then, once successful, to incite God's people to strike back.

"We are not going to let them take away our country," declared Ronna Romney McDaniel, the chairwoman of the Republican National Committee.

"We. Need. To. Pray," she said, emphasizing each word, before adding: "Because we have *got* to win in November."

For three days I watched Christians pray—not for God's will to be done, or for the forgiveness of their trespasses, or to be led away from temptation, but for a "red wave" in the upcoming election. The only thing more disingenuous than the appeal was its connotations of eternal significance.

"We are soldiers in God's army, and together we are engaging in spiritual warfare for our country. There are only two options: We can fight, or we can fail," said Bo Hines, a congressional candidate from North Carolina. Hines asked the crowd which option they would choose. When the response reached his anticipated decibel level, Hines cried out: "We're going to fight for religious liberty, so that we can worship the one true God!"

Sam Brownback, the former Kansas governor who served as Trump's ambassador for international religious freedom, followed Hines onto the stage. He told of a Finnish politician who had been "prosecuted criminally" for quoting scripture to explain her opposition to same-sex marriage. The crowd murmured as he swore that this sort of persecution was "coming to us" in America next.

Not bothering to share additional context—for instance, that prosecutors were seeking to fine, not imprison, the politician; or that the Finnish court unanimously dismissed all charges against her; or that the case served to underscore the sturdiness of freedom-of-speech provisions throughout the democratized world—Brownback began pounding on the podium. "We've got to fight back!" he said, as audience members leapt from their chairs.

These multitudes who'd come to Nashville claimed to worship a Prince of Peace, yet they roared at every mention of conflict. Some went out of their way to sound reluctant, like this call to rhetorical arms was a last resort. Because followers of Jesus no longer enjoy the constitutional safeguards afforded to other Americans—"The government is there to protect us. Or is it?" Jeanine Pirro, the Fox News host, asked ominously from the stage—some speakers suggested it was time Christians took matters into their own hands.

"How many of you love America? Say amen!" shouted Richard Lee, an Atlanta pastor and longtime conservative activist.

The audience bellowed as one: "Amen!"

"We've got a self-centered, mentally deficient old man in the White House," Lee continued. "Some people say he doesn't know what he's doing. Yeah, he does—because he's wicked. He's wicked. He's just not [following] a different philosophy; he's wicked. And his whole staff are wicked. They're all a bunch of weirdos themselves."

To booming applause, Lee argued that it was time for Christians to save the nation, to overcome the plotting of the wicked weirdos, to re-establish their rights and recapture control of their government.

"Thank God, I think the old man is going to go [away] in handcuffs, about January of next year," Lee concluded.

It wasn't clear whether Lee, like so many others at the conference, was predicting Trump's imminent return to the presidency. (One panel discussion featured Johnny Enlow, a QAnon conspiracy theorist and self-proclaimed "prophet" who has declared that Trump not only won the 2020 election but is secretly still the acting president of the United States, as well as "God's president for Earth.") For a fleeting moment, it was then-Texas congressman Louie Gohmert—never mistaken for a voice of reason—who seemed to be pushing back on expectations of Trump's messianic reappearance in the Oval Office.

"Our hope will not come on Air Force One," said Gohmert. "But unless we get back to teaching morality and discussing God in schools, we're on our way out."

The congressman then warned that our most precious freedoms—such as religious assembly and expression—were being shredded by dishonest people inside the government. It was a remarkable statement from Gohmert, who just two weeks earlier had reacted to the indict-ment of a Trump administration official by complaining, "If you're a Republican, you can't even lie to Congress or lie to an FBI agent or they're coming after you."

Gohmert closed this particular rant by thanking God for His many blessings, including that "Merrick Garland isn't on the Supreme Court."

(Surely the Maker of heaven and earth was similarly relieved that Senate Republicans had blocked one of Obama's judicial nominees.)

Things only got stranger as the event wore on.

One afternoon, while waiting in line at a pop-up kiosk selling coffee and pastries, I heard the woman behind me broadcasting her disgust at seeing Starbucks was being served. "They put baby parts in their coffee," she told her friends. (They stayed in line and got bottled waters.) During an evening time of communal worship in the ballroom, one of the singers onstage asserted that Jesus had been crucified because of "fake news." At the end of a panel on Hispanic political realignment, the moderator, one of Reed's staffers, concluded, "God is moving in the Hispanic community. And that's why they're going right. Because *God is right.*"

And then there was Stella Immanuel, the Texas pediatrician who gained social media fame during the pandemic because of her claim that hydroxychloroquine could cure COVID-19. Onstage for a discussion about "societal influence," she launched into such an oddball monologue about vaccinations and the Mark of the Beast that even her fellow panelists started to squirm. Having earned a medical degree in Nigeria, Immanuel operated a small strip-mall clinic outside of Houston next door to the church she pastors, Fire Power Ministries. Immanuel's influence on the fringe right was already well documented. As the journalist Will Sommer reported, Immanuel "has a history of making bizarre claims about medical topics and other issues." Among them: "gynecological problems like cysts and endometriosis are in fact caused by people having sex in their dreams with demons and witches . . . alien DNA is currently used in medical treatments . . . the government is run in part not by humans but by 'reptilians' and other aliens."

None of this disqualified her from addressing the Road to Majority conference. Her booth in the exhibit hall featured a pyramid of medicinal products—pill bottles, creams, sprays—that claimed to offer sleep aid and immune support and dietary health. They were visibly off-brand, bearing only a small logo: "DrStellaMD." Next to the makeshift pharmacy stood towers of her book, *Let America Live*, circulated by the Pentecostal publishing giant Charisma Media. Draped over the front of the table was a white shirt depicting two battle axes intersecting over an American flag. Blood dripped from their sides. In blue font were the words: I AM GOD'S BATTLE AXE AND WEAPON OF WAR. Below was a "DrStellaMD" logo and a citation from the Old Testament Book of Jeremiah.

These themes—of patriotism and divine commission, of nationalism and savage conquest—were ubiquitous in the hall. I saw one flag, black adorned with white revolvers, that read "God, Guns & Trump." They were sold next to decorative license plates that showed soaring eagles and cocked pistols: "God, Guns & Guts Made America," it read. "Let's Keep All Three."

One table over from where copies of *The First American Bible* were being sold (for a discounted price of $149.99), Road to Majority attendees crowded around a rack of T-shirts that carried slogans such as "Faith Over Fear" and "This Means War." The top seller, offered in at least seven different colors, was "Let's Go Brandon," a bowdlerized euphemism that conservatives chant as a substitute for "Fuck Joe Biden." The shirts even included a hashtag—#FJB—that jettisoned any plausible deniability.

When I asked Dave Klucken, the booth's proprietor, what brought him all the way from Loganville, Georgia, to peddle these goods, he replied, "We've taken God out of America."

Did he really think #FJB was an appropriate way to bring God back? Klucken shrugged. "People keep on asking for it," he told me. "You've got to give the people what they want."

As recently as five or six years earlier, even as the evangelical-political brand was becoming more disputatious, it would have been scandalous to see such vile and violent symbolism at an event associated with Christianity. But Ralph Reed didn't really care. He was giving the people what they wanted. He was giving them Donald J. Trump.

PLENTY OF PASTORS SPOKE AT ROAD TO MAJORITY. THERE WAS ROBERT Jeffress, my old sparring partner from First Baptist Dallas, who argued that because salt was used as an ancient preservative, Jesus *actually* wants Christians to preserve America a little longer so that more souls might be saved. There was Jentezen Franklin, the leader of Free Chapel church in Gainesville, Georgia, who sounded a rebel yell against "our enemies"—with a special emphasis on the "drag queens" allegedly invading children's locker rooms—and implored the Baby Boomer audience to make sure the next generation of evangelicals continued fighting the culture war.

But the holy of holies at this event—the only person treated with a Trump-like reverence—was the former president's spiritual adviser: Paula White.

To understand White's ascent to the pinnacle of evangelical influence is to study Trump's own takeover of the Republican Party. Neither had completed any formal education—White in theology, Trump in law or government—to justify their positions of authority. Both had several failed marriages behind them and were shadowed by whispers of infidelity. Both nearly saw their reputations irreparably marred by legal, ethical, and financial improprieties, only to somehow emerge more respected on the other side. They were outlaw survivors, conscience-free swindlers who possessed both the talent to detect what people wanted to hear and the shamelessness to say it to them. Trump knew how to market the nostalgia of an idyllic America. But White had something even better to sell: the prosperity gospel.

Also known as the "health and wealth gospel," what White preaches is straightforward: The more faith someone demonstrates, the more material comfort God provides them. How is faith most vividly demonstrated? By giving money, of course—to the church, to the televangelist, to related Christian ventures. This is hardly a fringe view. Much of the charismatic evangelical movement, which includes but is not limited to the Pentecostal denomination, subscribes to some variation of the prosperity gospel. Because God saves us from eternal damnation through faith, the thinking goes, that same faith delivers us from poverty and sickness here on earth.

The contradictions of scripture are blatant and innumerable—was Jesus insufficiently faithful, hence His penniless existence that culminated in being nailed to a Roman cross?—but the appeal is obvious enough for wealthy Americans. The prosperity gospel can be conveniently reverse engineered. Forget about the faith aspect: If you have lots of money, then clearly God has blessed you, and if God has blessed you, then clearly you are living a godly life. White has been riding this ruse since the early 1990s. It made her a spiritual guru to the stars, earned her endless millions, and won her an audience, long ago, with one especially prosperous American. White has repeatedly shot down the rumor that she converted Trump to Christianity—she insists that he's been a believer since childhood—and yet she savored the role of being his religious whisperer. She chaired Trump's evangelical advisory board, delivered the invocation at his inauguration, led prayer circles inside the White House, and enjoyed a direct line to the president of the United States. It is no exaggeration to call White the most politically accomplished pastor of the twenty-first century.

As she waited her turn to address the Faith and Freedom conference, Timothy Head, the organization's executive director, described White as a modern-day biblical hero. She was, if not a prophet, at the very least on par with Old Testament giants like Esther, Daniel, and Mordechai, people who amassed power behind the scenes, "shaping the destiny of nations" and doing God's will on earth. When she emerged moments later, White waved off the rapturous applause. She had come to Nashville to herald the arrival of someone even greater.

"I've never seen a family, or a person, go under such harsh criticism to stand for truth and do good in our land," White told the audience. Juicing that reliable comparison to King David, she credited Trump's "spiritual fortitude" for enduring the onslaught against him. She cautioned his supporters that they would need similar courage in the days to come.

"It's crystal clear that we live in a different America than we did under President Trump," White declared. Things were growing darker by the day. This promised land might soon be unsalvageable. What were God-fearing people to do?

"Politics matter," White continued. "We can't just sit back and let a group of people control the destiny of this nation. . . . I believe that we've been raised up, and we are responsible and required by God to make sure that we bring forth the best America possible."

White made it known, no wink or nod needed, that one man in particular had been raised up. He had been wrongly removed from power. But the day of his return was drawing nearer.

When Trump strode onto the stage, with Lee Greenwood's "God Bless the USA" rattling the solar plexus of every red-blooded patriot who stood inside the presidential ballroom of the Gaylord Opryland Resort, the anticipation was palpable. The former president had kept an unusually low profile since his disagreeable departure from office eighteen months earlier, which was made more conspicuous by the torrid pace of Trump-related news. Road to Majority occupied one side of a cable news split screen when Trump came to Nashville; the other side showed a special congressional inquiry into the January 6 attack on the Capitol. Before Trump spoke, the American people heard damning testimony from an esteemed conservative judge, J. Michael Luttig, who called Trump and his allies "a clear and present danger to American democracy." The former president was also under investigation in numerous jurisdictions for all manner of misconduct. And, just recently, *Politico* had published a leaked Supreme Court decision that would overturn *Roe v. Wade*, which would be a landmark achievement for the pro-life movement fifty years after the decision that legalized abortion. Meanwhile, Trump's inner circle kept teasing an announcement of his run for president in 2024. Evangelicals remained the most loyal cog in his political machine. Everyone in the ballroom was whispering: Would he launch his campaign here at Reed's event?

The speech proved anticlimactic. There was no announcement of another presidential bid. He mentioned the *Roe* leak only in passing (so much for the most pro-life president of our lifetime). He carped about January 6 being overblown and said the investigations were illegitimate and called the Republicans who opposed him "vicious losers." Trump seemed restless, even bored, like a musician tired of playing his own greatest hits. The crowd appeared fidgety as well. Then he mentioned his onetime vice president.

"Mike Pence had a chance to be great. He had a chance to be, frankly, historic," Trump said, grimacing. "I say it sadly, because I like him. But Mike did not have the courage to act."

The crowd booed the mention of Pence's name. The former president kept on attacking, and the crowd kept on booing. For the next five minutes—and for the first time publicly since their split on January 6, 2021—Trump tore into Pence for his role in formalizing Joe Biden's victory that day. He mocked his former vice president as a "robot" who would not deviate from his constitutional duty of counting aloud the certified Electoral College votes that had been sent by the states. Pence was too "afraid," Trump said, to embrace the creative legal theories that might have allowed them both to remain in office. He was too "afraid" to do what needed to be done.

It was an unforgettable scene. For two decades, Pence had been a darling of this community, an admired carrier of the torch once lit by the Moral Majority, a genuine born-again evangelical who introduced himself as "a Christian, a conservative, and a Republican—in that order." He had headlined this very event, counting as personal friends many of the people in this room. And now they had turned on him. Not for some biblical heresy or ideological apostasy. But for following the rule of law they so acclaimed; for obeying the Constitution they so adored.

What to make of this? I thought back to the beginning of Trump's speech. There was a rehearsed line that so neatly captured the narrative of the conference that I immediately suspected it had been written with the assistance of Reed. "The greatest danger to America is not our enemies from the outside, as powerful as they may be," Trump had said. "The greatest danger to America is the destruction of our nation from the people within."

Not long after, he added: "This is not just a political problem, but a spiritual problem."

That's when it became clear. This speech—like the entire Road to Majority event—had been executed with a double meaning. Yes, there was incessant talk about a radical "woke agenda" that was advancing Critical Race Theory and transgenderism and the like. But for every warning of progressivism run amok there was a rebuke of conservatism gone soft; pastors and politicians freely labeled as "cowards" anyone who shared their values but refused to go to war for them. The enemy wasn't simply those godless secularists on the left, but those gutless Christians on the right. The enemy was people who failed to appreciate how endangered their kingdom was, people who would let principles and laws obstruct their quest for power. The enemy was people like Mike Pence.

REED SAT AT THE HEAD OF THE TABLE BUT NEVER TOUCHED HIS FOOD. A handful of other reporters—from the Associated Press, Fox News,

National Public Radio—joined us for lunch in an upstairs boardroom. Trump had just finished his ninety-minute stemwinder and Reed wanted us to record his own victory lap. This was the seventh time Trump had spoken to the Faith and Freedom Coalition, Reed crowed, dating back to his days as a private citizen, and the organization had grown in strength and influence right along with The Donald himself. Reed began reciting the same statistics Trump had rattled off in his speech: Faith and Freedom would be responsible in the coming months for knocking on more than 8 million doors, making 10 million phone calls, sending 25 million text messages, and distributing voter guides to 100,000 churches. These numbers were impossible to verify, mind you, but there was no doubting the general trajectory of evangelical engagement. Reed's organization today boasts more than 40 million people in its voter file, compared to 8 million at the peak of the Christian Coalition in the mid-1990s.

Confident these numbers would translate to a Republican romp in November, Reed predicted the biggest turnout of evangelical voters in midterm history. "We have a president who's imploding," Reed told us. He argued that Biden's approval ratings, sagging under the weight of historic inflation, had no hope of rebounding before November.

But if Reed was being honest—and in this moment, he was—the real cause for electoral optimism wasn't Biden's poll numbers.

"They're scared. They're genuinely scared about the future of the country," Reed said, pointing toward the people in the ballroom. "I'm hearing things that I haven't heard since Jimmy Carter was president. Like, 'I don't know if the country is going to survive if these policies continue.'"

Reed paused, seemingly aware how pitiful this sounded.

"I'm not saying it's true or untrue," he added. "I'm just saying, these people are *scared*. And that's a big, big motivator when it comes to turnout."

He was right. These people were scared. They were scared, in part, because of economic and cultural instability. But mostly they were scared because people like Reed were trying to scare them; people like Reed *needed* to scare them. Sure, the Bible's most frequently cited command is "Fear not," but remember, Reed is no preacher. He's a political organizer. The job of a political organizer is to win campaigns. To win campaigns, Reed realized long ago, his most valuable tool was fear. And so, in Nashville, Reed unleashed a pack of starved partisan animals to feast on the fright of Christians. For three days, Reed looked on as thousands of believers were told that their children were being groomed; that their communities were under invasion; that their guns were going to be confiscated; that their medical treatments were suspect; that their newspapers were lying to them; that their elected officials were diabolical; that their government was coming after them; that their faith was being banned from public life; that their leader was being unjustly persecuted on their behalf; that their nation was nearing its end.

There's a reason that scripture warns so often and so forcefully against fear: It is just as powerful as faith. But whereas faith keeps our eyes steadily fixed on the eternal, fear disrupts us, disorients us, drives us to prioritize the here and now. Faith is about preserving our place in the body of Christ; fear is about protecting our own flesh and blood. Peter was doing the impossible—walking on the Sea of Galilee, just like Jesus—until the wind started whipping around him. Then he got scared and immediately began to sink. "You of little faith," Jesus said in that moment, grabbing Peter's hand and pulling him up. "Why did you doubt?"

No one should be surprised to see politicians and political hacks utilizing something so powerful in the name of winning an election. But it was disheartening all the same. Christians are called to transcend the patterns of this broken world; they also are called to be more perceptive than the nonbelieving person. If a jury full of atheists was brainwashed into believing that a criminal whose fingerprints were all over the scene was innocent, well, most Christians would shrug. It requires the gift of discernment, they would say, the *spiritual* gift of discernment, to see the truth. And yet, here we were, a whole ballroom full of Christians, clad in our "Faith Over Fear" shirts, doing everything backward.

"The far left takes their views and tries to shove them down people's throats like it's a religion. I'm not a crusader, but we have a real religion, and it's about people's rights," Randy Pitcher, a retired Army medic from Kentucky, told me in the lobby outside the event. He motioned at the scene around us. "You hear this stuff, and it makes you realize that we need more power. There are enough of us to take it."

"We're in trouble," said Lydia Maldonado, a pastor from South Florida. "God was kicked out of the White House as soon as Trump left office. When Trump left the White House, he took God with him."

Maldonado told me she'd run for state representative in 2020, but her election "was stolen" just like Trump's was. Perhaps sensing my skepticism, Maldonado said that Christians had a responsibility before God to expose voter fraud because "Jesus Himself was the first politician to walk the earth." I replied by mentioning how Jesus told Pontius Pilate, before His execution, that His kingdom was not of this world.

"No. It *is* of this world," Maldonado told me. "God gave us this country. We are the keepers of this kingdom. And right now, we are allowing the enemy to take it from us."

Her husband, Edward Maldonado, nodded along. Despite spending his career working for the federal government—doing exactly what, he would not say—Edward believed that Uncle Sam was hunting down Christians. He agreed with his wife: Secular progressives had hijacked the country and turned the government against believers. He agreed with Trump that time was running out to save America. He agreed with pretty much everything he'd heard at the conference. There was just one thing that bothered him.

"As Christians, why are we booing Mike Pence? I don't get it," Edward told me. "He's way more religious than—"

He paused. "I don't want to say he's more religious than Trump. But, you know . . ." He smiled as his voice trailed off.

To be clear, Pence had brought some of this madness on himself. Instead of using his credibility as a mature believer to steer his party away from the sacrilegious God-and-country claptrap being pushed by Trump and his party throughout 2020, the vice president had joined in. "Let's fix our eyes on Old Glory and all she represents," Pence declared during a speech to the Republican National Convention. "Let's fix our eyes on the author and perfecter of our faith and freedom, and never forget that where the spirit of the Lord is there is freedom. And that means freedom *always* wins."

At once, the ears of Christian viewers everywhere perked up. Pence had knowingly bastardized a precious passage from the New Testament. The epistle to the Hebrews states, "Let us fix our eyes on Jesus, the author and perfecter of our faith." In addition to substituting "Old Glory" for "Jesus"—a stunt that was nothing short of blasphemous— Pence deliberately conflated the freedom of being reborn in Christ with the supposedly all-conquering civil liberties enjoyed by Americans. It was a rhetorical sleight of hand aimed at rousing the very sorts of star-spangled Christians who would threaten his life on January 6, and who, a year and a half later, were booing him at Reed's conference.

Upstairs in the boardroom, over plates of glazed chicken and sweaty glasses of sweet tea, several reporters quizzed Reed about Pence's fall from grace. How had he—a longtime friend of the former vice president— felt listening to thousands of people booing him? How had he felt listening to Trump disparage someone who'd been nothing but loyal to him? How had he felt knowing Pence wasn't here to defend himself?

"He was invited," Reed said, holding out his hands as if wanting them to be washed. "He's been welcome here in the past. He would be welcome now."

Some of us laughed. Knowing his bluff had been called, Reed was putting on his best song and dance. With a hand placed over his heart, he called Pence a "dear friend" and said that he wished he had come to speak. Then he explained that Trump was also a "dear friend" and had the right to speak his mind about January 6. He continued to dodge and weave as the other reporters—even the one from Fox News—grew annoyed at his lack of candor.

"Does it bother you that one of your dear friends may have been trying to get your other dear friend killed?" I finally asked Reed.

He stiffened. "I'm not sure I would agree with that characterization," Reed said. Despite mounting evidence that Trump had been so furious with Pence that he'd shrugged at the prospect of him falling into the hands of the mob, Reed claimed this was inaccurate. He had talked to Trump personally about this, he said, and had been assured that Trump wanted Pence kept safe that day.

There was eye-rolling around the table. He knew nobody was buying it.

"Let me say this," Reed said. "I was in and around that White House as much as anyone who did not work there. I saw them interact, I know they prayed together, I know they were dear friends, and they genuinely cared about one another. There was tremendous affection between the two of them."

And?

"Umm, after the election, that was no longer the case."

Reed shrugged. "But I've been doing this a long time," he assured us. "You just have to face reality that in politics, that happens."

IN POLITICS.

Would a serious Christian see fit, I wondered, to condone this brutish behavior in any other area of life? Would they condone vicious ad hominem attacks if they were launched at the office? Would they condone the use of vulgarities and violent innuendo inside their home? Would they condone blatant abuses of power at their local school or nonprofit or church?

If the answer is no, then why do they accept it in politics? Because politics is about the ends, not the means. Since the ends are about power—the power to legislate, the power to investigate, the power to accumulate more power—the means are inherently defensible, even if they are, by any other measure, utterly indefensible.

This compartmentalization of standards is toxic to the credibility of the Christian witness. Many evangelicals have come to view politics the way a suburban husband views Las Vegas—a self-contained escape, a place where the rules and expectations of his everyday life do not apply. The problem is, what happens in politics doesn't stay in politics. Everyone can see what these folks are doing. Just as you might stop taking marital advice from your neighbor if you saw cell phone footage of him paying for prostitutes and cocaine in Vegas, you might stop taking spiritual guidance from your neighbor if you saw him chanting "Hang Mike Pence!" at the Capitol Building.

An extreme example? Perhaps. But bankruptcy—spiritual and otherwise—happens slowly and then all at once. In 2016, Christians condoned their preferred candidate talking on the *Access Hollywood* tape about grabbing women by their vaginas, because the election was a binary choice and the Supreme Court was at stake; by 2022 Christians walked around wearing "Fuck Joe Biden" on their chests because in politics the rules of decency, never mind the maxims of Christianity, do not apply.

This was what bothered me most about the Road to Majority conference. If Jesus warned us that what comes out of our mouths reveals what resides in our hearts, how can we shrug off lies and hate speech as mere political rhetoric? If Christians are called to reflect the awesome power of a God who renews minds and transforms hearts—who dwells within us, seeking our complete devotion to Him, commanding us to lead lives of truth and love that might shine His light in a darkened world—how can there be a special exemption for politics?

I thought about this while chatting with Reed on the final day of the conference. The headline of the event, even outdoing Trump's speech, was an appearance by Herschel Walker, the former college football star who was running for U.S. Senate in Reed's home state of Georgia. Days earlier, the *Daily Beast* had reported a bombshell: Walker was an absentee father to three out-of-wedlock children whose existence he had never publicly acknowledged. It was newsworthy not only because of Walker's crusade against Black dads who abandon their kids, but also because it underscored questions about his character: Walker had a documented history of lying about his academic achievements, grossly exaggerating his business successes, and allegedly threatening on multiple occasions to murder his ex-wife, including an incident in which she claims he pointed a pistol at her head and threatened to "blow [her] f'ing brains out."

When Walker took center stage at Road to Majority, sitting across from Reed for a fireside chat, there was reason to believe he might adopt a tone of humble contrition. Christians are a forgiving people, after all, and Walker had previously owned some of these personal failings, citing a mental illness and claiming that faith in Jesus had changed his life. But he and Reed had another strategy in mind. Assailing the biased liberal media, the two men turned the candidate into a martyr, a courageous follower of Christ who was being persecuted for his godly worldview and patriotic zeal. They didn't exactly dispute the substance of the reporting, but that was irrelevant. By the end of the program, it was Walker—not his traumatized ex-wife, not his fatherless children—who was the victim. "No weapon formed against me should ever prosper!" Walker told the crowd, which stood and cheered at his reference to the Old Testament Book of Isaiah.

This was a microcosm of Reed's entire event. Character didn't matter. Truth didn't matter. Honor and integrity didn't matter. Those were means, and all that mattered was the ends: winning elections. To achieve that end, Reed and his disciples were willing to invoke the name of Jesus Christ, the son of God, and argue that He was on their side.

Sitting backstage with Reed on a black leather couch, as the hotel staff dressed the ballroom tables with elegant white linens for that evening's formal dinner, I put the question to him as plainly as I could.

"You've said that politics is ugly; that this is just the way things go," I said. "But here's what I want to know: Should Christians hold themselves to a higher standard?"

"Well, obviously. *Sure*," Reed replied. "But then you have to define your terms."

He argued that dishonorable conduct in the eyes of one partisan Christian—such as Trump's strategy for litigating the election of 2020—was honorable in the eyes of another partisan Christian. This was a risky detour to take, but I couldn't help myself. I pressed Reed on that point. What about Trump asking the Georgia secretary of state to "find" him enough votes to win the state? What about Ronna Romney McDaniel teaming with self-confessed con artists to lead a coordinated campaign of deceiving the American people? What about all the other people involved in perpetrating that deception—people he'd brought to this event, people who appealed to the Almighty while peddling more lies, all in the name of winning some election? Was that not dishonorable? Did that not diminish the authenticity of the witness for Jesus Christ?

"You know, I—" Reed measured his words. "I think individual Christians have to make that decision about their own conduct. And you know, within the context of a campaign, I think it's fairly obvious that the partisans on both sides are likely to think that partisans on the other side are conducting themselves dishonorably, and think they are conducting themselves honorably. I think that's true whether you're a Christian or not."

Perhaps. But unlike nonbelievers, Christians have a code of conduct that is specific and exacting and unambiguous. Reed's assertion that "individual Christians" could interpret that code however they wished amounted to the kind of moral relativism that had inspired evangelicals to break away from mushy, mainline Christianity in the first place.

As I made this point to Reed, he suddenly looked beyond me, eyes lighting up. "Winsome!"

Approaching us was Winsome Sears, the recently elected lieutenant governor of Virginia. She was dressed casually; her two staff members carried a garment bag and several large portfolios. Reed sprang from the couch to greet them, telling Sears how excited he was for her keynote speech that evening. She seemed a bit anxious.

"So," she asked Reed. "What do you think I should talk about?"

Reed looked surprised. "Uh, didn't I get that to you guys?" he asked one of the staffers.

They said yes, they received his talking points but wanted further direction. Reed rubbed his hands together. He told Sears that she should tell of her upbringing as the daughter of an immigrant; about the "parental rights movement" she had helped champion in Virginia; about Biden "cutting and running" from Afghanistan; about the "radical agenda" that Democrats were forcing on Christians like them; about how the Republican triumph in Virginia the previous fall was "the foreshadowing of what can happen in America in one hundred and forty-three days."

Sears was expressionless.

"But whatever you say, it's gonna be great!" Reed concluded, breaking into a grin.

"Whatever He gives me to say," Sears replied, looking upward.

"Right. Amen to that," Reed said, his face turning solemn. "Because, well, what we've been praying all weekend is that the Holy Spirit would be in charge. That every word uttered by every speaker would be what His will is." He paused a moment. "And what they need to hear."

Sears nodded. "A call to action?" she asked.

The grin returned to Reed's face.

CHAPTER TEN

WASHINGTON, D.C.

*For God did not send his Son into the world to condemn
the world, but to save the world through him.*

—JOHN 3:17

I had begun to tune out the Faith and Freedom speakers by the time
Jim Jordan was introduced. The Ohio congressman's set was indistinguishable from the dozens of others that preceded him. He slammed
"the lefties" who "don't like freedom" and "have disdain for the folks in
flyover country." He observed, "Next to Jesus, the best thing that ever
happened to this world is the United States of America." It felt like the
teleprompter had been stuck on the same page for hours. I stood up to
leave the ballroom.

"I love the comment that Cal Thomas made one time," Jordan told
the audience.

Just like that, I sat back down. Of all the names I expected to be invoked at Ralph Reed's shindig, Thomas's would have been the very last.

Jordan continued, "Cal Thomas had a great line. He said, 'Every
morning, I read the Bible and the *New York Times*, so I can see what each
side is up to.'"

This was close enough to the quote Thomas had famously given
during a 1994 C-SPAN interview promoting his book *The Things That
Matter Most*. A witty and wily observer of American life, Thomas was
at one time among the most-read journalists in the country, with a

syndicated column that appeared in more than five hundred newspapers nationwide. That particular quip about the Bible and the *Times*,
delivered with a playful smirk, was a nod to his past. Thomas had spent
five years working as Jerry Falwell Sr.'s spokesman at the Moral Majority. He was an evangelical Christian and a political conservative—and,
once upon a time, he had used those labels interchangeably.

What Jordan didn't mention is that five years after giving that
C-SPAN interview, Thomas wrote another book. It was a contrition-
laden confessional called *Blinded by Might*, coauthored by Pastor Ed
Dobson, the onetime Liberty University dean and Falwell confidant
who had been present at the founding of the Moral Majority. The authors provided a damning window into the rise of the religious right:
Given how the Scopes Trial had humiliated fundamentalists in the
1920s, and how progressives had hijacked both Church and culture in
the 1960s, Thomas and Dobson recalled believing that Ronald Reagan's presidency represented "the greatest moment of opportunity for
conservative Christians" since the dawn of the twentieth century. "We
were on our way to changing America," the authors wrote. "We had the
power to right every wrong and cure every ill."

But they didn't change America—at least, not in the manner they
had hoped.

Thomas and Dobson acknowledged, in the pages of their book, that
they had not ushered in the sort of kingdom-on-earth spiritual utopia
about which they and so many American evangelicals fantasized. In
fact, there was evidence to suggest that the country was angrier, more
antagonistic, more fearful, more divided—less Christlike—*because* of
the Moral Majority. If Jesus was known for hating sin and loving sinners, American evangelicals were known for hating both. The movement's short-term electoral gains had come at a steep cost. Not only had
the culture moved further away from them; the Church had sacrificed its
distinctiveness in the process. "We think it is time to admit that because
we are using the wrong weapons, we are losing the battle," Thomas and
Dobson wrote.

What they called for was radical: "unilateral disarmament" by the religious right. Christians need not be "political quietists or separatists,"
they wrote, but a wholesale reestablishing of boundaries and priorities

was in order. The Moral Majority's use of shameless scare tactics had tempted the masses of American churchgoers to put their faith in princes and mortal men. This "seduction by power," the authors wrote, was sabotaging the message of Christ. Winning campaigns had become more important than winning converts; scolding the culture had become more important than sanctifying the Church. Mustering some fire and brimstone of their own, Thomas and Dobson warned their old boss Falwell—and his many descendants, biological and otherwise—to stop confusing "spiritual authority for political authority."

The book's publication in 1999 caused a furor inside American evangelicalism. *Christianity Today*, the venerated magazine founded by Billy Graham in 1956, devoted an entire issue to a debate of *Blinded by Might*. (The cover asked: IS THE RELIGIOUS RIGHT FINISHED?) Defending its thesis were former Reagan aide Don Eberly; Paul Weyrich, who had coined the term "Moral Majority" during that fateful meeting two decades earlier; and Thomas himself. Prosecuting the case against the book were Falwell Sr.; Focus on the Family chieftain James Dobson; and Ralph Reed, whose Christian Coalition had grown to become the nation's largest, wealthiest, and most influential evangelical-political organization.

Reed's piece was especially telling. Its headline: "We Can't Stop Now." Listing their many victories in recent years, Reed boasted of how he and his allies had defeated pro-gambling initiatives in numerous states. It would be another six years before Reed was exposed for taking millions of dollars in laundered payments from Indian tribes who enlisted him to mobilize Christian voters against *rival* gambling initiatives in nearby states. This was but one part of the sweeping scandal that took down and imprisoned Reed's close friend, lobbyist Jack Abramoff. Although Reed had technically broken no laws (if duplicity were criminal, he'd be serving a life sentence) the revelations confirmed many a suspicion about the man and his movement.

Hence my surprise to hear Cal Thomas's name mentioned at Ralph Reed's event. I couldn't think of anyone who would be more repulsed by this right-wing revival than Thomas.

A few months later, I met him for breakfast in Washington. The U.S. Capitol Building—its post–January 6 protective fencing having been removed—was visible a couple of blocks away. As we sipped coffee, Thomas, tall and slender and sharp as ever approaching his eightieth birthday, asked what I'd been up to. I told him about attending Reed's event in Nashville. He put his coffee down.

"When Trump mentioned Pence and the evangelical audience booed their brother in Christ, I said to myself, this is the final compromise," Thomas told me. "Here is your brother. Here is a man who worships the Lord that you claim to worship. Here is a man who goes to church every Sunday. Here is a man who has had only one wife and never been accused of being unfaithful. And you're booing him? As opposed to a serial adulterer? A man who uses the worst language you can think of and does every other thing you oppose? Explain that to me from a biblical perspective. Please."

Thomas was not a Never Trumper. In fact, he admitted to me, he'd actually voted for the man twice. Despite his published takedown of the religious right, Thomas still identified as both an evangelical and as a conservative Republican. The difference between the old Thomas and the new Thomas, he explained—the whole point of *Blinded by Might*—is that those identities were now rigidly and properly ordered. This gave him an intellectual autonomy to which his brethren could not relate. Thomas had no issue lauding Trump one day and lashing him the next; taking Republicans to task for falling short of certain moral standards and praising Democrats for meeting others. His organizing principle was not a party platform, but the Sermon on the Mount. Instead of considering his faith in the context of his politics, Thomas considered his politics in the context of his faith.

He was still widely read, still publishing columns that examined social and economic and political questions through the prism of his belief in Christ. But the world around him was unrecognizable.

"I got a letter the other day when I wrote something critical of Trump. The guy accused me of not even being a Christian," Thomas said. "You can't have a legitimate conversation with these people who are all in on Trump. Because if you find any flaw in him, even flaws that are demonstrable, they either excuse it or attack you."

What's interesting, Thomas added, is that nobody went all in on Trump quite like Pence did. Once a respected arbiter of ethical matters, the former vice president forfeited his reputation—not to mention some longtime friends and admirers—by subjugating himself so thoroughly to his boss. But even that wasn't enough to satisfy the MAGA mob. The moment Pence thought for himself, choosing the rule of law over the ego of a president, Trump's minions turned on him. Thomas found himself pitying the former VP.

I did not. Pence, I reminded Thomas, described himself as "a Christian, a conservative, and a Republican—in that order." To lead with that identifier—to profess publicly, time and again, that you're a follower of Jesus before anything else—is to invite and deserve perpetual scrutiny. Unlike all the craven, self-indulgent schemers who had surrounded Trump, the vice president knew the difference between right and wrong. He deserved to be held to a higher standard. Pence did the courageous and honorable thing on January 6, but he was the one who'd spent four years ignoring and excusing all the abuses of power and violent rhetoric and authoritarian impulses that set January 6 into motion.

Thomas wore a stoic expression. Then he began to nod.

"I do wonder if he should have resigned," Thomas said. "He and I talked about this once. I think his view was that he was being salt and light. He was privately counseling the president—I don't know about personal things, but certainly about legislative things. And he felt that he would at least have some effect by remaining on the inside."

Thomas cocked his head sideways, as if struggling with that rationale. "For the president to keep saying the things he was saying, especially asking him to do something unconstitutional—I can see the argument for resigning," he said. "But I can also see the argument for staying there and fighting for what's right."

This had been a defining dilemma of the Trump era for many Republicans, especially Christians who held high-ranking offices. Should those who claim to follow Jesus stick around a situation that requires violations of their conscience, sensing that they might in fact be mitigating an even worse outcome? Or should they flee the scene with their individual honor intact, despite knowing that things might get even worse for the collective in their absence?

During my previous visit to Washington, I'd confronted this same question from a very different perspective.

* * *

IN THE FALL OF 2021, I SAT DOWN TO DINNER WITH TWO MEN WHO, LIKE Thomas, knew something about relinquishing their tribal membership: Russell Moore, who'd recently quit the Southern Baptist Convention; and Adam Kinzinger, a Republican congressman from Illinois who'd become persona non grata to the GOP for serving on the congressional committee that was investigating January 6.

Moore wasn't just traversing the country offering counsel and re-assurance to religious leaders. His post-SBC ministry was aimed at propping up any believer in a position of authority, particularly those who found themselves in the crosshairs of the extremist right. Lots of politicians had sought out Moore's advice on navigating the Trump phenomenon—though few were keen, given Moore's known rivalry with Trump himself, to make that relationship public. Kinzinger didn't much care. He was one of few living souls who knew as well as Moore did what it was like to be assailed, repeatedly, by the president of the United States. It bonded the two men, made them members of a quirky club. Still, they hadn't planned this dinner for the purpose of commiserating. They were meeting because Kinzinger had a fateful decision to make.

He first ran for Congress in 2010, a year characterized by Tea Party fervor and antipathy toward the new president, Barack Obama. Kinzinger was a blue-chip recruit. Raised by a schoolteacher and a leader of faith-based organizations, he had resigned local political of-fice in 2003 to join the Air Force, where he earned pilot wings. He went on to fly missions in Iraq and Afghanistan. Switching to reserve duty, Kinzinger came home to run in a crowded GOP primary and clobbered the field with the help of an endorsement from Sarah Palin, the former Alaska governor and vice presidential nominee who'd become a conser-vative kingmaker. He routed the Democratic incumbent in November and was on his way to Washington.

Over the ensuing decade, Kinzinger proved to be one of the smarter, more levelheaded members of an otherwise boisterous and self-sabotaging House Republican Conference. He helped to negotiate deals and break through congressional gridlock, earning him the "moderate" tag, even as he consistently opposed abortion rights, Obamacare, and tax hikes. Kinzinger was better understood as a pragmatist, someone who valued incremental gains over interminable grandstanding. He did draw lines in the sand. When it came to certain things—national security and political ethics, above all else—Kinzinger considered himself an absolutist. It was not terribly surprising, then, when in 2016 he became one of the first Republicans in Congress to announce he wouldn't vote for Trump in the general election. "I'm an American before I'm a Republican," he told CNN, noting that he wouldn't vote for Hillary Clinton, either.

From that moment on, Kinzinger was a pariah inside the party. It didn't matter that he'd done good work in Washington, or that his constituents loved him, or that he wound up voting with Trump's policies 90 percent of the time. (Kinzinger even voted against Trump's first impeachment in 2019 and for Trump's reelection in 2020.) None of that changed the reality that he was on the wrong side of a binary equation: You were either faithful to Trump or you were his nemesis.

Kinzinger didn't mind being in the barrel. In fact, he found it liberating to be one of a handful of Republicans who could speak candidly about the president without fear of losing their next election. He had dominant showings in both 2018 and 2020, the last remaining Republican to represent the Chicagoland area in Congress. Having survived the worst—the Trump presidency—he was eager to help lead the Republican Party into a post-Trump era.

And then came January 6. Kinzinger knew there would be trouble. According to an interview with journalist Jeremy W. Peters, the congressman told his wife and his office staff to stay away from the Capitol that day. He brought his .380-caliber Ruger LCP to work with him, and when the Capitol Police locked down the building, Kinzinger holed up in his office with the pistol in hand. Later that night, after the complex had been cleared and multiple Americans had died, Kinzinger was sickened to see 147 of his Republican colleagues vote against certifying the results of the election—essentially bowing to the demands of the terrorists who'd stormed the cathedral of American democracy hours earlier. A week later, Kinzinger was one of just ten House Republicans who voted to impeach Trump for inciting the violence and obstructing the transition of power. The rest of his party had shed any pretense of integrity or accountability. His colleagues had made their choice. Now Kinzinger made his: Along with Liz Cheney, the dynastic Republican from Wyoming, he agreed to join the committee investigating January 6.

"Everybody has a responsibility to do what they think is right," he told me at the time. "This is what I think is right."

If Kinzinger's previous criticisms of Trump made him an apostate to the MAGA true believers, investigating January 6 made him downright satanic. This is not figuratively speaking: Kinzinger told the *New York Times* he received a handwritten letter from his cousin, and signed by another eleven family members, accusing him of fighting for "the devil's army" and betraying his fellow Christians. "Oh my, what a disappointment you are to us and to God!" the letter read. "You have embarrassed the Kinzinger family name!"

The congressman said they'd been "brainwashed" by their right-wing churches. And they weren't alone. As the investigation got underway, and Kinzinger got louder about Trump's alleged crimes, the holy war against him intensified. People in the district confronted him with apocalyptic bombast; people from across the country wrote to inform him that he was going to hell with all his Democrat friends. The death threats became relentless. His wife was petrified. By the time we sat down with Moore for dinner, four months into the congressional inquiry, the combat-veteran lawmaker looked like a man who'd hobbled out of a field clinic.

"It just feels like enough is enough," Kinzinger told Moore. "Some days I think about retiring and never running again. Some days I think about quitting the Republican Party and running again. But the one thing I'm not gonna do is run as a Republican again. I just—I *can't* do it."

Moore understood why the congressman no longer wanted to identify with the GOP. He also understood why abandoning the party was harder than anyone on the outside might realize.

"When you leave the tribe, you're going to keep looking back, wondering if you should have stayed, wondering if you could have made a difference," Moore said. "I felt that way when I left the SBC. Watching them struggle, I kept thinking, maybe I could have helped them through this. Maybe it's *my fault* for walking away."

Kinzinger nodded. "That's what I want to know. Can I call it quits, even knowing things will get worse without me here?" he asked Moore. "How do you know when it's time to go?"

Moore told the story about his son suspecting that his father had committed some great moral failure because of all the scrutiny on him, and his wife telling him to prepare for interfaith marriage if he remained a Southern Baptist. Moore said he'd spent years justifying his continued role at the SBC because of "the illusion that if I lose my seat at the table, it will be taken by somebody worse, and therefore it will be my fault that the institution suffers." But his very presence at the table, Moore finally realized, was doing a different kind of damage.

Kinzinger confessed that this was his greatest fear. He shared with us the news that his wife was pregnant with their firstborn. It was a boy. Kinzinger was already preoccupied with making sure that his son one day understood that his father had been on the right side of history.

He sat in silence for a little while. Then, as the check arrived, the congressman told us that he'd been reading that day from the apostle Paul's final letter to his pupil, Timothy.

"I've fought the good fight, I've finished the race, I've kept the faith," he quoted.

Kinzinger announced his retirement a few weeks later.

CAL THOMAS WAS BORN IN THE CAPITAL CITY, CRADLED IN THE CRADLE of power. He went to college there and got his first job there, working as a copyboy for NBC News. His goal was to become "rich and famous by the time I was thirty," and he was well on his way, reporting for NBC's radio and television mediums by his mid-twenties and gaining acclaim as a budding star in the industry. But he was unhappy—deeply, strangely unfulfilled. Then, at thirty, he self-destructed—the details are unimportant, he says—and was fired by NBC.

Thomas began to spiral. His wife, a serious Christian who did volunteer work for the National Prayer Breakfast, asked her husband to meet some of the men she knew through the organization. Thomas was not a serious Christian; he believed abstractly in God, and sometimes attended church out of social habit, but was unschooled biblically. He resisted his wife's appeal.

"She said, 'You won't be a success until you thank God for losing your job,'" Thomas recalled. "She was right. My job was my god. It was the center of my life around which everything else, including my wife and kids, were to circulate."

He gave in. One day, at an intimate gathering in Washington, Thomas listened to a federal judge speak of his "personal relationship with Jesus Christ." The language, so alien to Thomas, utterly captivated him. Before long, Thomas was "born again," assuming a new persona in Christ and vowing to submit himself to God's will. It would prove a halting journey. Like so many D.C. contemporaries, secular and Christian alike, Thomas was a political addict. He saw no issue with fusing the zeal of his Christianity with the convictions of his conservatism. This was how he came to fall in with the Moral Majority. Falwell Sr. needed an ambassador to the Washington press corps, someone reporters knew and liked and trusted. Thomas, with his deep connections to the city's social and political scenes, fit the bill; he was that rare firebrand who regularly dined with his ideological counterparts and considered them close friends. Thomas, adrift since getting axed by NBC, joined the Moral Majority in 1980 and rose to become the organization's vice president. At long last, he felt fulfilled.

Until he didn't. There was no Road to Damascus moment, Thomas says, that made him question his work with Falwell Sr. Rather it was a steady accumulation of doubt, a growing sense of guilt about how the furiousness of their messaging—on any given subject—did not reflect the realities of the matter at hand, never mind the example of Christ Himself. Thomas was all for trying to win elections. But invoking the wrath of God to collect twenty dollars from a retiree in Tulsa started to feel less like a strategy and more like a scam.

"I would go to these fundraising meetings. They would start in prayer and end in manipulation," Thomas recalled. "We had this one fundraiser who was working both sides of the street, like a cheap hooker. His wife was a member of NOW"—the National Organization for Women, a feminist pro-choice group—"and he was raising money for her while also raising money for Falwell. He'd hit his goals, we'd go off to the bar and have a drink, and he would celebrate the stupidity of these people giving to him."

Almost forty years later, Thomas still felt ashamed. This practice of preying on unwitting believers was central to the business model of the Moral Majority and its successor groups.

"You get these letters: 'Dear Patriot, We're near collapse. We're about to be taken over by the secular humanists, the evil pro-abortionists, the transgender advocates, blah, blah, blah,'" Thomas said. "They're always the same. 'If you donate, we'll do a double-matched gift!'"

Little has changed. There were emails in my inbox at that very moment—from Reed's Faith and Freedom Coalition, from Chad Connelly's Faith Wins—that deployed similar language.

"There's always a threat. Look at Tucker Carlson every single night: 'They're out to get you.' And it works," Thomas said. "One time, I actually asked one of our fundraisers, 'Why don't you ever send out a positive letter about what you're doing with people's donations?' And he looked at me with this cynical look. He said, 'You can't raise money on a positive. If the goal is bringing in money, you have to scare them.'"

Little by little, Thomas told me, the limits were pushed. The successes of the Moral Majority became self-justifying: The money raised by dubious methods was evidence of God's blessing on the project, thereby sanctioning ever-more-dubious methods to raise ever more money.

"The worst one I ever saw was where Jerry compared himself to Jesus. It actually said, 'Now I know what it was like for Jesus in the Garden of Gethsemane,'" Thomas said. "And I told him, 'Jerry, you can't say that.' And he said, 'Huh, it must have gone out without my approval.' But nothing went out without his approval. That's just how radical we had become. We had no problem saying that Jesus would have been a Republican. Even though his kingdom's not of this world. How do you get around that?"

Actually, getting around it was simple enough. American evangelicals have a talent for what some theologians call "baptizing the past." That means propagating the tale of George Washington asking a chaplain to dunk him in the icy waters at Valley Forge when no supporting historical record exists; insisting that Thomas Jefferson was a God-fearing humanitarian when he was in fact a slaveholding epicurean deist; seizing upon Lincoln's appropriation of scripture to paint him as an evangelical when he was known to mock revivalists and rarely attend church; and one day, no doubt, citing photos of Trump in an Oval Office prayer circle to argue that the forty-fifth president was himself an earnest follower of Christ.

This is the scaffolding upon which the Moral Majority constructed its edifice of Christian America. It took Thomas a long time to see it. Once he did, he couldn't look away. He was maturing in his faith, and part of that maturation meant questioning his own dogma, challenging his own lifestyle choices. Thomas searched the scriptures to find validation for what he and his friends were doing. What he found instead was a rebuke—and a call to repent. Praying ahead of a meeting with newspaper syndicate executives for a columnist position that would find him published in hundreds of outlets nationwide, he promised the Lord that if he was given this opportunity, he would use it to honor God and not America. Thomas got the gig, quit the Moral Majority in 1985, and has spent the decades since trying—however imperfectly—to keep that promise.

"The Book of Isaiah says that God views all the nations of the world as nothing but a drop in the bucket. All means *all*," Thomas told me. "Now, has America been uniquely blessed? Sure. But it could also be uniquely cursed. You better be careful, because patriotism quickly turns into idolatry. There's more than one way to be an idol worshipper. In the Old Testament, you had Moloch and child sacrifices and all this stuff. But Satan is subtle. We don't have statues now; we have political parties and presidential candidates."

Thomas thought he'd done his penance by writing *Blinded by Might* in 1999. As we refilled our coffee mugs, a quarter century later, he wondered out loud whether something more needed to be done.

"WHEN YOUR IDOLS BEGIN TO DISAPPOINT YOU," RUSSELL MOORE SAID, "it can lead you back to God."

He was speaking to a conspicuously youthful audience at the American Enterprise Institute, the renowned Washington think tank. Here, at a place the right's preeminent scholars have called home since before World War II, Moore was addressing a roomful of grad students, Hill interns, and entry-level political staffers (along with a quorum of tweed-jacketed academic types) who were just getting their start in

Washington. Most of them had never been to AEI before. Most of them had never *heard* of AEI before.

Moore was there to speak about the challenge of decoupling faith from politics. Which explains why the room skewed baby-faced: Years of social science had demonstrated the degree to which young people, even and especially young believers, were alienated from organized religion by the perception of its ulterior motives. Their parents, desensitized by decades of incremental boundary crossing inside the Church, didn't think anything was wrong. But these kids sure did. This was the generation that would make or break American evangelicalism. These were the children of the Moral Majority.

There was no tiptoeing around the disillusionment in the room. Moore opened his speech by suggesting that the popular image of evangelicalism was "Mister Rogers with a blowtorch"—genteel in theory, militant in practice. Heads bobbed up and down. He wanted these young people to know there was potential, even a certain promise, in their disillusionment. This tracked with what I'd heard Moore preach to people of all ages and statuses and locations. But here, addressing the potential future power brokers of Washington, he was even more explicit: All the weakness of our earthly affiliations—to family, to political parties and cultural tribes, even to churches—highlights the strength of our eternal identities.

"Remember, only those with no home are desperate to find one," Moore said. "The normal state of the Christian life is, in some sense, to live in a state of homelessness. If we see that as our normal situation . . . then we can actually engage with the outside world and not be terrified when we're out of step. We can be free."

Moore did not present this reality as optional to the Christians in attendance. In his southern soft-yet-direct manner, he argued that there was no room for interpretation when it comes to the spiritual sequencing of one's life.

"If the gospel is true, that means the gospel is not a means to an end. It's not a tool to excite nationalistic passions, or to form social bonds, or to teach civics. The gospel is the announcement that God has raised the crucified Jesus from the dead and seated Him in the heavenly places at the right hand of God as the heavenly ruler of the cosmos. If that is true, then every other allegiance is subordinate," Moore said, his voice now rising. "Jesus teaches us to pray by asking first of our Father, holy and set apart, for the coming of the kingdom on earth as it is in heaven. And only *then* does He turn to the question of our daily bread."

Our transposal of these priorities—seeking first "all these things" that Jesus promised would be given to us after we'd sought His kingdom—has drained the Christian message of its grandeur. Too many believers have rationalized this, Moore said, by avowing that God is most glorified when Christians hold the commanding heights of society. But this is exactly backward.

"A Christian witness is always best when *not* from a position of power as defined by the outside world," Moore said. He quoted the essayist Wendell Berry: "If change is to come, it will have to come from the margins."

As Moore transitioned into a time of Q&A after the speech, nobody seemed interested in litigating the tactics of the left or in rationalizing the actions of the right. Question after question was searching and introspective. Everyone seemed to agree with Moore's assertion that "the outside world is repulsed by us," but nobody seemed interested in talking about the outside world. The young Christians here wanted to discuss why things had gone wrong in the Church—and what might be done to fix it.

A good place to start, Moore suggested, is for Christians to worry less about perceived enemies and more about supposed allies. I knew just what he meant: Today's evangelicalism preaches bitterness toward unbelievers and bottomless grace for churchgoing Christians, yet the New Testament model is exactly the opposite, stressing strict accountability for those inside the Church and abounding charity to those outside it.

"Throughout the gospels, there are people panicking around Jesus when He's calm," Moore said, offering several examples. "But then there are moments where He shows a flash of anger, and it's not when anyone else is angry. You have the temple courts; the pushing back of marginalized people; the turning of the holiness of God into a commodity. Jesus is incensed. Why?"

The answer, Moore said, is that Jesus has higher expectations for people who profess to know God. Christians are instructed to operate in this same way. When Moore was asked how this could be accomplished practically—how to "balance grace and accountability" for their brothers and sisters in Christ, one student asked—he went straight to the writings of the apostle Paul, starting with his first letter to the dysfunctional early church in Corinth, Greece.

"When he told them not to associate with someone who is immoral, he wasn't saying that with the implications of the world, but of someone who bears the label as a Christian," Moore explained. In the words of Paul: "What business is it of mine to judge those outside the church? Are you not to judge those inside? God will judge those outside."

Moore closed by sharing the story of a former mentor who'd reminded him that "Christianity is not genetic." The point was that some of the most powerful advocates for Christ—from Saint Paul to Saint Augustine, from C. S. Lewis to Charles Colson—once lived far outside of God's family.

"When I talk to atheists and agnostics, most of them are genuinely curious. Some of them are really, really angry. But I know that 99.9 percent of the time they're not angry about theism. They're angry at some parent who used religion in a destructive way, or a pastor who hurt them. . . . This is a person Jesus loves, a person for whom Jesus died, a person who is *hurting*," Moore said. "My responsibility is not to try to win the argument. My responsibility is to stand in [God's] place and say, 'Come, all you who are weary and heavy-laden and I will give you rest.'"

He concluded, "There is no one, no matter how upset we are with their opinions and their actions, who is impossible to reach with the grace of God."

THOMAS AGREED THAT AMERICAN EVANGELICALISM WAS LONG OVERdue for a reckoning. *Blinded by Might* hadn't done the trick, though he and Dobson, his coauthor, were successful in at least forcing a conversation. (Dobson died of ALS in 2015; he caused a firestorm in evangelical circles in 2008 by sharing that, despite still being staunchly anti-abortion, he voted for Obama because the Democratic nominee better represented the teachings of Jesus.) Thomas doesn't know what more he could do to take that conversation to another level. He does know that the problem is worse than it was in 1999.

"We wrote the book to warn the future about the past," Thomas said, conceding that perhaps their warnings weren't stark enough. "Look at this new generation. Over twenty percent of young people have no faith at all. I think part of that is our responsibility—our being evangelicals—because of what we've modeled. These kids don't want to be caught up in the 'us versus them' thing. They have friends who have different points of view, and they think they have to hate them to go to church."

He continued, "The great fault in the evangelical movement today, is that we're disobedient to the commands of the one we claim to follow. What were those commands? Love your enemies. Pray for those who persecute you. Feed the hungry. Clothe the naked. Care for widows and orphans. Visit those in prison. Seek first the kingdom of God."

There are millions of Christians in America who follow these commands with rigor. But there are millions more who do not—or who, at best, follow them selectively and inconsistently. I recalled what Pastor John Torres told me about his congregation at Goodwill Church in the Hudson Valley: Some of his most politically feverish people were also his most generous. It's certainly possible for believers to have warm hearts *and* misplaced priorities. The problem is, the first two commands Thomas cited—love your enemies, pray for those who persecute you—are simply incompatible with the culture-warrior mentality so many otherwise kind and benevolent evangelicals have adopted. The public doesn't see their support of single moms or their donations to African clean-water initiatives. What they do see is a belligerence that overshadows those good deeds and in fact makes the possibility of them seem remote.

"When you ask the average person, what do you think it means to be a Christian? They'll say, pro-Trump, Republican, right-wing, anti-abortion, don't like gays. They'll go down the list," Thomas told me. "Well, why would they say that? Because that's what we're modeling before the world. Those are our public priorities—not these other things, which get so little attention from man but all the attention from God."

That sounded harsh, and perhaps Thomas was utilizing some hyperbole to make his point. But he wasn't wrong. Unlike the Catholic Church, which at least offsets its scandals with bountiful, centralized, highly visible social programs—for the hungry, the disabled, the drug addicted, the abused, the sick, and anyone else who needs help—the evangelical

Church is not exactly synonymous with charity. This isn't because evangelicals are not themselves charitable; to the contrary, research has shown time and again that Christians, both Protestant and Catholic, are more generous with donations than their non-religious peers. It's really a matter of emphasis—as influenced by theology. Whereas Catholics stress the "works" that must accompany faith, Protestants adhere to the doctrine of salvation by grace alone. Intrinsically, then, the "public priorities" of many evangelicals skew away from the social good even as their churches make profound contributions to it.

I was reminded of a conversation with Robert Jeffress at First Baptist Dallas. After touring his quarter-billion-dollar facility, complete with the designer coffee shop and hundred-foot-tall fountains, I asked Jeffress what his church was doing to serve the community in Dallas. It seemed a fair question. Extravagant wealth aside, he and his church were constantly in the news for their political activities; surely he would also want to be known for helping his fellow man. Jeffress mentioned a homeless shelter and a women's health center—commendable projects both—but then hurriedly pivoted away from the subject, not wanting to elaborate on these or any of the other community welfare projects sponsored by First Baptist Dallas. "We're not a sanctified social agency," he said. "That's not what I believe the Church is about."

The remark had echoed through my brain for months. I relayed it to Thomas, who frowned. "Does Jeffress regret going all in for Trump? Feels like we haven't heard from him in a while," he said.

I told Thomas about the arc of my conversations with Jeffress, and reported that, no, the pastor did not have any regrets. Thomas rolled his eyes. He recalled how this was the same Robert Jeffress who'd lectured him and other leading evangelicals—as a means of defeating Mitt Romney—not to settle for anything less in an American president than a Bible-believing, born-again Christian.

"It's like being for civil rights *and* a member of the Klan," he chuckled.

The irony was that Thomas himself was no stranger to the culture wars. Even after *Blinded by Might*, he continued publishing a column that regularly took polarizing positions on already-divisive subjects. Yet he wasn't a villain to the left. This was a man who called Ted Kennedy and Nancy Pelosi friends; a man who wrote conservative op-eds by day and dined with the country's most prominent progressives by night. What was his secret?

"I want to be like Jesus. He ate with 'publicans and sinners'—or, as I like to say, Republicans and Democrats," Thomas said, beaming mischievously. "He hung out with tax collectors and prostitutes. That's what I want to be known for. I want them to see Him in me, so that they will be attracted to Him. That is the purpose of my life."

The words Jesus spoke to His disciples at the Last Supper—"Greater love has no one than this: to lay down one's life for one's friends"—are phenomenal and inspiring. Yet, read in a vacuum, they can create a misconception about God's truly charitable nature. Jesus didn't take on flesh to play favorites with a chosen few; according to Paul, God's love is revealed in the fact that His son died for us *while we were still His enemies*. This is the gospel we are to proclaim both in word and in deed: To be a Christian is to sacrifice not for the benefit of those we already have around our table but for the betterment of those we have never considered to invite.

It's a funny thing about loving your enemies: Once you love them, they cease to be your enemies.

"That's right. When you love somebody, regardless of their politics, it's very difficult for them to hate you. And then you can have a real conversation," Thomas said. "Do you want to convert them, or do you want to condemn them?"

The Bible's best-known verse is John 3:16, in which Jesus reveals God's plan to sacrifice His only son in order that sinners might believe in Him and have life everlasting. But, as Thomas pointed out, the verse that follows—quoted far less frequently—is every bit as momentous: "For God did not send His Son into the world to condemn the world, but to save the world through Him."

He and Russell Moore were making the same point in different ways. Evangelicals have successfully accumulated a type of power that would condemn their enemies and protect their kingdom here. Yet they have squandered the real power that God offers us.

CHAPTER ELEVEN

MT. JULIET, TENNESSEE

*Am I leading a rebellion, that you have come out
with swords and clubs to capture me?*

—MATTHEW 26:55

Nestled in a wooded stretch of exurban Wilson County, Tennessee, the campus of Greg Locke's Global Vision Bible Church felt more like a compound. Heaps of felled oak trees bordered the property, evidence of hurried expansion. A rutted gravel parking lot climbed high away from the main road. At the summit was an enormous white tent. Out front, a sign read: THIS IS A MASK FREE CHURCH CAMPUS.

Inside, men wearing earpieces and camouflage pants guarded the entrance. Behind them, many hundreds of people jumped up and down on a floor of cedar chips. Pastor Locke saluted them as "soldiers rising up in God's army." Some heard this more literally than others: a significant number were carrying guns.

Most evangelicals don't think of themselves as Locke's target demographic. He has suggested that autistic children are subjugated by demons. He organized a book-burning event to destroy occult-promoting Harry Potter novels and other books and games. He called President Biden a "sex-trafficking, demon-possessed mongrel."

If this all sounds a bit strange—ominous, or even "dangerous," as one local pastor warned me the night before I visited—well, sure. But strange compared to what? By this point, I'd been desensitized to all the rhetoric of militarism and imminent Armageddon. The churches that hosted election fraud profiteers and weeknight speakers denouncing the pseudo-satanic agenda of Black Lives Matter—churches that consider themselves mainstream—were starting to feel like old hat. Spectacles that would have appalled and shocked generations of American churchgoers had become commonplace, garish manifestations of a spiritual ecosystem spun so far off its axis that the falcon could not hear the falconer (even with all the yelling, battle axes, and Pence jeering).

It was time, I decided, to visit the furthest fringes. It was time to go see Greg Locke.

Not long ago, Locke was a small-time Tennessee preacher. Then, in 2016, he went viral with a selfie video, shot outside his local Target, skewering the company's policies on bathrooms and gender identity. The video collected more than 18 million views and launched Locke as a distinct evangelical brand. Casting himself on social media as a lone voice of courage within Christendom, he soon aligned himself with figures like Trump henchman Roger Stone, propaganda filmmaker Dinesh D'Souza, and right-wing rabblerouser Charlie Kirk to gain clout as one of the evangelical world's staunchest Trump supporters. All the while, his congregation swelled—moving from their old church building, which seated 250, into a large outdoor tent, then into an even bigger tent, and eventually into the current colossus. The tent holds three thousand people and would be the envy of both Barnum and Bailey.

Which is fitting—because Global Vision is less a revival than it is a circus. On the Sunday morning of my visit, Locke, pacing the stage, asked how many people had traveled to his tent from outside Tennessee. Scores of people raised their hands. "And this is every weekend!" Locke cried in his hickory drawl.

Eager to put on a show for the visitors, Locke announced that his special guest—he tries to book one every Sunday—was the actor John Schneider, who played Bo Duke on *The Dukes of Hazzard*. The crowd erupted. Everyone hoisted their phones in the air, heralding Schneider's arrival like Catholics awaiting the pope.

Schneider had come to speak and sing. There was such energy inside the tent that even some very serious-looking men—dressed in paramilitary gear, firearms strapped to their sides—bounced on their toes and clapped along. Between songs, Schneider offered a different catalog of greatest hits. He talked about the flu shot making people sick. He decried the Christian elites who look down on believers like him. He referred to Biden as "Brandon" and suggested that Christians should prepare to join a violent uprising.

"We are born for such a time as this. God is calling you to do something," Schneider said. "We have a country to get back. And if that fails, we have a country—yes, I'll say it—to *take* back."

Not that one might expect theology from a guy whose claim to fame was portraying a bootlegger who named his Confederate-themed car "General Lee," but this was a curious take on scripture. The notion that God was "calling" on Christians to "take back" their country—especially by force—is laughably incompatible with the teachings of Christ. It was Jesus who subverted the authorities with teachings of obedience and edicts of nonviolence; it was Jesus who mocked His captors for brandishing weapons as they arrested Him. "Am I leading a rebellion, that you have come out with swords and clubs to capture me?" He asked.

After a series of meandering anecdotes that lacked any coherent theme, Schneider finally made clear why he'd come to Global Vision, asking people to go to JohnSchneider.com and support him. Before playing their final song, Schneider's musical partner, a man named Cody, plugged his own album for sale. Then, after an awkward segue into describing the campaign against Jesus in America, he announced they would be closing with a patriotic song. Its title: "Rise Up."

Locke's sermon that day was about the Philistines of the Old Testament stealing the Ark of the Covenant from the Israelites, because they sensed that the only way to defeat God's chosen people was to separate them from God. The same thing was happening in America today, Locke warned. The enemy—liberals—had devised a plot to separate Christians from God, by weaponizing a fake "plandemic" to close down the Church. And all too many Christians were content to let it to happen.

"Let me tell you something," Locke said, his voice snarling. "I ain't never had a prostitute mad at me for keeping this church open! I ain't never had a wino or a drunkard [come] in here and say, 'I can't believe you!' I ain't never had a crackhead mad for keeping this church open! But I get letters from preachers all the time: 'Oh, Brother Locke, you just need to take a chill pill. We feel like you've shamed us.'"

Locke started nodding. "I have! Every last one of them cowards, I've shamed all of them!" The audience went berserk. "Shame, shame, shame!" the pastor shouted, wagging a finger.

At the beginning of the service, Locke had marveled at the turnout, likening this to a Billy Graham revival. It raised an interesting question: How *would* Graham feel about all this?

The most celebrated evangelist of the twentieth century, Graham took his "crusades" to hundreds of nations and preached to millions of people. Whatever his initial political inclinations—warning against the evils of communism in the 1950s, allying himself with Richard Nixon in the 1960s—Graham grew openly suspicious of partisanship as his career wore on. He distanced himself from the religious right, eschewed the Moral Majority, and became known as "America's pastor," the man who met with and prayed over every U.S. president spanning nearly seventy years. Before his death, Graham repented for his early political activism, saying he'd "crossed the line" in ways that harmed his witness for Christ. Still, even in his most unscrupulous moments, Graham was a paragon compared to the self-seekers who would follow him, from the televangelists of the 1970s and '80s all the way to the Ralph Reeds and Greg Lockes of today. There was no foaming, mad-as-hell partisanship to be found at a Graham rally. There certainly were no guns, no calls for violence, no swarms of people dressed—and visibly ready—for combat.

Locke was on a very different crusade, one that more closely aligned with the vanquishing mentality of the Middles Ages than the evangelistic efforts of modern Christian history. Reveling in the sudden rise of Global Vision on that Sunday morning, the pastor said that Christians were done being pushed around. If secularists wanted a war with the Church, Locke said, then a war is what they would get.

"It's time to stand up, it's time to push back, it's time to fight," the pastor thundered. "I've read the back of the book, and we're on the winning side. The left don't win! The socialists don't win! Nancy Pelosi don't win! The devil don't win!"

* * *

LOCKE WAS SIXTEEN YEARS OLD—A WARD OF THE STATE AT GOOD SHEP-
herd Children's Home in Murfreesboro, Tennessee—when he professed
faith in Jesus Christ. This conversion may well have changed the trajectory of his life. But it didn't correct certain behaviors that led to his
teenage detention in the first place.

A self-described "hellion," Locke was arrested five times before going into the state's custody. This had long seemed his destiny: Locke was
a toddler when his father went away to a maximum-security prison on
charges of drug dealing and armed robbery, according to a profile in the
Nashville *Tennessean*. He hated his stepfather and escaped into a rebel
existence of violent music, perpetual fistfights, and eventually crime.

His time at Good Shepherd might have been a minor-league stop-
over, preparing him for a life of professional incarceration, had he not
attended a revival one night. The minister denounced the very activities Locke had been involved with, and at first the youngster didn't take
it well, tracking down the pastor and screaming at him afterward. But
then Locke decided to go back the next night. This time he listened
carefully and, at the end of the program, responded to the altar call and
prayed to be saved.

Soon after, Locke felt called to preach. He began practicing at the
boys' home, then worked odd jobs so he could pay for airtime at a local
radio station. At age nineteen, Locke married an older woman—she had
worked on staff at Good Shepherd—and began attending Bible college.
For parts of the next ten years, he worked as a traveling evangelist with
the independent Baptist movement, visiting forty-six states and fifteen
countries. By the time he was thirty, Locke had gotten tired of life on the
road. He came home and planted Global Vision not far from his childhood home.

It would be some time before Locke started making headlines. In
fact, for a decade after returning to Tennessee, his only controversy was
splitting from the small, fundamentalist Baptist denomination to which
he'd belonged and declaring Global Vision an independent church. To
the extent Locke was known in wider Nashville—an area home to many
hundreds of evangelical churches—it was for Global Vision's dramatic

acts of generosity and community outreach. He staged public events around the area, raising money for the homeless and drug addicted and donating it directly to those in need. (The church continues that practice today.)

Locke's behavior, and his reputation, began changing around 2015. Just before the Supreme Court ruled in *Obergefell v. Hodges* to legalize same-sex marriage, Locke shot a selfie video, titled "I'm Coming Out of the Closet," declaring Christianity to be under attack and encouraging believers to launch a counteroffensive. Locke said that local churches should be "the governing authority" on earth, suggesting that the American political system had become illegitimate for followers of Christ. The video was viewed more than six million times—not bad for a self-described "hillbilly preacher"—and grew Locke's Facebook following tenfold in the space of just a few weeks.

Before long, Locke, once a reluctant user of social media, was living online. On one occasion, he videotaped himself outside a local school accusing teachers of "indoctrinating" kids with lessons about Islam. (Educators in deep-red Wilson County, most of them Christians, explained that the curriculum was standard and had been taught for years.) Another time, Locke ranted on camera against the state's Republican governor, Bill Haslam, for vetoing a bill that would have established the Bible as Tennessee's official state book. ("The men that laid the framework for this nation," Locke taunted Haslam, "didn't use the Quran to do it.")

The formula was simple enough: Just as Donald Trump was weaponizing Twitter, bullying his opponents and building a small army of MAGA enthusiasts en route to the presidency, Locke was using Facebook as a recruiting tool for his campaign against the enemies of Christianity in the broader culture. It was an unqualified success. By the time he shot the video skewering Target's bathroom policies, Locke was gaining hundreds of new online followers every day and scores of new attendees at Global Vision every week. The Target video elevated him from guerrilla scrapper to general in God's American army.

Not everyone was comfortable with Locke's tactics. Some of his original congregants defected from Global Vision, concerned that their missional outreach would suffer from the church's changing reputation.

Locke worried about this himself. The church had been established on the concept of "radical compassion," but now it was known as just plain radical. Whatever money Global Vision raised for the hurting was being dwarfed by the proceeds Locke generated by inflicting pain onto others. Suddenly the reward found in loving one's enemies seemed trivial relative to the reward found in hating them.

If the Trump presidency was a gold rush for right-wing grifters, Locke struck it positively rich, growing Global Vision in proportion to his own bulging celebrity in evangelical circles. He became difficult to ignore. The churn of controversy was incessant—sometimes about his tirades against transgenderism, sometimes about his alliances with MAGA figures, sometimes about his personal life (following an ugly divorce, Locke scandalized some in the church by marrying his ex-wife's closest friend). Where others might have pulled back, Locke always charged ahead, picking any and every fight he could.

The payoff came with COVID-19. Refusing to close Global Vision, and publicly degrading any pastor who decided differently, Locke portrayed himself as an avenger fueled by religious vindication, the lonely voice of boldness inside a retreating American Christendom. His following kept increasing and he kept pushing the limits. His viral videos became ever less about Jesus Christ and ever more about Greg Locke: railing against medical authorities, jeering Biden, discrediting vaccines, protesting in D.C. on January 6. In one of his most-viewed videos of 2020, the pastor accosted a Dunkin' Donuts employee who asked him to wear a mask inside the store.

Locke hadn't responded to my requests for an interview when I visited Global Vision. But several months later, he called me on the phone. I expected hubris and hostility. What I got was something else: skittishness and self-doubt.

"DO I BELIEVE AMERICA'S IN DECLINE? ABSOLUTELY. DO I BELIEVE we've come a long ways from our original values? Yeah. Do I believe the Constitution and the Bible are under attack? A thousand percent. That doesn't mean I'm gonna take up arms against the government," Locke assured me.

Then he added: "I certainly believe in gun ownership. And I've told people, look, we still believe in our First Amendment right. If they show up at our tent to stop us, then we'll meet them at the door with our Second Amendment right."

This rhetorical turnabout—making clear in one gulp of air that he draws the line at violence, then suggesting in the next that his congregants would shoot anyone who tried to prevent the church from convening—was representative of our longer conversation. The pastor was surprisingly pensive and receptive to tough questioning. He would regularly admit to having taken something too far, and lament how a stray sound bite that went viral had distracted from the substance of his sermon. Then he would double down on that sound bite, as if fearful that I took his contrition for cowardice.

Early in the interview, Locke shared a concern. Although he was thrilled with the booming numbers at Global Vision—they were averaging well over two thousand attendees each week, and hundreds of those were first-time, out-of-town visitors—Locke feared that certain people were coming "for the wrong reasons." Some expected an America First festival. Some hoped the church was plotting a seditious uprising. Some believed that Locke would prophesize the arrival of "Q," the fabled forerunner of the QAnon movement, and tell them when to expect military tribunals and public executions of America's leading leftists.

"Everybody thinks I'm automatically Q because I believe that child sex trafficking [is real] and because I believe the election was stolen and things like that. So these people came over and they couldn't switch it off," Locke said. "It's almost like a lot of the Church took on the Q movement, when the Q movement and the Church are really two diametrically opposed organizations."

I told Locke that it sounded like the Q people worshipped a different god entirely. He agreed.

"I don't wanna be put into that mix and amalgamated into the whole QAnon movement, or any other conspiracy theory movement," Locke said. "I think that can be detrimental to the gospel, because what I'm preaching about Jesus is not a conspiracy theory."

But, as Locke had just told me, he *did* think Trump's reelection was stolen. He *did* subscribe to certain beliefs, about vaccines and globalist

schemes and a deep-state regime, that are commonly described as conspiracy theories. Might he grasp why some people who heard him
preach with such authority and conviction—about the central truth
of Jesus *and* about the peripheral truth of these other matters—were
merging the two beliefs systems into one?

"You know, I think that's a fair argument. No doubt," the pastor replied. His counterargument: Most Sunday mornings, his sermons are
ninety percent biblical—"Verse by verse, line by line, word by word"—
and ten percent political. But the popular perception of him is inverted.
People who know him only from a viral video, Locke complained, think
that his material is ninety percent political and ten percent biblical.

"I am flamboyant and animated and demonstrative. When I believe
something, I *really* believe something. So, yeah, I get where somebody
would think, 'This is crazy, this guy's dangerous,'" Locke told me. "But if
they talk to me or sit down with me over a cup of coffee or actually come
to a service, they'd be like, 'Oh, wow, that wasn't nearly as abrasive as I
thought it would be.'"

He laughed. "I think people have a certain perception of me and of
our church—it's Jim Jones and Kool-Aid and all this kind of stuff—when
really we're just a bunch of people that preach verse by verse and line by
line," Locke said. "I just get carried away sometimes."

In his epistle, James likens the human tongue to a small rudder that
directs a massive ship. Locke didn't seem to grasp this concept, shrugging off concerns about his deranged commentary while simultaneously
complaining that he was misunderstood. There was, I suggested, one
surefire way to prove his detractors wrong. If Locke stopped mixing priorities, wouldn't people stop thinking he had his priorities mixed up?

"I think there could be some validity to that," he acknowledged. "We
can operate sometimes in a spirit of fear, because we see our rights being
stripped from us and what our kids are being taught and things that are
glaringly and polar opposite from what we would've grown up with. . . .
But I mean, even from my standpoint, I've grown. I'm almost forty-six
years old now. Are there times that it's been perceived that I cared more
about the kingdom of earth than the kingdom of heaven? Probably. And
that was probably my fault. I probably shot myself in the foot and got a
little too animated about things."

One of those times, Locke said, was the Dunkin' Donuts confrontation. When he learned that the employee in his video had been flooded with threats and hate mail from Locke's followers, the pastor issued a tearful apology to his congregation, admitting he'd been a "jerk for Jesus." (Locke told me, more bluntly, that he'd acted like "a colossal prick.") The pastor asked Global Vision to take up a special offering for the man, then delivered him a check for three thousand dollars along with a personal apology. "What I've learned about the size of our platform is, it does a lot of good, but if I'm not careful to harness its power, it could hurt a lot of people," he said.

Locke proceeded to explain how things were now "very different" at Global Vision. Even in the short time since I'd visited, the pastor said, his approach to leading the church had changed. God had given him a platform over the past decade that he used to draw thousands of people to that hillside tent in middle Tennessee. He now had a flock to shepherd, Locke told me, and didn't have time for any more distractions.

"I'm really focusing on pastoring our people. We have tens of thousands of people all over the world that consider me their pastor, and I've never even met 'em," he said. "I've been canceling a lot of meetings. I've not been going to these rallies. I mean, I got people who want me to go down to Mar-a-Lago. And it's like I've outgrown it, you know? I'm bored with it, to be honest with you. I just want to pastor our people."

Locke didn't stay bored for long.

In the months following our conversation, he returned to those rallies and resumed his old routine from the pulpit. He accused Tom Hanks and Oprah Winfrey of being "pedophiles." He suggested that the president's son, Hunter Biden, should be executed by a firing squad. He called Democrats "God-denying demons" and said, "You cannot be a Christian and vote Democrat in this nation." He boasted about his collection of assault rifles—making noises to mimic the cocking of a firearm—and claimed that Christians had biblical authority to take America "by force." He warned, pointing a finger directly into the camera, "You ain't seen an insurrection yet!"

No doubt Locke was a talented showman. Either he was putting on an act for these people, or he had played a part for me. Which was it?

Locke obviously did believe some of what he said from those stages.

But it was equally obvious that much of his bellicose cruelty was performative. This was a man who assured me, "I'm not against people. You and I, there's no doubt if we sat down, you and I would disagree on a lot of things, but that doesn't make us enemies. It makes us human." Locke had all but winked and nodded at me over the phone, explaining that there was a strategy behind his firestorms; that by kicking up so much fuss he was attracting masses of outsiders to Global Vision, then stealthily converting them to Christ.

But those masses weren't necessarily wise to the game Locke is playing. The thousands of people making the pilgrimage to Mt. Juliet every week aren't aware that Locke actually thinks QAnon is a joke, or that he actually wishes people didn't bring guns to his church, or that he actually believes "Christian nationalism" is a contradiction in terms. They aren't aware of any of that because Locke doesn't tell them. Like so many celebrity shot-callers on the Christian right, Locke sees this charade for what it really is, but does everything possible to make sure that his followers don't.

Coming to the realization that Greg Locke is somewhat rational—a guy who's perceptive and self-aware, contrary to the persona who prowls the stage at Global Vision—might make one feel better about the prospect of restoring some sanity to the American evangelical movement. But I didn't feel any better after that conversation with Locke. In fact, I felt a whole lot worse.

LOCKE IS A GENUINELY GIFTED PREACHER. WHILE HE DEFINITELY spends more than 10 percent of his pulpit time on political rants, his presentation of the other material can be quite compelling. He has an ability to snap off entire chapters of scripture, no notes required, effortlessly lacing Old Testament law and New Testament application with sharp, self-deprecating quips. When he stays disciplined on the substance, Locke's style can be startlingly effective. There is every reason to believe that had he tapped into that rational side, pursuing a career of preaching the gospel and nothing else, Locke might have become every bit as influential as he is today.

Instead, Locke took a shortcut. He discovered that there was a market for being irrational. He came to appreciate that wrath is a business model, that crazy is a church growth strategy, that hating enemies is far more powerful—at least in the immediate sense—than loving them.

The results are hard to dispute. Some of the most prominent conservatives in America have lined up to speak at Global Vision. The president of the United States invited him to Washington for the 2020 Republican convention. Franklin Graham even posed with him for photos at the White House. For that long-ago-troubled kid who dreamed of becoming Billy Graham—and who'd since been shunned by many of the most respected voices in evangelicalism—this must have felt like divine validation.

Locke achieved this legitimacy without surrendering to the evangelical establishment. In fact, Locke made the evangelical establishment surrender *to him*. Prior to COVID-19, his delusional anti-leftist shtick made him an outcast in the evangelical world. But when the virus arrived, and the question of shutting down became a defining litmus test for churches nationwide, Locke went from pariah to prophet. As the country emerged from the fog of 2020, pastors who had defied the government—especially those pastors who made a show of it, then watched attendance double and donations triple as a result—learned what Locke already knew: This was the new normal. They had chosen a permanent side. They had committed themselves to something bigger than an individual public health policy. No longer could the culture wars be selected à la carte. Talking politics was now as much a part of church life as taking communion.

"I don't think there's any going back," Locke told me. "That train's left the station."

Extremism in American churches is nothing new; recall Westboro Baptist Church, the Kansas congregation that achieved notoriety at the turn of the century by hoisting signs claiming that God hates Jews, gays, and dead soldiers. But Locke embodies a distinct Trump-era phenomenon. The most revealing part of my trip to Global Vision was the peculiar sort of indifference I felt at the end of the service. There was nothing sui generis about Locke. He said the same things I'd heard from other pastors on my trips around America. Atmospherics aside—it's not every day you worship inside a tent next to a pistol-toting man wearing an Alex Jones shirt—the substance was familiar and predictable to the point of tedium.

Of course, this would come as a shock to many self-respecting Christians who still want to believe that their pastors are nothing like Locke; that their churches are nothing like Global Vision; that they themselves are nothing like the people in that tent. These self-respecting Christians are in denial. It's easy for evangelicals to dismiss Global Vision as an outlier, the same way they did Westboro Baptist. It's much harder to scrutinize the extremism that has infiltrated their own churches and ponder its logical endpoint. In this environment, if a pastor begins to dabble in conspiracies and political deception, what guardrails exist to keep him from going off the grid altogether? And what if he does go off the grid—does it even register? Just as with our politics, there is no longer a clear line of demarcation between the fringe and the mainstream. Ten years ago, Global Vision would have been considered a cult. Today, Locke preaches to 2.2 million Facebook followers and poses alongside Franklin Graham at the White House.

Walking out of Global Vision, I wondered: How many pastors at smaller conservative churches—pastors like Bill Bolin at FloodGate in my hometown of Brighton—Michigan, would have felt uncomfortable sitting inside this tent listening to Locke? The answer, I suspected, was very few. Global Vision and FloodGate may be different in degree, but they are not different in kind.

What binds them together—Locke and Bolin and the scores of other right-wing pastors I'd encountered over the past few years—is that they are now expected to be something more than mere church leaders. They are political handicappers, social commentators, media critics, information gatekeepers. And they have only themselves to blame: It turns out, when a pastor decides that churches should do more than just worship God, congregants decide that their pastor should do more than just preach.

This might be precisely what some pastors had always hoped for, the opportunity to guide and shape every aspect of their congregants' lives. But spiritually speaking, this is a doomed proposition. Pastors already struggle to provide all the answers written down inside their book. In a modern evangelical culture that punishes uncertainty—where weakness is wokeness, where indecision is the wrong decision—asking pastors to provide all the *other* answers is a recipe for institutional ruin. Because what their congregants crave, more and more, is not so much objective religious instruction but subjective religious justification, a clergy-endorsed rationale for living their lives in a manner that might otherwise feel unbecoming for a Christian.

Down this path, disaster waits. The pastor who finds himself offering religious justification today might find himself inventing it tomorrow. In the darkest chapters of Church history—the Crusades and Inquisition, the slave trade and sexual abuse scandals—the common denominator has been a willingness on the part of Christian authority figures to distort scripture for what they perceive to be some greater good.

This explains why, long after leaving Global Vision, I could not rid myself of its violent imagery—all the guns and the paramilitary gear and the swaggering talk of the Second Amendment. Locke swore this rhetoric was defensive in nature. That's always the case, until it isn't.

CHAPTER TWELVE

SAINT-JEAN-CAP-FERRAT, FRANCE

*In this world you will have trouble. But take
heart! I have overcome the world.*

—JOHN 16:33

The short man in the black turtleneck, the one with the glasses and the salt-and-pepper beard, was no ordinary wartime dissident. His name was Cyril Hovorun.

An Orthodox monk, Hovorun spent a decade in Moscow as the theological aide-de-camp to Patriarch Kirill, head of the Russian Orthodox Church and the second most powerful man in Russia. Hovorun was born in Ukraine and taught around the world, but felt duty bound to lend his intellectual talents to the Soviet mother ship. (The Ukrainian Orthodox Church had existed for centuries under the umbrella of the Russian Orthodox Church.) A special opportunity awaited the young monk in Moscow. Unlike in his native Ukraine, Hovorun explained, only a fraction of the Russian people are practicing Christians. For the vast majority—80 percent of the country's citizens, he estimated—Christianity is "an identity thing, a cultural thing."

Fortunately for the Kremlin, doctrinal conviction is not a precondition for religious tribalism. As the historian Mara Kozelsky observed, "Orthodox Christian nationalism has been on the rise in Russia from the collapse of the Soviet Union," the by-product of a state desperate to rediscover legitimacy in the eyes of a chastened and aimless populace.

Hovorun remembers being alarmed in 2007 when Vladimir Putin announced at a global security forum his desire to recreate the old Soviet empire. What concerned him even more was how, around that same time, the Kremlin began deploying obtrusive language around the restoration of "traditional values." It seemed clear that the strategy of Russia's government—in partnership, Hovorun began to suspect, with Patriarch Kirill and the Orthodox Church—was to create a spiritual rationale for policies that might otherwise prove unpopular.

This church-state alliance seemed mostly ceremonial at first, projecting a renewed Orthodox piety that invited the nation's downtrodden subjects to feel distinctive once more. Russia refused entrance to the pope; targeted evangelicals with a law criminalizing missionary work; and, in a symbolic flex of state power, arrested three female rock stars who protested Putin on stage at a Moscow cathedral. When Russia passed a 2013 law banning "propaganda of nontraditional sexual relationships," it was evident that Putin, in contrast to leaders of the liberalizing and secularizing West, was successfully depicting himself as a global champion of religious and cultural fundamentalism.

But the Kremlin's scheme soon took a more sinister turn. In 2014, Russia invaded and annexed Crimea, a Ukrainian territory of historical import to the Russian people. This blatant violation of international law—as well as the bloody campaign that ensued in the Donbas, a disputed region of eastern Ukraine—was made palatable to the Russian people thanks to Moscow's rhetoric of divine destiny. Gone was any pretense of institutional independence for the Orthodox Church. Vladimir Putin and Patriarch Kirill were now operating in tandem. A host of Kremlin-backed separatists fought to topple Ukrainian sovereignty in the Donbas, but one special battalion stood out. An on-the-ground report from NBC News called them "shock troops." They called themselves the Russian Orthodox Army.

By the time Putin launched a full-scale invasion of Ukraine in 2022, the Kremlin had perfected a propaganda that casts nationalist aggression in terms of cultural defense, geopolitical conquest in terms of religious obligation. This was a throwback to pre-Enlightenment casus belli. Russia had entered both world wars on protective grounds; now Putin was harkening back to a time before the last tsar, and nobody could stop him. The Russian people were convinced, Hovorun said, that they were fighting "a sacred war" to liberate Ukraine from secularists, apostates, even Nazis. And though much of the heavy lifting was done by Patriarch Kirill—who told Russian troops mobilizing toward Ukraine to "remember that if you lay down your life for your country, you will be with God"—history would record a new canon being authored by Russia's president.

"This phenomenon," said Hovorun, who went into self-imposed exile prior to the Crimean conflict, "I would describe as the political theology of Putinism."

IN THE FALL OF 2022, AS THE RUSSIAN INVASION OF UKRAINE WAS limping toward an inglorious stalemate, Hovorun spoke to a small gathering of journalists and academics in the south of France.

The setting was incongruous with the subject matter. Perched atop a luxury resort overlooking the French Riviera, the soft-spoken monk analyzed the ongoing atrocities in his native Ukraine. This juxtaposition was not by design—the event, hosted by the nonprofit Faith Angle Forum, also featured panels on China and democratic breakdowns in Europe—though it did serve as a useful device for framing the conversation. So many of the Westerners gathered, Americans and Europeans alike, were "going about our daily lives," Faith Angle moderator Josh Good said, largely ignorant to the "strange reality" that a ferocious land war was raging one thousand miles away.

The war wasn't going well for Putin—that much was known. The Ukrainians were staging an inspired defense of their homeland, and Russian morale was crumbling. One reason for that, Hovorun told us, was that the Kremlin's religious rhetoric had worn thin on the Russian *troops*. Whereas notions of an ordained offensive had worked in Crimea, as well as at the outset of the Ukraine invasion, there was now substantial evidence of Russian soldiers discovering that they'd been duped by Moscow. There was no legion of Nazis awaiting them in Kyiv. They weren't being greeted as holy liberators. There was nothing hallowed about shelling this friendly neighboring nation.

This sounded to us Americans like excellent news. But Hovorun did not seem particularly hopeful. The propaganda campaign was still highly effective back at home. With the aid of state-run media and a blockade against Western information, the Kremlin had convinced much of the Russian public that their sons were engaged in a sanctified struggle. It wasn't just the Russian people being brainwashed: Tucker Carlson, at the time still the top-rated Fox News personality, spent the first year of the war defending Putin's honor, downplaying his savagery, and describing America's aid to Ukraine as a secular "jihad" aimed at toppling "an orthodox Christian country with traditional values." (He was joined in this effort by far-right American lawmakers, such as Republican congresswoman Marjorie Taylor Greene, who ranted on Carlson's show about "this war against Russia in Ukraine.") Carlson's programming was played in a loop on Russian state television to reinforce the Kremlin's talking points. That Putin was losing this holy war—death tolls can be manipulated, but not concealed entirely—only gave him cause to escalate.

"The intensity of the theological language has really increased" from Putin, Hovorun warned us. "His rhetoric has made a long journey from de-Nazification to de-Satanization."

Putin's troops mostly knew by this point that they weren't fighting against Lucifer in Ukraine. But it hardly mattered anymore. The stir of national humiliation, on top of persuasive economic incentives—warriors are paid three times the median wage in Russia, according to news reports—had guaranteed a longer and uglier war than anyone had imagined. As we gathered in France, the list of documented war crimes committed by Putin and his troops was impossible to ignore. Mass grave sites with civilian bodies. Strikes against hospitals and children's refuge homes. Evidence of torture and potential genocide.

"When you have a special mission from God, then you are not bound by moral norms," Hovorun said. "You are free to do whatever your mission requires you to do."

Hovorun was quick to clarify something: Putin is not *really* a religious man. The Russian leader practices "an eclectic theology," he said, that cherry-picks whatever spiritual concepts support his ideological agenda. The one constant—the one thing Putin believes in—is power. By weaponizing religion, Hovorun said, Putin had accumulated more of it than ever before.

Russia wasn't merely using Christianity to endorse its ambitions. Russia was using Christianity to define its enemies. It was the kind of identitarian programming that presaged some of history's greatest crimes—and, in the case of Russia's butchery in Ukraine, it would not have been possible without the blessing of the Church.

"IDENTITY IS NOT BARBARITY," MIROSLAV VOLF TOLD US. "BUT IT CAN lead to it."

Volf would certainly know. A renowned theologian who heads Yale University's Center for Faith and Culture, Volf had traveled to France to share the dais with his fellow scholar Hovorun. Raised in the former nation of Yugoslavia, Volf was the only Protestant in his high school. He was the son of a Pentecostal minister who, like most Protestants, was monitored closely by the governing authorities. Volf grew up buffered by ethno-religious boundaries: The republic of Croatia was predominantly Catholic, the republic of Serbia was predominantly Orthodox, the republic of Bosnia and Herzegovina was predominantly Muslim, and the churches in these and other states preached a dogmatic nationalism as Yugoslavia careened toward civil war in the late 1980s.

"The world was uniting but Yugoslavia was falling apart," recalled Volf, a lanky, bald-pated professor, his accent still distinctly Eastern European. "What we experienced was a religiously motivated reassertion of ethnic identities."

The result was a decade of genocide and ethnic cleansing. The carnage is difficult to quantify, but scholars generally believe that some 150,000 people were killed and as many as 4 million others were displaced by the violence in the Balkans. The chief instigator was Serbian president Slobodan Milošević, who rose to power by vilifying the Muslim Kosovans within his state. Historians point out that Milošević, in delivering a national address that sparked the civil war, cited the recorded persecution of *his* people by rival religious factions. He delivered the message flanked by Orthodox priests.

This is the world from which Volf emerged. Having returned to his native Croatia to teach after completing his theological studies in the West, Volf left in 1991, the year Croatia declared independence, and watched from the United States as his homeland was ravaged by internecine violence. The professor has since dedicated much of his career to preventing a historical encore. His advocacy of nonviolence—"I take seriously the commandment of Jesus that one should love one's enemy," Volf said, citing it as a cornerstone of the Christian faith—can only accomplish so much. To head off what he fears is a resurgence of religious totalitarianism, Volf was attempting to reclaim his own faith tradition from the extremist fringe.

The narrative arc of the Bible tells of an aspirational evolution in mankind's thinking, Volf said. What began in Exodus—the story of God's chosen people escaping bondage and eventually coming into the covenant state of Israel—was finished by the arrival of Jesus, who taught His disciples to take His message to *all* the nations. The transformational effect of this cannot be overstated. Immediately, all but overnight, a people who had refused to associate with anyone outside their ethnic tribe began calling them brothers and sisters. "There is neither Jew nor Gentile, neither slave nor free, nor is there male and female, for you are all one in Christ Jesus," Paul wrote in his letter to the Galatians.

The Bible's final book, Revelation, paints a utopic vision of Christ living among His followers in a New Jerusalem. This is the believer's pluralistic destiny, a heavenly melting pot where descendants of every nation, ethnicity, and race are unified, forevermore, in the body of Christ. That vision can be difficult to see, Volf said, when professing Christians are engaged in a "twisting of the religious landscape" that rationalizes social antagonism, clannish nihilism, and even physical violence.

None of this is unprecedented. Religion and politics are natural enemies; both provide a sense of belonging and self-actualization to the masses. Tension between the two is healthy and necessary. When one appropriates the other, history shows that oppression—leading to death and human suffering at a woeful scale—is the inevitable result.

What Volf watched take root in Yugoslavia has been seen throughout the centuries and continues to repeat itself. In his view, there are three features of creeping totalitarianism in the name of religious conviction. The first can be seen when leaders assert the primacy of an ethnic or cultural identity over shared humanity. The second is when they stress the purification of those identities (inevitably leading to forms of ethnic cleansing). The third is when violence becomes legitimized for the protection of group identities.

People of the modern world are "living in a gap," Volf said, stuck between a pre-technology age that is fading away and a futuristic world that has yet to fully arrive. The resulting anxiety—around the crumbling of institutions, the instability of cultures, the insufficiency of economies—creates a crisis at the intersection of religion and politics. Volf fears that Christians are *claiming* to navigate this rupture via religious identity but are *actually* navigating it via political identity. When believers invoke eternal symbols to advance an earthly goal, those symbols become cheapened to the point of ultimately meaning nothing. This is what happened in the Yugoslavia of Volf's youth. This is what is happening in Ukraine today at the hands of Vladimir Putin and Patriarch Kirill. And this, he warned us, is what could happen elsewhere if current trends go unchecked.

Volf threw up a hand symbol—like a peace sign, but with the thumb jutting out—that was commonplace among Christian soldiers in Eastern Europe. Its aim was religious. Instead of two fingers calling for peace on earth, three fingers, representing the Trinity, meant to summon God's blessing.

"But if you see a fighter riding on a tank flashing this sign, none of that theological content is on their minds," Volf said. "That is a religion that has been completely hollowed out of its internal content. It is functioning simply as a marker of identity."

I could think of a few markers like that.

ALTHOUGH THIS WAS A CONVERSATION BETWEEN TWO EASTERN EUROpean scholars, taking place in France, about a war between Russia and Ukraine, the subtext very much centered on the American evangelical Church. Hovorun fought a smirk while describing how Putin manipulated his countrymen into buying a revisionist "founding myth" of their nation, his ultimate goal being to "Make Russia Great Again." Volf, noting the hard conversations he's having with his American students, detailed the ways in which religion and nationalism were motivating "today's totalitarian movements" (the plural was not lost on anyone in the room). Neither one of these erudite, dignified gentlemen seemed eager to discuss the sordid details of what was transpiring across the pond. But the rest of us were.

America was not engulfed in a land war; it was not waging holy war against a sovereign nation. There was, however, a war for the essence and the character of American Christianity, and it was reverberating the world over. In recent years, I had spoken with missionaries and evangelists spanning multiple continents, and they all shared the same fundamental concern. Was all this nationalistic talk from the American evangelical Church just that—talk? Or was it indicative of a serious effort to restructure the relationship between the state and the country's dominant religion? And if it was the latter, why weren't sane Christians doing more to stop it?

This last question haunted me most. In the years following September 11, 2001, as the Taliban and al-Qaeda and ISIS slaughtered innocents in the name of Allah, Western intellectuals fixated on the idea of finding and elevating "moderate Muslims" who could help reclaim the religion from its violent extremist fringe. The wisdom and efficacy of this strategy was dubious, yet it struck me that Christianity was probably overdue for a similar conversation—globally, in Russia, and in the United States. This was not to equate suicide bombers with January 6 rioters, or to compare body counts between Putin and Osama bin Laden, but rather to observe that there are consequences when religious doctrine becomes infected with political ideology. While the scope of the American crisis at present seemed trivial relative to, say, the Crusades, things had gotten very bad very quickly and would only get worse unless something was done about it.

But what? Having spent a lifetime immersed inside this world, it was unclear to me what—or, more realistically, *who*—might help to bring American evangelicalism back from the brink. There was no longer reason to believe that some calamitous intervening event could unify the Church; we had just endured a once-in-a-century pandemic, and it made existing divides that much deeper. The situation seemed almost hopeless. It was an unfair fight for the soul of American Christianity. On one side were decorated veterans of the culture wars, archconservative Christians who live for conflict. Meanwhile, their more "moderate" counterparts—in temperament, not theology are inherently reluctant to enter the fray. (Those who believe that their struggle is not against flesh and blood, I had learned, were the least likely to struggle against flesh and blood.)

Unpacking all this for Volf and Hovorun—with an apology for viewing their universal discussion through a narrower prism—I asked what hope they had for the American evangelical Church.

"I'm wondering how many American Christians, even conservative evangelicals, think in those purely spiritual terms," Volf replied. He didn't think it was a fair fight, either, though for somewhat different reasons. Whereas I was suggesting that the silent majority needed to speak up, Volf wasn't sure they were a majority anymore at all.

He told us that something had changed during his decades spent teaching and engaging with Christians in America. A generation earlier, this militant approach to theology was discernable only below the surface. But the Church had since been "captured by nationalist ideals" that saturated the evangelical ecosystem. Volf said he believed that Christian nationalism was now "the predominant form of evangelical Christianity" in the United States—and he "frankly had no idea" what to do about it.

"There's something really powerfully insular about this vision that it's almost like I have experienced it as impenetrable," he told us. "Just as it's very difficult to talk to your neighbors who disagree on political grounds, so also it's difficult to have theological discussions at all."

I asked Volf whom he held responsible for this tapering of our theology in the American Church.

"There is a loss of educated, thoughtful leadership," he said. "Leaders of evangelicals have become media personalities. Paula White is a very good example of somebody who is highly, highly influential, but has the thinnest of all possible understandings of the complexities of faith."

The gates to Mar-a-Lago were flung open now. Emboldened by the mention of Trump's pastor, the British journalist Emma Tucker—who, soon after this convening, was named editor in chief of the *Wall Street Journal*—followed my question with an even better one. She asked Hovorun whether, given the nature of Putinism as a "secular religion" in Russia, he saw the same forces at play with Trumpism in the United States.

"Certainly, we are dealing with a similar sort of secular religion," Hovorun replied. Under this canopy of secular religion, however, he stressed a key distinction: "political religion" versus "civil religion." The former is imposed by the state, while the latter is practiced voluntarily. As Hovorun explained the history behind these definitions, it became obvious why he was so invested in our understanding of them.

"Political religion is [not] optional," he said. "That was exactly Hitlerism, Nazism, communism. They were political religions. They were much more violent, and that is exactly the transformation that happened to Putinism. It started as a civil religion with a set of rituals, quasi-religious rituals, ideas that were optional for the Russian people. Now it's not optional anymore. It's a political religion with [the] power of imposition upon the Russians."

He added: "In Trumpism, we are still dealing with civil religion—a form of civil religion. It's not *yet* political religion."

Hovorun stabbed a finger into the air as if to suspend his thoughts. After Trump won the presidency in 2016, he told us, he submitted an article to the conservative ecumenical magazine *First Things* arguing that Trumpism could become America's first political religion. The article was rejected. Surely the editors found his premise a bit exotic. The brilliance of our kingdom is in its curbs on autocracy: term limits, checks and balances, a peaceful transition of power. And yet, long before the mayhem of January 6, Hovorun argued that all of this was beside the point: Just as the political theology of Putinism was now bigger than Putin himself, Trumpism as a religious ideology was taking root in ways that would endure after Trump left office. The magazine editors spoke for most American Christians in refusing to entertain the notion that what had transpired in Russia—an abrupt, ensanguined transition from civil religion to political religion—could happen here.

"I still believe it is possible, unfortunately," Hovorun said.

* * *

TO THE EXTENT HOVORUN REMAINED OPTIMISTIC, IT WAS BECAUSE OF A
basic difference between American evangelicalism and Russian Orthodoxy. "Political evangelicalism, at least rhetorically, is Christ-centric,"
he said. "Political Orthodoxy is not. It avoids speaking about Christ.
If you take Putin or others, they don't speak about Christ. They speak
about other things in the faith."

But Volf wasn't sure that the rhetoric mattered anymore.

"I've come to believe . . . that the Christ of the gospel has become a
moral stranger to us," he said. "If you read the gospels, the things that
profoundly mattered to Christ, they marginally matter to most evangelical Christians. And the things that really profoundly matter to them,
marginally mattered to Christ."

He added: "In the sense in which Christ is the key to Christianity—
you cannot have Christianity without Christ—we are, in a certain sense,
in this crisis of Christianity precisely because of a certain alienation
from Christ."

One of the journalists asked Volf to be more specific. Could he offer
some examples of the things that mattered profoundly to Christ? The
professor's eyes danced at this open-ended invitation to proselytize.

Christ concerned himself greatly with the poor, Volf said, but the
poor are "hardly mentioned" in today's evangelical discourse.

Christ actively avoided fame, Volf said—asking the people on whom
He performed miracles not to tell anyone—but today's evangelical leaders are "drunk on fame."

Christ demanded that we love our enemies, Volf said, but "not even
lip service is being paid to this" in today's evangelical churches.

"I can go down the line of the fundamental values of modernity—the
fundamental values of most of us—and contrast them to what one finds
in the gospel. You find incredible discrepancy," the professor concluded.
"I find it deeply, deeply disturbing."

Thomas Chatterton Williams, a Paris-based journalist who was born
in the United States, offered a final thought on "the American situation"
Volf was describing.

"My maternal family are evangelical Christians, and my aunt is someone that I think of as keeping Christ very personally in her life," Chatterton Williams said. "She voted for Trump twice and said that he's a very flawed human being, but the only way she could get herself motivated to block a truly evil woman"—i.e., Hillary Clinton—"was to think that God works with flawed human beings all the time to do a greater good."

That same aunt, he said, had just moved from California to Georgia. During a recent phone conversation, she told him that she was planning to vote for Herschel Walker, the Republican candidate for U.S. Senate. It didn't matter that a proliferating number of news reports, beginning with a blockbuster story in the *Daily Beast*, offered credible and compelling evidence that Walker had paid for at least one abortion. It didn't matter that Walker's son—the one child he had publicly acknowledged, not the three others—had responded to the news by tweeting that his father, a self-professing "moral, Christian, upright man," had in fact abandoned him and his mother to "bang a bunch of women" and then "threatened to kill us." None of these flagrant character flaws were relevant to his aunt, Chatterton Williams said, because Walker, like Trump, was playing for the right team.

"I'm trying to square this," he said to Volf. "How can Christianity accommodate itself to such appalling anti-Christian conduct? And once you get to a point where you can say anybody's conduct can be excused because God has a larger plan and uses flawed vessels, then what is left of an actual Christianity at that point?"

Volf could only shake his head, searching for the words.

"I think you've identified the problem really well," the professor said.

THAT HERSCHEL WALKER WOULD CLOSE THAT U.S. SENATE CAMPAIGN BY likening his Democratic rival to Satan incarnate was not surprising. After all, the success of Putinism and Trumpism owes to a *literal* demonizing of the other—casting adversaries as not just wrong or obnoxious but as wicked and diabolical. Because these political-religious movements depict opponents as evildoers, it is intrinsically difficult to defeat them on theological grounds. And yet, both Volf and Hovorun argued, this is the *only* way of defeating them. Denouncing cruelty and

malice and violence in a political context only achieves so much, because politics are naturally cruel and malicious and violent. To expose
the shallowness of these secular religions, Hovorun told us, "they need
to be deconstructed theologically."

That term, *deconstruct*, had come to represent a great rift within
American evangelicalism. The concept was hardly new, yet it took on
heightened significance during the Trump era: Christians who'd been
raised in the evangelical tradition—reared in churches that effortlessly
synthesized conservative theology with the zero-sum tribal politics that
led to Trump—began to question their beliefs. If their parents and pastors had been so mistaken about the politics, the thinking went, what
had they gotten wrong about the theology?

I never considered myself a deconstructionist, though I empathized
with the underlying sensibility. In my view, biblical Christianity requires a constant reassessing of one's beliefs and biases; deconstruction
is something that should be done every single day, not in response to
some black swan event. Tellingly, much of the modern evangelical lobby
had condemned deconstructionism writ large, claiming (wrongly) that
it was some progressive political device and fearing (rightly) that it
would stir uneasiness in their churches.

Hovorun and Volf were prescribing deconstruction on an industrial
scale. This went far beyond challenging individual interpretations of
scripture. What they envisioned was a collective and decentralized effort on the part of serious, kingdom-first Christians of all partisan persuasions to strip these secular religions of any theological legitimacy.
The best antidote to bad religion, as Volf noted, is good religion.

Hovorun pointed to a hopeful precedent. It was Volf's mentor, the
German theologian Jürgen Moltmann, who helped to lead an in-
terconfessional effort that rectified so many deadly distortions of
Christianity in post–World War II Europe. This was no easy feat.
For decades, Hovorun said, "totalitarian theology" had seized much
of Europe. Christo-fascists had a foothold inside the Roman Catholic Church. The Deutsche Christian faction in Germany was rabidly
antisemitic. Orthodox leaders in Romania and elsewhere in Eastern
Europe spewed antidemocratic propaganda. It took the extermina-
tion of six million Jews—at the hands of soldiers wearing a twisted

cross—for Christians to deconstruct this fascism, antisemitism, and authoritarianism. "Putinism is a mosaic consisting of all those pieces," Hovorun said. "We need to come together and figure out how to deal with this new monster, which is so similar to the totalitarian theologies of the thirties."

What made the old monster so difficult to slay, Volf told me over lunch afterward, was that it feasted on the trembling heart of man. Jesus instructed His followers to "take heart!" because He had overcome the troubles of this world. But most of us don't listen. Christians remain just as susceptible to panicky groupthink and identity-based paranoia as anyone else. Despite Jesus promising His followers that they would suffer—or perhaps *because* of this promise—Christians since the age of Constantine have run anxiously into the arms of the state, desperate to be protected by the rulers of their time and place. The irony, Volf said, is that Jesus Himself was killed by the state because He was daring enough to "offer an alternative to the powers that reigned in the domain where He was."

A willful blurring of lines—between those powers and the alternative—led to calamity in the last century. History might repeat itself, Volf warned, if we don't heed the words of Karl Barth, the legendary Swiss theologian who prosecuted the theological case against Hitler and Nazism. If the Church is to practice the teachings of Christ, Barth wrote, it must be "an unreliable ally" to every social, political, and government order of this world.

This is not always an easy message to preach. Volf's mentor, Moltmann, possessed a singular credibility because of his proximity to the Nazi cause. Drafted into the German army at age sixteen, he surrendered to the first British soldier he encountered and spent three years as a prisoner of war. An American chaplain supplied the Bible that would alter the course of his life. Moltmann's reflections on the atrocities of Auschwitz—and his teachings on the benevolence of a sovereign God, one who took the form of man in order to bleed and grieve alongside us—did as much to shatter the spell of Nazism as any B-17 bomber.

Listening to Hovorun during our time in France, I could tell he was following a similar blueprint. The onetime Russian Orthodox insider turned dissident-in-exile was traveling the world at considerable personal risk to warn of the dangers of Putinism. He was proving highly effective.

It made me wonder about Trumpism and the American evangelical movement. Was deconstruction even possible without atonement from the people who'd been part of the problem? We probably shouldn't expect any sweeping, transformational contrition from the likes of Robert Jeffress or Greg Locke. Maybe the best we could hope for was a course correction at the grassroots level, a model of reconciliation in miniature, some wrongs made right by the rank-and-file pastors who'd led their churches into crisis.

The problem with this hope: Most of these pastors couldn't see the crisis at all.

CHAPTER THIRTEEN

ERIE, PENNSYLVANIA

*You would have no power over me if it were
not given to you from above.*

—JOHN 19:11

Inside the Bayfront Convention Center, an architectural peninsula
bounded by the shimmering indigo waters of Lake Erie, men with artifi-
cially enhanced muscles strutted around the lobby grunting and jogging
in place and bending in ways that tried the elasticity of their spandex
suits. They carried powders that assured them of Samsonian size, vitamins vowing vascularity, pills promising paradisiacal pectorals, all
manner of almost supernatural betterment.

Just down the corridor, security officials manned giant magnetometers. It was a jarring sight—there was no president or head of state here,
only a long-shot candidate for governor—but Doug Mastriano, the Republican running to lead the Commonwealth of Pennsylvania, wasn't
taking any chances. Since announcing his candidacy in January 2022,
Mastriano, a military veteran and would-be theocrat with extensive
ties to far-right Christian nationalist groups, had portrayed himself as
a commander in our great religious conflict. Forces of evil were laying
siege to the country, Mastriano had warned, and Christians needed to
expel them. As his campaign progressed, this doomsday talk escalated.
The metal detectors in the hallway served as a visual reminder: The
enemy was out to get Doug Mastriano.

As it turned out, the checkpoint was surprisingly useful. Despite posted signs at the entrance—"No guns, No knives"—several people had walked up to the event with weapons on their person, only to be turned back. (The ones I saw retreated to their vehicles, stashed the items, then returned to the rally.) Violence was an undercurrent of the event. Just past the magnetometers, dozens of people clustered around folding tables in the foyer outside a large ballroom. Some were clad in camouflage and paramilitary gear; I recognized them as members of Mastriano's personal security detail, guys from his church who escorted him around the state, arms at the ready, willing to lay down their lives for the Republican candidate. Others in the crowd were more casual; they wore shirts with bull's-eyes and Second Amendment expressions. Even the little old ladies volunteering behind the tables, selling buttons and bumper stickers and yard signs, wore olive-green shirts with military-style campaign font.

One of them greeted me warmly as I hovered over a pile of campaign literature denouncing Critical Race Theory. "I'm so excited," she told me. "Can you believe *Jack Posobiec* is here?"

I could, actually.

A conspiracist luminary, Posobiec rose to fame on the far right in 2016 by championing #Pizzagate, the internet rumor that alleged Hillary Clinton and a cabal of top-ranking Democrats were running a child sex-trafficking ring from the basement of Comet Ping Pong, a trendy pizza joint in Washington, D.C. Posobiec was no casual participant in #Pizzagate; he personally visited the restaurant to investigate, surreptitiously livestreaming footage of what he later described on Alex Jones's *Infowars* channel as "demonic artwork" and "a secret door" that seemed suspicious, given the presence of so many "little kids." The video exploded on social media after being uploaded to YouTube. Two weeks later, a man drove to D.C. from North Carolina, walked into Comet Ping Pong, and opened fire with his AR-15 rifle. (The man told police that he'd come to save the children, only to realize the restaurant had no basement; thankfully, nobody was hurt.) Posobiec never apologized for his starring role in fomenting what law enforcement agencies declared to be a brazen, dangerous falsehood. Indeed, he was just getting started.

Over the next four years, Posobiec, a protégé of Trump henchman

Roger Stone, distinguished himself—even inside the crowded MAGA ecosystem of professional radicals and for-profit reprobates—as especially prolific. He spread the despicable lie that Seth Rich, a young Democratic staffer who'd been murdered one night in Washington in 2016, was killed as part of a cover-up after he'd leaked sensitive party documents. He speculated about U.S. immigration policies being part of a planned "white genocide." He cultivated ties with a sprawling network of anti-government extremists, antisemites, and white nationalists. In 2020, months before the presidential election, Posobiec helped to popularize the phrase "stop the steal," which Trump and his allies would use to rally millions of Americans against the peaceful transition of power.

In this effort, Posobiec found an ally in Mastriano. A state senator from southern Pennsylvania, Mastriano had claimed that Biden's victory in the commonwealth was "compromised," proposing that he and his fellow legislators could unilaterally switch the state's electoral votes to Trump. This cannot be viewed in a narrowly political context: Mastriano, who described himself as an agent of God's will, felt unbound from the pesky laws and procedures that govern American elections. Sure enough, when his legislative subterfuge failed, Mastriano joined a Zoom call organized by prominent Christian nationalists in December 2020—well after the Electoral College had voted to install Biden as the next president—and, according to video unearthed by *Rolling Stone*, prayed that God would empower Republicans to "rise up with boldness" and "seize the power" before Joe Biden's inauguration. A week later, Mastriano not only joined the January 6 protests in Washington but used campaign funds to charter buses to Washington so that his constituents could attend.

When he launched his campaign for governor a year later, in Gettysburg, Pennsylvania, an elaborately robed minister blew a shofar to signal Mastriano's entry into the race. The message was unmistakable: Americans were approaching a second civil war. A *spiritual* civil war.

The people of Pennsylvania seemed less than enthused about this. Nor did they seem receptive to his plan, which he'd casually spoken out loud, to use his executive power to withhold Pennsylvania's electoral votes from the Democratic candidate in the next presidential election.

By the time Mastriano and Posobiec came to Erie in October 2022, the Republican nominee trailed his Democratic opponent, Josh Shapiro, by double digits. In an electoral environment highly favorable to the GOP—Biden's popularity had cratered earlier that summer due to historic inflation—it was curious to see a Republican getting thumped in one of America's most competitive battleground states.

But Mastriano wasn't concerned. The stage was being set, he told supporters in Erie, for a miracle of biblical proportion.

"We're gonna take our state back by storm!" Mastriano declared, predicting that he would "shock the prognosticators" on Election Day. The audience roared. "Something is happening, something really incredible," he said. "And I think our founder, William Penn, would be proud."

Switching into professor mode, Mastriano told of how Penn "founded our state to be the seat of the nation." It was part of a "holy experiment" to establish a God-fearing government of men. "America owes everything to Pennsylvania," he argued, and in turn, America owes everything to William Penn, a man whose contemporaries said "belonged to the wrong religion" and "talked about Jesus too much" and "had the wrong political beliefs."

Mastriano pitched himself as a twenty-first-century iteration of the Quaker legend. But whereas Penn had overcome the persecution of his times, Mastriano worried openly about falling to his enemies. It would represent more than a political loss; it would be a defeat of the idealized nation that Christians had fought and bled for since coming to this land.

"It's an incredible dream, and we've come close to achieving it," Mastriano said. "But the light is flickering. It's about to be snuffed out." Mastriano repeated what other speakers had said: This was the most important election of our lifetimes.

If that wasn't dramatic enough, Jack Posobiec, in a stemwinder that outlasted the candidate's own remarks, identified eight strategies Democrats used to "destroy Pennsylvania" and "dismantle America." It wasn't terribly well organized; Posobiec kept veering off script, making fun of Mitt Romney, telling a laughably fabricated tale about Mother Teresa and Hillary Clinton, and at one point challenging Shapiro, the Democratic nominee, to a fistfight. Still, the thematic chord was consistent. The nation's eyes were on this race, Posobiec declared. If Mastriano could "save Pennsylvania," then America, too, might be delivered from annihilation.

"God has raised him up for this purpose. He has raised all of *you* up. That's why we're all here," Posobiec cried.

He appeared tempted to elaborate on God's plan for Mastriano and the United States. But after some unintelligible comments about the Virgin Mary, Jesus's birthday, and his own trip to the Holy Land, Posobiec nodded toward the front row and concluded: "I'll leave the theology to the pastor."

Jonathan Wagner, a minister from nearby Garden Heights Baptist Church, offered remarks that were notable both for their brevity and sanity. Thrust into a lineup of frenzied, fearmongering speakers, Wagner, clad in a black "Mastriano for Governor" shirt, looked like he belonged—but sounded as if he'd arrived from another planet.

"Encourage our hearts," Wagner prayed from the stage. "Help us to understand that while we enjoy freedoms in this country, and we don't want to see those diminish, Lord, the only true freedom is what's offered through Jesus Christ, and that's freedom from our sins."

Wagner exhaled. "Lord, may we understand that."

It was the quietest ovation awarded to any of the speakers in Erie. When the event wrapped, Wagner dashed toward a side exit from the ballroom. I stopped him, introduced myself, and asked if we could talk about what we'd just witnessed. The pastor looked dazed.

"I don't really understand politics," he said.

TO UNDERSTAND POLITICS—OR AT LEAST, TO UNDERSTAND WHY FRINGE figures like Mastriano had achieved such prominence within the Republican Party—was to accept that extremists were now the establishment. Those fabled gatekeepers who once kept crackpots away from positions of authority no longer existed. Those fanciful unwritten rules that dictated who did and didn't deserve our attention no longer applied. This was true for American politics, and it was true for American Christianity. The same asymmetrical forces that lifted Donald Trump to the presidency made pastors like Greg Locke overnight evangelical celebrities.

Consider the case of Lance Wallnau. Once an obscure Texas businessman who moonlighted as a wannabe media personality and Christian "futurist," Wallnau gained fame in 2015 after prophesying that Trump was "anointed" to become president. He parlayed this newfound relevance into an all-purpose enterprise—podcasts, motivational videos, online training seminars, all of it powered by insights gleaned from the Almighty—that gained him millions of new followers.

It wasn't long before the Republican politicians came calling. In hindsight, this was inevitable. Elected officials have a nose for money, and by teaming with Wallnau, they were betting that the same fanatics who forked over $87 for his "Supernatural Living Bundle"—a combination of DVDs and CDs and online courses, marked down from the original price of $397—would chip in to help them defeat their evil Democratic opponents.

It was inevitable for another reason. The Republican ranks had, since Trump's victory in 2016, swelled with the sort of cartoonish misfits who found significance in spreading metaphysical divinations about the Church, the country, the president, and the future of mankind. Some of these were shameless opportunists; to be sure, not everyone who preached the politics of Armageddon was a true believer. But plenty of them were. And it became clear, soon after the Democratic president took office in 2021, that they would treat the 2022 midterm campaign like a modern crusade. It wouldn't just be a struggle between Republicans and Democrats; it would be a showdown between heaven and hell.

"Lord, strengthen them in the name and the blood of Jesus," Pastor Steve Holt prayed at a Colorado revival in the spring of 2022, as he stood beside two Republican members of Congress. "May this state be turned red with the blood of Jesus, and politically."

One of the lawmakers, Doug Lamborn, appeared mildly uncomfortable during the prayer, which was captured on video and circulated widely online. But Lauren Boebert looked right at home. She closed her eyes and mouthed silent words of supplication, raising her left palm skyward in a gesture of worship. Boebert wasn't bothered by this pastor praying for Jesus's blood—His precious, sacrificial blood, shed for the salvation of sinners—to win an election, because, well, she wasn't bothered by much at all.

A small-town restaurant owner who'd been arrested four times in the decade before seeking political office, Boebert was fond of boasting that God told her to run for Congress because her unlikely victory "would be a sign and a wonder to the unbeliever." If the unbeliever paid attention to Boebert, the only signs they saw were of psychosis. As a candidate in 2020, she was the Republican Party's most outspoken ally of the QAnon deception. After getting elected, she joked about a Muslim colleague being a suicide bomber, calling her "the jihad squad." Forging close ties with Trump, Boebert played a leading role in spreading disinformation about the election results in 2020, and declared on the morning of January 6 that it was a "1776 moment."

It was after Biden's swearing-in, however, that Boebert became fully unhinged. At various forums—some political, some religious, most of them barely distinguishing between the two—Boebert made remarks that in my experience had no precedent when it comes to members of the United States Congress. She said that "we are in the last of the last days." She prayed out loud for Biden's death. She said Jesus didn't have enough AR-15 assault rifles to stop the Roman government from killing Him.

Boebert's most striking comment came while addressing a church congregation in the summer of 2022. "I'm tired of this 'separation of church and state' junk," the congresswoman huffed, according to the *Denver Post*. "The church is supposed to direct the government. The government is not supposed to direct the church."

Here was the explicit endorsement of theocracy that generations of Christian conservatives had studiously avoided. But Boebert was sick of dancing around the debate. She was done rejecting the accusation of being a "Christian nationalist." And she wasn't alone. As the midterm elections drew closer in 2022, a number of prominent evangelicals, inside and outside of government, started coming around to the label.

"I'm a proud Christian Nationalist. These evil people are even calling me a Nazi because I proudly love my country and my God," Marjorie Taylor Greene, the Georgia congresswoman, tweeted in the summer of 2022, less than a year before the *Daily Beast* reported that she called Boebert a "little bitch" while the two argued over whose impeachment resolution of President Biden should take precedence.

Greene followed up with an Instagram post. It showed her in a fighting position, fists cocked, with a shirt for sale: PROUD CHRISTIAN NATIONALIST.

Nobody embodied this evolution quite like Al Mohler. Once named the "reigning intellectual of the evangelical movement" by *Time* magazine, Mohler, the president of Southern Baptist Theological Seminary, had long been known for his consistent, scripture-first position on matters of politics and culture. He objected to Trump's candidacy in 2016—writing, "Honest evangelicals would not want him as a next-door neighbor," much less their president—and slammed the "idolatrous" Christians who stormed the Capitol on January 6. "Nationalism is always a clear and present danger," Mohler wrote in the aftermath of the insurrection.

But suddenly, in the summer of 2022, Mohler seemed to be rethinking this position. "We have the left routinely speaking of me and of others as Christian nationalists, as if we're supposed to be running from that," Mohler said on a podcast. "I'm not about to run from that."

Mohler's friends and admirers in the evangelical world were distraught. They prayed that he didn't really mean what these comments implied; that he'd spoken ineloquently, hurriedly, without considering the ramifications of his words. Their prayers went unanswered. Not long after the podcast controversy, Mohler told a gathering of evangelicals that if they "vote wrongly" in 2022—which, he made clear, meant voting for Democrats—they were being "unfaithful" to God.

"The vote is a powerful stewardship. And we need to remind Christians of that," Mohler said. "We need to remind Christians of what's at stake."

SCRIPTURE HAS A FUNNY WAY OF CUTTING POLITICAL LEADERS DOWN to size. Pharaoh, the most powerful man on the planet, is utterly impotent in the face of God's plagues. The gospel of Luke catalogs all the kings and rulers of the era, then tells of how the authority they believed was theirs was given instead to a primitive-living prophet named John and a carpenter's son named Jesus. The Messiah Himself—who physically runs and hides from the people who desire to make Him king—dismisses the Pharisees by telling them, "Give back to Caesar the things that are Caesar's, and to God the things that are God's," the implication being that only one deserves from us that which truly matters.

The word *power* can be found hundreds of times in English versions of the Bible. It is translated from several Greek words: *exousia*, which refers to authority; *ischus*, which refers to natural strength; *kratos*, which refers to supremacy and dominion. By far the most common root word is *dunamis*, which refers to explosive force, explosive potential, explosive might. (*Dunamis* is the origin of our *dynamite*.) The New Testament recounts in detail the reign of many earthly rulers—yet those Greek words for "power" are almost never attributed to any of them. Instead, the words are reserved for God, who rules the universe; for Jesus, who gives His life to save humanity from its sins; and, tellingly, for His followers, who are divinely equipped to take this message of hope to all the nations.

There is at least one notable exception. In the Book of John, after Jesus is arrested and handed over to the Roman authorities, Pontius Pilate attempts to interrogate the defendant to discern whether He deserves punishment. But Jesus refuses to answer Pilate's questions. Indignant, the Roman governor says to Jesus, "Don't you realize I have power either to free you or to crucify you?"

"You would have no power over me if it were not given to you from above," Jesus replies.

This English phrase "from above" is translated from the Greek *anothen*, a word used throughout the New Testament in reference to that which is established by God and comes from heaven. This makes for an astonishing rebuke to Pilate. Even though the Roman governor will decide whether He lives or dies, Jesus is telling him that God set these events into motion from the beginning of time; that He cast Pilate in these proceedings as an actor who would read lines from a divine script; that neither Rome nor its rulers have inherent power of their own.

Jesus's words to Pilate echo throughout all of scripture. True power is not reflected in kingdoms, administrations, or campaigns, because these things are counterfeits of God's original, supreme authority. The power to raise taxes is not the power to raise Jesus from the dead; the power to seat senators is not the power to seat Jesus at the right hand of the Father. Every biblical reference to power—every prayer, every reflection, every instruction—affirms that *God* is all-powerful, and that to the extent He vests that power in man, it is to proclaim *God's* kingdom, *God's* power, and *God's* glory.

Why, then, does Doug Mastriano pray for Republicans to "seize the power" ahead of January 6? Why does Al Mohler emphasize that "the vote is a powerful stewardship"? Why do the speakers at Ralph Reed's conference, politicians and pastors alike, talk fearfully about the Democratic Party remaining "in power" for another two years?

The simplest explanation—at the risk of hermeneutical overload—takes us back to Greek linguistics. Among the weightiest biblical concepts is *aphiemi*, which means to detach, to abandon, to leave alone, to let go. Simply put, many American evangelicals cannot let go. They cannot detach themselves from national identity or abandon the notion that fighting for America is fighting for God. Hence the creeping allure of "Christian nationalism." William Wolfe, an ex–Trump administration official who has embraced the term and regularly traffics in ad hominem attacks against fellow believers on social media, distilled the "animating principle for my Christian political engagement" in one succinct tweet. "If it was good, right, and noble to fight against communists when they're in power," Wolfe wrote, "it's good, right, and noble—even better—to fight to ensure they never get power."

People like Wolfe do not hide from an essential truth: theirs is an *offensive* fight. No longer can Christians engage with politics as though they are preserving something, the thinking goes, because there is nothing left to preserve. The aim is to take something back—religious revanchism. However "noble" the intent, the result is a blurring of the line between a love of country and a lust for hegemony. In the name of objectivity, it's worth recalling what a known atheist, George Orwell, the author of *Animal Farm* and *1984*, said differentiated patriotism from nationalism. "Patriotism is of its nature defensive, both militarily and culturally," Orwell wrote. "Nationalism, on the other hand, is inseparable from the desire for power."

When the apostle Paul wrote to the church in Ephesus, Greece, he offered this instruction: "Finally, be strong in the Lord and in his mighty power. Put on the full armor of God, so that you can take your stand against the devil's schemes." Notably, most of what Paul describes—the weapons of Christian warfare—is defensive: the belt of truth, the breastplate of righteousness, the shield of faith, the helmet of salvation. The only offensive weapon Paul names is the "sword of the Spirit, which is the Word of God." (Evangelicals my age probably remember "sword drills" from Sunday School, in which we raced to locate a particular Bible verse cited by the teacher.)

But politicians have purposely misappropriated this language. Ron DeSantis, the Florida governor who harbored designs on winning the White House, frequently invoked the Book of Ephesians while traveling the country in 2022 to raise money and rally the conservative base.

"Put on the full armor of God," DeSantis would say, "and take a stand against the left's schemes."

In substituting "the left" for "the devil," DeSantis wasn't just counting on the biblical illiteracy of his listeners. He was banking on a nationalist fervor that rendered scriptural restraint irrelevant. He was confident that evangelicals in the audience would agree that he knew better than Paul; that the real enemy is the left; that the real struggle is against flesh and blood; that the real power belongs to a politician who can ignore Anthony Fauci's coronavirus protocols and eliminate Disney World's tax exemptions.

Eventually, DeSantis did away with any subtlety. Steamrolling toward reelection in the fall of 2022, the Florida governor was aiming to put the nation—and Trump, his looming rival for the Republican nomination come 2024—on notice. DeSantis decided to release a campaign advertisement, cinematic frames shot in black and white, that borrowed from radio host Paul Harvey's famous speech, "So God Made a Farmer." But one important change was made.

"On the eighth day," rumbled a deep voice, with DeSantis pictured standing tall before an American flag, "God looked down on His planned paradise and said: 'I need a protector.' So God made a fighter."

The two-minute video was so comically overdone—and so thoroughly panned for its rampant self-glorification—that its appeal went unappreciated. Tempting as it was to believe that DeSantis had overplayed his hand in depicting himself as an anointed guardian of God's promised land, there was ample evidence to suggest that this message was exactly what the evangelical base of the Republican Party wanted to hear. Not long before DeSantis released his ad, the University of Maryland published a survey of more than two thousand Americans who were asked about the separation of church and state. The results were astounding: 61 percent of Republicans said they would support a formal declaration by the United States government that America is a "Christian Nation." Among the evangelicals who were polled, 78 percent supported making such a declaration.

In this context, it was becoming easier to make sense of the absurd.

Why was Jim Caviezel, the actor who portrayed Jesus in Mel Gibson's *The Passion of the Christ,* talking about the blood harvesting of children at a conference alongside a roster of Trump confidants? Why would the lieutenant governor of Idaho hold a gun in one hand and a Bible in the other during a staged protest of COVID-19 policies? Why were high-profile evangelicals like Al Mohler lining up to speak at the National Conservatism Conference, whose organizers signed a "statement of principles" that explicitly endorses theocratic rule? ("Adult individuals should be protected from religious or ideological coercion in their private lives and in their homes," the statement reads.) Why was Kari Lake—the Republican running for governor of Arizona, who friends say identified as a Buddhist before declaring herself a born-again vessel of God's vengeance—palling around with Mark Driscoll, the disgraced pastor whose Mars Hill megachurch collapsed under the weight of scandal? Why would pastors invite Duane Chapman, aka Dog the Bounty Hunter, to their evangelism summit—and moreover, why did they sit by while he speculated that Biden would soon commit suicide like Adolf Hitler did?

Something was happening on the religious right, something more menacing and extreme than anything that preceded it. This was no longer about winning elections and preserving the culture. This was about destroying enemies and dominating the country by any means necessary. There was no rhetoric too appalling, no alliance too shady, no biblical application too sacrilegious. Letting go—*aphiemi*—was not an option.

The scariest part, I thought to myself while talking to Pastor Wagner in Erie, Pennsylvania, was that not everyone could see it.

* * *

THE FIRST POLITICAL EVENT WAGNER EVER ATTENDED WAS IN THE
spring of 2022: a Mastriano for Governor rally. It was an otherworldly
experience. The pastor, who avoided politics and rarely voted in local
or national elections, was taken aback by the tone of the environment.
People seemed restive, dismayed, fearful. When he went to leave, one
of the campaign workers asked if he would walk the blocks vouching for
Mastriano.

"And I was like, 'No, but I'll go around and talk to 'em about Jesus
Christ,'" Wagner recalled with a broad smile. "I'm not talking to people
about politics. It's just not that important to me."

Wagner, a man in his mid-forties with a thin goatee and a gentle demeanor, described himself as blissfully ill informed of current events.
He doesn't "waste time with the news—no TV, no talk radio, no newspapers." Wagner's only window into the world of politics is his Facebook
feed. Back in 2020, when he saw Christian friends recommending Mastriano's "fireside chats"—daily, direct-to-camera videos in which the
senator talked about his faith and his views on COVID-19, among other
issues—Wagner tuned in. The pastor wasn't sold on everything Mastriano said. But he appreciated how the man was unapologetic about his
Christian beliefs. When Mastriano announced his campaign for governor, and swung through Erie, Wagner decided to check it out.

He was encouraged by some of what he heard. To the extent Wagner
had political priorities, the big one was abortion, and Mastriano had
staked out a hard-line position. His number one priority as governor,
the Republican candidate had said, would be outlawing abortion without any exceptions. The pastor approved. But some of the candidate's
other obsessions—such as whipping up outrage over the "stolen election" of 2020—were lost on Wagner. He planned to vote for Mastriano in
the fall election but decided that one political rally was enough.

And then, six months later, a local Republican called Wagner and
asked him to deliver the invocation for Mastriano's return event in Erie.
The pastor felt conflicted. He hadn't given Mastriano much thought
since that rally and wasn't keen to relive the adventure. Praying over
the proceedings wouldn't be a problem with his congregation—Wagner

said his church is overwhelmingly conservative—but he did worry about sending mixed signals to his flock. The pastor had a long-standing policy: The only time politics were mentioned in the church was when they prayed for their leaders on Sunday mornings. Accepting Mastriano's invitation, he fretted, might give outsiders a false impression about "the real purpose of our church."

Ultimately, Wagner felt compelled to say yes. The rally would be held just a few miles from Garden Heights Baptist—a quaint, brick-and-tan building in a residential neighborhood—and lots of local nonchurchgoers would be in attendance. He viewed it as an opening to evangelize the community.

As we spoke afterward, it was clear that Wagner was processing the event. He seemed a genuine political greenhorn; some of my small talk about the national electoral climate, and even some recent happenings in Pennsylvania, were met with a blank stare. At one point, I mentioned the protesters outside the event, some of whom held signs accusing Mastriano of being a "Christian nationalist." The pastor told me he was unfamiliar with that phrase.

"I think he just loves his country, and he's a Christian, so people attack him," Wagner told me. "I think some people just don't like Christians."

I asked him why that might be.

"We're not living in a Christian country. We haven't lived in a Christian country for a long time." He shrugged. "When I was young, it was a common thing to go to weekly revival meetings. . . . My parents talk about crusades that would last for weeks on end. Nothing happens like that anymore. You can't even get somebody to come to a free event at the church. It's just not something people want to be part of."

I asked him, again, why that might be.

"I wish I knew. I really don't," the pastor replied. One theory was that children have been "indoctrinated" for decades by the public schools and universities to "think a certain way" about God and American life. This was a popular complaint, Wagner told me, that he heard from Christian friends. Many of them were upset that schools weren't teaching about the biblical founding of America.

Then he surprised me.

"I don't really get that," Wagner said. "Many of the founding fathers *weren't* Christian. And I'm sorry, but I don't think we should aspire to be a Christian country anyway. I don't see America in the Bible, you know?"

He sighed. "Look, God's gonna do what God's gonna do. I'm not too concerned about America," Wagner said. "I'm just supposed to read my Bible and preach the word and be faithful."

Wagner was in a lose-lose situation. If he declined the invitation and kept his distance from the event, he would be called "weak" and "spineless" and "cowardly." By accepting the invitation and allying himself with Mastriano, he would be called a "Christian nationalist." He was clearly neither, but instead a decent guy who had unwittingly signed up for something he didn't understand. He had cast his lot with people who supposedly shared his priorities, only to begin questioning, once he got up close, what those priorities were.

"Joe Biden is the president. I didn't vote for him, but he was sworn in, and I'm praying for him, and these Republicans need to move on," Wagner told me.

I started to interrupt him. But Wagner wasn't done.

"Honestly, I voted for Trump, but I'm not a fan of his," the pastor said. "The language he uses, and these moral issues, he's just not an upstanding person. I'm tired of him, too."

Wagner glanced around the empty ballroom. "If I said that up there"—he grinned, motioning toward the stage—"I would've gotten kicked out."

I asked him if his opening prayer—a warning against fear and idolatry—was his coded way of getting the message across.

Wagner nodded. "Let me put it this way. We've had a lot of people wanting to put an American flag up on the platform at our church, especially around the Fourth of July and times like that. But every time, I've said no. We're there to worship God, not America," he said. "We love America, but that's a separate thing."

What about the light of our nation flickering? What about this being the most important election of our lifetimes?

The pastor rolled his eyes. "They've said that during every election for the last two hundred years."

CHAPTER FOURTEEN

BRANSON, MISSOURI

Let your light shine before others, that they may see your good deeds and glorify your Father in heaven.

—MATTHEW 5:16

It was several hours into the program—just before the attractive blonde with an explicit OnlyFans page warned of the nation's decline, and right after the mystic with a Brooklyn accent said that the coming blood moon on Election Day portended victory for the Republican Party—when Brian Gibson, a pastor from Kentucky, got to the point.

"Is anybody ready for a red wave?" Gibson shouted. "Anybody want to see us take this nation back? Anybody want to see D.C. turned upside down and right side up for the glory of God?" The concert hall shook with applause.

Gibson, a stocky man with a graying beard—you might recognize him from photos he shared posing alongside the "QAnon Shaman" of January 6 infamy—warned that depraved leftists were undermining America in order to defeat its spread of Christianity. But there was reason to take heart. Because Democrats in the state of New York had approved pro-abortion laws—laws that would kill unborn babies, "the apple of God's eye," Gibson said—God had spoken to Gibson, revealing to him that Republicans were going to take back "the Big Apple" on Election Day, routing the Democrats on their home turf as punishment.

It was November 4, 2022, just a few days before the midterm election, and I found myself in the middle of a most unusual political pep rally. Organized by a retired three-star general and a marketing guru who'd recently been baptized—literally and figuratively—into the church of Christian nationalism, the event brought together an assortment of conservative clerics, Trump-inspired politicos, patriot crusaders, culture-war capitalists, and a few thousand people who were willing to pay $250 each (or $500 for VIP seating) to hear the gospel of an imminent Republican triumph at the polls. The "ReAwaken America Tour" was the hottest ticket in the underworld of right-wing evangelicalism.

Sitting in the second-floor gallery of the Mansion Theatre, looking out across a standing-room-only crowd of people clad in garish cross necklaces and QAnon sweatshirts and red MAGA hats, I could practically hear the voice of the Old Testament prophet Jeremiah, who declared sometime around 600 BC that the people of Israel possessed "no shame at all." They had, Jeremiah said in one translation, "forgotten how to blush." In fifteen years of political journalism, I had witnessed chicanery and skulduggery of every sort. Nothing could surprise me anymore; I was immune to outrage, bereft of the ability to recoil from iniquity. And then I discovered the ReAwaken America Tour.

Over the course of two days, hucksters and spin doctors and straight-up sociopaths took turns preying on the anxious masses of Missouri. These people had traveled to Branson, just north of the Arkansas border, in search of hope. Their nation was nearly expired. Their politicians appeared powerless, and their God seemed indifferent. They were desperate to believe that America might yet be saved; that revival was within reach.

Marty Grisham, purveyor of a web-based business, "Loudmouth Prayer," told them that it was. He had just received a vision from heaven that depicted "an army of red." This was no reference to the Chinese military, Grisham assured us, but rather to the people of God, the people in this very room, Christians and conservatives who were fighting for the future of the nation. The red didn't merely signify a Republican victory on Tuesday; it also meant that they were "covered with the blood of Christ," and therefore could not lose. (Going over his allotted time, Grisham shouted repeatedly as the music played him offstage: "Loud mouthPrayer.org!")

Not all swindles were spiritual in nature. One person was screening trailers for his forthcoming documentary about education. Another was raising money for his fight against election fraud. Yet another was pushing his specialty diet and warning about the dangers of "big agriculture." My personal favorite was the guy peddling "Kingdom Fuel," a powdered shake mix, which he pitched as a means of staying healthy, living longer, and defying the malevolent medical regime. (It comes in two flavors, vanilla and chocolate.)

If there was an organizing theme to the proceedings, it was presented by the brains behind the ReAwaken America Tour: Michael Flynn and Clay Clark. Taking the stage together at one point, the two men explained that globalists had weaponized the COVID-19 pandemic to push lockdowns that would give them control of the world population. The supposed mastermind was Klaus Schwab, who they said was using his position atop the World Economic Forum to pursue a "Great Reset" that would result in a secular, tyrannical one-world government. Hence the need for a "Great ReAwakening." Flynn and Clark declared that theirs was a mission to defend not just American sovereignty, but Christian supremacy.

Once a respected military mind who'd overseen counterterrorism strategy in the Middle East, Flynn's descent into conspiracy-fueled madness had rendered him a punch line. The former Army lieutenant general was spiraling long before he resigned under duress as Trump's national security adviser—capping three turbulent weeks on the job— but that episode seemed to mark a point of no return. (He eventually pleaded guilty to lying to the FBI and was pardoned by Trump after the 2020 election.) Flynn spoke incessantly of a New World Order. He accused Bill Gates of planting tracking devices under the skin of unsuspecting vaccine recipients. On July 4, 2020, Flynn shared a video showing him taking an oath associated with QAnon, and soon after, he began organizing what would become the ReAwaken America Tour.

Clark made for the ideal partner. Slick, witty, and almost comically impervious to humiliation, the Oklahoma-based businessman saw in Flynn the market for martyrdom and brought it up to scale, recruiting an all-star cast of the country's most-shunned Christian and conservative influencers to band together in the name of airing grievances and saving the country and making lots of money, not necessarily in that order. Clark was perfectly preposterous as Flynn's sidekick, parroting all the same sinister views but with a mirthful disposition, giggling and wisecracking and radiating such sprightliness that one could forget the apocalypse was nigh.

Tailing Flynn outside after their "Great Reset" routine, I ran headlong into a security detail that was escorting him to a designated zone outside the large white tent erected in the theater's parking lot. Looking to my right, I noticed a line—several hundred people long—snaking all the way back to the building's entrance. These were Flynn's superfans, bearing photos and posters and products from his signature clothing line (branded with the hashtag #FightLikeAFlynn). Soon, another guest of honor joined Flynn: Mike Lindell, the "MyPillow" inventor who'd become the most vocal (and most frequently debunked) advocate of nonsensical stolen-election theories. Together the two men worked the receiving line for nearly an hour, signing autographs, taking selfies, giving hugs, promising their disciples that America wasn't finished just yet. Flying behind them was an American flag emblazoned with that familiar Old Testament passage: "If my people, who are called by my name . . ."

Standing just ten feet away, leaning against the corner of the tent, I marveled at the scene. Here, people panicked about Big Pharma's trickery were toting around boxes of unregulated vitamins. People upset by the brainwashing of America's youth were buying paintings that depicted Trump inside a lion's den. People fearful of God's judgment were sporting T-shirts that read: "Jesus Is a Badass."

Surely, I thought, some of these folks were in on the joke. One table peddled children's books authored by former Trump aide Kash Patel. (*The Plot Against the King*, which depicted a deep-state coup against a fearless monarch, sold for $20.) For sale nearby were filtering contraptions marketed as "Living Water." At a neighboring booth, one young woman handed out pamphlets for Rhema Bible Training College in Oklahoma. ("You don't get a degree," she noted sunnily. "But you do get to learn about the Bible.")

It was a scam artist's Super Bowl. Traveling from station to station, gamely chatting up the proprietors—Can this book *really* cure my son's autism? Can this presentation *really* decode prophecy to predict war with China? Can this supply kit *really* help me survive nuclear winter?— I went from amused to annoyed. Every question I posed about the sincerity of these schemes was met with a far-off gaze. I suddenly felt parched, stranded in the desert, thirsting for an oasis of sanity.

What I found instead was a mirage. His name was Stephen E. Strang.

MAYBE IT WAS THE EXPERTLY TAILORED SUIT, THE SHARP RED TIE, AND the careful comb-over. Maybe it was the heap of books that bore his name. There was something about Strang that stood out inside that circus tent. He was quiet, studied, visibly mortified by his surroundings, like a librarian who'd been shoved inside a locker room. A prolific Christian author and publisher, Strang was selling and signing copies of his books for five dollars apiece. When I asked if he'd like to take a break and chat with me—he was being upstaged by the miracle pills a few booths over—Strang did not hesitate to agree.

"There has to be a standard for these things," he grumbled, shaking his head.

We went inside and grabbed two seats on a tan couch just outside the second-floor gallery, overlooking the swarm of humanity moving between the tent and the theater. Strang sat upright, looking self-consciously proper, the only man in Branson wearing wingtips, pretending not to notice the guy in the QAnon hat sitting across from us munching on a hot dog. I asked Strang what he made of his surroundings.

"Every group has its weirdos," he replied. "But there's something about 'the enemy of my enemy is my friend.' And a lot of these people feel like America's going in the wrong direction. . . . I don't agree with a lot of the stuff here. But I am concerned about the direction of the country."

Strang, a man in his early seventies, has been concerned for quite some time. He was born not far from here, in Springfield. Both his father and grandfather were preachers and his parents kept active within the charismatic, ultraconservative Assemblies of God denomination. It was a rigid upbringing. Strang was taught that most activities in which a young man might indulge—smoking, drinking, dancing, watching television, going to the movies—were wrong and sinful. (At least he wasn't a woman; they were additionally forbidden from wearing makeup.)

I assumed Strang was telling me all this to illustrate, approvingly, how the Church had adapted to modernity. "It almost seems laughable now with how things have changed," he said. The longer we talked, however, the more I sensed his nostalgia for this bygone age. Strang spoke repeatedly of "backsliding," reflecting on how the average Christian's scruples had relaxed in proportion to their diminished zeal for Christ.

Strang said he was "on fire for God" as a young man. But he wasn't cut out for the clergy. Looking for a novel way to influence society for Christ, Strang turned to journalism. After a stint in the secular press, he caught the entrepreneurial bug and decided to marry his journalism skills to his church background. "I started a little magazine," Strang said, "and by God's grace, it's grown into a media company."

That company is better described as an empire: Charisma Media. It is the de facto publishing arm of the Pentecostal movement in North America. Strang once led a staff of two hundred that worked out of a 67,000-square-foot headquarters near Orlando, Florida. The operation has slimmed down, but Strang still employs a large workforce that prints a bimonthly magazine, produces an expansive suite of podcasts, and publishes dozens of books each year. Back in 2005, Strang earned a spot on *Time* magazine's list of the "25 most influential evangelicals in America." At that time, he was mostly a behind-the-scenes player. That changed in 2017 when Strang wrote a book that rocked the charismatic world: *God and Donald Trump*.

The book portrayed Trump not as the odious, spiteful cretin his opponents made him out to be, but rather as a bighearted (and, to borrow some hagiographic rhetoric from Mike Pence, broad-shouldered) family man who was fundamentally misunderstood. As for Trump's moral shortcomings, the book leaned into them, contending that they made him uniquely capable of restoring the nation's Christian character. It required a man from the secular world to defeat the forces of secularism. This, Strang wrote, is why God raised up Trump, ordained him as America's leader, and delivered him the presidency in such seemingly transcendental fashion.

The book sold like crazy—and backed Strang into a corner. He had not always admired Trump, but now, having found commercial success arguing that the man was an imperfect instrument of God's will, Strang had every incentive to nurture the narrative. The president's myriad and manifest deficiencies would only underscore the original premise. No matter how bad things would get for Trump in the years to come, the savvy move for Strang was to double down.

So that's what he did. Like Homer revisiting the consequences of the Trojan War he had chronicled, Strang went on to churn out a series of books that played off the original theme: *Trump Aftershock* (foreword by Jerry Falwell Jr.); *God, Trump, and the 2020 Election* (foreword by Eric Metaxas, who would endorse martyrdom in response to Trump's defeat); *God, Trump, and Covid-19* (foreword by Lori Bakker, who co-hosts a show with her husband, disgraced televangelist Jim Bakker, that hawked a "miracle cure" for the virus); and *God and Cancel Culture* (foreword by Lindell, who was finding it harder to sell pillows amid his crusade to prove mass voter fraud, at one point saying he had "enough evidence" to put "300 and some million people" in prison for life).

There was a curious unintended consequence of his parasitic attachment to Trump. Strang had spent so much time defending the forty-fifth president, explaining the ways in which he was *actually* virtuous and *actually* an ally of American Christianity, that he'd overlooked the larger questions about American Christianity itself. This became more and more apparent as our own conversation progressed. Strang would repeatedly bring up Trump, then say he didn't want to talk about Trump, only to later steer the conversation back to Trump.

We had begun by discussing the deterioration of American values. He said "right and wrong" were once clearly defined: "It was right to get married. It was right to raise your kids. It was right to be honest." Strang believed it was a relentless secular onslaught against these values— these *Christian* values—that invited, and ultimately justified, the slash-and-burn tactics of the religious right.

I struggled with his logic. Why should Christians allow the coarsening of the world to justify the coarsening of Christianity itself?

Strang wore a blank expression. "I'm not understanding the point you're trying to make."

I tried to clarify. He was citing concerns about the decaying standards of American life—sexualized curricula, drag shows, transgender bathrooms, the works—to explain why the future of American Christendom depended on cartoonish heretics like Lindell and Flynn and Trump. Forget about what *the world* is getting wrong. Aren't Christians called to a higher standard?

"Listen, I believe that Donald Trump changed—"

Strang stopped himself. He began explaining that during the "Stormy Daniels mess"—code for the episode in which a porn star was paid by Trump's lawyer to keep quiet about an alleged sexual encounter when Trump's third wife was home with their newborn son—CNN had brought him on-air to offer commentary. The network was hoping for an evangelical to denounce such activity, Strang said, but "they picked the wrong one." He was not about to abandon Trump in that moment.

Why not?

For one thing, Strang said, Trump had told him in a private conversation that the Daniels affair never happened. And even if it had, "I think he's changed," Strang assured me, recalling how people he knew had prayed with Trump in the White House. Strang believed the man had become a born-again Christian during his presidency. How else to explain his bold stand on behalf of the evangelical movement in America?

"He's our hero," Strang said. "He stands up for the values that we have. That's why we support him."

I arched an eyebrow. *Our hero.* Strang just shrugged.

"No politician is perfect," he said. "But interestingly, they hold him to a much higher standard."

By "they," Strang was referring to those condescending Christian elites, those Never Trump conservatives who held high-profile postings in academia and media. He was especially fed up with "evangelicals like [the ones at] *Christianity Today*, which has been my chief competitor."

Strang couldn't understand me, and I couldn't understand him. The man who had started our conversation by saying "There has to be a standard" now seemed to be arguing that there should be a standard for everyone except Donald Trump and the Christians who supported him.

He wasn't totally lacking in self-awareness. Hoping to win back some credibility, Strang explained that he would remain objective when it came to Trump and the rest of the 2024 Republican presidential field.

"I have a friend that's bugging me to get on the Trump bandwagon. There are people trying to encourage him to run, and I'm staying totally neutral," Strang said.

Then, a moment later: "If he runs, of course I'll support him."

Finally, Strang said—and he meant it this time—that he didn't want to discuss Trump anymore. Neither did I. There were more important questions to be asked.

STRANG HAD TRIED TO PERSUADE ME—AND PERHAPS HIMSELF—THAT this particular event was not organized around religious beliefs. Rather, he said, it was a political and cultural jamboree with some spiritual undertones. It would not be fair to judge Christianity writ large based on the happenings in Branson.

He was wise to distance his faith from his affiliation with the Re-Awaken America Tour. Strang, one of the featured speakers, had shared the stage with people who had told absurd and verifiable lies, openly advocated violence, and trafficked in all forms of unwholesome talk. Not long before Strang and I sat down together, Patrick Byrne, the former CEO of Overstock.com, delivered a breathless rant that lasted nearly an hour. In it, Byrne boasted about lobbying Trump to seize voting machines and declare martial law after the 2020 election; called Amazon founder Jeff Bezos a "pussy" and Secretary of Defense Lloyd Austin a "fat fuck"; suggested that some combination of the Russian KGB and American deep state was trying to neutralize him; and claimed that he'd uncovered a secret government plot to install Michelle Obama as the future president. ("You mean Michael Obama!" a man shouted from the audience, referencing the popular far-right belief that the former first lady is, in fact, a man. The people around him went wild. Soon people were chanting: "Michael! Michael! Michael!")

The obvious flaw with Strang's argument—that all this should be considered outside the context of Christianity—was that praise hymns had been sung from that same stage, inside that same theater, by those same people, before and after Byrne dropped his countless f-bombs. And there was something else to consider. Despite Strang's eagerness to dismiss some of these speakers as sideshow freaks who were in no way representative of Christianity, many of the foulest acts were put on by *preachers.*

Brian Gibson, the Kentucky pastor who shared God's plan for taking back the Big Apple for the Republican Party, warned that believers needed to prepare for a cosmic showdown with the "Marxist manipulators" inside the Church and the "demonic" Democrats in government who were colluding to destroy American Christianity.

Greg Locke, the Tennessee tent revivalist, roused the crowd with call-and-response shouts of "Jesus!" and "America!" He then declared himself a "Christian nationalist," said it was "time to start fighting and stop talking about it," and boasted that he was "the most dangerous pastor in America."

Kevin Garner, a minister from Illinois, was the most colorful clergyman in Branson. Perhaps feeling pressure to outdo his fellow pastors—not to mention Clay Clark, who during his introduction mocked the Democratic governor of Illinois as "retarded"—Garner wove an elaborate tale connecting the sons of Noah (yes, he of the Ark) to the present crisis in America. For it was Noah's oldest son, Japheth, who supposedly fathered the European peoples that came to America and birthed a Christian nation. It was no coincidence, Garner went on, that Philadelphia—our first capital—was named in the Book of Revelation. This was proof of God's divine plan for America.

But then everything went awry in 2020. Noah's middle son, Shem (supposed father of the Asiatic nations), brought the "Asian virus" to America's shores, while Ham, the youngest son (and supposed father of the African nations), brought the Black Lives Matter protests. Lest anyone lose the plot of Garner's tale—and glancing around, it seemed more than a few people had—the pastor brought it home with a flourish. "Philadelphia was all of a miracle, with the calling and the power and the freedom to spread the gospel all over the world," he said. "But in 2020, where did the worst election fraud happen? Philadelphia! Where did Joe Biden go last September to slam all MAGA followers and half the voters in this country? Philadelphia!"

Garner began pounding his fist against an invisible pulpit: "Gee," he cried, "do you think maybe God is trying to tell us something?!"

In that moment, the only thing God was telling me was to get out of that theater. Closing my notebook, collecting my belongings, and shuffling through the throngs of people, I could hear Garner's closing prayer: "God, we cry out now, even though we do not deserve it, by your mercy, which is renewed every day, we just cry out and pray, Lord, that it would fall to this nation, especially next Tuesday, that all the cheating in the world would not stop a red wave."

Talking with Strang a little while later, I would concede one important point to him: Most of the people here hadn't come for the preaching. Sure, they shouted *hallelujah* in response to Bible verses that were cited to dehumanize Democrats or to ridicule gay teenagers as "gender-queer unicorns," but this spiritual feeding wasn't going to satiate their ultimate hunger. They needed something more. They needed something nakedly political. They needed something *Trumpy*.

But even the former president wasn't about to stoop to hanging around this crowd. (As Strang said, there has to be a standard.) So, Clark recruited Eric Trump—not the most articulate or entertaining of Trump's progeny, but a Trump progeny nonetheless—to speak in Branson. He strode onto the stage like he'd just knocked down the walls of Jericho himself. Cheers cascaded down from the rafters. No man had ever been celebrated so much for accomplishing so little.

"This is real America. This is what we fight for. This is what we love," Trump declared, arms extended as if receiving some red-state life-force.

There was nothing novel in his winding homily. He won applause for identifying as a Floridian instead of a New Yorker; boasted about his dad building a border wall; stirred a low-energy "lock her up!" chant; and decried the amorphous evils of "the swamp" in Washington.

"It's unthinkable what these people are doing to this nation. The way they want to destroy Christianity; the way they want to destroy our families; the way they're destroying our children; the way they're destroying our history; the way they're rewriting our textbooks," Trump said. He called it "a war" for the country.

That war might already have been lost, he noted, if not for the 2016 election. His father's victory was "divine intervention" that gave America a fighting chance to survive. Now, he said, observing the damage done by Biden's illegitimate presidency, the Trump family possessed a sacred duty.

"We have to do it again!" Eric Trump announced. The crowd shot to its feet, delivering a prolonged standing ovation paired with chants of "U-S-A!"

A little while later, after Trump affirmed that Biden did not possess "one redeeming quality" as a human being—then bragged that he, Eric, owned "a shit ton" of guns and ammunition—the spectacle wound down with a surprise video montage. Flynn joined Trump on the stage to present Clark with a highlight reel of the ReAwaken America Tour to date. There was certainly lots of material to choose from. At one event, during the opening prayer, a pastor asked God to remove the "RINO trash" from Trump's inner circle. At the most recent stop, just weeks earlier, a self-proclaimed prophet named Bo Polny had displayed a collage of prominent political figures—Biden, Kamala Harris, and Hillary Clinton, among others—and said the "Angel of Death" was coming for them by year's end.

As it turned out, the director's cut was a sanitized synopsis of the tour. It did include cameos from the likes of Alex Jones and Roger Stone; it even showed Clark getting baptized. After the screen went black and the applause died down, a local pastor grabbed the microphone to adjourn the afternoon session. But not before making a final announcement: If anyone wanted to follow Clark's example, a group of clergymen would be hosting a baptism event later that evening at the Wyndham hotel down the street.

"Remember," the pastor said, "this is all for the glory of God."

MAYBE IT WAS THE SIGHT OF PEOPLE WEARING "JESUS IS A BADASS" shirts cheering expletive-laden calls for violence against political opponents, but something told me that devotion to the Reformation-era creed of Soli Deo Gloria—"to God alone be glory"—was not what brought these folks to Branson. No amount of singing or praying or Bible quoting from the religious leaders onstage could conceal the true aims of this event. They may have honored the Almighty with their lips, but their hearts were far from Him indeed.

I asked Strang whether this worried him. If Christians were so perceptibly failing to seek first the kingdom of God—instead prioritizing national identities, cultural squabbles, political agendas—who could blame unbelievers for concluding that the kingdom of God wasn't worth seeking at all?

Strang shook his head. "You could get this nice little perfect thing"—by which he meant a healthier, more credible Christian movement in America—"and you would feel better about it. But it's not gonna move the needle," he said.

How could he be sure? Jesus called on His followers to "let your light shine before others, that they may see your good deeds and glorify your Father in heaven." Paul instructed us to "let your conversation be always full of grace, seasoned with salt," so that we can draw outsiders to Him. Was it so far-fetched to believe that those outsiders might be more attracted to Christ if Christians ceased to associate with the ugliness we'd witnessed in Branson?

"A lot of the people that gripe about that—if we correct it, they'll gripe about something else," Strang said. "They're not interested in being saved. They're not interested in living for the Lord. They're just not."

Back at First Baptist Dallas, Robert Jeffress had argued this same point: The collective integrity of the Christian witness had no bearing on the individual's desire for a relationship with Jesus. This struck me as a pivotal battle within the war for American evangelicalism. Whereas some leaders such as Russell Moore stressed the diminished reliability of the Church as directly proportional to the declining numbers of church attendees and professing believers, others such as Jeffress and Strang dismissed such theorizing as the lazy finger-pointing of Christians who don't have the stomach for preaching the hard truths of eternal condemnation.

This schism carried major implications for the future of the Church. But Strang believed the debate was already settled. To hear him tell it, I was giving voice to a viewpoint that was marginal within American Christendom. The people who held to it—those do-gooder evangelical elites who subscribed to Moore's magazine, *Christianity Today*—were flirting with theological and statistical irrelevance.

"In my world, nobody takes *CT* seriously," Strang said.

I asked him why not.

"They think they're woke."

"What does *woke* mean?"

Strang frowned at me. "Well, we didn't develop the term," he said. "It's pretty far left."

"You think Russell Moore is pretty far left?"

"Yes," he nodded.

My job wasn't to defend Moore's honor. But I was genuinely curious, in terms of substance, how Strang could describe the man—a conservative by most traditional measures, theologically and politically and otherwise—as "pretty far left."

He wouldn't answer. Instead, Strang started venting about his long-running feud with *Christianity Today,* how the *New York Times* had once taken him out of context, and why he doesn't normally give interviews like this one. "Really the best way to find out what I believe is to read either *God and Cancel Culture,* which is the newest one, or *God and Donald Trump,* the first one," he told me, forty-five minutes into our conversation.

I probed a bit more, but Strang was shutting down. He was done indulging these questions about the health of the Church. His congregation was doing just fine, thank you very much, and if people like me and Moore wanted to critique evangelicalism, well, that was our problem. Strang told me it was time to wrap up the interview.

"Last question," I said. "What's your greatest concern for the American Church?"

Strang scratched his head. Then he launched into a detailed description of how several major Christian denominations had, over the course of generations, been liberalized, pacified, sapped of their spiritual intensity. Recalling a passage from Revelation—that Jesus preferred people to be either hot or cold when it came to following Him—Strang said he worried that "instead of being on fire for God, that we become lukewarm and meaningless and incorporate the values of the world and try to Christianize them."

Now, nearly an hour into our meandering discussion, we were getting somewhere.

I had been taught that "being on fire for God" meant deliberately cultivating a relationship with Him—through prayer and meditation on the word—that would equip a Christian to spread the message of His love. But it was becoming clear that it meant something quite different to some of the people I'd been spending time with.

To people like Strang—and people like Chad Connelly, who went around the country portraying any politically passive churchgoer as fraudulent in their faith—the Christian's devoutness was measured not by their striving and self-perfecting on the inside, but by their scrapping and self-aggrandizing on the outside. In this context, all the shady alliances and moral compromises made sense. The quest for political clout was not a deviation from their faith in Jesus; it was a *demonstration* of it.

For someone who worried about Christians conforming to the patterns of the world, Strang had certainly proven its viability as a business model. Praising Trump for advancing sound policies was one thing; even the man's fiercest detractors had lauded specific decisions he made as president. But Strang had chosen to take it further, connecting those policy decisions to something supernatural. He had used specific ends to rationalize all means. He had Christianized—*literally*, Christianized—a man and his political movement, despite knowing that many of that man's values were antithetical to the example of Christ.

The most disturbing part: Strang wasn't limiting this practice to Trump. The foreword to his newest book was written by Mike Lindell, who had spent the last two years spewing such laughably demonstrable lies that even many of his erstwhile MAGA allies had cut him off. When I raised once more the question of credibility—was it helpful to the witness of Christ to align with Mike Lindell?—Strang shot me a dirty look, personally vouched for Lindell's sincerity as a Christian, and ended the interview.

Shutting off my recorder, I grabbed my five-dollar copy of *God and Cancel Culture* and walked outside. The sun was diving below the rock quarries that formed a jagged border around Branson. I had made plans to attend Sunday morning worship on the opposite side of the state.

For the next four hours, I thought about Stephen Strang. I thought about the decisions he'd made; I thought about the questions I still wanted to ask. Little did I know, driving northbound through the cool Missouri night, that some answers awaited me in the city of St. Joseph.

PART III

THE
GLORY

CHAPTER FIFTEEN

ST. JOSEPH, MISSOURI

*What good is it for someone to gain the whole
world, yet forfeit their soul?*

—MARK 8:36

The first thing I noticed was the parking lot—how gigantic it looked and how desolate it was. There must have been spaces for eight hundred vehicles outside Word of Life Church, but on this chilly Sunday morning, maybe one in ten of those was occupied. It was an unfamiliar sight. Parking at most megachurches I'd visited required prayer and careful strategic planning; men in orange vests directed drivers to overflow lots so far from the church building that the steeple faded from view. That was not the case at Word of Life.

Then again, this was not a megachurch. Not anymore.

Pastor Brian Zahnd had told me, prior to my visit, that his congregation was a fraction of its former size. But that notice did little to brace me. Once inside the sanctuary, I was agape all over again. The imposing space, with its tiers of elongated wooden pews spilling backward from a darkened stage bathed in blue overhead lights, looked capable of seating close to a thousand people. But there couldn't have been more than 150 in attendance. Pulling out my phone, I double-checked the church website, thinking perhaps I'd arrived for the lighter of their worship services. But there was no other service. Word of Life met once on Sunday mornings. This was everybody.

For his part, Pastor Zahnd didn't seem fazed. At sixty-three, Zahnd looked and acted like a younger man. He wore an outfit of all black—jeans, T-shirt, leather jacket, thick-rimmed glasses—that was offset by a graying beard and bushy dark hair. This morning, he announced, practically skipping across the stage, was the forty-first anniversary of Word of Life Church. "I feel *good* today," he said, paying brief homage to James Brown. His energy was infectious. For a while already, the people around me had stood, arms outstretched, singing about God and His mercies. As Zahnd thanked the Lord for blessing this church, its people bowed their heads and lifted their palms, then jumped up from the pews and began hugging and laughing with one another. (Zahnd had instructed us to greet at least seven people; that quota was surpassed and then some.)

After the singing and praying and hugging, Zahnd launched into a sermon centered on the story of Haggai, a Jewish prophet, in 520 BC. Zahnd provided the historical backdrop: It had been sixty-seven years since Jerusalem—all of it, including Solomon's temple—was destroyed and the Jews were taken as exiles to Babylon. Eventually Babylon was overthrown by the Persians, and the Jews had come under the rule of the Persian king, Cyrus the Great. It was Cyrus, Zahnd explained, who allowed the Jewish exiles to return to Jerusalem and build a second temple. They got started on construction, but the work slowed and eventually stopped. For fifteen years the second temple sat unfinished. Enter Haggai.

The prophet blasted the priorities of God's people. In fact, he told them that their suffering—from drought and other afflictions—was punishment for becoming consumed with their own narrow needs and neglecting the work of God. Reminding the older generation of Jews of the splendor of Solomon's temple, Haggai shocked them by prophesying that the sequel would be even greater. He said God planned to establish His ultimate kingdom in a New Jerusalem, with a new temple, that would redeem mankind.

This motivational tactic worked. The Jews completed the temple. But Haggai's words—at least, as the people understood them—didn't come true. This rebuilt temple was a far cry from Solomon's magnificent structure. Even when King Herod kicked off a building drive centuries later and made spectacular renovations to the temple, it still didn't compare to the original.

What the Jews couldn't comprehend, Zahnd said, is that Haggai was prophesying a different kind of kingdom, a different kind of temple. He was telling of Jesus and His eternal sovereignty. The people were so attached to their identity, to the tangible glories of earthly power, that they missed the greater thing promised them.

"The more glorious latter temple that the prophet Haggai foretold has nothing to do with impressive buildings or national interests or imperial aspirations. These things are the petty ambitions of pharaohs, caesars, and other wannabes. It's the false glory of the kingdoms of this world that the devil offered to Jesus in the wilderness temptation, and Jesus rejected," Zahnd said.

"The more glorious temple of which the prophet spoke is nothing more than the new temple that is the body of Christ," the pastor added. "We've been given a new temple, one that can never be destroyed, and we're often too busy looking back at the old temple—something beautiful but ultimately fleeting—to appreciate the new temple in front of us."

Nothing of man lasts. Jesus promised to raise up the temple three days after it was destroyed—a foretelling of His death and resurrection—but also prophesied that the second temple, the one built at the behest of Haggai, would be demolished. The Romans took care of that in AD 70. By that time there was no need to build another: a growing number of Jews who believed that Jesus of Nazareth was the promised Messiah—calling themselves Christians—preached that a new, indestructible, eternal order had been established.

This changed everything. After centuries of worshipping on Saturdays, these Jews declared Sundays to be holy. They began eating pork and consorting with gentiles and ignoring the Jewish priests—behavior that would have been unthinkable throughout their history. Suddenly these early Christians no longer cared about the strictures and power struggles that had consumed them. Their validation came not from a physical stronghold but from a spiritual fortress. Zahnd pointed out how, in the New Testament epistle of Hebrews, the writer harked back to the words of Haggai, rejoicing that while God would continue to subject the world to disruption and uncertainty, "we are receiving a kingdom which cannot be shaken."

The pastor's implication was hard to miss: If only American Christians, two millennia later, could exude such confidence. Not that we're alone in getting mixed up. Ever since the baptism of Emperor Constantine in the middle of the fourth century, "the development toward an imperial Church and finally toward a state religion was almost a matter of necessity," Zahnd said, quoting the German theologian Gerhard Lohfink.

Zahnd continued with Lohfink verbatim: "It was a grandiose attempt to create a Christian 'empire' and thus to unite faith, life, and culture. Only a careful look at the people of God in the Old Testament, their experiment with the state and the collapse of the experiment, could have preserved the Church from repeating the old mistake. But it was not possible in late antiquity or in the Middle Ages for people to read the Old Testament so analytically. . . . Only the history of the modern era shattered the dream. Today the experiment is truly at an end and can never be resumed."

Zahnd's tone became more direct. "The writer of Hebrews understands that the glory of the latter temple is not a nation of this world, but the unshakable kingdom of Christ," he told us. "If you place your hope in the politics of this world, you will be *greatly* shaken."

The sanctuary was silent.

"I have so little faith in America. But fortunately, I'm sustained by a faith placed elsewhere," Zahnd said. "It doesn't mean I don't care about America; it just means I place my faith elsewhere. I place it in a kingdom that cannot be shaken, and that is the kingdom of Christ, and that is the glory of the latter temple that is greater than anything that has ever been or ever will be. Amen and amen."

"Amen," nodded the people around me.

"Now," the pastor said, pointing toward the communion elements, "let's come to the table and participate in the body of Christ."

ZAHND'S STORY OF FAITH BEGINS AT AGE FIFTEEN. RAISED AN HOUR outside of Kansas City, Missouri, the son of a prominent attorney who helped run the Missouri Republican Party, Zahnd was a compulsory churchgoer. But his real religion was music; his gods were Led Zeppelin and Jimi Hendrix. Jesus of Nazareth was little more than an abstract character.

Then, one night, he attended a youth revival at Missouri Western State University. There Zahnd had such a vivid encounter with Christ that he became a self-proclaimed "Jesus freak." He began proselytizing everyone he met and joined the Jesus Movement that sprang from the charismatic renewal of the 1960s. (Recall that the Greek word *charism* refers to a gift or favor that is bestowed, often in a supernatural context.) With its emphasis on spiritual endowments, the Jesus Movement aimed to restore to modern churches some ancient practices of the apostles: healing, prophesying, speaking in tongues. This was a decentralized undertaking, a nonconformist groundswell drawing its strength from the notion that Western Christianity had become complacent and consumeristic. For kids like Zahnd, who was raised in a respectable Baptist home, the draw was irresistible.

When he was seventeen, Zahnd began organizing an avant-garde ministry called the Catacombs. It was part church, part music venue, part coffeehouse and became a headquarters for young members of the Jesus Movement in the Kansas City metro area. In 1981, Zahnd decided to spin off the Catacombs into an actual church. He called it Word of Life, and despite having no theological training whatsoever, appointed himself lead pastor. He was twenty-two years old.

The church was a sensation. Attracting loads of college-aged and young professional Christians disillusioned with the stodginess of their congregations, Word of Life quickly outgrew its original venue. It moved and then moved again. Finally, just over a decade after he'd founded the church, Zahnd broke ground on a vast new property, with designs for a grand state-of-the-art sanctuary that would represent Word of Life's arrival as a megachurch.

These were heady times. Throughout the 1990s, Word of Life would explode in size and influence. Zahnd went from garage band leader to rock star headliner, regularly preaching to thousands of people every weekend. "We went through a period of time when, almost every single Sunday, it was a new record attendance," Zahnd said. "By the metrics that Americans use to measure success in ministry, we had achieved it all. People. Money. Power."

Around the turn of the century, however, Zahnd began to sense that something wasn't right. His church was full of nice people. They had grown up together, if not literally then by association, from subversive teenage zealots to refined, middle-aged church folk. But they hadn't grown up spiritually. Theirs was a Christianity, Zahnd began to realize, so heavy on style and feeling and expression that it eschewed doctrinal substance. In this sense they had become every bit as complacent and consumeristic as the churches they'd once rebelled against.

"There wasn't anything counterculture about what we were doing. This *was* the culture, just with a few Bible verses drizzled over it," Zahnd said. "We started off as these radical Jesus freaks, but over time, we'd turned into a bunch of Republicans with Jesus fishes on our SUVs."

It all began to feel facile and thin. Zahnd had never been insecure about his lack of theological training, but now it gnawed at him. He would come home Sunday afternoons feeling strangely unfulfilled, like a man leaving a banquet with his stomach still rumbling. "I had a crisis of faith, but it wasn't about Christ. It was about Christianity. *American* Christianity," the pastor recalled. "I just came to the conclusion that Jesus deserves a better Christianity than this. And I needed to go looking for it."

He had no idea where to start. Zahnd, by then in his mid-forties, had spent his entire adult life "stuck in this cul-de-sac of charismatic Christianity, where everyone reads the same stuff and it's very insular." After stumbling for a while, Zahnd finally discovered the Church Fathers. These were the experts who helped establish Christian doctrine in the ancient world: Augustine of Hippo, Gregory of Nyssa, Irenaeus of Lyons, Maximus the Confessor. Known in academic settings as "the patristics," these men merged Christian philosophy with applied theology, furnishing Zahnd with an intellectual understanding of Christ he never knew existed.

"It was thrilling. I had been embarrassingly ignorant of this stuff, and I couldn't get enough," Zahnd told me. "I found this thread. After studying all the Church Fathers, now I'm starting to read N. T. Wright and Walter Brueggemann and Stanley Hauerwas and David Bentley

Hart and all these preeminent theologians. I'm learning and changing. I'm loving every second of it."

On this metamorphic journey, Zahnd was slow to shed his former self. He was still leading a massive religious enterprise, after all, one that had certain expectations of its pastor. The 9/11 attacks had amplified nationalistic sentiments inside the church. Fights over abortion and gay marriage were hotter than ever. For a while, Zahnd kept on playing along, indulging the culture wars and lending his pulpit to Republican politicians. Finally, in the summer of 2004, he decided enough was enough.

"I stood up in front of the church and said, 'I'm moving on. We're going in a new direction,'" Zahnd recalled.

The pastor did some nipping and tucking at first, adjusting congregational norms and tweaking his preaching style at the margins, not wanting to scare anyone off. And then he got a phone call. It was October 2004, in the thick of the campaign pitting President George W. Bush against Democratic challenger John Kerry. The local GOP boss told Zahnd that Vice President Dick Cheney was coming to town for a rally. Would the Word of Life pastor deliver the invocation? Zahnd was paralyzed by the request. He did consider himself a nominal Republican—both his father, a judge, and his brother, a prosecutor, had been active in the state party—and besides, it was an honor to be asked to pray over the vice president of the United States. So, why did he feel sick at the idea of saying yes?

After a few tortured days of deliberation, Zahnd accepted the invitation. He met with Cheney personally. He got the VIP treatment. Then he was pushed out onto the stage, tasked with kicking off the event. Staring out at the sea of people, nearly ten thousand of them, Zahnd was overcome with guilt. He saw members of his church everywhere, draped in red, white, and blue. And they saw their pastor, the guy who'd sworn to take the church in a new direction, lending his religious authority to the Republican Party.

"The crowd is going absolutely wild," Zahnd recalled. "And I just heard Jesus saying, 'Brian, Brian, why are you politicizing me?'"

That moment, Zahnd believes, was God ordering him once and for all to abandon the world he'd known. And that's what he did. After muttering "the most innocuous prayer possible" into the microphone, Zahnd exited the stage, walked past the designated chair for him in the front row of the arena, found the parking lot, and got into his car, all the while praying silently for the Lord to forgive him.

The following Sunday, and in the Sundays that followed, Zahnd made clear to his congregation what the new Word of Life Church would be about. "I began to critique the American empire as not a kind of biblical Israel, but a kind of biblical Babylon. I told them that God was not on our side; that God raised up Jesus, not America," the pastor recalled. "I was pretty direct about it. You didn't have to read between the lines any-more. They got it. And then they left."

It was a slow leak at first—a Sunday no-show here, a Bible study ab-sence there—and then a gusher. Entire cliques and social networks quit the church together. People defected by the dozens, and then by the hun-dreds. Within a few years of Zahnd's announcement, the church had lost more than 1,500 members.

The pastor was prepared for casualties, but he couldn't have pre-dicted the scale of the exodus. Looking back, the hardest part was overhearing all the accusatory whispers—how he'd succumbed to a weakened, watered-down Christianity—when precisely the opposite was true.

"They would say, 'Brian's backsliding,' and if anything, I was *front-sliding*," he said, laughing. "Suddenly, I'm more committed to Jesus than I've ever been. But they saw it differently. Because when you're stuck in that left-right paradigm, that's all you can see. They would say, 'Brian's become a Democrat.' But I'm not a Democrat. I'm a kingdom person."

I TRAILED THE PASTOR'S JEEP TO A ROADSIDE SUSHI JOINT AND PARKED alongside him. Rummaging through my belongings on the passenger seat, I grabbed a notebook, two pens, and my recording device. Then I spotted *God and Cancel Culture*. I was still chafing from my chat with Stephen Strang the night before in Branson. On a whim, I grabbed the book, walked into the restaurant, and placed it on the seat beside me.

This, Zahnd said, drumming on the table between us, was one of his favorite study spots. It could be hard to concentrate inside the church; everyone always needed something from the senior pastor. Here he could achieve solitude, reading and praying and reflecting without interruption. It was inside this restaurant that he conceived of his book *Postcards from Babylon: The Church in American Exile*, which was published in 2019. He wrote the book in the format of letters to his former comrades in the charismatic evangelical world, pleading with them to recognize the disservice they were doing to Christ and His gospel.

"I've asked myself repeatedly, why did I wake up and so many of my contemporaries didn't?" Zahnd said. "I still don't have the answer."

There was an old pastor friend in particular, Zahnd said, whom he thought about often: Jentezen Franklin. Immediately I flashed back to the Faith and Freedom conference in Nashville. Franklin had been one of Ralph Reed's marquee speakers. I had watched the pastor whip the crowd into a frenzy describing how "our enemies" aimed to destroy Christianity in America.

"That used to be my routine," Zahnd told me. "If you want to know what I preached, back when we had the four thousand people, go find Jentezen's sermons on YouTube. It's the same kind of stuff."

The two men had been close friends and kindred spirits, a pair of rising stars in the charismatic movement. Franklin was stunned by Zahnd's decision to leave that world behind. They remained friendly for a while. It was Franklin who reached out to Zahnd, in the middle of the evacuation at Word of Life, and introduced him to a Christian publisher called Charisma Media. Years earlier, Zahnd had self-published a short book, *What to Do on the Worst Day of Your Life*, that had caught the attention of Charisma. Now the publisher was asking Zahnd to write an updated version for mass distribution. Zahnd felt compelled to say yes. His church was in trouble—attendance was barely two hundred on some Sundays—and he was beginning to wonder if it might expire altogether. A book could at least help pay the bills if he found himself unemployed.

When it came time to publish, in January 2009, Charisma began booking Zahnd on every major religious television and radio program in the country. There was one hitch: He refused to appear on Paula White's show. The prosperity gospel preacher was attracting huge audiences

with her "health and wealth" spiritualism, but Zahnd wasn't just bothered by her bad theology. He was offended by the fact that White, a professing Christian minister, would regularly host Donald Trump, the
vulgar playboy billionaire, on her evangelism platform, all because she
was enamored with his worldly success.

"This turns into a big fight, because I'm refusing to go on her show,"
Zahnd told me. "So, finally, the president of Charisma Media, the big
boss, this guy named Stephen Strang, he calls me up personally and
pleads with me to do the show. He tells me how many books it's going
to sell. And I tell him, 'Stephen, I don't care if it sells one million books.
You have to understand, Paula White and I do not belong to the same
religion.'"

Startled, I reached over and grabbed *God and Cancel Culture*, holding
it up to Zahnd.

"This guy?"

Zahnd inspected the cover of Strang's book. "Why do you have that?"
he asked me.

"I was just with him last night. In Branson."

Zahnd pressed his palms against his cheekbones. "He was *there*?"

"Yes."

"Did he know you were coming *here* today?"

"No."

Zahnd stared ahead. Then he began to laugh. "The Lord works in
mysterious ways," he said. "Let me tell you about Stephen Strang."

The two had quite a history. After Zahnd's 2009 book sold relatively
well, Strang, taken with the pastor's conviction—the man had torpe-
doed his own megachurch in the name of theology!—offered him a deal
to write three more books. Zahnd accepted. In 2011, he published *Unconditional: The Call of Jesus to Radical Forgiveness* (with a foreword
written by Miroslav Volf, the Yale theologian I befriended on the French
Riviera). Strang loved the book so much, Zahnd told me, that he flew the
pastor to Charisma's headquarters in Orlando to address the staff. Too
much of their work during Barack Obama's presidency had been hostile
and acrimonious, Strang told his employees. Zahnd—with his emphasis
on reconciliation and the rejection of political tribalism—was demonstrating a different path forward. Strang was so smitten with Zahnd

that he asked him to begin writing a column for *Charisma* magazine. It looked to be the dawn of a great partnership.

And then capitalism got in the way. *Charisma* readers complained about the pacifistic undertone of Zahnd's columns. *Unconditional* flopped with the publisher's core demographic. ("You had a lot of Methodists buying that book," Zahnd said with a chuckle, "but not a lot of charismatics.") It made for an awkward situation. Charisma Media had poured resources into promoting Zahnd and his book. But it was outsold—badly—by one of the publisher's other offerings that year, *The Harbinger*, a book that connected the 9/11 terror attacks to the ancient destruction of Israel, prophesying a full-circle threat to American Christians.

Zahnd was undeterred. Ignoring market feedback, and the not-so-subtle hints of editors and executives at Charisma Media, he wrote the next book, *Beauty Will Save the World*, as a repudiation of materialism and political striving. The book sold well, but Zahnd's iconoclastic streak—not to mention his blunt denunciation of the prosperity gospel—made him the resident bête noire. His *Charisma* column was canceled. By the time Zahnd wrote the third book, *A Farewell to Mars*, which argued for nonviolence as a foundational Christian principle, Charisma had turned on him. Strang refused to print the book, then tried to stop Zahnd from publishing it altogether.

In this context, my misadventure in Branson took on new meaning. I had been bewildered by Strang's unwillingness to acknowledge what was manifestly amiss all around us; by the latest *Charisma* magazine issue he handed me, the cover of which promoted a new book by the *Harbinger* author warning of ancient gods wreaking havoc on American culture; and by Strang's own books, which, to make his allusions to a divine indwelling of Donald Trump all the more questionable, included forewords from the likes of Jerry Falwell Jr. and Mike Lindell.

Zahnd's story made it all click.

"These people have lost their souls," Zahnd told me, tapping on the cover of Strang's book. "That's not being dramatic. That's being analytical. Stephen Strang knew better than this. He could have done the right thing. He chose not to."

It was evident that Zahnd took no pleasure in saying any of this. There was an anguish in his eyes, a stinging melancholy in his voice.

Too many of his old friends—Franklin and Strang, just to name two—
had been seduced by prominence and power, by fame and fortune. And
Zahnd could not understand why.

There is a warning issued repeatedly in the scriptures, about boasting
not in one's own accomplishments but boasting only in the knowledge
and glorification of God. That word, *glory*, can seem vague in certain biblical contexts. But typically, derived from the Hebrew *kavod*, it implies
weight, importance, heaviness—something of substantial value. When
Christians achieve something of substantial value, be it a megachurch
or a publishing empire, the impulse to self-glorify can become overpowering. But it must be resisted. Because the dynamic is very much
binary: You can glorify God or glorify yourself, but not both.

This, Zahnd said, explains why Jesus insisted that His followers
"deny themselves" and prepare to throw away their lives for His sake.
The pastor quoted one of my favorite verses, Mark 8:36.

"What good is it for someone to gain the whole world," Jesus asked,
"yet forfeit their soul?"

LOOKING BACK, ZAHND IS GRATEFUL FOR LOSING MUCH OF HIS CONGRE-
gation all those years ago. Downsizing so dramatically allowed the pastor to connect with his people more intimately, to make sure everyone
was on board with his mission and his message. This not only made for
a healthier church; it insulated Word of Life from the turmoil of the
Trump era.

In fact, Zahnd told me, at a moment when many of his clergy counterparts were bleeding members from their churches, Word of Life was
experiencing real growth for the first time in over a decade. The chief explanation: YouTube. This was not a COVID-specific phenomenon; Word
of Life had begun streaming its services online years before the pandemic arrived. Zahnd was skeptical of the practice at first. He believed
in gathering physically, in taking communion as one body, in the power
of corporate worship. He wasn't terribly interested in pastoring people
thousands of miles away. But then he got to know some of them. He listened to their stories, heard their prayers. Online church wasn't *their*

preference, either. They would love to join a solid, unified, kingdom-first congregation in their community.

"They just can't find one," Zahnd told me. "These people feel like they have nowhere to go. I just heard from someone yesterday who lives in Texas; apparently, the county she lives in voted for Trump in a higher percentage in 2020 than any other county in America. And she told me, 'Pastor, I cannot find a normal church.' What do I say to that?"

Zahnd is happy, on some interim basis, to offer an online community to the displaced masses. But it's not a sustainable solution to the problem of "normal church" scarcity. These people watching Zahnd online—particularly the less seasoned believers—need a permanent home. They need a pastor to love and disciple them; they need a church family to grow alongside them and hold them accountable. To this end, Zahnd is trying to help the only way he knows how: by mentoring young preachers.

"I had these four pastors here yesterday, from a fairly large church in Oregon," Zahnd said. "And I told them, 'You're going to have to lean into the great tradition. Don't allow your preaching to be driven by the news cycles. Start paying attention to the Revised Common Lectionary; preach from that. Pay attention to the liturgical calendar; preach from that.'"

Hours earlier, at the Word of Life entrance, a kindly old gentleman had handed me a church bulletin. The first thing I noticed was the date: "November 6, 2022. Twenty-Second Sunday After Pentecost." Zahnd's church observes days tied to the deaths of saints, sacred moments from scripture, and the onset of seasons such as Lent and Advent. American holidays—Memorial Day, Independence Day, Veterans Day—are not recognized. "What do those dates have to do with us?" Zahnd said with a shrug. "We're the Church."

It's not easy to break away from American traditions, Zahnd said. But if evangelicals are to regain lost standing, it's necessary.

"Christianity is inherently countercultural. That's how it thrives. When it tries to become a dominant culture, it becomes corrupted. That's been the case from the very beginning," Zahnd said. "This is one major difference between Islam and Christianity. Islam has designs on running the world; it's a system of government. Christianity is nothing like that. The gospels and the epistles have no vision of Christianity being a dominant religion or culture."

The Bible, as Zahnd pointed out, is written primarily from the perspective of the underdog: Hebrew slaves fleeing Egypt, Jews exiled to Babylon, Christians living under Roman occupation. This is why Paul implored his fellow first-century believers—especially those in Rome who lived under a brutal regime—to both submit to their governing authorities *and* stay loyal to the kingdom built by Christ.

It stands to reason that American evangelicals, themselves born into the bosom of imperial might, can't quite relate to Paul and his pleas for humility, or Peter and his enthusiasm for suffering, never mind that poor vagrant preacher from Nazareth and his egalitarian rhetoric. The last shall be first? What kind of socialist indoctrination is that?

"You see, the kingdom of God isn't real to most of these people. They can't perceive it," Zahnd said. "What's real is America. What's real is this tawdry world of partisan politics, this winner-takes-all blood sport. So, they keep charging into the fray, and the temptation to bow down to the devil to gain control over the kingdoms of this world becomes more and more irresistible."

Zahnd has studied the rise and fall of Christian civilizations; he understands that, as the Book of Ecclesiastes tells us, "there is nothing new under the sun." Still, it's hard for him to accept just how quickly this particular American experiment went south. When he created Word of Life Church at age twenty-two, riding high on the generational momentum of the Jesus Movement, he was convinced that the United States was experiencing a real-time revival. Forty years later, he is witnessing the sort of crash that will be studied by pastors in the centuries to come. "I think about it every day. I can't believe it came to this," Zahnd said. "I'm totally baffled by it. I'm not depressed; I'm not unhappy. I'm just *baffled*."

The pastor was quick to clarify something. He's not baffled by the 1,500 people who left his church almost two decades ago. He's not baffled by the people who go to Greg Locke's circus tent or listen to Paula White's podcasts or buy VIP tickets to Mike Flynn's ReAwaken America rally. These people are called *sheep* for a reason. No, Zahnd is baffled by the so-called shepherds. Scripture says God demands more from these Christian leaders. And yet, whether it's Strang platforming the My-Pillow lunatic, or Liberty University's leadership trading evangelism for electioneering, or the pastor down the road in St. Louis, a onetime friend who now leads his Sunday services with a fifteen-minute political segment called "Ron's Rants," Zahnd sees a reckless abdication of duty on the part of the people in charge. They are, as Jesus said of the Pharisees, blind guides, leading their followers to fall into a pit.

"You are forming your people in anger and hate. You are helping to intensify their capacity to hate other people," Zahnd said. "You are giving them permission to carry around this permanent rage."

I countered by telling Zahnd what these pastors would say about *him*—that he's woke, that he's lukewarm, that he's a coward for not taking a stand and fighting to advance biblical principles in a broken world.

"Taking a stand," Zahnd scoffed. "There's this false assumption of action we're called to take. The task of the Church is simply to be the Church. All of this high-blown rhetoric about changing the world—we don't need to change the world. We're not called to change the world. We're called to be the world *already changed* by Christ. That's how we're salt; that's how we're light."

He looked incredulous. "I talk about Jesus all the time. I talk about Jesus constantly. But I talk about Jesus in the context of *His* kingdom," Zahnd said. "The idea that Jesus is some mascot for the donkeys or the elephants—it's a catastrophe for the gospel."

The pastor told me he was offended—not upset, or hurt, or angry, but *offended*—by what the American Church had become. God does not tolerate idols competing for His glory, Zahnd said, and neither should anyone who claims to worship Him.

"You can take up the sword of Caesar or you can take up the cross of Jesus," Zahnd told me. "You have to choose."

CHAPTER SIXTEEN

KENNESAW, GEORGIA

No one can serve two masters. Either you will hate the one and love the other, or you will be devoted to the one and despise the other.

—MATTHEW 6:24

Herschel Walker had a joke to tell.

It was about a man who suddenly dies and meets Saint Peter at the pearly gates, only to learn that due to some mix-up his soul had not been designated for either heaven or hell. Because of the unusual circumstance, Peter gives the man a chance to tour both places. They ride the elevator down to hell first. It's a giant party. The man, living it up with old friends, is reluctant to leave. Finally, he goes with Peter to see heaven, and while it's nice enough, he decides he'd rather spend eternity down south. But when the man descends back to hell, everything has changed. It's torturously hot. People are crying and screaming. "What happened?" the man asks aloud. "A couple hours ago there was a party."

"Satan shows up," Walker deadpanned, "and he says, 'A couple hours ago I was campaigning!'"

Everyone laughed. But this was no incidental comedic detour. The U.S. Senate race in Georgia had become the most-watched campaign in America, and not just because it was likely to determine control of Congress's upper chamber. The snowballing claims of personal scandal against Walker, the Republican nominee, had turned the contest into a made-for-Jerry-Springer spectacle. Walker's campaign had responded by bludgeoning his opponent, Democratic senator Raphael Warnock, stressing his church's history of threatening to evict tenants from a rental property and dredging up an unsubstantiated claim that he'd run over his ex-wife's foot with a car. That Warnock was a pastor—the pastor, in fact, of Ebenezer Baptist, the Atlanta church once led by Martin Luther King Jr.—lent an air of divine consequence to the campaign. As November 8 drew closer, each candidate accused the other, in so many words, of being a phony follower of Jesus. By the time Walker stepped to the podium on Election Day eve, he made it known that the next day's choice was not just between a Republican and a Democrat.

"The left is campaigning right now for you. They're campaigning. *My God*, Senator Warnock is campaigning," Walker said, referring back to his punch line. "They're trying to take you down in that elevator."

The insinuation was hard to miss—even the conservative *Washington Examiner* ran a headline reading WALKER LIKENS WARNOCK TO 'SATAN' IN CONTENTIOUS GEORGIA SENATE RACE—but the Republican nominee left nothing to chance.

"I'm that warrior for God!" Walker declared. "He prepared me for this moment, because He knew I was going to have go up against that wolf in sheep's clothing."

The hundreds of people around me, pressed shoulder to shoulder in the floodlight-bathed parking lot of the Governors Gun Club in exurban Atlanta, had signed up for just this sort of spiritual conflict. Every likening of Warnock to the devil stirred snarling cheers; every mention of his own dauntless persecution at the hands of the left inspired awestruck ovations. Walker was accustomed to being a hero—he'd won the Heisman Trophy as a punishing tailback at the University of Georgia—but this was a different sort of exaltation. He was more than a homecoming king; he was a crusader. Standing before a Bulldog-red tour bus that featured his smiling visage stamped over the word HERSCHEL, the Republican candidate pledged to stop Warnock from dragging the good people of Georgia down to hell with him. They danced and chanted and celebrated as though the election was already won. Maybe it was.

Republicans looked to have momentum in the late stages of the campaign, and party officials were swelling with confidence about winning Georgia. This would be a triumph made all the sweeter by what Walker had endured. Though he denied allegations of having ever paid for an abortion, the pile of evidence in one particular case—including a personal check covering the cost of the procedure and a handwritten "get well" card, both synced to the date in question—left little doubt that he had. ("I thought we all knew this," Erick Erickson, a conservative radio host in Georgia, tweeted in response to the *Daily Beast* bombshell that dropped one month before Election Day. Erickson added that "people do change over time.")

That October surprise was most notable for what it *didn't* do: change the trajectory of the race. The fallout from the abortion story—even the social media scorning from Walker's own son, who had once been a visible supporter of his dad's campaign—did little to sour the state's conservative Christian voters on Walker. Even the revelation that Walker had allegedly pressured that same woman to have a second abortion—and a subsequent on-camera accusation, from *another* ex-girlfriend, that he'd paid for her procedure—didn't hurt his candidacy. Why would it? What mattered was that Walker had an *R* next to his name. What mattered was power.

"*Winning* is a virtue," Dana Loesch, a conservative Christian talk-show host, said on her program. "I don't care if Herschel Walker paid to abort endangered baby eagles. I want control of the Senate."

And so it came to pass in Georgia, the night before the election, that these hundreds of people gathered for a performative ritual of make-believe martyrdom. As Walker's surrogates took turns at the microphone denouncing the character assassination of this good and decent man, the people in the crowd played along, booing and hissing and feigning outrage, even as one after another admitted to me that they believed the charges against Walker were true.

"This is a tough business. The difference between football and politics is you don't have a helmet. And there are no rules. You can cheat," Lindsey Graham, the senator from South Carolina, said from the stage. "I've been in this business a long time. I don't think I've ever seen anybody belittled, dehumanized, treated so poorly as my good friend Herschel Walker."

Soon after, Gina Phillips, who had been applauding Graham's impassioned defense of Walker's integrity, stopped on the sidelines of the event to chat with a pastor named Raymond Porter. The minister, wearing a silver-and-burgundy clergyman's robe, was there to protest Warnock's pro-choice policies. Phillips worked at a pregnancy help clinic and was eager to compare notes with Porter. As I stood chatting with them, I was struck by the nonchalance of their shared observation about Walker: *Of course* he paid for those abortions as a private citizen, they agreed, but what counted moving forward was his opposition to abortion as a public official.

"I'd rather have Herschel Walker pay for an abortion, repent, get right with God about it, than elect Raphael Warnock who'd allow everyone to have unlimited abortions," Phillips said.

There was one problem: Walker had not repented. At least, not publicly. The candidate had stubbornly denied the allegations, claiming an innocence that was utterly implausible and yet, somehow, totally acceptable. I asked Phillips if repentance is possible while clinging to a lie.

"He's not telling *us* the truth. But I think he's done the right thing with God," Phillips replied.

If abortion is murder, as pro-life advocates like Phillips believe, then can someone who committed murder be forgiven without admitting to it? She shrugged at the question. I decided to simplify things. Doesn't the public deserve to know whether a politician running on a specific promise has broken that promise in his own life?

"It doesn't bother me," she replied. "Because Raphael Warnock wants to let full-term babies be born and left on a table to die."

Phillips was referring to Warnock's vote—which he cast along with every other Democrat in the Senate, save for Bob Casey of Pennsylvania and Joe Manchin of West Virginia—against the Born-Alive Abortion Survivors Protection Act. The bill would require health practitioners to provide medical care to any baby that survives an attempted abortion. This one vote did not occur in a vacuum: Much of the Democratic Party, which once emphasized that abortions should be "safe, legal, and rare," had more recently come to support abortion at any time, for any reason, a position well outside the mainstream. Both before and after the *Dobbs* ruling that overturned *Roe v. Wade*, polling consistently showed that while most Americans support abortion rights, an overwhelming majority of them—across the ideological spectrum—also believe abortion should be illegal in the third trimester.

What made Warnock's extremist position all the more notable was his training in the clergy. The son of a Pentecostal preacher, Warnock spoke eloquently, in Congress and on the campaign trail, about mankind being made in the image of God. He littered his speeches with references to scripture while advocating for human rights. In 2022, he told voters that he has "a profound reverence for life." Given all that, one might assume that Warnock would break from his party on this issue. Yet he remained unapologetically pro-choice under any circumstance, stressing that the decision should be left between a woman, her doctor, and, if need be, her pastor. "Even God gave us a choice!" Warnock told voters at one rally, in a clip that quickly went viral. (Pressed during a debate to clarify what he meant, a flustered Warnock responded, "I think it's self-explanatory," which, theologically, it most certainly was not.)

Walker took plenty of pot shots at Warnock over his other positions, from supporting transgender rights to expanding the social safety net to condemning institutional racism in America. But it was Warnock's abortion position that lent itself to Walker's strategy of portraying the senator as Lucifer incarnate. As the campaign wore on, Walker went from challenging Warnock's policy choices to questioning his legitimacy as a Christian. "He wants to throw these Bible verses out and say he's doing a good job," Walker sneered at the Election Day eve rally.

Warnock wasn't the only one throwing Bible verses out. While making his closing argument that night, Walker alluded countless times to scripture, often in disjointed fashion. He said Warnock failed the country by not holding Biden responsible for the withdrawal from Afghanistan—the way God held Adam and Eve responsible for eating the forbidden fruit. He said Warnock failed his community by ignoring Matthew, twenty-five ("When I was hungry, you fed me . . .") and threatening to evict those tenants. He said Warnock failed his Black church by preaching about racism instead of promoting America's innate goodness. "God says, 'Together we stand, divided we fall,'" Walker declared. "Right now I'm not ready to fall!" (These and other arguments were continually punctuated with the now-familiar warning, "They're trying to take you down that elevator!")

That Walker was not always biblically literate made no difference to the crowd in Kennesaw. They were eating up every word. He had convinced them, no matter his own personal failings, that he was playing for the right team—politically and otherwise.

"We need those warriors [in] Washington," Walker said, building to his rhetorical grand finale. "When I go up there, Jesus Christ is coming with me. He can block and I can run!"

With the pulsing lights and screaming crowd rousing memories of his athletic zenith, Walker shared what one of his offensive linemen used to tell him: "Herschel, follow me. I can take you to the promised land."

The candidate extended his arms. "I'm going to tell all you: Vote for me, and I'll help us to get to the promised land!"

As the music blasted and a throng of supporters circled around their hero for pictures and hugs and last-minute prayers, I glanced over at the entourage standing in the shadows of Walker's tour bus. There were five of his confidants, applauding and shouting through cupped hands. One of them was doing nothing at all. He was just standing there, arms crossed, soaking it all in, a knowing smile spread across his face. It was Ralph Reed.

THE NEXT MORNING, OVER AN ELECTION DAY BREAKFAST IN THE STYL-ish Buckhead neighborhood of Atlanta, Reed told me he had a feeling: This was Walker's day. Unlike some who believed the race was too close to call—or others who predicted that neither Walker nor Warnock would clear the 50 percent mark needed to avoid a runoff under Georgia election law—Reed was bullish on Walker's chances of winning outright. The Republican governor, Brian Kemp, was running away with his race and could have coattails down the ticket. Democrats nationally looked to be limping toward the finish line, playing defense over untamed inflation, rising crime, and lawlessness at the southern border. The history of midterm beatings taken by new presidents boded poorly for Joe Biden and his party.

And yet, Reed told me, what informed his outlook more than those political fundamentals was a gut feeling that the attempt to destroy Walker had failed. Not only that—it had *helped* him. Republicans who had been slow to embrace their party's nominee, Reed said, had rallied around him in the wake of the allegations, sensing that this was yet another orchestrated attack on a virtuous Christian man. Hence the language of sacrificial suffering that became central to Walker's cause down the homestretch: If Democrats were weaponizing the familiar trope of evangelical hypocrisy against him, it only made sense for Republicans to tap into the tried-and-true persecution complex of their base.

"The drubbing of evangelicals as hypocrites and frauds and phonies—candidates like Herschel, and voters who support candidates like Herschel—is unrelenting," Reed told me. "I think people are honestly tired of that kind of politics. The politics of fear and smear, the politics of personal destruction, the politics of trying to tear people down and produce somebody out of thin air. . . . It's gutter politics. And it's sometimes practiced by both sides, but it has become a wholly predictable and key part of the Democratic playbook."

The fact is, Reed said—dutifully reminding me that he trained as a historian—that these ad hominem strikes have rarely been successful. Thomas Jefferson's ownership of human beings didn't prove relevant to most voters. Neither did Grover Cleveland's out-of-wedlock child. Coincidentally, one seeming exception came in the 1990s, when Republicans, *led by Reed*, capitalized on Bill Clinton's libido and persuaded the conservative churchgoing public that morality was a prerequisite for political leadership. "We care about the conduct of our leaders, and we will not rest until we have leaders of good moral character," Reed told a Christian Coalition gathering in 1998, according to a contemporaneous account in the *New York Times*. "The American people are hungry for that message."

But not as hungry as Reed hoped. Democrats won surprising victories in the 1998 midterms—right in the thick of the Monica Lewinsky scandal—and Clinton's popularity rebounded to historic highs. This was a hard lesson for Reed. Republicans had overplayed their hand, assuming that voters cared more about character than they actually did. By the time Trump came along, Reed said, voters were deaf to the acoustics of personal indignity. This explains why he bought into Trump's candidacy long before other evangelical leaders did: Reed had concluded that voters are far more forgiving than most political analysts give them credit for.

If Reed's performance in the aftermath of the Walker allegations came across as shameless—his emotional vouching for a "dear friend" he'd known for all of two years; his organizing of a "Prayer Warriors for Herschel" event at an Atlanta church that he barred reporters from attending; his comparison of Walker standing tall against these charges to Trump surviving the *Access Hollywood* tape—he didn't particularly care. Reed did what he had to do. His theories of primitive human nature, American political history, and the modern Republican Party were connected by a common thread. People, he said, are fundamentally self-interested. So was he.

"Voters are really pragmatic. There is nothing new about giving candidates the benefit of the doubt about past moral failings," he said, scooping a spoonful of berries and oatmeal. "And by the way, generally speaking, I'm happy about that." Reed broke into that inculpable grin. "Now, I'm *more* happy when that grace is extended to the candidate that I'm supporting."

It reminded me of the conversation I'd had with Pastor Robert Jeffress at First Baptist Dallas. Both he and Reed drew a similar narrative arc to make sense of Trump's relationship with the evangelical voter. But the two men seemed to diverge on one key point: Jeffress believed that evangelicals came to champion Trump not because they were full of grace, but because they were full of *fear*. The universal stench of scandal may have inured the evangelical mind, Jeffress told me, but it was the rejection of Christian values in the culture—the "under siege" mindset—that truly changed the game. I asked Reed if he thought this was a fair way to understand the appeal of both Trump and Walker.

Reed bristled at the notion that evangelicals were mobilized by fear (this, months after he told us in Nashville that his conference-goers were scared that the country might not survive much longer). Rather, Reed said, Christians were rebelling against their views being treated as "inherently intolerant and undemocratic." He recalled Barack Obama's observation that some voters would cling to their guns or their religion as the nation changed around them; he assigned a spiritual subtext to Hillary Clinton's comments about "deplorables" and "irredeemables." In these cases and many others, Reed said, America's political and cultural elite had gone out of their way to ostracize conservative Christians, treating their political calculations as illegitimate and inciting growing hostility against the evangelical Church.

"There's no honest conversation anymore. They're not saying, 'I understand these are tough issues. You have to wrestle with your faith and your moral beliefs, and this is where you came down.' No. It's, 'You're a hypocrite. You're a phony. You're a fraud,'" Reed told me. "All those things are lies. And they're not just lies; they're slurs on the character of these people. Because it suggests that their movement is based on some reactionary fear, rather than an admirable, robust expression of their citizenship."

Once upon a time, Reed might have been right in observing that Christianity was getting a raw deal from the culture. But not today. Just as with the unraveling of the Republican Party, the Church had been destabilized from within, its fringe infiltrating the mainstream in ways that warranted systemic criticism. There was a reason Christian views writ large were now summarily dismissed as "inherently intolerant and undemocratic." For generations, white evangelicals had been overwhelmingly supportive of both immigrants and refugees entering the United States; by 2020 they were, far and away, the least likely of any religious subgroup to advocate for either one. And this was not some outlying development. In the year after Trump left office, polling repeatedly showed there was one demographic group most likely to believe that the election had been stolen, that vaccines were dangerous, that globalists were controlling the U.S. population, that liberal celebrities were feasting on the blood of infants, that resorting to violence might be necessary to save the country: white evangelicals.

None of this justified the sweeping censure of tens of millions of people. Having spent Trump's presidency traveling the country, meeting religious voters in small towns and big cities alike, I knew how many serious, sane evangelicals were still out there. These people have no place in the left-wing fever dreams that inform cable news punditry and op-ed pages. They are reasonable and realistic, making prudential political judgments that often reflect something quite limited about their core values, their commitment to others, their complex set of religious convictions. They are dismayed by the hysteria and hyperbole that has captured their movement and want nothing more than to reclaim it. Their character deserves respect and the crackup of the evangelical Church is not their doing.

But Reed rejects this analysis. He scoffs at the suggestion of a self-inflicted crisis. In his narrative, evangelicals have been in the barrel since the courts banned prayer in public schools and legalized abortion and sanctioned the government to regulate religious institutions. This unfair and systematic shunning of evangelicals, Reed insists, is nothing new. He's dedicated his career to fighting back against it. The only recent development, he told me, is that now he's got an army behind him.

"We've always been marginalized. We're marginalized today," Reed said. "The challenge was, could we ever change it? And we did. I mean, it took forty or fifty years. But we've changed it."

Changed *what*, exactly? The public's perception of evangelical Christianity is worse than at any point in recorded history. Church attendance is steadily eroding and will nosedive as Baby Boomers die off in greater numbers. Meanwhile, the rhetoric around their supposed persecution—Reed told Stephen Strang, on his podcast in 2019, that it would be "open season" on Christians if Trump lost reelection—hasn't been updated since the heyday of Jerry Falwell Sr. The only thing that seems changed, I observed to Reed, is disposition. Whereas the evangelical movement once downplayed its alliances with those who might undermine its moral credibility, today it openly champions the likes of Donald Trump and Herschel Walker.

Reed set his jaw. "I believe as a theological matter that someone can find redemption in Christ and become a new person," he replied. "And I believe that Herschel Walker is a new person."

Maybe he was. I didn't know the man's heart. If the allegations against Walker were true, then it would be consistent with scripture for him, as a new person who found redemption in Christ, to take responsibility for his actions, to admit his deceptions, to ask for the forgiveness that accompanies being a new person, and to radiate the transformative mercy he had been shown. But Walker wasn't doing any of that. Instead, he was asking for cheap grace. He was promoting a surface-level sanctification. He was using Christianity as a lowest common denominator—a way to gloss over the mistakes of his past, to explain his persecution at present, and to guarantee voters a political reward in the future.

I flashed back to Walker's defiant appearance at Reed's event in Nashville a few months earlier. "No weapon formed against me shall ever prosper," the candidate had said, quoting the prophet Isaiah, as reports swirled about the out-of-wedlock children he'd neglected to raise. Reed had looked smitten. Now, with the campaign in its final hours, I asked Reed: If Walker won, would it prove that Georgia voters really *believed* he was a new person? Or would it reveal that they care more about power than principle?

"I think what it shows is that people have rejected a really dirty gutter-level campaign of character assassination, and an attempt to destroy a good and decent human being," Reed answered. "And I think that what it says is that with few exceptions, elections tend to be about the economy and they tend to be a referendum on the policies of the party holding the White House with regard to the economy."

He paused for emphasis. "I think the Democrats and their allies tried to dodge that bullet by trying to run an alternative campaign of character assassination and personal destruction," Reed said. "And it failed."

NOT EXACTLY.

Walker failed to hit the 50 percent needed to win the Senate race outright, and so did Warnock, sending the election to a December runoff election. The signs were most ominous for the Republican candidate. Walker ran a full 5 points behind the top of the ticket, GOP governor Brian Kemp, and also lagged noticeably behind other Republicans on the ballot. The explanation was straightforward: Exit polling showed that for whatever concerns independent voters had about Warnock's policies, they were even more concerned about Walker's character and judgment. Despite framing his race as a proxy war between heaven and hell, Walker won a smaller share of white evangelical voters than did Kemp. He won a smaller share of pro-life voters than did Kemp. He won a smaller share of conservatives than did Kemp. These margins were small—a few points—but small margins made all the difference.

A month later, Walker lost the runoff to Warnock.

The Republican nominee delivered a gracious concession speech, pleading with his voters to "believe in America and continue to believe in the Constitution and believe in our elected officials most of all." There were no foolish claims about voter fraud, no manufactured appeals to the Almighty. Just a divisive candidate going out on a unifying note. In truth, Walker looked relieved at the result. Whatever his faults, this man did not deserve to be used by powerful people to advance their agenda. All the tough-guy talk they coached into him—a fighter for Georgia, a warrior for God—couldn't conceal the fact that he was unprepared, unstable, and fundamentally unfit for the office he was seeking.

"Don't beat women, hold guns to peoples heads, fund abortions . . . leave your multiple minor children alone to chase more fame, lie, lie, lie, say stupid crap, and make a fool of your family," Walker's son, Christian, wrote on Twitter after the race was called. "And then maybe you can win a senate seat."

In fairness to Walker, he was hardly the only Republican to come up short in 2022.

Defying the odds, the GOP laid an egg on Election Day. Republicans did recapture the House of Representatives by a thin margin. But they blew a chance to win back the Senate, lost key governor's races, and forfeited control of several state legislative bodies. The analysis was elementary. In some of the nation's most competitive states, Republicans had nominated radical candidates with views and rhetoric that scared away the moderates and independents who decide elections. Certainly, it was no coincidence that the prime examples of this—Walker included—were candidates who espoused some version of Christian nationalism.

In Pennsylvania, Republican Doug Mastriano—who prayed for Trump to "seize the power" before Joe Biden's inauguration, and later launched his campaign for governor to the sound of a shofar blowing—did not get the biblical miracle he promised in Erie. He lost by 15 points, an impressive feat in a state where the last two presidential elections were decided by less than 2 points *combined*. And in Arizona, Kari Lake, the onetime Buddhist-curious television anchor who found religion in bashing any Republican apostate who doubted the saving power of

Donald Trump, snatched defeat from the jaws of victory. Though she faced a forgettable Democratic opponent—and claimed that God "chose" her to be governor—Lake suffered critical defections from moderate Republican voters in Maricopa County, the state's largest voting jurisdiction, and lost the country's tightest race.

She refused to concede. Insisting the election was rigged against her, Lake dialed up the religious fanaticism to rally her faithful. She spoke of praying to God, telling Him to "make this victory come whatever way you want," even if that meant overcoming "the BS" that election officials were trying to pull. She joined a livestreamed prayer session pleading with heaven to overturn the results; one speaker asked God to "avenge us" against the Democrats. She told supporters that "the power of prayer" was leading to a successful legal effort to install her as governor, proclaiming: "We're taking these bastards to trial!" A week after the election, Lake's disciples performed a "Jericho march" around the Maricopa County elections office, believing that upon the seventh lap the deep-state deception would come tumbling down like those city walls of Old Testament lore. Despite these efforts—and half-baked lawsuits challenging the results—Lake's loss was finalized, and her Democratic opponent was sworn into office.

NO MAN CAN SERVE TWO MASTERS.

Any politician who runs for office sensing a divine mandate soon confronts a bracing reality: Campaigns are built around the accumulation of money, power, and influence, currencies of a kingdom to which Christians do not belong. Dual citizenship is not a biblical option. When Jesus spoke of the metaphorical "two masters," He explained, "Either you will hate the one and love the other, or you will be devoted to the one and despise the other." Jesus concluded with the famous line: "You cannot serve both God and money."

This quote has long been used to shame the extravagantly wealthy. But Christ's message was more nuanced. Instead of *money*, the term used in most translations is *mammon*, from the Greek word *mamōnas*. Drawing from roots in Hebrew and Aramaic, *mamōnas* has historically been understood as referring not just to material wealth but to any entity that encourages greed, prestige, self-glorification. Some early Christian scholars, including Gregory of Nyssa, believed that Jesus meant "Mammon" as an alias for Satan himself. The reason politics are such a dangerous trap for Christians isn't that they lead to devil worship per se, but that they tempt even the most disciplined believer to pursue that which inevitably distracts from—and comes into conflict with—their allegiance to God.

Matthew 6:24 isn't simply a rebuke to the Doug Mastrianos and Kari Lakes and Herschel Walkers of the world. The road to hell, as that old unsigned proverb cautions, is paved with good intentions.

Consider the pro-life cause. Millions of evangelicals identify as single-issue voters, having formed their political sentience around stopping what they see as the moral atrocity of killing unborn babies. After fighting for two generations to overturn *Roe v. Wade*, evangelicals heralded the *Dobbs* ruling in June 2022 as deific validation of the efforts put forth—and the compromises made—to end the scourge of abortion. Some went out of their way to mock Christian leaders who had preached any modicum of partisan restraint. William Wolfe, the ex–Trump administration official and avowed Christian nationalist, blasted Russell Moore, David French, and like-minded evangelicals who had opposed Trump's candidacy in 2016. "Will they admit they were wrong?" Wolfe tweeted.

But the ruling *didn't* end the scourge of abortion. The *Dobbs* case certainly changed the landscape of abortion policy in America, but not in the ways people like Wolfe had envisioned. Once a controlled and regulated medical issue, abortion became a wild-west patchwork of policies in the aftermath of *Dobbs*. Some red states rushed to ban the procedures entirely. But many more blue and purple states, now liberated from any overarching federal framework, pursued laws that made *Roe v. Wade* look conservative by comparison. On Election Day 2022, the citizens of six states voted on ballot measures that would shatter old precedents by dramatically increasing access to abortion. All six measures—including three in Republican-dominated states—ended in defeat for the pro-life side. The fifty-year campaign to overturn *Roe v. Wade* had succeeded, and the result was *more* abortions in America.

Winning elections does nothing to woo persuadable people. Confirming Supreme Court justices does nothing to convert skeptics. The evangelical movement's exercise of raw political power was doomed to fail even as it succeeded. According to Gallup, in early 2023, the number of Democrats who supported looser abortion laws had reached an all-time high. No surprise there. But that same poll also showed a historic number of *Republicans* supporting looser abortion laws. The trend line was devastating for the pro-life community: Republicans now supported liberalized abortion laws at rates higher than Democrats did just two decades earlier.

How could this have happened? One explanation is that too many evangelicals have taken the path of least resistance. Holding up signs is easy. Posting on Facebook is easy. Voting for a candidate is easy. But providing sustained support to babies and their mothers—by donating disposable income, by volunteering for long shifts at that clinic in a rough part of town, by considering adoption of a newborn with fetal alcohol syndrome—is much, much harder. Not every pro-life advocate has the capacity to do these things, of course, and that doesn't make their beliefs any less sincere. Plenty of pro-life advocates *have* done these things and will continue to do them. Yet none of those people—and I've known hundreds of them—would argue that their efforts are anywhere close to the scale necessary to change the American public's heart on this issue. None of them would pretend that the sum total of these grassroots efforts is remotely proportional to the raw political engagement surrounding abortion rights. It's worth wondering how different this debate might look a half century later had millions of single-issue voters invested in something other than electoral politics as a solution to the problem of unwanted pregnancy.

There is nothing inherently wrong with legislative engagement. People of faith *should* advocate on moral grounds for the betterment of their fellow man. But politics are one tool to help construct a movement; politics are not the movement itself. Slavery would not have been abolished by bumper stickers and annual marches with hashtags. The struggle for civil rights was powered by people who were unrelenting in their on-the-ground activism, who toiled in the trenches without reward, who did dangerous and unpleasant work with humility and grace. These fights were waged block by block, city by city, to rally public consciousness to the cause. There were no shortcuts to legislating a more just society. More often than not, winning a political battle first requires winning the public argument.

The pro-life movement has not won the public argument—and, arguably, it hasn't really tried. The message of abortion as a moral evil, as an affront to the loving God who made humanity in His own image, has proven curiously ineffective. Why?

For one thing, that message seems wildly inconsistent with the politics otherwise practiced by those who claim the "pro-life" mantle. If one is driven to electoral advocacy by the conviction that mankind bears the image of God, why stop at opposing abortion? What about the shunning of refugees? What about the forced separation of babies from their mothers? What about the hollowing out of programs that feed hungry kids? What about the lifelong incarceration of nonviolent offenders and the wrongful execution of the innocent? What about the Darwinist health-care system that prices out sick people and denies treatment to poor people and produces the developed world's highest maternal mortality rate? What about the fact that, in 2020, guns had become *the number one cause of death* for children in the United States? Surely even the most devoted anti-abortion advocate could spot the problem when Sarah Huckabee Sanders, the former Trump press secretary who was running for governor of Arkansas, declared, "We will make sure that when a kid is in the womb, they're as safe as they are in a classroom." Indeed, America set another new record for school shootings in 2022, and the evangelical movement was silent.

The other problem with the pro-life message: *the messengers*. Can we really expect Americans to take lessons on virtue from a president who brags about grabbing women by their vaginas? Can we really expect voters to entertain the argument of unborn lives having inherent dignity coming from a man who lies about having ended unborn life himself? Evangelicals can rationalize all this—going on about "binary decisions" and "the lesser of two evils" until they convince themselves it's true—but the unwillingness to demand and enforce a higher standard has sapped their arguments of moral urgency.

There is no blanket answer to complex questions of making compromises for the greater good. Inevitably, some citizens will choose to form uncomfortable associations, like civil rights leaders did with a president who held retrograde racial views, Lyndon B. Johnson, in the name of passing the Voting Rights Act into law. But the unbelieving world must always know that earthly alliances are subordinate to eternal allegiance. This is the great failing of today's evangelical lobby. Instead of testifying confidently to the presence of a supreme and sovereign God—a celestial chess master rolling His eyes at our earthly checkerboard—Christian conservatives have acted like toddlers lost at the shopping mall, panicked and petrified, shouting the name of their father with such hysteria that his reputation is diminished in the eyes of every onlooker.

It's not just a lack of confidence that undermines the Christian witness, but a carelessness, a casual way of communicating the Lord's priorities. If a politician claims God's support, and that politician goes on to lose, can we blame unbelievers for concluding that *God* lost, too? And if God lost something as trivial as a political campaign, how can He possibly triumph over the grave?

This is the problem with politics as a substitute religion. Jesus commanded us to love the Lord with all our heart, soul, mind, and strength, and to love our neighbors as ourselves. *This* is the recipe for reaching the unchurched. *This* is the recipe for convicting the unconvicted. *This* is the recipe for effecting change—whether over abortion or sexual ethics or any other issue of importance.

Donald Trump promised a transactional relationship with evangelical voters: He would give them pro-life policies in exchange for their unconditional support. That transaction went through, but the receipt isn't pretty. Abortion rates spiked during his presidency. The celebration that accompanied toppling *Roe v. Wade* was short-lived. In 2022, for the first time in memory, *Democrats* were the single-issue voters when it came to abortion, turning out in historic numbers to support abortion rights. It proved to be decisive, swinging dozens of competitive races against the Republican Party. The only thing more predictable than this crushing defeat of the pro-life movement was its immediate scapegoating by Trump himself.

"It wasn't my fault that the Republicans didn't live up to expectations in the midterms," the former president wrote on social media.

It was, Trump insisted, the "abortion issue."

CHAPTER SEVENTEEN

PHOENIX, ARIZONA

It is not the healthy who need a doctor, but the sick.

—MARK 2:17

Two thousand souls filled the sanctuary's lower bowl one night in February 2023, yet they hadn't come for sanctification. They kicked off the event with a blaring, rock-band rendition of "Christ Be Magnified"—"I won't bow to idols, I'll stand strong and worship you / And if it puts me in the fire, I'll rejoice 'cause you're there too"—but there was little rejoicing. Although they gathered inside Dream City Church, this wasn't a church service. It was the first Wednesday evening of the month. At Dream City, that meant it was "Freedom Night in America."

Pastor Luke Barnett greeted the first-timers in attendance. He explained that this was a chance to "talk about what's happening in our nation" and "draw a line in the sand" to preserve its traditional Christian values. He couldn't take credit for the idea. Freedom Night, the pastor said, was the brainchild of a "visionary" Christian, "a wonderful, wonderful man of God who loves the Lord." As Barnett built up the introduction, like the announcer at an NBA All-Star Game—"He's a friend of Dream City Church . . ."—the crowd rose to its feet.

Charlie Kirk played it cool. After all, he was used to big entrances.

Once a doe-eyed misfit with an outsize self-image, he was now a doe-eyed misfit with seven million social media followers, having grown his youth-activist organization Turning Point USA from scrappy upstart into industry behemoth. Kirk had cannily tapped into the quick-twitch instincts of his fellow Millennials, building an empire of memes and merchandise, takedowns and talking points, recognizing early in Trump's rise how "owning the libs" could be monetized. Fighting faux outrage on the left with faux outrage from the right, he became a profiteer of the American culture wars. Kirk, still shy of his thirtieth birthday, usurped the old guard of the conservative movement with such ease that even the right-wingers wise to his game had to play along. He enlisted volunteers and earned downloads and won headlines at an extraordinary clip. A few weeks before this Dream City event, Kirk had hosted the second annual "AmericaFest," a four-day carnival of politics and culture, just down the street at the Phoenix Convention Center. The event attracted GOP heavyweights, Fox News celebrities, internet luminaries—and a crowd bigger than most of the year's other right-wing gatherings combined.

Despite these many successes, Kirk, like the folks in his audience, was in no mood to celebrate. "It was a tough November for me, personally," he admitted. Studying the subdued expressions in the sanctuary, Kirk admitted to feeling "demoralized." Heads nodded all around me. Kirk said that he'd spent the month of December in prayer, seeking to understand what had gone wrong and what God was trying to tell him.

The conclusion Kirk reached?

"We need to *redouble* our efforts," he stressed. No matter how exhausted Christians were feeling—no matter how futile the fight to "get our country back" could seem at times—surrender was out of the question. "The enemy" wanted Christians to give up so that America might be conquered. Now they needed to prove themselves. It was, Kirk suggested, God's plan to withhold Republican victories in the midterm elections, to test their mettle. How would they respond?

"We've got to fight harder. We've got to organize," Kirk said. "We've got to continue to educate ourselves on where we come from in our biblical tradition, and from our history, to understand what we're fighting."

At some level, this was the same rah-rah rhetoric Kirk had been deploying since he founded Turning Point USA in 2012. But there was something newly distinctive about his approach. Having spent the past decade waging a war that was, at least superficially, ideological in nature, he was now hyping a struggle with higher stakes. This would be a spiritual battle, with implications much larger than any one election. He wanted the Dream City faithful to understand that they had entered a new phase of the war for America, one that couldn't be won by politicians and voters alone. To defeat the left, Kirk explained, patriots would need to be led into battle by the people who'd been hanging back for too long: their pastors.

"The enemy would love nothing more than for the American Church to remain silent and complicit," Kirk declared from Barnett's pulpit. "Tyranny and totalitarianism will continue to grow if the American Church does not stand up."

Kirk had come to issue a challenge to the clergy. There was a time, he said, when it was defensible to avoid partisan disputes. But now, given the overt efforts to destroy the nation's Judeo-Christian culture—including a state-ordered shutdown of churches—there was no excuse. Any pastor who declared political neutrality was a weakling at best or a traitor at worst.

This was chesty stuff coming from a twenty-nine-year-old whose sole theological exploit was getting his name, image, and likeness dropped by Liberty University. And yet, one could see how Kirk felt emboldened to lecture the nation's ministers. He wasn't merely speaking to a crowd of several thousand professing Christians, but doing so from the pulpit of one of America's largest megachurches. For this successful appropriation of clout—if not credibility—Kirk could thank one person: Pastor Barnett.

The leader of Dream City wasn't known for his discernment. In the summer of 2020, as the coronavirus raged nationwide, he lent his stage to then-president Donald Trump for a campaign rally, boasting that his church operated a cutting-edge air filtration system that killed "99 percent" of the virus. (The pastor's sidesplittingly absurd claim, which was quickly debunked and later removed from the church Facebook page, distracted from the more pressing question of why he'd sanctioned a presidential campaign event inside his sanctuary.) Still, what Barnett lacked in guile he made up for in sincerity. Unlike so many other pastors

I'd encountered, Barnett came across as credulous to a fault, a man who seemed thoroughly convinced of both the righteousness of his cause and the utter, no-time-to-waste urgency of advancing it.

On this particular night, Barnett previewed a promotional video for his audience at Dream City. It told of an upcoming conference—"On This Rock"—that his church would host later in the month. About two thousand pastors would be coming to Dream City to learn how to "take a stand" and defeat the leftist agenda.

As the lights dimmed, two gargantuan monitors depicted a violent storm moving in. "Now is the time . . ." the banner read, "for church leaders to stand for Christ." Soon typhoon waves were crashing against a church building, and the famous words Jesus spoke to Peter scrolled across the screen: "On this rock I will build my church, and the gates of hell will not prevail against it." For a grand finale, the video showed a promotional reel of the pastors who would be headlining the event. Among them were Barnett; his father, Tommy Barnett; his brother, Matthew Barnett; and, naturally, Jentezen Franklin.

Barnett and Kirk made for a formidable tag team. Barnett, whose dynastic ministry had deep ties to the charismatic movement, could reach millions of Stephen Strang–reading churchgoers; Kirk had well-placed political allies, including but not limited to the entire Trump family, and was fast becoming a player in the evangelical world. Having established a religious foothold several years earlier with "Freedom Night in America," Kirk began hosting *his own* pastor's conferences in 2022. That same year, he launched the "Saving America Tour," which played in church sanctuaries from coast to coast. For an encore in 2023, Kirk had announced the "Kingdom to the Capitol Tour," a traveling revival that would bring music, prayer, and advocacy to each of the fifty state capitals before year's end.

Kirk was preparing an all-out blitz on American churches. It didn't appear to be a bluff: He certainly had the resources and the organization—and the chutzpah—to succeed where other right-wing agitators had failed. At one point, describing how atheism had led to mass violence in centuries past, Kirk, without a trace of self-awareness, announced to his audience, "God will not honor those that try to do big, majestic, and temporal things not in His name."

Kirk was doing a big, majestic, temporal thing with Turning Point USA—and with its newest division, TPUSA Faith. The only thing standing between conservatives and control of the nation's key institutions, he believed, was impotent pastors. Teaming with their outspoken counterparts in the clergy, Kirk was preparing to crank up the pressure. And if he couldn't get through to these church leaders and their congregations—with the conferences and tours, the radio ranting and social media shaming—Kirk knew someone who could: Eric Metaxas.

AMERICAN EVANGELICALISM HAS LONG BEEN PLAGUED BY A CERTAIN pedagogical insecurity. Whatever their collective influence amassed in certain arenas—politics and business, certainly—evangelicals have chafed at their seeming exclusion from elite social, academic, and intellectual circles. This hunger for relevance can result in the lionizing of men who infiltrate society's innermost sanctums, seemingly on *their* behalf, representing their views and validating their beliefs and giving them a metaphorical seat at the table. Simply put, evangelicals hate feeling like outcasts, and are quick to uncritically follow those who make them feel accepted, relevant, enlightened.

Eric Metaxas understood this sentiment—the Church's gnawing sense of marginalization—and knew just how to take advantage of it.

Raised in the Greek Orthodox tradition, Metaxas embraced the evangelical movement after graduating from Yale in the mid-1980s. Unlike many young Christian conservatives who rushed headlong into politics, Metaxas pursued the arts. He authored numerous children's books; wrote for *VeggieTales*, the Christian cartoon for kids; and became an understudy of Chuck Colson, the former disgraced Nixon aide who'd become born again and later launched the Prison Fellowship ministry. (Metaxas cowrote Colson's widely distributed "Breakpoint" media bulletins.) Having cultivated deep roots in evangelicalism, Metaxas branched into secular society. He began hosting live events in Manhattan, known as "Socrates in the City," that drew erudite crowds for discussions of the finer things over wine and hors d'oeuvres. He wrote a book on the British abolitionist William Wilberforce and followed that project with a biography of Dietrich Bonhoeffer, the German preacher who was martyred for his opposition to Hitler. This earned Metaxas an invitation to keynote the National Prayer Breakfast in 2012. By the time he'd finished goading then-president Obama and then-Speaker Nancy Pelosi over the issue of abortion—both of them sitting a few feet away on the dais, television feeds broadcasting the event live—he'd become a singular celebrity on the Christian right.

I could see why Metaxas was alluring to people like my mom and dad. Here was a witty and winsome Christian intellectual, sartorially flawless and linguistically fearless, displaying an evangelicalism that seemed immune to caricature. But red flags were everywhere. Metaxas possessed a bottomless appetite for self-promotion. He chased media exposure with voracious abandon, making no secret of his longing to land a Fox News show. At the prayer breakfast, he badgered Obama so insistently to read his Bonhoeffer book that the president finally held it up playfully, providing a photo that Metaxas would spend years milking for publicity. And his grandiloquent style could not conceal questions about the substance: Even as Christian audiences devoured *Bonhoeffer*, the book came under intense scrutiny from historians who had spent their careers studying the German pastor and ripped many of Metaxas's analyses and conclusions. Something about Metaxas was off. For a man whose celebrity owed to such a seemingly inimitable and authentic persona, he carried the eerily familiar scent of superficiality.

It was little surprise, then, that Metaxas went all in on Trump's presidency. Having once skewered the Republican candidate and his manifest foibles, Metaxas declared soon after Trump clinched the GOP nomination that Christians "must" vote for him in the general election. As with so many others, this marked a crossing of the Rubicon for Metaxas. Once a passive political onlooker, he now argued that Democratic Party rule would imperil America's very existence. "This is for the survival of the nation," Metaxas pronounced in 2016.

Jon Ward, a Christian journalist, captured the reaction thusly: "Conservatives sent me unsolicited emails of outrage. One email simply quoted from a passage in Metaxas' Bonhoeffer book, where he described Hitler's rise to power: 'The German people clamored for order and leadership. But it was as though in the babble of their clamoring, they had summoned the devil himself, for there now rose up from the deep wound in the national psyche something strange and terrible and compelling.'"

The ensuing debate over what had become of Metaxas traced a well-worn dichotomy. Was he knowingly shedding his principles in the pursuit of fame and influence? Or was he *actually* convinced that America needed saving and that Donald Trump was our national Messiah?

Both answers may have been correct. Corruption and psychosis are not mutually exclusive. Metaxas had become accustomed to a level of commercial success and spiritual relevance that would be forfeited by opposing Trump's candidacy. But it also did appear as though his views, like those of so many Christians, had become radicalized in the Obama era. This would continue apace into Trump's presidency.

Metaxas went on to defend the forty-fifth president with a convert's vigor. He wrote children's books titled *Donald Builds the Wall* and *Donald Drains the Swamp*. When Franklin Graham remarked to him that citizens protesting Trump's policies were "almost demonic," Metaxas objected to the use of the word *almost*. At the 2020 GOP convention in Washington, Metaxas sucker-punched a demonstrator who was bicycling around the premises. In a livestreamed debate with David French—a fellow evangelical intellectual who opposed Trump's reelection—Metaxas left their Christian college hosts slack-jawed when he responded to French's opening argument by quipping an old *Saturday Night Live* joke: "Jane, you ignorant slut!"

Given the intensity of this evolution, Metaxas became a predictable champion of Trump's crusade to overturn the election result in late 2020. He promised that people were going to prison—or worse—for rigging the results. He insisted that Trump would stay in office, likening his faith in this outcome to his faith in Jesus rising from the dead. He even booked the president on his radio show and suggested that martyrdom was an appropriate Christian recourse to the crisis at hand. "I'd be happy to die in this fight," Metaxas told Trump on the show. "This is a fight for everything. God is with us."

These antics permanently alienated Metaxas from some longtime friends in the uppermost echelons of the evangelical movement, people who had clung naïvely to a hope that his Trump spell would ultimately break. But, in another predictable pattern, it did nothing to diminish his standing within the Christian conservative community. If anything, his reckless rallying cries only further endeared Metaxas to the multitudes who felt betrayed by their own leaders for not fully backing Trump's election denial.

This explained why, several nights before I saw Kirk in Phoenix, more than one thousand worshippers greeted Metaxas like a biblical prophet inside the sanctuary of a suburban Seattle church.

It was Sunday night at Westgate Chapel, a large congregation in the town of Edmonds, Washington. An aging, bald pastor named Alec Rowlands opened the proceedings by confessing to a terrible failure. For many years, Rowlands said, he had refused to engage with partisan political causes. "Basically, I thought if I didn't say anything controversial, that people who were more sensitive or maybe on the fence would hang around, and eventually the gospel would get to them. Probably what a lot of pastors think," Rowlands said. "And then, when COVID hit, and we watched the systematic attack on the Church, it really opened my eyes."

Rowlands recalled how he'd repented to his congregation in 2021. But repentance wasn't enough. He needed to atone. And so "Apologia" was born: Every other month, Rowlands would bring an A-list guest speaker to address Westgate Chapel on a Sunday evening, discussing the overlap of conservative theology and conservative policies and urging believers to get more involved. The guests included Fox News characters and right-wing internet brawlers. But this event in early 2023 was the biggest draw of all: Eric Metaxas.

With his swoop of silver hair, tortoiseshell glasses, and gold-festooned navy sport coat, Metaxas took the stage to a wild standing ovation. Rowlands said it was "a record crowd for Apologia," and Metaxas did not disappoint. For the next two hours, he and a friend he'd brought along, conservative pundit John Zmirak, roused God's people with a message of scorching certitude on all things political, cultural, and theological.

It was a race to the rhetorical bottom. Zmirak blamed America's demise on "RINOs"—Republicans In Name Only—and "the squish Christians" who won't fight, calling out "the David Frenches of this world" as "the real enemy." He referred to the vice president as "Camel A. Harris," then started in on Michelle Obama, calling her "the American Winnie Mandela." (Nobody in the racially homogeneous audience seemed to mind.) He mocked "crackhead" Hunter Biden and asked if anyone had seen the YouTube video of "the crackhead singing 'Amazing Grace,'" which he found to be amusing beyond words. He said, with a straight face, "The next January 6 should be open carry."

Metaxas was less nakedly incendiary and yet, somehow, more disturbing on the substance. He claimed the imprisonment of Americans who stormed the Capitol was part of a deep-state cover-up, "and by God's grace, very slowly but surely, the truth is coming out" thanks to the efforts of Julie Kelly. (Kelly, a professional misinformation artist who claimed that January 6 was an FBI inside job, once called Michael Fanone, the Capitol policeman nearly beaten to death by rioters, "a crisis actor.") Metaxas made at least four direct comparisons to Nazi Germany, arguing that by accepting the government's policies—on vaccines, for instance—Christians were doing "the exact same thing" they did in appeasing Adolf Hitler. He emphasized again and again, with increasing ferocity, that believers would be "judged" before God for refusing to confront these injustices.

"If you're in the middle, playing it safe, you are enabling the devil to destroy the culture. There are a lot of good people who have been fooled into silence, and God will deal with them," Metaxas said. "God will hold you accountable. Because you're supposed to believe that He has deputized you to be His voice and His hands and His feet wherever you are. The silence in this nation—of the Church—is a scandal."

He took a late-night-infomercial pause. "And that's why I wrote this book."

Sure enough, Metaxas had pegged his Apologia appearance to the publication of a treatise, *Letter to the American Church*. The book encouraged Christians to follow the example of Bonhoeffer—and Metaxas himself—by combating the "regime" that aimed to inflict evil on the world. He echoed the argument made by Kirk: God was using the turmoil of recent years to test American believers. Were they willing to pursue righteousness, even if it entailed persecution and suffering? Metaxas was proud to say that he had done so. (The half dozen members of law enforcement on hand, two of them guarding either entrance of his book-signing event, and another two personally escorting him around the church, was evidence of his supposed persecution, if not of any material suffering.)

Even the most unhinged portions of the conversation failed to faze the people in attendance. Zmirak repeatedly offered casual calls to violence, at one point citing the Islamic fundamentalist takeovers of Middle Eastern societies as a model for how Christians "can take this one back." Metaxas grew openly conspiratorial as the program wore on, referencing his "friend" Roger Stone's work on the assassination of JFK, suggesting that Biden's presidency was not what it appeared, and predicting that Harris would soon be forced to formally assume office.

That none of this nonsense appeared even mildly surprising to the folks at Westgate Chapel reflected the systematic inurement of evangelicals everywhere. Listening to his radio program in the weeks preceding Metaxas's visit to the church, I had to wonder if it was being produced from inside a padded room somewhere. He compared January 6 to July 4 as a birth of liberty that would one day be celebrated. He hosted Mike Lindell and Jenna Ellis—the former Trump lawyer who was censured by a judge and admitted to spreading numerous falsehoods about Biden's victory—for "election integrity updates." He discussed "the underbelly of Hollywood" and "the permanent lockdown" being pushed by global elites. Metaxas speculated that Biden had been replaced by a body double, encouraging his listeners to study the so-called president's earlobes as evidence of the switcheroo.

None of this stopped a prominent pastor from allowing Metaxas to feed his sheep. None of this disqualified Metaxas from giving religious instruction to a sanctuary full of professing believers. None of this excluded Metaxas from the conversation over the future of American Christianity.

In fact, if Charlie Kirk got his way, Metaxas would soon be leading that conversation at an extraordinary scale.

JUST AS PASTOR ROWLANDS HOSTS A SPECIAL GUEST FOR EACH APOLOgia event, Freedom Night in America is programmatically designed around Kirk interviewing a Christian conservative influencer. On the night I visited Dream City Church, Kirk sat down with Jeff Myers, an evangelical academic who'd recently written a book about rediscovering absolute truth in an age of epistemological confusion.

Kirk began with a surprise question. He wanted to know, before they got into Myers's book, whether the guest had any thoughts on Kirk's opening rant against churches that weren't "taking a stand." Myers hesitated to respond, shifting in his seat.

"Only about twenty percent of the people who even go to church have a biblical worldview," he told Kirk. Now the people around me shifted in *their* seats. "It's hard to imagine, but if you see in any given church a row of ten people, two of them are there to figure out what God has to say and apply it to their lives. The other eight are asking, 'Well, does the pastor's story inspire me? Does his truth somehow match up with my truth?'" Myers said.

"As long as people who ought to know better are not seeking the truth," he concluded, "I can see why it's very discouraging for a lot of pastors."

Although it wasn't clear whether Myers meant it this way, his comment set the tone for a tightrope-walking conversation with Kirk. One of these two *did* know better: Myers held a doctorate in philosophy, was learned and well-read, and appeared uncomfortable with some of Kirk's adolescent commentaries. At the same time, Myers knew the market for his book—and even more so for his educational programs aimed at teenagers and college students. Progressives weren't ponying up two thousand dollars to send their kids to a "biblical boot camp." It was conservative churchgoers—like the ones in Phoenix, like the ones in Edmonds—who paid Myers's bills. And so, the one who knew better modulated his responses to the one who didn't, indulging Kirk on certain topics and sidestepping others.

Following up on Myers's point, Kirk asked him, without a hint of self-reflection, "If you have the truth and you don't speak the truth, then what good is actually having the truth?"

Myers referenced a venerated Harvard sociologist, Pitirim Sorokin, who had studied civilizations all the world over and reached a harsh verdict. "In the absence of a belief in God, in the absence of moral absolutes . . . the only binding imperative left is power and physical force," Myers explained.

Kirk nodded, but the irony may have been lost on him. For all his talk about the "absolute truths" of certain topics—gender, sexuality, and the like—Kirk specialized in muddying the waters about matters of basic fact. He was uniquely brazen about peddling bad information when it came to election laws, January 6, Russia's invasion of Ukraine, racial violence, education curriculum, and the science and side effects of vaccination. (Several weeks before the Dream City event, Kirk had been the tip of the MAGA spear in blaming the on-field collapse of NFL player Damar Hamlin on the COVID-19 shot.)

By definition, the pursuit and application of absolute truth cannot be discriminatory. Yet Kirk was famous for picking and choosing the certainties his base wanted to hear—the things he could package into slick sound bites, market to the indignant masses, and monetize with breathtaking velocity. What Myers had articulated fit Kirk and his disciples all too well: a belief in nothing except the imperative of power.

In an act of infantile projection, Kirk peppered his Freedom Night performance with mentions of "tyranny" and "tyrants." This was usually in the context of Christians being pushed around by the woke secularists who control government bureaucracies, corporate boardrooms, and leading social media channels. Christians were constantly being censored for "misinformation," Kirk complained, but progressives who asserted their own "truth" were celebrated. In this vein, Kirk launched into a mean-spirited tangent about a "lesbian in a wheelchair" claiming a certain truth that "white cisgendered males" could not understand.

Myers looked dazed by the commentary. "Wow," he said to Kirk. "There was a lot there."

There certainly was. And the church was a most fitting backdrop: The more these two men spoke about "absolute truth"—about this next generation being morally adrift and detached from reality—the less effective any political program seemed as a solution. If tens of millions of young people were as badly damaged as Myers and Kirk claimed, the only answer was Christ. Yet the tone and tenor of this conversation rendered Christ, or at least *Christianity*, thoroughly off-putting to anyone who might otherwise be interested in seeking Him. Perhaps sensing as much, Myers finally spoke up.

"The core truth that's been lost, and needs to be recovered in our time, is that every human has value because they bear the image of God," Myers said.

The line won some polite applause—from the same people who'd been howling at Kirk's "lesbian in a wheelchair" crack. Hence my distinguishing between Christ and Christianity. When Jesus walked the earth, He went out of His way to minister to the broken and the shunned. He didn't show mere mercy to the adulterer and the prostitute and the tax collector; he showed *favoritism* toward them because these were the people who needed him most. He showered affection on them, regardless of their lifestyles. This was disgraceful to the Jewish authorities monitoring Jesus's activity. They demanded an explanation from His disciples: Why was their rabbi keeping such company?

"It is not the healthy who need a doctor, but the sick," Jesus responded, overhearing their objections. "I have not come to call the righteous, but sinners."

Christianity in today's sad manifestation treats the "lesbian in a wheelchair" as a punch line. Christ would have treated her then—and He regards her now—as a treasure.

The scandal is that Christians, someplace deep in their hearts, possess that categorical, Christlike love. But they have been conditioned to subdue it. They have been taught to selectively practice habits that are meant to be universal. They have been acclimatized to applaud when Myers talks about the danger of dehumanizing people—like Hitler with "vermin" or abortionists with "fetuses"—but ignore the implications that challenge their own prejudices, like migrants as "aliens" or Democrats as "demons" or LGBTQ youth as the "lesbian in a wheelchair."

When Kirk opened the session to audience questions, one college-aged woman expressed concern about going into her chosen field, teaching. She wanted to know how to engage with LGBTQ students while still "speaking the truth" as a Christian. Myers suggested that the best place to start is Genesis—with its emphasis on God making humans male and female—and basic biology, which documents thousands of differences between the sexes. He emphasized, however, that "gender dysphoria is real," and said Christians ought to extend compassion toward those people suffering from it. "We should walk alongside them," Myers concluded.

Kirk didn't bother hiding his smirk. He ridiculed Myers for being "so sweet," and then declared, "This entire trans thing is one of the most evil things happening in our society, and we cannot tolerate this evil."

He proceeded to liken gender-dysphoric people to animals—"They think they're a zebra, a giraffe, a lion"—and said doctors "should be put in prison" for prescribing treatments to minors.

Both of these men—both of these answers—earned distinct waves of applause. For the first time all night, the friction was palpable. Clearly, even in this self-selecting audience of Christian conservatives, a tension nipped at the margins of their shared identity. Not all evangelicals, even at a place like Dream City Church, were sold on the uncompromising, scorched-earth spirituality of Kirk and his kind.

This was a risk that Kirk could not afford to take. He had invested too much in this crusade to see it fail—the pastors' conferences, the church speeches, the capital tour. He was promoting TPUSA Faith as the crown jewel of his activism empire; losing his target market over some lily-livered misgivings about extending grace to those who fell outside the accepted rubric would not do. Now, at Dream City, he was sharing some breaking news: Kirk was working with Eric Metaxas to produce a film version of *Letter to the American Church*, and together they were aiming to screen it in sanctuaries nationwide.

Kirk preened as the crowd buzzed at his announcement. Like a developer snatching up real estate, the young ideologue was making a play to monopolize the conservative church market. He didn't bother pretending that the goal was to glorify God or make disciples or reach the nations. Kirk was building a movement to take back America—and churches, he said, would be "the backbone."

FOR THE FIRST TIME IN A LONG TIME, THIS MOVEMENT KIRK SPOKE OF lacked a single leader.

Donald Trump had declared his candidacy in November of the previous year, not long after blaming pro-lifers for the GOP's letdown in November. This scapegoating hadn't gone over well with social conservatives. But in truth, many of the evangelical figureheads who'd backed Trump in 2016—including close allies during his four years in the White House—had already begun to hedge their bets on the former president.

Mike Evans, an original member of Trump's evangelical advisory board, told the *Washington Post* that Trump "used us to win the White

House" and then turned Christians into cult members, "glorifying Donald Trump like he was an idol." James Robison, a well-known televangelist who also advised Trump, compared him to a "little elementary schoolchild" while addressing a group of Christian lawmakers. David Lane, a veteran evangelical organizer whose email blasts reach many thousands of pastors and church leaders, wrote that Trump's "vision of making America as a nation great again has been put on the sidelines, while the mission and the message are now subordinate to personal grievances and self-importance." Everett Piper, the former president of Oklahoma Wesleyan University, reacted to the midterms by writing in the *Washington Times*, "The take-home of this past week is simple: Donald Trump has to go."

Even Robert Jeffress, the most loyal of Trump loyalists, worked to create some distance from the former president. In several media interviews after the election, Jeffress explained that while Trump was still a close friend—"And the best president of our lifetimes"—there would be a large, competitive field of Republican candidates running for president in 2024, and he wasn't ready to commit to any one of them.

When I got Jeffress on the phone in March 2023, not long after those interviews, he admitted to running game on the reporters who'd been calling. "Absolutely" he was going to back Trump, Jeffress told me. But what good would his endorsement do at this early stage? Jeffress explained that he and Trump had an understanding: In order to maximize impact, he would hold off on endorsing for now, then weigh in later in the primary contest when Trump most needed a boost. "I'll always support him," Jeffress said. "The country's going to hell, and he's the only one who can save it."

If Trump really was in on this arrangement, he did a heck of a job of concealing it. The former president fumed to friends and advisers about the "ungrateful" evangelicals who were holding out. When he learned that Jeffress was hosting an event at First Baptist Dallas with Mike Pence, his personal Judas who was now exploring a 2024 bid of his own, Trump turned a new shade of tangerine.

Not that Trump had anything to fear from Pence. Sure, the Hoosier State's favorite son was an *actual* Christian who cared about the issues—abortion, religious liberties, traditional ethics around sexuality and gender—that had been purely transactional to Trump. But none of that much mattered. Evangelicals had been habituated to a new political reality. More important than questions of what a given candidate *personally* believed, by this point, was the question of how far that candidate would go to advance the beliefs of the evangelical Republican base.

I witnessed this evolution up close. A few months after the midterms, Pence traveled to Michigan for a lecture at Hillsdale College, the small and highly influential Christian university. The subject was "Faith in Public Life." Pence, looking preternaturally comfortable in the elevated pulpit of Hillsdale's gorgeous, European-inspired campus chapel, delivered an eloquent address that articulated his views on the most pressing cultural matters of the day. The former vice president made clear that he would stand strong in defense of traditional values. But, Pence said, unlike *certain* Republicans, he would do so with a graciousness and humanity that kept the country intact. This had always been his calling card. Pence reminded the audience that, as far back as his days in conservative talk radio, he was known as "Rush Limbaugh on decaf."

The line got some laughs. But it also underscored his limitation as a prospective candidate. After the event, I heard the same thing from attendees over and over: Pence was not tough enough to meet this moment. Many folks still admired him. They thought he was an honorable man and a model Christian to boot. But a Sunday School teacher wasn't going to win this fight. They needed a warrior.

"I'm tired of nice guys letting us down. The Bushes were nice. Mitt Romney was nice. Where did that get us?" said Jerry Byrd, a churchgoing attorney who'd driven from the Detroit suburbs to hear Pence speak. "Trump is the only one who stood up for us. The Democrats are ruining this country, and being a good Christian isn't going to stop them. Honestly, I don't want someone 'on decaf.' We need the real thing."

Were Pence to seek and fall short of the presidency in 2024, this line would warrant strong consideration for his political epigraph. It said so much about him, and about the movement that for decades he'd helped to lead. Surely Trump would take comfort in knowing that he'd sabotaged his former vice president; that his own boorish provocations had conditioned Christians to expect an expression of their faith so pugilistic that Pence could not pass muster.

At the same time, Trump could be excused for feeling perplexed. He *did* go to war with Democrats. He *had* delivered evangelicals the policy wins they always wanted. He *was* promising to do it all over again. So, why weren't they embracing his second run for the presidency?

One reason is that Trump had become politically toxic. The electoral win-loss record—his own, and the Republican Party's under his leadership—was dreadful. His defeat in 2020 might have been forgiven, and his election fraud rubbish might have been overlooked, had he not insisted on carrying it over into the 2022 cycle, throwing his weight behind clownish candidates who doomed the GOP in crucial races. The November midterms seemingly affirmed that Trump's brand was broken with moderates and independent voters. The man who'd convinced evangelicals that winning was everything now couldn't shake the stench of defeat.

In this sense, it was difficult to separate Trump's decline from the rise of another Republican, someone who looked to be both a warrior *and* a winner: Ron DeSantis.

No politician had a better Election Day 2022 than Florida's young governor. Running for a second term in one of America's premier battlegrounds, DeSantis beat his Democratic rival by nearly 20 points, carrying the state by an astonishing one and a half *million* votes. More impressive than the margin was how DeSantis ran it up. He hadn't courted the middle of the electorate, emphasizing bipartisanship and good governance. Nor had he campaigned on a traditional conservative platform of free markets and limited government. Instead, with Ivy League precision and populist flair, DeSantis had weaponized the state to crush the left, seeking and destroying progressivism wherever it could be found—state agencies, public schools, private corporations. Every victory further emboldened the governor. In one publicity stunt, DeSantis used state funds to round up illegal immigrants *in Texas*, put them on a charter plane, then drop them in the blue enclave of Martha's Vineyard, Massachusetts, using the suffering and desperation of human beings to make a point about immigration policy. (The people of Martha's Vineyard, perhaps unwittingly embracing biblical dicta, welcomed these strangers and sojourners.)

DeSantis's dominant reelection showing provided a mandate to do more. Soon after winning a second term, DeSantis set about broadening his prohibition on discussions of sexuality in public schools. He stripped colleges of the ability to teach certain curricula around race and gender. He punished "woke" corporations like Disney, stripping the company of its autonomous development status and imposing control over its governance with a new five-member board, all in retaliation for Mickey Mouse employees voicing opposition to the governor's agenda.

"We find ourselves in Florida on the front lines in the battle for freedom," DeSantis declared in his state of the state address in early 2023.

On paper, this made DeSantis the prototype for leading the Republican Party into 2024 and beyond. He embodied all of Trump's willingness to scrap and claw and pulverize opponents, yet he carried none of the petty personal baggage.

"Donald Trump came onto the playground, found the bully that had been pushing evangelicals around, and he punched them. That's what endeared us to him," said Tony Perkins, the president of the Family Research Council, a onetime Trump foe who helped to rally evangelicals around the GOP nominee before the general election in 2016. "But the challenge is, he went a little too far. He had *too much* of an edge sometimes. . . . What we're looking for, quite frankly, is a cross between Mike Pence and Donald Trump. We want someone like Mike Pence, with the strong moral convictions—but Donald Trump had the fight in him. We're looking for someone with that mix."

When I responded that it sounded quite obvious who he was describing, Perkins just chuckled.

"I've sure been cheering him on in Florida," he said.

Whether or not Trump could fend off DeSantis to remain atop the Republican Party, his imprint on evangelicalism would endure. The forty-fifth president had foundationally altered the expectations and incentive structures within American Christendom. He had persuaded the churchgoing class that it was better to win with vice than to lose with virtue. He had blinded believers to the means and fixed their eyes on the ends. Most significantly, he had shown evangelicals that their movement need not be led *by* an evangelical.

This was evident enough in the emerging love affair with DeSantis, a casual Catholic for whom faith had never been a known part of his life. But this phenomenon was bigger than politics. Consider the case of Charlie Kirk. That a twentysomething without any college education or theological training could have a think tank named after him at the world's most influential Christian university might once have prompted some disbelief from evangelicals. Not anymore. Nobody blinks when Kirk speaks at America's largest churches, flippantly dropping insults and hateful innuendo from the pulpit. It raises no eyebrows when Kirk invites an atheist, the "anti-woke" polemicist James Lindsay, to his pastor conferences, or when Donald Trump Jr. disparages the teachings of Christ at one of Kirk's Turning Point USA jamborees. "We've turned the other cheek, and I understand, sort of, the biblical reference," Trump Jr. said. "But it's gotten us nothing."

Simply put, Trump the elder created a new moral-political framework in which people like Kirk and Eric Metaxas and John Zmirak convince evangelicals to distrust any believer who dares stray from their absolutist ideology. They do so by fomenting fears of a crushing, coordinated assault on Christianity—and by attacking anyone who refuses to adopt a militant posture in response. This is how Metaxas justifies portraying Tim Keller, the widely admired New York theologian, and Rick Warren, the author and leader of Saddleback Church in California, as "Hitler's favorite kind of pastors." This is how John Zmirak gets away with likening David French, a staunch defender of social conservatism and of religious liberty, to Nazi collaborators. This is how Tucker Carlson blasts Russell Moore and his aforementioned friends as cowards who don't have the guts to defend their faith against a secular onslaught.

"Where's Russell Moore and all the other *breastfeeding* Christians as that happens—as the U.S. government cracks down on Christianity?" Carlson asked on his Fox News show in March 2023, showcasing that familiar snarl while slinging an adjective nobody quite understood.

Walking out of Dream City, I thought about that question: Where *were* those Christians?

The forces of political identity and nationalist idolatry—long latent, now fully unleashed in the form of Trumpism—were destroying the evangelical Church. I had seen it for myself, over the past six years, in every corner of the country. Pastors had walked away from the ministry. Congregations had been shattered by infighting. Collective faith communities and individual relationships had been wrecked. This turmoil, once largely organic, gestating in the back pews and coffee parlors of local churches across the country, was now being sown by powerful outside actors—by people like Kirk—at a frightening clip. They did not concern themselves with the credibility of the Christian witness. Churches were not a bride to be loved, but a battlefield to be conquered.

This was nothing less than a war for the soul of American Christianity. And church by church, believer by believer, it appeared to me that Kirk and his allies might be winning it. This wasn't just because their side had more resources to deploy and fewer ethical guidelines to observe. It was because they were encountering no resistance. This was always going to be an unfair fight, but it was becoming painfully clear how uneven the two sides really were. Pastors who wanted to host a lobbying workshop or voter registration drive or anti-vax rally at their churches had a sprawling, sophisticated network to tap into. Pastors who wanted to push back on tribal mutinies could send an email to Russell Moore or David French, pray it earned a response, and then prepare a sermon written in code so as to not scatter the remnant of their flocks.

I knew the leaders of the opposition—figures like Moore and French— and I knew they were horrified by this hostile takeover of evangelicalism. These were people who had suffered, personally and professionally, by swimming against the currents of their own faith subcultures. It seemed most of them had given up, or least retreated, and I couldn't blame them. They had every excuse to ignore the institutional struggle and look inward, toward their own families and their own faith journeys; to settle on loving the Lord and letting him sort out this mess in America.

But they had not given up. They had not retreated. They had been underground, regrouping and organizing and plotting the path forward. Finally, after so many years on the defensive, they were poised to launch a counterattack.

CHAPTER EIGHTEEN

BRENTWOOD, TENNESSEE

'Do to others as you would have them do to you.

—LUKE 6:31

The first thing David French did, when Russell Moore flopped into our booth, was to offer him a drink. "You're not a Southern Baptist anymore," French said, grinning as he twirled an old-fashioned in his left hand.

Moore snorted and shook his head. It was almost the end of 2021—some eight months after his departure from the Southern Baptist Convention—but for all the changes in Moore's life since then, taking up alcohol wasn't one of them. He studied the sweet tea being sipped by the fourth member of our party, author and Christian communicator Daniel Darling, and asked the waitress to please bring him the same.

"Not that I couldn't use it," Moore said, nodding toward French's half-drained cocktail.

We all laughed. Moore had been through a lot, as had these other two gentlemen. Indeed, it was their mutual torment—and their shared home base, in metropolitan Nashville—that brought us together this late November night at a Mexican restaurant in the suburb of Brentwood. All three men were losing sleep over the trajectory of American evangelicalism, because all three men had seen, from the inside, the very worst it had to offer.

Moore, of course, had been bullied into leaving his role atop the

Ethics and Religious Liberty Commission, the influential public-facing policy arm of the SBC. Darling had recently been fired from his job at the National Religious Broadcasters, where he'd served as senior vice president of communications, for the sin of promoting COVID-19 vaccines during an interview on the MSNBC show *Morning Joe*. ("Our family has lost too many close friends and relatives to COVID, including an uncle, a beloved church member, and our piano teacher," Darling said on the cable news program.)

French had probably endured more than either of them. Ever since announcing his opposition to Trump in 2015, while writing for *National Review*, French had occupied a special place in the crosshairs of the Christian right. Perhaps it was because of his pedigree. A distinguished lawyer who had represented major conservative organizations in federal court, French had long been regarded as a steadfast opponent of the progressive left. Back in 2005, after stepping down as the president of a prominent civil liberties organization in order to join the U.S. Army—and deploy to Iraq to join the war on terror—French told a conservative gathering: "The two greatest threats to the United States of America are radical jihadists abroad and radical leftists at home, and I feel called to fight both."

But then French went to war. "And I saw what the enemy actually looked like," he told us at dinner.

The jihadists who were beheading journalists and mutilating young girls and burning apostates alive were nothing like the progressive political activists he'd encountered back home. In fact, French, a Kentucky native, had spent most of his adult life in deep-blue communities. His son was born in Ithaca, New York, not long after the reign of a socialist mayor. His introduction to the evangelical Church—after his fundamentalist upbringing—came in Cambridge, Massachusetts. His wife had accepted Christ at a church in Manhattan. French cherished these places and the people in them. As he matured in his faith, he told me, "I was very chastened. I was still a conservative, still a Republican, but I began to fall out of step with the tone and the direction of my tribe."

French's wandering in the political wilderness attracted little attention at first. It wasn't until he declared his opposition to Trump in the pages of *National Review*—and condemned the figures and forces of the white nationalist "alt right" who supported Trump's candidacy—that he became a target. The campaign against French and his family was vicious. Twitter trolls bombarded him with death threats. They flooded the internet with messages accusing French's wife, Nancy, an outspoken survivor of sexual assault, of sleeping with groups of Black men during his deployment to Iraq. They photoshopped images of his youngest daughter, who'd been adopted from Ethiopia, inside a gas chamber (Trump, depicted in a Nazi SS uniform, was shown with his finger on the ignition button). The specter of physical violence was inescapable. Both David and Nancy began carrying pistols.

Nor was the harassment limited to anonymous social media accounts. As French raced to keep up with blocking the thousands of Twitter users who stalked him, he noticed some familiar names. They belonged to fellow churchgoers.

This was perhaps the most wrenching part of French's ordeal. He had hoped, during these trying times, to at least find refuge in his house of worship. No such luck. Throughout the 2016 campaign and into Trump's presidency, French was regularly confronted by his fellow congregants at their church in Columbia, Tennessee, about his political writings. He would always try to deescalate. But the tension kept building. Families whispered about them when they walked into a room; some even made a show of turning their backs to the Frenches. One Sunday morning in 2018, things boiled over. An elder at the church—a fellow veteran whom they considered a friend—accosted David and Nancy inside the sanctuary, after the worship service, about an article David had written. "After all he's done for us," the man said, "how can you still be opposed to our president?"

When David began by citing Trump's basic moral failings—his degradation of women, his penchant for sexual conquest—the man scoffed. "Trump's just an alley cat!" he said.

Nancy interrupted. She asked whether he'd been bothered by Bill Clinton's womanizing. The elder responded that yes, he had been. "But you're okay with paying hush money to porn stars and bragging about grabbing women by the pussy?" she asked.

The elder gritted his teeth. "You," he said, turning to David, "had better get your woman under control."

David demanded an apology. The elder refused. Storming out of the sanctuary, the Frenches found the rest of the congregation in the refreshment lobby, sipping coffee and making small talk before the Sunday School hour. David grabbed a spoon and rapped it several times against a mug. "Hey everyone, just an announcement," he shouted, eyes ablaze, restraining the rage now curdling inside of him. "No one is allowed to talk to me and Nancy about Donald Trump while we're at church! You can come to our house; you can do it over coffee. But not here!"

When they moved, a short time later, to the Nashville suburb of Franklin, the Frenches hoped to start over at their new church. It didn't last. One of the first Sundays there, as David stood in a semicircle around the communion table with a small group of other congregants, a man drank from the cup, set it down, then looked over at him. "You're David French, aren't you?" he asked. David nodded. The man told him—right there, at the communion table—that he strongly disagreed with French's political opinions. Then he introduced himself. French was astonished: This man had been one of his most prolific online abusers. His words had been so venomous that French, having long ago blocked his Twitter account, still recognized the name at an instant.

The Frenches didn't last long at that church. More striking than any one detail from French's account was the reaction from Russell Moore and Daniel Darling. They offered little more than shrugs and eye rolls. It wasn't that they lacked for sympathy; they just knew that what French was describing wasn't isolated or entirely unique. This was the new reality of the evangelical movement in America. This is what they—and Christian leaders everywhere—were up against.

"And let's be clear, none of this started with Donald Trump," Moore said. "It was easier to get an argument going in the church parking lot over whether there were death panels in Obamacare, than it was over the trinity or the inerrancy of scripture. Trump just took it to a new level."

Moore recalled how, back in 2014, Trump had reacted to the Ebola outbreak by arguing that Christian missionaries working in Africa—whom the Obama administration was working to bring back to the United States—should not be allowed to reenter the country. "THE UNITED STATES HAS ENOUGH PROBLEMS," Trump had tweeted.

"People that go to far away places to help out are great—but must suffer the consequences!" Moore paused, blinking rapidly, struggling to summon the words. "And it was like, *come on*, this one is as easy as it gets: Missionaries caring for the sick get to come home," he said. "But you had evangelicals defending Trump's position. Why?"

The answer, French suggested, was complacency. Christians had spent the previous decade watching the left take control of major cultural institutions and win defining battles over sexuality, marriage, and the like. Overwhelmed, they had retreated ever deeper into the echo chamber of conservative talk radio and Fox News, where every disagreement over policy was treated as a proxy war for the soul of the nation. This formed a new catechesis for believers—one that French, like so many Christian leaders, saw but never took seriously enough until it was too late. What once seemed like heightened—but not unhealthy—political engagement turned out to be toxic, malevolent, paranoiac thinking that Trump skillfully harnessed in his rise to the presidency.

Moore agreed with that assessment. And he, like French, accepted some of the blame. Evangelicals should have seen this coming—not because of the right-wing-media-induced freakouts over immigration patterns or Obama's birth certificate, but because of the for-profit propagandizing of Christians that had been successful for decades. Long before your average churchgoer was addicted to Fox News prime time, "these same people were listening to four or five hours of fundamentalist, prophecy-charting, conspiracy preachers on the radio and TV every single day," Moore said. "So, it's not all that different. There's just a lot more of it now, and it's more explicitly political in its aims."

The proliferation of content that preys on Christian audiences—catastrophizing events for profit, via podcasts and blogs, social media sites and forum subgroups—makes it impossible for church leaders to police what their people are consuming. Whereas any pastor in the 1970s or '80s could identify the threats by name, and warn their flock to stay away, today churchgoers are imbibing information from sources their clergy have never heard of. This has bred a certain resignation. Because the sheer volume of external noise is so overwhelming, lots of church leaders have given up trying to block it out.

"When I was a kid, my parents and my pastors were hard-core about controlling our content. Any movies or music or TV that even hinted at violence, sexuality, drugs, disrespect for authority, you name it, that stuff was absolutely forbidden," Darling said. "What we need is for Christians to apply that same standard to political content. Because it's way more subversive than that pop-culture content."

Moore chuckled. "There's been this amazing shift. It used to be the parents coming to me, worried sick about what their kids were watching and listening to, asking what they could do to pull them back," he said. "Now, almost everywhere I go—this just happened at a church I visited the other night—it's the *kids* coming to me. They say their evangelical parents have gone totally crazy, binge-watching Fox News or Newsmax or One America News, and they want to know how to pull *them* back."

Darling noted how there were people at his church who had strayed "really far into the conspiracy stuff, and sending them legitimate news articles with facts does not work." These people have lost trust in institutions across the board, Darling said, and are effectively living in a different reality. Arguing with them was pointless. The only way to reach them, he said, was for pastors to "accept the burden of meeting these people where they're at, and try to help them live more responsibly in the information age."

French took exception to this point.

"I'm really tired of this talk about how these poor people don't trust anything anymore. Oh no—*you trust*. You just trust all the wrong stuff. You trust awful people, with awful intentions, for no good reason other than they tell you what you want to hear," French seethed. "You come home after work, put on Fox News, and leave it on until you go to bed. You trust Fox News—despite the Seth Rich conspiracy theory, the election bullcrap, all the revisionist history on January 6. You sit there for hours, listening to this garbage, rotting your soul. And then you turn around and say, 'Why would I trust the *New York Times*?' Really? Why would you trust Tucker Carlson?"

We all agreed that these ideological die-hards whom French was describing were not a majority of the evangelical movement. There is a difference between the people who prefer the 6 p.m. hour of programming at Fox News to those of its cable rivals, and the people who marinate in right-wing misinformation all day long. That latter group, everyone estimated, was still no more than 15 or 20 percent of most church congregations they knew of. The problem is, as Moore pointed out, "That vocal minority will always push around a timid majority. The people who care the most usually get what they want."

French nodded. "The people who care about an institution, define an institution. This is the problem for pastors dealing with that crazy fifteen or twenty percent," French said. "If they had a just-as-committed twenty percent to push back on them, their churches would be just fine. But they don't."

I asked what it would take to equip that other 20 percent; what it would take for these pastors to regain control of their churches. Nobody said a word. Finally, Moore spoke up.

"I don't know. Honestly, I'm more concerned than I was a year ago—and that's saying something," he said. "It may sound like Chicken Little. But I'm telling you, there is a serious effort to turn this 'two countries' talk into something real. There are Christians taking all the populist passions and adding a transcendent authority to it. And nobody is stopping them."

AN AIR OF DESPONDENCY HUNG OVER THAT DINNER IN LATE 2021. THE events of the previous few years haunted each of my companions in unique ways. All vowed to one another that they would spend the *next* few years fighting this contagion inside the American Church. But they struggled with a basic question: Where to start?

Darling, who was reeling after being axed by the National Religious Broadcasters, landed on his feet at Southwestern Baptist Theological Seminary. Moving his family from Tennessee to Texas, Darling became the director of the university's Land Center for Cultural Engagement, a prized perch from which he could reach a large Southern Baptist audience while mentoring the next generation of theologians and preachers.

French focused his energies on journalism. Having left *National Review* near the end of Trump's presidency to join a new website, The Dispatch, French became one of the most indispensable conservative voices in American media. In columns published twice a week, French used his Judge Advocate General background to investigate abuses, adjudicate bad-faith arguments, and offer nuanced perspective on the most pressing political, legal, and social issues of the day.

Moore's journey was the most ambitious. Splitting the difference between teaching doctrine and practicing journalism, he joined *Christianity Today* as the magazine's public theologian. Moore began writing a widely read newsletter and hosting an eponymous podcast, using the *CT* platform to expose and contextualize the sausage making of the professional evangelical industry. He brought a sharp, inquisitory voice to this effort. Most famously, in May 2022, when a third-party firm released the shocking summary report of its probe into the handling of sexual abuse by the Southern Baptist Convention's leadership, Moore—who'd been terrorized for requesting this very investigation—wrote a scathing column titled "This Is the Southern Baptist Apocalypse." Moore, the SBC exile whose years of alarm sounding were vindicated by the findings of the report, got lots of attention for his flamethrowing censures of America's largest denomination. But all the while, behind the scenes, he was spending much of his time battling the blaze that was engulfing evangelicalism writ large.

One of the first things Moore did, after quitting the Southern Baptist Convention, was link up with other Christian refugees. They were of different generations and races and political persuasions; they came from all different denominational backgrounds and worship traditions. What united them was the hard-earned knowledge that something had gone very wrong within American Christianity. Starting in the spring of 2021, Moore had convened a series of private gatherings about how to rebuild the Church. The first meeting, at a friend's home in Maryland, counted twenty-five participants. The next convening, at a resort in Vermont that fall, included twice that number. Every time I spoke with Moore over the ensuing year, he reported that the group had grown larger. Yet its footprint became no more visible. There were no creeds or open letters or mission statements. And that, Moore explained, was the entire point.

"A few people have argued for forming a group—you know, the 'National Association of Sane Evangelicals' or something—but most of us don't think that would be effective in this moment," Moore told me in the summer of 2022. "All it takes is one of our members to be recognized as 'woke' or 'liberal' or whatever, and suddenly the entire effort is infected. The people we're trying to empower, they don't need to be signing on to manifestos on organizational letterhead. They need to be in a safe space where they can ask questions and figure out how other people are dealing with these problems."

His group aimed to "empower" two different categories of Christian. The first were high-level operators, people with deep connections in the evangelical world who were undertaking myriad efforts to depollute their own denominations and affiliated churches. Because these efforts were often overlapping, Moore came to view his secret society, which ran the demographic and ideological spectrum, as being "in charge of directing traffic." They made sure that groups working toward racial reconciliation, like Undivided, out of Cincinnati, were communicating with groups focused on misinformation, such as the D.C.-based American Values Coalition, and that grassroots efforts to combat Christian nationalism at evangelical colleges were coordinated with well-funded studies at secular universities. Plenty of believers had responded to the crises facing the Church by leaping into action, Moore said, but they had struggled because nobody was systematizing their efforts.

Moore called this "the air war" he and his allies were fighting. And I could tell, from our conversations as the months went by, that he considered this effort a success. At the same time, I could sense Moore's growing angst about the other part of their operation: "the ground war."

He always had a heart for pastors. Preaching was in the man's blood, after all. Nothing gave him a thrill like seeing one of his former seminarians in the pulpit, answering God's calling on their life. But the thrill had in recent years given way to terror: Moore watched helplessly as pastors he knew and loved quit the ministry, overwhelmed by the moment and unable to continue on in their work.

This was the other component of Moore's charge, and it looked to be consuming him. Every time we spoke it seemed he was in a different city, meeting with a different crowd of local pastors, trying to prop up the whole of the American clergy like Atlas himself. Moore worried that many pastors were simply ill equipped to meet the challenges

of the times. They had gone to Bible college or seminary to study the
scriptures; some had received advanced degrees, perhaps in divinity
or counseling. But none of them had learned how to soothe tribal political tensions in their churches; none of them had been trained to navigate an ascendant nationalist excitability in their congregations. They
were losing a game for which they had never practiced. This sensation
of failure could drive even the most gifted and confident preacher to
despair. I had seen it myself—Chris Winans at Cornerstone, John Torres at Goodwill, and so many others. Moore felt a manic urgency about
their plight. These pastors were a redoubt. They were, in so many cases,
the only thing standing between the Christians in their communities
and forces that would destroy the Church. They needed to be fortified—
and fast.

"We are losing our most stable people. In Mississippi right now, one
out of every four Baptist churches are without pastors. A lot of these
guys, they won't say it in a room in front of people, but they'll whis-
per to me afterward: 'I'm not sure how much longer I can hang on,'"
Moore said. "And pretty soon, it's a choice between quitting and self-
destruction. There's a lot of pastors who are very isolated, and they're
giving into numbing mechanisms—alcohol, substance abuse, affairs.
Subconsciously, it gives them an off-ramp. We're seeing a lot of that
right now."

Moore couldn't hope to save all of these individuals himself. What
he aimed to do, by convening groups of clergy all over the country, was
to build networks of pastoral brotherhood. Rivalries between religious
factions—and even within shared traditions—have long prevented the
kind of collaborating one might expect from men of the cloth. This moment, Moore argued, *demanded* that collaboration: Not only were these
pastors experiencing something that could only be related to by other
pastors, but they were experiencing it at a time of massive realignment
within the Christian world.

"That's what makes it such a challenge—all this crazy political stuff
is happening just as the denominational structures are imploding,"
Moore explained. "Most of these pastors don't have institutional support. It doesn't matter what kind of polity they're in. Whether they have
a bishop or a presbytery or whatever, it doesn't matter. It's similar to

how the political parties have dissolved. Back in 2015 and 2016, I would hear people say, 'Don't worry about Trump, the party won't let him win.' And then I'd meet with Reince Priebus"—the chairman of the Republican National Committee, and subsequently Trump's first chief of staff—"and he'd say, 'You think *we* can stop Trump?' It's the same thing in these denominations. Most pastors can't count on a structure behind them to help, because those structures don't exist anymore."

The good news, Moore told me, was that pastors were beginning to adapt to this new reality. Unlike in 2015 and 2016, when so many of his brethren clung to the belief that this was a passing storm, most of them now accepted that the tempest would endure. The result was a new and notably proactive attitude toward engaging these divisions. The demand for Moore's private network-building seminars had exploded beyond any reasonable supply. He was speaking in four different cities that week alone. There was no keeping up with the outcry from pastors and church leaders who were pleading to be outfitted. It was a good problem to have, but a problem nonetheless.

Moore wasn't sure he could scale up his efforts. There was already so much to balance: He had recently been named editor in chief of *Christianity Today*, and in addition to leading the magazine's staff, he was writing a book, receiving constant speaking requests, and raising five kids. Transforming his unofficial, loosely structured pastor-rehabilitation program into a formal, public-facing initiative wasn't in the cards. "God is up to something," Moore told me. But for once, it wouldn't necessitate his leadership. Someone else needed to do the heavy lifting.

CURTIS CHANG KNEW A THING OR TWO ABOUT THE PRESSURES OF PASToral ministry.

The Harvard-educated son of Chinese immigrants, Chang bypassed lucrative careers in business, law, and government to serve the Lord. He spent his twenties working for InterVarsity Christian Fellowship, the nation's largest campus-based ministry, and in his thirties he assumed the role of lead pastor at a vibrant young evangelical church in San Jose, California. This was long before the Trump era, yet the pressures were just as intense. The dot-com bubble was beginning to burst, which led to an exodus of money and human capital from Silicon Valley. As the young pastor's congregation dwindled, and he informed some staff members that they would need to be let go, Chang began to spiral. He had battled anxiety since childhood but it now began to crush him. He went weeks without sleep and suffered from crippling panic attacks. The anxiety gave way to a severe depression. Chang found himself hardly able to function; he could not lead his family, let alone his large church.

He took a leave from pastoring and eventually stepped down for good. It was a humiliating, traumatizing ordeal. Chang stuck around as a lay leader—he still serves the church to this day—but he knew that his clergy career was finished. (Certain professions are not conducive to panic disorder; preaching is one of them.) Retreating from what he thought had been God's design for his life, Chang decided to tap into another skill set, launching a Bay Area consulting firm focused on serving corporations and universities, secular nonprofits and government agencies. He was enormously successful. Chang earned loads of money and a superb reputation among Silicon Valley's elite. For a decade after leaving the ministry, he felt healthy—personally, professionally, spiritually—and content.

Then, around the time of Trump's election, Chang began to detect in his church—and in the broader evangelical movement—those same undertones of anxiety that had tortured him years earlier. *Economic* anxiety. *Cultural* anxiety. *Racial* anxiety. *National* anxiety. All of it was palpable; none of it was productive. Chang had a unique vantage point. An evangelical who subscribed to conservative theology, he was politically left of center, someone for whom issues of refugee settlement and gun violence mattered as much as abortion and same-sex marriage. He had never fit neatly into any particular category or clique. Troubled by Trump's presidency and its radicalizing effect on the Church, Chang in 2019 launched a religious nonprofit, Redeeming Babel. The group's mission was to reimagine the methods by which evangelicals engaged with society. It was a noble enough idea.

And then COVID-19 arrived. Chang found himself at the intersection of an evangelicalism that recoiled at pandemic policies—church shutdowns, mask wearing, vaccines—and a secular Silicon Valley that possessed zero understanding of this faith community or its objections to said policies. He attempted to serve as a conduit between these worlds. Contracted by health agencies to promote vaccination, Chang worked to build an alliance between evangelical and secular organizations. But too often it was like translating between tribes. Recalling one particular meeting with a high-powered health-care executive who could not fathom the evangelical resistance to vaccines, Chang walked her through arguments touching on everything from abortion and stem-cell research to bodily temples and end-times prophecy. Her expression was blank. Finally, the passive and unfailingly polite Chang blurted out, "Does the term 'Mark of the Beast' mean anything to you?" The woman, wide-eyed, said it did not.

Distressed by this disconnect, Chang began pouring himself into dual education efforts—teaching evangelicals about the vaccine, while teaching everyone else about why evangelicals were forgoing the shot at rates exceeding any other demographic. He authored essays for the *New York Times*. He testified before the U.S. Senate. He created video content explaining the science and efficacy of the vaccines. These efforts absolutely moved the (pun intended) needle; a peer-reviewed study from Stanford and Columbia left no doubt that Chang's initiatives saved lives in the evangelical community.

Still, he felt inadequate. The bloody conclusion to Trump's presidency had unleashed sentiments far more menacing than vaccine hesitancy. Even as he gained ground in one battle, Chang feared that Christians like him were losing the war.

In July 2021, Chang and his wife hosted some friends for a stay at their California home. One of those friends was David French. They had known each other for thirty years—a relationship built not on religion or law or politics, but on something even more profound: fantasy baseball. Having bonded decades earlier over the ritual of stat casting and simulated roster building, Chang and French were now comrades sharing a foxhole. Although their politics were quite divergent—Chang a moderate pro-life Democrat, French an archconservative who'd abandoned the Republican Party—they shared religious convictions to which everything else was subordinate. Both men had witnessed the unraveling of the evangelical movement. Both men had watched bad actors strong-arm the Church in pursuit of a partisan agenda. Both men agreed that something needed to be done about it.

One afternoon, while hiking the Grey Whale Cove trail along the spectacular San Mateo Coast, Chang laid it all out for French. There needed to be an organized, visible, well-funded effort to counter the work done by the likes of Charlie Kirk, Eric Metaxas, Ralph Reed, David Barton, and so many others on the MAGA right. Chang didn't envision some puritanical campaign to banish politics from the Church alto-gether; what he hoped to articulate was an alternative to the manic, enemy-at-the-gates mindset that was infecting American evangeli-calism. This would best be accomplished by a systematic curriculum, something that could be studied by individuals and small groups, some-thing focused not on the "who" or "what" of politics—who to vote for, what policies to support—but on the question of "how" Christians are called to engage the culture.

"The one thing that's unambiguous, where we can take direct in-struction from Jesus, is on the *how* of politics—when it comes to loving our enemy, having humility, showing mercy, pursuing truth," Chang told French. "And those *hows*, while being deeply biblical and pointing people to Jesus, also happen to be really congruent with the basic val-ues of democracy and pluralism."

Chang was onto something: How many disputes, theological and political and otherwise, might be amicably resolved by practicing the so-called golden rule we all learned in kindergarten? That old adage—meant to ensure harmony, dignity, community—was first spoken by Jesus, as He taught His followers *how* to deal with people they didn't like or agree with. "Do unto others as you would have them do to you," Jesus said.

French listened carefully. He and Chang had noodled on these ideas before, but this was a new level of detail—and commitment. He had so many other obligations and so little time to give to such an ambitious new venture. But he knew it needed to be done. As long as Chang was willing to lead the charge from an organizational and fundraising standpoint, French told his friend, "I'm in."

At that very moment, the two men rounded a curve in the trail. Outstretching before them was a panoramic view of the Pacific Ocean. Chang thought of the old fisherman's prayer: "O God, thy sea is so great and my boat is so small." The man driven from the ranks of professional preaching by chronic anxiety was about to climb into an even wobblier pulpit.

The first step, Chang and French agreed, was to throw up a flag and see who rallied to it. They soon created the *Good Faith Podcast*, a weekly conversation situated at the nexus of Christianity and current events. The podcast launched in November 2021 and quickly climbed into the top 0.5 percent of global podcast downloads. The response was a revelation. Until that point, Chang and French had only hypothesized about the appetite for their novel approach to politics and evangelicalism. Now the audience was proving larger and hungrier than they could have imagined. Chang assumed, given basic market dynamics, that raising money for their initiative would be easy enough.

"In my mind, this is an evangelical problem. We allowed this to happen, and so I felt like it was important that Christian funders take the lead," Chang told me. "But what I discovered very quickly was that the same paralysis—the same fear of stepping into the fray that has gripped evangelical pastors—has also gripped evangelical funders. Just like the pastor fears the blowback if they speak out, the Christian funders and foundations do as well. Because they're dealing with the same dynamics on their boards and with their constituencies. So even though I had relationships with these people, I had worked with them before, I kept coming up empty."

Even without any clear sense of how the resources might materialize to power this project, Chang embarked on a determined talent-recruiting tour. Throughout the spring and summer of 2022, he traveled the country pitching well-placed evangelical leaders on the initiative. Slowly, painstakingly, he won important allies, among them, former George W. Bush adviser (and prolific writer) Pete Wehner; Cherie Harder, who runs the D.C.-based nonprofit Trinity Forum; Andrew Hanauer, who leads the One America Movement; and Shirley Hoogstra, president of the Council for Christian Colleges & Universities, an organization long vexed by the question of how to handle the incursion of Charlie Kirk's Turning Point USA into its affiliated campuses.

The biggest catch was Russell Moore. Better than anyone, he understood the necessity of a teaching program that could be introduced at the lay level, something to relieve the pressure on pastors to have to tackle everything from the pulpit. Moore simply didn't have the time to do it himself; he had been praying and waiting for someone else to shoulder the load. Suddenly, here was Curtis Chang, offering to do just that.

Made in heaven or not, the match was perfect. Chang, Moore, and French decided to call their venture *The After Party*. It was a double entendre: They aspired to a postpartisan Christianity, but even more so they looked forward to the promised feast awaiting Jesus's followers in eternity, a place where divisions will vanish, replaced by a celebration of unity in Christ.

With the gang put together, Chang charged ahead even harder on the fundraising front. Striking out, time and again, with Christian individuals and entities, he began to entertain a strange idea: What if *unbelievers* footed the bill for this project?

Walking into his initial meetings with secular funders, Chang halfway wondered if he was losing his mind. These were some of the same people who couldn't fathom vaccine hesitancy among evangelicals; who had zero understanding of the Church's conflicts regarding politics, policy, and culture. Now they were going to bankroll his Christian curriculum enterprise?

Yes. That's what all of them said—*yes*. In retrospect, Chang told me, it shouldn't have been a surprise. The people he approached, while predominantly progressive in their personal views, were invested in issues of democracy, pluralism, national cohesiveness. In one particularly impactful meeting, after Chang began with a mea culpa—explaining that this was a problem of evangelicals' own making, and a problem they were responsible for solving—the man across the table, a non-Christian, abruptly cut him off.

"No, no, no. This isn't just your problem. This is everyone's problem," the man told him. "The truth is, some of us *have* marginalized evangelicals. We *have* given them reason to be suspicious of us. This is our problem, too."

Chang became emotional when recalling this exchange. "It was really, really heartening to me," he said. "I've come around, since then, to realizing that these partnerships need to be part of the solution to shar-ing this society together. There has been so much hostility for so long. And it's inexcusable on both sides—but *we're* the ones called to be wit-nessing to the culture. Right? So, let's see. Maybe if we use the resources of the secular world to heal the evangelical Church, then we can also use the spirit of the evangelical Church to heal the secular world."

Flush with seed funding, Chang, French, and Moore got to work crafting their curriculum. What they wound up producing—as an initial offering—was a six-session series, designed to be plug-and-play for small groups that host sixty- to ninety-minute Bible studies. A typical session might feature an opening video lecture, followed by a time of conver-sation around certain prompts, then conclude with a structured group exercise and a period of individual reflection. The plan was to steadily build out a library of content, available online and via smartphone apps, that can be accessed anywhere and taught by anyone.

In December 2022, *The After Party* was awarded a large grant to execute a pilot project in Ohio. Announcing the launch of his group at the National Press Club in March 2023, Chang explained how they were partnering with networks of pastors and Christian colleges in the Buckeye State and hoped to distribute the curriculum to some fifty churches later that year. If all went according to plan, Chang said, they would receive enough positive feedback to start scaling the project up in 2024—just in time for a presidential campaign. The timing, Chang said, is not coincidental.

"Pastors have been white-knuckling their way through politics for the last six years," he told me after the launch. "It's time we helped them out."

THERE WAS SOMETHING DIFFERENT ABOUT RUSSELL MOORE WHEN WE spoke in the spring of 2023.

For the past number of years, our regular conversations had been marked by a persistent heaviness. And yet, on this March afternoon—just days after Tucker Carlson ridiculed him on his television show, and days before the launch of *The After Party*—Moore sounded lively, cheer-ful, *light*. I had to wonder if there wasn't a certain validation in being mocked by Carlson at this stage. Recent court documents, revealed due to an ongoing lawsuit against Fox News, had exposed the staggering extent of Carlson's duplicity. The Fox host had promoted election-fraud profiteers while privately deriding them (and his own viewers) as buffoons for believing any of it; he'd publicly championed Trump while telling one colleague via text, "I hate him passionately." None of this mattered to the professional class of grifters—"I'd rather the men in my church be discipled by Tucker Carlson over David French," tweeted MAGA mascot and Christian nationalist mouthpiece William Wolfe—but it did serious damage with the common viewer.

Moore acknowledged that he was encouraged by this. In fact, he told me, he'd recently gotten a double dose of related good news. A revival had broken out at Asbury University, a small evangelical school in Kentucky, and thousands of Christians had flooded the campus to share in the experience of spiritual ecstasy. This was precisely the type of moment Moore had been praying for—but he worried, almost immediately upon hearing the news of Asbury's revival, that it would be hijacked by bad actors for the sake of their own agendas. Asbury refused to let that happen. When he called to check in with friends at the college, Moore was told that in an attempt to safeguard the beauty and sanctity of the occasion, school officials were guarding the campus against performance artists. That included Fox News: Carlson's team had asked to broadcast a show live from the revival, Moore was informed, but the Asbury staff refused.

"One of the things that's really extraordinary about what's happened at Asbury, both at the institutional leadership level and with the organic, on-the-ground presence of students there, is they haven't let these outsiders come in and leverage what God was doing there for their own means-to-an-end purposes," Moore said. "That gives me real hope that something is changing for the better."

This amounted to an impossibly optimistic sentiment from Moore. *Changing for the better*? Who was this upbeat individual, speaking in such buoyant tones? I recalled to Moore what he'd told us at dinner in Tennessee sixteen months earlier: "It may sound like Chicken Little. But I'm telling you, there is a serious effort to turn this 'two countries' talk into something real. There are Christians taking all the populist passions and adding a transcendent authority to it. And nobody is stopping—"

Moore interrupted before I could finish. "I'm in a better place now. *We're* in a better place now," he said.

One reason for that, Moore noted, was the resilience of the young generation of believers. They had not only held the line but helped to pull their parents back from the brink. "Put it this way: The Turning Point USA youth rallies and the Asbury Revival are just two very clearly different things in a way that would not have been the case a couple of years ago," Moore said. "These kids, even though they'd have every right to rebel against the older generation, they're not. Instead, they're finding ways to love and honor and bring along their pastors, their parents, their grandparents. And that's actually forcing a lot of these parents and grandparents to begin seeing things through the rubric of their children or grandchildren, which is incredibly positive."

This was not, however, the primary explanation for Moore's surging confidence. Beyond the Asbury Revival and other recent developments—the emergence of efforts like *The After Party*, the continuing implosion of Carlson, who was soon fired by Fox News—there was reason to believe that, despite having all the resources to stage a serious institutional takeover of American Christianity, people like Charlie Kirk and Eric Metaxas were floundering. No doubt they would continue to spend even bigger and push even harder, making life miserable for pastors and sowing incessant instability in their churches. But that was worlds removed from what seemed possible not long before when, in the two years after Trump left office, they seemed poised to capture the controls inside of the American Church. Somewhere along the line their momentum had stalled. I could see it on Kirk's demoralized face in Phoenix; I could hear it in Metaxas's strained, desperate voice in Washington State. These were not men beholding a great victory that was within reach. These were men bracing for further losses.

"Obviously, we still have enormous challenges. But one of those challenges is *not* an organized Christian nationalist movement gaining the power, at a grassroots level, to hijack institutions," Moore said. "That has now shown itself to be the case over and over again, whether in denominations or campus ministries or colleges themselves. Those institutions that are doing the work of church-based evangelicalism have not fallen to this nationalist political movement, and they don't appear to be in danger of falling."

He added: "There was an almost-universal sense in many of those institutions, not long ago, that this populist Christian nationalist takeover had an appearance of inevitability. And that has proven to not be the case. It's a surprise—a very pleasant surprise."

I asked Moore if there was a specific example that came to mind.

"Believe it or not," he said with a reticent chuckle, "it's the Southern Baptist Convention."

CHAPTER NINETEEN

ANAHEIM, CALIFORNIA

Go and do likewise.

—LUKE 10:37

When Daniel Darling was fired by the National Religious Broadcasters back in 2021, after voicing support for the coronavirus vaccine, his life went sideways. The father of four was cast away, abruptly without work, battered by internet bullies—many of them self-identifying Christians—who reveled in his misfortune. Yet it was also Christians who rode to his rescue: reaching out with prayers and encouragement, offering job leads, even sending money directly to his family so they could pay the bills.

"Man, I've been hurt by the Church. But I've also been blessed by the Church," Darling said. "Getting fired like that revealed the best and the worst of what Christianity can be—so ugly, but also so beautiful. And the real problem is, the public only sees the crazy side of Christianity. They don't see the love behind the scenes."

Stocky, bearded, and in his mid-forties, Darling wore a teal fishing shirt on the morning we met for breakfast in June 2022. A blue lanyard swung from his neck. It announced the Southern Baptist Convention's annual meeting, which was unfolding at a convention center three blocks away. The theme of the gathering—displayed on literature and banners and Darling's lanyard—was "JESUS: The Center of It All."

Except Jesus *wasn't* the center of it all. This year's SBC meeting—like every other SBC meeting in recent memory—would be dominated by extrabiblical headlines. There was the fight over Saddleback Church, headed by renowned pastor and author Rick Warren, who had antagonized some SBC mates by allowing women to teach inside his church. There was a hotly contested election for the SBC presidency pitting a far-right candidate against a more agreeable (but still quite conservative) opponent. Perhaps most consequentially, there was a historic vote over whether to adopt recommendations from a third-party investigation—the one that produced the "apocalypse" report Russell Moore wrote of—that would set up a database to track sexual predators inside of the denomination.

This was Darling's entire point.

"Our North American mission board raised something like $66 million this year to help the most impoverished people around the world. We've sent $11 million to Ukraine in the last year alone. We have people on the ground there. We have people on the ground *everywhere*. I mean, literally anywhere you see human suffering, you see Southern Baptists, you see evangelicals," Darling told me. "But we spend so much time doing and saying crazy stuff—stuff that hurts people—that it distracts from all the good we're doing in the world. It distracts from Jesus."

Some of this, Darling complained, was the product of incentive structures in the media industry. He had spent years living and worshipping in Mt. Juliet, Tennessee, the town where Greg Locke pastored his tent-revival church. Darling explained that an alliance of evangelical leaders there had done heroic work in the community, including starting a public-private cooperative to help feed, clothe, and educate underserved youth. They got no coverage from the Nashville press—and they didn't want any. "But when Greg Locke starts spouting all this crazy nonsense, guess who makes the cover of the *Tennessean*?" Darling said.

The resilience shown by many congregations in the face of these insurgent threats, he told me, was as big a story as the insurgency itself.

"A lot of people expected that your average evangelical church had turned into some kind of MAGA hothouse on Sunday mornings. And that's definitely happened in some places, but it's nowhere near the numbers that people think," Darling said. "For all the problems we've seen, with people arguing over COVID and racial justice and Trump—people leaving their churches because of their own political biases—those churches have held on. And in a lot of cases, they're actually healthier than they were before."

This sentiment was beginning to sound familiar. I had heard it in conversations with pastors who had been through the ministerial meat grinder since 2016; who had watched a quarter of their congregations defect due to partisan grievances; who had suffered so greatly in the process that they themselves nearly quit the Church or the clergy altogether; but who, with the passing of time, if not yet the proverbial storm, had seen their ministries fortified. Fears of a mass exodus faded. Church life returned to some semblance of normal. Newcomers popped up in the pews. Pastors could finally breathe again, focusing on their jobs instead of worrying about the next turn of the news cycle.

"This is the mistake Tom Ascol is making," Darling told me, referring to the Florida pastor who was running for SBC president on a hard-line conservative platform. "Most pastors are thinking about their sermon for Sunday. They're tied up with the person they're visiting in the hospital, the marriage counseling they're doing—and oh yeah, they've also got a troubled kid at home. They don't want to get sucked back into this political junk."

It wasn't for a lack of conviction. Indeed, many of the pastors I'd encountered over the previous few years held strong personal beliefs on the most pressing issues of the moment. In certain cases, such as with abortion, they might feel obliged as a matter of conscience to share those beliefs with their flocks. But by and large they kept quiet. There was no upside to engaging in political discourse, because too many of their congregants simply could not observe the boundaries necessary to keep that discourse centered on Christ. What the military calls "mission creep"—a bombing of some munitions hut turns into a ground war against the entire continent—confounds much of the modern evangelical movement. A specific ethical cause, such as advocacy for the unborn, gives way to wide-ranging, knee-jerk, intellectually untethered promotion of partisan crusades. The key to healthy

Christianity, Darling said, is discerning where that line is—and rejecting the pressure to cross it.

"There's nothing wrong with presenting our views in the public
square. If we really see the world as our mission field, then we should try
to shape society as best we can," Darling said. "But we can't do it from a
place of overrealized patriotism. We can't do it from a place of red versus
blue. We can't do it from a place of fear. Because to those people watching from the outside, that's the only thing they see—fear."

Plenty of people were watching from the outside in Anaheim. The
SBC had credentialed scores of reporters, many from major mainstream news outlets, to cover the conflicts over women in ministry,
over the leadership of the SBC, and especially over the handling of sexual abuse in the denomination. Some Southern Baptists recoiled at the
presence of such interlopers. They felt these journalists were there to
ridicule and caricature them, to gleefully document the Southern Baptist imbroglio for their vindictive secular audiences.

Perhaps some of them were. But I had to wonder, in talking with Darling, whether this wasn't the best thing for the SBC—and for American
Christianity on the whole. A public shaming was long overdue. Maybe,
after seeing nothing but cover-ups and self-preservation, these reporters would finally see contrition and repentance. Maybe that behavior
would point them and their audiences to the reason that thousands of
people were meeting in Anaheim. Maybe, just maybe, they would start
to see Jesus as the center of it all.

"Credibility matters. Every institution fails, but the Christian Church
has failed spectacularly," Darling said. "What the Christian Church
has—its secret weapon—is the ethic of forgiveness and reconciliation.
But we've got a lot of work to do. We need to get this right."

I asked Darling if he was optimistic about getting it right. He said
the outcomes in Anaheim would do much to color his outlook.

"The thing is, Christianity is exploding across the globe—in China, in
Iran, all over Africa. But we're struggling in America. If we don't humble
ourselves, if we don't start treating people in a way that glorifies God,
we're going to squander what's left of our credibility here," Darling said.
"I think we'd all do well to remember: God's plan for the ages has nothing to do with America. We need Him. He doesn't need us."

* * *

THE FIRST THING I SPOTTED, AFTER WALKING INTO THE LUMINOUS, warehouse-aesthetic exhibition hall inside the Anaheim Convention Center, was a sprawling blue banner promoting a company called Brotherhood Mutual. Its stated mission: PROTECTING CHRISTIAN MINIS- TRIES.

A middle-aged man named Charlie Cutler, clad in a navy blazer and jeans, leaned against the booth with brochures in one hand and a fly- swatter in the other. A longtime executive with ChurchWest Insurance Services, the parent company of Brotherhood Mutual, Cutler ex- plained to me that ChurchWest had for generations worked exclusively with churches, Christian schools, and religious nonprofits. Most of their efforts focused on fires and floods, storms and sewage—typical insur- ance stuff. Not anymore.

"Reputation," Cutler said, "is becoming our specialty."

Hence the flyswatter. Branded with a ChurchWest logo, the plastic instrument carried a three-word warning: NOT TODAY SATAN. This was the message Cutler and ChurchWest were advertising at the SBC's an- nual meeting. Their services were specifically designed to help Chris- tian organizations deal harshly with unwelcome species; to protect them against an infestation of abusers, predators, and pedophiles.

For a long time, Cutler told me, this represented just a rump portion of their firm's business. "The Catholic Church scandal was a wake-up call for a lot of Americans, but not necessarily a lot of evangelicals," Cut- ler said. "There was really a refusal to accept that this could be hap- pening in *their* churches."

Faith-based organizations have always cleaved to the notion—or at least, to fragments of it—that they are somehow uniquely impervious to the woes that plague secular institutions: thievery and fraud, harass- ment and intimidation, abuses of power and denials of justice. Religious people, Christians in particular, want to believe that their communi- ties are safer, better, more virtuous than those of nonbelievers.

But in fact, those communities are often worse *because* of the tradi- tions and misapplied teachings of the Church. Trust can seem incompat- ible with transparency. Deference to authority can seem irreconcilable with demands for accountability. Finding fault can seem unnecessary given the overarching emphasis on mercy.

"One of the great challenges in running a church is that they are self-governed, self-regulated," Cutler said. "They answer to no one but themselves. And that breeds a lot of problems. So, part of what we do is try to help them meet standards of care that govern other organizations, especially organizations that deal with children."

Cutler shrugged. "Let's face it. If you're a pedophile, the church is a very inviting target," he said. "It's a place built on trust. You're not necessarily looking for those red flags."

Finally, that was beginning to change. Just down the hall from us, in the main ballroom, thousands of delegates from SBC churches around the country—known as "messengers"—were on the verge of adopting measures that might transform the Southern Baptist Convention. Taken together, these reforms would compel transparency and make those red flags a whole lot harder to miss.

"It's about time, isn't it?" Cutler said, nodding in the direction of the ballroom. "When these horrible things continue to happen inside the Church, the message of Christ—His love for us, and the work Christians do to share that love with the world—is totally lost."

That work was on display all throughout the exhibition hall. This was not the Road to Majority Conference or the ReAwaken America Tour; there were no kiosks selling miracle cures or militaristic slogans. Instead, sprawled out over some ten thousand square feet, the SBC exhibitors showcased causes more readily identifiable with Christ.

One booth promoted the Prison Fellowship ministry, soliciting donations for an initiative that delivers gifts to the children of incarcerated persons at Christmastime. Another booth, sponsored by Voice of the Martyrs, offered education on the underground church in parts of Africa and the Middle East, and raised funds to support the frontline workers who were risking their lives to support Christians in hostile locations. Some organizations fought childhood poverty with their meal-packing operations; others battled online porn addiction with free software downloads. Talk of stopping human trafficking—the real thing, not those Reddit rumors targeting Tom Hanks and Oprah Winfrey—was everywhere. At one point, a crowd swarmed around the stall where SBC disaster relief officials signed up volunteers who would, at indeterminate times over the years to come, drop everything and rush to sites of devastation in the United States and abroad.

Most prominent were the stations dedicated to a holistic view of the pro-life movement. Catering to single mothers, and mothers in dire economic straits, these organizations specialized in forming support groups at the local level; offering food, clothing, and diapers; providing free child care; and supporting them financially before and after birth. It was an impressive display, both in terms of generosity and self-awareness, as many of the representatives spoke to me in regretful tones about what had long been a myopic approach to the anti-abortion cause. One organization, Embrace Grace, even handed out pamphlets declaring, "Pro-Love is the new Pro-Life."

Herbie Newell, the president of Lifeline Children's Services, said he was heartened to see his pro-life allies starting to catch up. Since 1981, his organization has been a leading advocate for what he calls "human flourishing through the love of Christ." They are widely (and rightly) perceived as a pro-life organization, but they are best understood as a Christian social agency: serving vulnerable women, training new parents, placing kids through adoption and foster care. "True human flourishing is not just when life is protected at the outset, but when it's *sustained*," Newell said. "We want to manifest the gospel of Jesus Christ—not proclaim it, but manifest it."

Traditionally, Newell told me, his organization has focused on poverty—maternal poverty, childhood poverty—as a social ailment to be addressed. They have not abandoned that mission. However, they have begun incorporating a new mission: "relational poverty." One of Lifeline's burgeoning programs focuses on family reunification. By mobilizing local churches to minister to parents who gave up their children, either via adoption or foster care, Lifeline hopes to help them with education, job skills, and biblical discipleship. The idea is to build long-term relationships between the biological parents, their children, and the families raising them.

When I commended this idea—and offered praise for the other work that Lifeline does—Newell arched a skeptical eyebrow in my direction, as if to question whether these efforts should be in any way remarkable to a follower of Jesus.

"We in the United States have such an inadequate view of what a Christian is called to be," Newell told me. "The Bible tells us that we are broken beyond repair—*all of us*—and that Christ came to heal us. Churches are supposed to be hospitals for the sick. And once we're healed, we're supposed to be helping others get healthy, too."

I asked Newell, whose work has taken him all over the world, why his critique was focused on American Christianity.

"Our disease in America is the same as anywhere else: sin. But in America, we've used our prosperity to hide it. I think we've grown accustomed to worshipping the blessings of God instead of the blesser," he said. "Those blessings have become our god. That's why you see Christians gripping on to the things of this world with sweaty palms. We're too busy trying to stay on top, trying to be in charge of things, instead of being misfits who are saved by grace."

A former Southern Baptist, Newell copped to a certain awkwardness given the setting. He'd grown up in the SBC, raised his kids in the SBC. But those concerns with the American Church, readily apparent in his own local congregation, eventually caused him to walk away. Just recently, Newell and his family had begun attending a Presbyterian church in their hometown of Birmingham, Alabama. He had come to Anaheim this week expecting to feel like a spectator. Instead he found himself hanging on the proceedings down the hall, hoping that his brothers and sisters would get out of their own way.

"Look, I'm sick about all this stuff—the abuse, the cover-ups, the corruption. It's got to stop. But, at the same time, I'm not concerned about God getting His glory. God always gets His glory, because God is always sovereign," Newell told me. "The question is, are we going to keep on living for our own glory? Or are we going to die to ourselves and beg for His forgiveness?"

EVERY ONE OF THE STACKABLE METAL CHAIRS WAS OCCUPIED. THOU-sands of them had been arranged throughout the main ballroom, wrapping around painted steel columns and unfurling across endless sections of the cavernous event space. The messengers sat in them quietly, listening to the arguments being made at the microphones nearby. They wore small badges—name, church, hometown—and gripped yellow voting placards the size of business envelopes, waiting for the action to begin.

One year earlier, at the contentious 2021 SBC meeting in Nashville, the messengers had voted to create a temporary task force that would oversee a probe into allegations of sexual abuse and cover-ups within the denomination. That vote had set history in motion. The newly created task force hired a third-party firm, Guidepost Solutions, to investigate the SBC's Executive Committee, which led to the publication of its bombshell report in May 2022, just a few weeks before this annual meeting.

In light of Guidepost's findings, the task force came to Anaheim armed with a package of recommendations. One would create a *new* entity—the Abuse Reform Implementation Task Force—to handle all such ongoing matters in the denomination. Another would form an independently maintained database, known as Ministry Check, that would allow churches to share "properly vetted information" about people who had been "credibly accused" of abuse.

The first proposal received no real pushback. Virtually everyone in the denomination, even the head-in-the-sand hard-liners who recoiled at the hashtag #SBCtoo, acknowledged that they had a serious, long-term problem on their hands, and that some governing body would be needed to deal with it.

It was the second proposal, pushing the formation of a database of credibly accused abusers, that came under fire from the SBC's arch-conservatives. What did "credibly accused" mean, anyway? How could they trust that such a system wouldn't be weaponized by opponents of a particular pastor—or enemies of the Christian faith—to sow chaos in the Church? Why would they trust a secular third-party firm to handle the most sensitive inner workings of Southern Baptist polity? After all, Guidepost Solutions, as several messengers noted ruefully from the microphones, had just that very month issued a tweet celebrating Pride Month.

Finally, Bruce Frank put an end to the cantankerous debate. The muscular, middle-aged pastor of Biltmore Church in Asheville, North Carolina, Frank had been appointed chairman of the original task force a year earlier. Now, as he listened to certain messengers—people who had opposed his group from the very start—suggest that its recommendations were tainted because of an external corporation's Twitter account, Frank was running low on patience.

"Our book tells us that God is so sovereign, that He can even take pagan nations and use them to chastise His own people," Frank declared from the ballroom stage. "The issue here is not what Guidepost thinks about LGBT issues; it's what Southern Baptists think about abuse."

When it came time to vote, the room hummed with anticipation. Then, suddenly and more than a bit theatrically, it fell silent. Seconds felt like minutes as the messengers received their final balloting instructions per Robert's Rules of Order. A group of outspoken sexual assault survivors, seated together near the front, joined hands and closed their eyes. People glanced side to side, looking to see who had their placards at the ready, like amateur forecasters parsing exit polls on election night. The call from the chair came, instructing all those in favor to say so at this time. Yellow ballots blasted into the air. *Thousands of them.* It wasn't close. For all the fuss, the task force's recommendations were adopted with what appeared to be at least 80 percent of the vote.

The ballroom erupted with applause. People began hugging and weeping and praying, arms outstretched, rejoicing in the justice of this triumph—relatively incremental and ridiculously overdue as they knew it was. As the messengers began pouring out of the hall, praise music boomed from the stage behind them: "I have built an altar where I worship things of men / I have taken journeys that have drawn me far from You / Now I am returning to Your mercies ever flowing / Pardon my transgressions, help me love You again."

A short time later, in a small windowless space on the second level of the complex, Frank and his task force colleagues stood at a makeshift dais before dozens of assembled media. The air was drenched with catharsis. Before the press conference began, one of the task force members, a famous young woman who wore a long brown ponytail, huddled with a group of abuse survivors in the back of the room. One of them cried out what the rest were thinking: "Three years ago," she said, when they'd faced scorn and ridicule for going public with their allegations, "this would have been impossible!" Their sobs were captured by snapping cameras all around them, images that would rocket around the web in the days to come.

One by one, Frank and his associates tackled questions from the press about the practical implications of the vote we'd just witnessed. Yes, they said, the work in constructing the database would begin immediately. No, they said, attorney-client privilege could not be invoked to keep abusers from being named. Yes, they said, the database would be retroactive to include past offenders.

In the scrum of sorting out these details—about dates and organizations, legal mechanisms and denominational proceedings—the essential underlying question went ignored. Why did it take leaders of the Southern Baptist Convention so long to take such basic steps toward protecting the people inside their churches?

Before I could ask, Marshall Blalock, a pastor from Charleston, South Carolina, and the vice chair of the task force, offered an unsolicited window into his own experience and evolution.

"From my perspective, when these kinds of incidents come up, I think our first instinct is . . . about protecting the institution. And we've got to have a culture change in our thinking," Blalock said. "And that's the one place where I've changed the most in my own life."

It wasn't that he had actively ignored the problem, Blalock continued. He had simply been oblivious to it. He was too busy pastoring his church, looking out for his own flock, to see how systemic the abuses had become and to engage with the scale of deception and exploitation. It took hearing the harrowing tales of survivors he'd met through his work on the task force to realize the extent of the crisis and repent for his own culpability. Something needed to change, Blalock declared. Rather than worrying about containing the damage and guarding its good name, the first impulse of the Church moving forward must be to care for the people who have been hurt.

Alas, the irony of it all. Churches had been so preoccupied with safeguarding their reputations that they behaved in ways that destroyed their reputations. It took generations of getting it wrong for pastors like

Blalock to recognize that the best way to do right by the Church was doing right by the people hurt inside of it.

"I viewed this as an assignment from God, to bring glory to His name," Pastor Bucas Sterling III, a member of the task force, told me after the press conference. "I believe we have done that. We are openly repenting. We are agreeing to do what is good and righteous in protecting the most vulnerable people in His Church. What God does with this now, that's up to Him. But we've gained ground for His kingdom today."

Frank, walking with us down a corridor, frowned at his friend's optimistic note. He had seen too much ugliness inside the SBC—over his career, and particularly over the last year—to get carried away with this one victory. He assured me that the heaviest lifting was yet to come.

"Trust is earned," Frank said. "Today was a great day. But in many ways, it's just the beginning."

IN THE CASE OF A VAST, COMPLEX, CLIQUISH INSTITUTION LIKE THE Southern Baptist Convention, doing the right thing depends on having leaders who *want* to do the right thing.

Russell Moore's departure from the denomination in spring 2021 had seemed like a knockout blow landed by the SBC's radical faction. They had spent years making an example of Moore, bullying him with mafioso-like tactics, sending a chilling signal to other like-minded reformers. When he quit, they were sufficiently emboldened to believe it was their time to retake total control of the denomination. They saw an opening in the summer of 2021 for a sequel to the great "conservative resurgence" of the late 1970s, pushing back once more on the perceived liberalism and supposed biblical infidelity that were permeating the denomination.

But there were obvious problems with this strategy. For one thing, no evidence existed to support the idea of leftward drift within the SBC. According to political scientist, statistician, and ordained minister Ryan Burge, the average white Southern Baptist voted 9 percent more Republican in 2020 than in 2008. Partisan loyalties aside, nobody could plausibly claim that Russell Moore was some sort of ideological or theological progressive. Turning Moore into the poster boy for weak-kneed wokeness—and hoisting his scalp as the rallying cry for a second conservative resurgence—would only work if their *real* reasons for hating Moore stayed secret.

But the secret got out. In May 2021, a few weeks before the SBC's annual meeting in Nashville, one of Moore's allies had leaked a copy of the damning letter he'd written to the SBC Executive Committee a year earlier. Moore quite obviously did not leak the letter himself; the time to do that would have been right when he sent it, in 2020, as he was under investigation by the Executive Committee and fighting to maintain his own leadership role inside the SBC. But the publication and proliferation of Moore's letter nonetheless proved ruinous to his adversaries—starting with Mike Stone, the Georgia pastor who had led the Executive Committee and directed the probes into Moore.

Stone was an immensely powerful figure within the Conservative Baptist Network (CBN), a sect of right-wing pastors who counted themselves as descendants of that fundamentalist takeover of the 1970s. Stone, it so happened, was also a candidate to become the Southern Baptist Convention's president in 2021; in fact, many considered him the favorite. But the contents of Moore's letter, which went viral inside the denomination, swung public opinion sharply against Stone. In the weeks leading up to the 2021 annual meeting, he and his CBN allies had taken to calling themselves "pirates" who aimed to storm the Southern Baptist ship and steer it hard to the right. But their mutiny failed. Stone lost the presidential race to Ed Litton, a pastor from Alabama sympathetic to Moore and his followers.

The attempt to destroy Moore had backfired in more ways than one. Not only did Stone and his brigands lose out on the presidency, which, given their hold on the Executive Committee, would have given them total control of the SBC leadership structure; they also unwittingly created a groundswell of support for the very thing Moore had been seeking: an independent probe into the denomination's handling of sexual abuse. The Executive Committee tried to head this off, announcing days before the 2021 annual meeting that it would be commissioning an outside firm to do the investigating. But the SBC messengers, in a stunning show of defiance, overruled the Executive Committee. It was fast becoming apparent, even to many loyal conservatives within the denomination, that the Executive Committee could not be trusted to police itself. The messengers insisted on a different arrangement: The incoming president would appoint a special task force to oversee the investigation. That's just what Litton did, tapping Frank to lead the effort that, one year later, would result in the historic vote in Anaheim.

Yet for all the fanfare, SBC messengers realized that adopting the recommendations wouldn't mean a thing if the denomination's president refused to keep pressing the issue forward. Litton had announced he was stepping down after just one year on the job—a result of the pressures he felt navigating this denominational civil war. This presidential vacancy created the conditions for a dramatic and devastating backlash: The pirates, humiliated in Nashville and at risk of losing their grip on the SBC with another defeat, would be inclined to pull out the stops.

Indeed they did. On the morning of the presidential vote in Anaheim, members of the Conservative Baptist Network gathered in an event space not far from the convention center. They spoke of a showdown for the soul of their denomination. They handed out copies of *Rules for Radicals*, the book about guerrilla political tactics written by left-wing cult hero (and right-wing bogeyman) Saul Alinsky. They vowed never to surrender to the limp-wristed Church leaders who would let the Southern Baptist Convention descend into a shapeless spiritual utopia.

And then they brought out a special guest: Charlie Kirk.

Straddling the twin roles of motivational speaker and MAGA cleric, Kirk issued an impassioned fatwa against the *other* pastors in Anaheim. Their weak-willed SBC colleagues would do nothing to stop the bombardment of the American Church; in fact, they were abetting it. By sidestepping the political maelstrom—at a moment when Christianity was "under attack from within"—these pastors were "complicit" with the leftists and secularists who sought to purge the Almighty from public life. Kirk suggested that they might as well hang LGBTQ rainbow flags below their steeples and get it over with. There was only one way to stop this madness: Kirk endorsed the CBN's presidential candidate, Florida pastor Tom Ascol, portraying him as a bulwark against a sequence of events that might well lead to the collapse of Christianity in America.

But Kirk and his allies were attempting to usher in a second conservative resurgence at a moment when the failures of the first were becoming all too obvious. Inside that very room Kirk spoke to, on the morning of the presidential vote in Anaheim, was one of the last living architects of the 1970s fundamentalist takeover: Paige Patterson.

A pastor and theologian who served as SBC president in between stints of presiding over two of the denomination's most prestigious seminaries, Patterson had refashioned the SBC into a hard-nosed, play-for-keeps entity. He had stressed "inerrancy of scripture" as a means of not only suppressing heterodox thinking about culture, but blocking outside voices that might challenge internal practices on things like, say, sexual abuse. Now the Southern Baptist Convention was reaping what Patterson and his allies sowed. The Guidepost report implicated numerous SBC luminaries, including Patterson himself, who'd been fired by Southwestern seminary in 2018 for his repeated mishandling of rape cases, including one instance of an outright cover-up. (One week after the report dropped, Patterson was Robert Jeffress's guest preacher at First Baptist Dallas.)

The folly was inescapable: At the very convention where messengers voted in overwhelming fashion to modernize the good-old-boy culture of the SBC, Patterson showed up to the CBN breakfast pushing for a return to the past. (Paul Pressler, a former Texas judge and SBC kingmaker who'd been Patterson's closest ally in the 1970s, at least had the good sense not to show up to Anaheim, given the mounting legal troubles related to his alleged sexual assaults of underage males.) According to journalist Robert Downen, who attended the breakfast, Patterson "compared himself to the Apostle Paul and said Jesus 'forgave my sins'" though he declined to specify them.

Ascol lost the 2022 presidential vote in lopsided fashion. The winner, Bart Barber, a pastor from small-town Texas, made plain after the election his concern that political extremism had infiltrated the Church.

"Sometimes we let the tail wag the dog in Southern Baptist life," Barber told reporters.

"I don't think if you tried to plot me politically you could find me anywhere other than the right wing of American politics," he added, confessing his love for Ronald Reagan. "But the most important thing is where my home is spiritually, and that's with the gospel of Jesus Christ. . . . And I do believe we've seen some unhealthy ways in which secular politics have dominated the conversation in the Southern Baptist Convention."

Asked about becoming president, Barber choked with emotion. He downplayed any exaltation that one might typically associate with the job. Instead he spoke of "the scars" he collected from his previous stops in the SBC—and the fresh wounds he knew to expect in this role.

"But the Church is worth it. It's worth enduring the slings and arrows," he said. "Sometimes we treat people in ways that must make it hard for people to believe that we believe in the inerrancy and sufficiency of a book that says, 'The fruit of the spirit is love, joy, peace, patience, kindness, goodness, faithfulness, gentleness, and self-control.' I knew all of that coming into this. But praise God. I give thanks to Him for the things that happened before. Because now I look on Twitter, and see the things people say about me, and not only do I ignore it . . . but I get to the point where I can love them."

It was hard to imagine a more winsome human being. Barber answered every question by returning to the same central message of ratcheting down the partisan rancor, restoring the Church's reputation, and reaching unbelievers with renewed credibility. He even mentioned the heifers back on his ranch in Farmersville, Texas—the actual name of his town—that he needed to get home and tend to.

Only once did a fire flash in Barber's eyes. Recognizing the implications of his own victory in tandem with the historic vote a day earlier—Ascol almost certainly would have subverted the database effort—Barber declared that the Southern Baptist Convention was never going back to the way things were. Calling out the "wolves" who stalked SBC congregations for far too long, he delivered a message that sounded very much like a threat.

"Sexual predators have used our decentralized polity to try and turn our churches into a hunting ground," Barber said. "The tables have turned. The hunter is now the hunted."

BARBER HAD SOUNDED A BULLISH NOTE, BELIEVING THAT THE SWEEP- ing reforms adopted by SBC messengers in Anaheim boded well for the future of the denomination and the wider Church. Yet Frank's words from a day earlier echoed all the louder: "Trust is earned."

Maybe Barber was right. Maybe this was the moment when Southern Baptists would stop the bleeding and begin the process of restoring con- fidence in their churches. But that process was bound to be plodding. So much trust had already been squandered—and for certain people there could be no restoration of it.

Outside the convention center following Barber's press conference, I came upon two of the unsung heroes in Anaheim: Jules Woodson and Tiffany Thigpen. Both women were survivors of sexual assault in SBC churches, and both women had persevered through years of mockery and malice to force the issue in front of rank-and-file Southern Bap- tists. Their sobs of joy and release a day earlier, in that viral moment caught on camera, were well deserved. For the first time since they were abused, Woodson and Thigpen told me, they had some measure of faith in the Church getting things right.

"The old guard had such a hold on all these people. Even as victims, we thought we were doing the right thing by staying silent, by doing what they told us, by protecting the institution," Thigpen said. "I think those days are over. I think—I hope—that this younger generation, a gen- eration that really is concerned with justice, will take the Church in a better direction."

Woodson, lighting a cigarette while we sat on neighboring benches, told me that she held on to the same hope. But she wanted to make some- thing clear: She wouldn't be sticking around to see that new direction for the Church. In fact, she had left the SBC long ago. Thigpen had, too. They were expatriates from the denomination of their youth, and ex- iles from organized religion altogether.

"Confronting my history of abuse, especially in these last few years, I've been thinking about my morals and my values. And I've just come to realize that the Jesus I know is not the Jesus of the Church any-more," Woodson told me. "The Christ that has loved me at my most bro-ken and most vulnerable, is not the Christ that is demonstrated by the Church. So, my faith used to be very outward facing, but now it's very private. I still identify as a Christian, but I find it very hard to identify with the Church."

Thigpen nodded toward the building behind us. "I still love corpo-rate worship. Being in there, even though it's painful, it was beautiful. I still love the singing and worshipping. I would love to trust the Church again," she said. "But we've been hurt so many times, so many different ways. And at a certain point, I just can't risk going—I can't afford to lose my faith. I need to be closer to God, but I feel like every time I've been a part of a church, it just pushes me farther away."

She thought a moment. "I'll tell you something," Thigpen said. "Guidepost and their investigators showed us more of God—their com-passion, their fighting for us, their believing us, their validating us—than we *ever* got from the Church."

"Yes!" Woodson exclaimed. She was reminded of the Good Samar-itan, a parable Jesus taught about a Jewish man who was robbed, beaten, and left "half dead" while walking the treacherous road from Jerusalem to Jericho. He was ignored by two of his fellow Jews, both of whom were religious leaders. It was ultimately a Samaritan—sworn en-emy of the Jews—who stopped, tended to the man's wounds, took him for medical care, checked up on his recovery, and even paid his hospi-tal expenses.

This was an astounding, incendiary illustration to make. Jesus had chosen as the protagonist of His story a hated outsider who, despite not adhering to Jewish teachings, practiced them better than believers did. When He finished, Jesus pointedly asked one of His listeners—a Jewish religious leader himself—which of these three witnesses had treated the hurting man like a neighbor.

"The one who had mercy on him," answered the religious leader, surely mortified by this exchange.

"Go," Jesus told him, "and do likewise."

Two thousand years after Jesus told that parable, religious leaders were still failing to tend to their own, and outsiders were still showing the type of neighborly compassion that God requires of us.

"When I went public with my story in 2018, it was the *secular* world that had my back. It was the *secular* world that believed me and supported me," Woodson said. "It wasn't the Church."

Thigpen told me that her trauma had brought her into a closer relationship with God—and fundamentally changed the way she reads scripture. Whereas she once primarily studied the teachings of Jesus, she had, in recent years, developed a fondness for the front of the book.

"I used to have a hard time reconciling the God of the Old Testament— all that doom and gloom and anger—with the idea of a loving God," Thigpen said. "But now, having lived this hell with the SBC, I *like* God's anger and judgment. I understand it. I relate to it. I can see how betrayed God must have felt watching people mock His name with the way they treated each other."

Thigpen and Woodson were struggling to make peace with the Southern Baptists who had mistreated them—not merely their original abusers, but the legions of loyalists who had prized the Church's name over the children of God inside of it. Both women know their Bible well enough to appreciate the imperative of forgiving others as Christ forgave us. Still, having witnessed enough acts of halfhearted penitence to last several lifetimes, they weren't prepared to offer absolution until it felt completely authentic.

"These guys live off the message of cheap grace. They prop each other up by stressing God's forgiveness," Woodson said. "And obviously, that's an important part of His word. But God also talks about bringing darkness to light; about truth; about justice; about discipline; about the qualifications for pastors and leaders. You can't take one part of the Bible and dismiss the rest."

"Sure you can," Thigpen scoffed. "They do it all the time!"

They shared a laugh. But then Woodson turned introspective. She was clearly wrestling with feelings of hardheartedness, unsure of how to reconcile the progress of the past two days with the years of agony she had endured. Woodson looked around us and shook her head in amazement. "I will say, when I went to Birmingham for the annual meeting in 2019, the year after I went public, I never could have imagined *this*," she said. "People have been coming up to me nonstop here—some of the same people, I'm pretty sure, who were giving me dirty looks at previous meetings—and saying, 'Thank you.'"

Her eyes filled with tears. She tried to finish her thought, to no avail.

Thigpen rubbed her friend's back. "That's the love of Jesus," she said.

Woodson put out her cigarette—she had chained three in the course of our twenty-minute conversation—and we all stood up. Soon we were strolling along the campus of the Anaheim Convention Center. As we prepared to part ways, I congratulated the women on what they had accomplished at the 2022 annual meeting. Regardless of what came next, I told them, it was a moment for history.

They didn't deserve any congratulations, the women told me flatly. Yes, their stories had helped to shock the system of the denomination, but those stories would have stayed hidden if not for the heroics of so many people around them. There had been third-party investigators who worked tirelessly to bring the truth to light. There had been journalists, secular and Christian alike, who excavated and exposed that which was meant to stay buried forever. There had been attorneys who leveraged the law in ways that compelled churches to finally, at long last, come clean.

If the Church was going to be reformed—really, truly reformed—Woodson and Thigpen said it would need to happen this way. It was going to take people working from the outside in. Churches might improve their self-policing, but they would never hold themselves fully accountable. The blind spots were too big. The best hope for the Church, Thigpen and Woodson said, were people like that well-known woman they'd tearfully embraced a day earlier, the one with the long brown ponytail. She was no Southern Baptist, but she'd shaken the denomination to its core. And her work was only just beginning: Christian organizations across the country were seeking her counsel in responding to abuse crises and reforming the rules that govern their institutions. She was fast becoming a Joan of Arc figure in modern evangelicalism—heroic and hated, divinely inspired and widely despised.

Her name was Rachael Denhollander.

CHAPTER TWENTY

JEFFERSONTOWN, KENTUCKY

Well done, good and faithful servant! You have been faithful
with a few things; I will put you in charge of many things.

—MATTHEW 25:21

"I was the evangelical darling," Rachael Denhollander remembered,
"until I started talking about abuse in the Church."

Raised in culturally pious West Michigan, the daughter of conservative Christians who homeschooled their three kids, Denhollander was
born with a maternal instinct. As the firstborn, she vigilantly nurtured
plastic dolls and gravitated toward babies from the time she was little
older than one herself. Once, she physically confronted a bully who'd
been picking on her younger siblings at a McDonald's playpen. All she
wanted was to be a mother.

As she aged, however, Denhollander realized there was something
embedded even deeper into her spiritual disposition than this love of
children. She still desired a family of her own, but her true passion was
defending the vulnerable. At eight years old, she announced to her parents that she wanted to go to law school. When asked why, she replied:
"to protect kids."

That calling soon would take on a personal dimension. Denhollander
was sexually abused by a pedophile in her childhood church, and later,
as a teenager, she was groomed and repeatedly molested by a physician.
Larry Nassar was one of the most celebrated names in sports medicine.

The head doctor of USA Gymnastics, Nassar cared for numerous Olympic gold-medal winners in addition to hundreds of other elite athletes as part of his work at Michigan State University. Denhollander was no Olympian, just a competitive gymnast from the city of Kalamazoo. Still, she was serious enough about the sport, and had suffered serious enough injuries from it, to drive an hour and a half for a consultation with Nassar. During that initial exam, with Denhollander's mother present in the room, Nassar digitally penetrated the fifteen-year-old girl. The abuse, committed under the guise of legitimate medical techniques, was accompanied by playful talk, gushing compliments, and practiced affection to disarm both the victim and her mother. This pattern continued over successive visits. The abuse escalated to include fondling and arousal. In one visit, Nassar, perhaps sensing Denhollander's growing alertness to his predatory behavior, and knowing of her love for children, asked her to meet and hold his newborn daughter. It was the last time she visited his office.

Sixteen years later, while tending to her three young children one summer morning, Denhollander pulled out her laptop to finalize a grocery shopping list. Spotting an open Facebook tab, she clicked on her feed and immediately saw an *Indianapolis Star* story trending. It detailed a systematic cover-up by USA Gymnastics of sexual abuse cases involving dozens of coaches who had gone on to assault countless girls after initial allegations had gone ignored. Denhollander was shocked but hardly surprised. She had by then spent half of her life—while attending law school, passing the bar, starting a family—convincing herself that any attempt to expose Nassar would fail, because nobody would believe her word over his. This was the crux of the USA Gymnastics scandal: Powerful, respected coaches received boundless benefit of the doubt from those invested in safeguarding the reputation of the institution, all while young girls were robbed of their innocence.

Denhollander felt ill reading the article. But she also, strangely, felt a twinge of optimism. The *Star* journalists had done outstanding work in documenting these abuses and cover-ups. They had brought the public's attention to a scandal. They had helped to prevent these monsters from further preying on defenseless children. They had listened to the victims and *believed them*.

Then and there, with a nursing baby, toddler, and five-year-old boy in tow, Denhollander stopped what she was doing and wrote an email to the *Star* offering the rough overview of her own ordeal. She identified Nassar—who had not been a subject of that initial news story—by his name and position. She volunteered to go on the record with her accusation. Little did she know, Denhollander was setting in motion one of the most extraordinary criminal cases in modern American history.

Nearly two and a half years later, in January 2018, Denhollander stood up inside a Michigan courtroom. Cameras flashed with her every movement. She had effectively started a stampede: Hundreds of women, inspired by Denhollander's decision to go public with her story of Nassar's abuse, had since come forward with their own. Now, after 155 of her fellow survivors had read their victim statements to the court, Denhollander was going last.

"How much is a little girl worth?" she asked the judge.

For the next forty minutes, Denhollander delivered a riveting speech. Surpassingly composed and surgical with her every word, she spoke of the scars that would never fully heal. She shamed those who had accused her of wanting fame or money for going public. She blasted the institutions that had provided shelter for degenerates like Nassar. Then she turned to Nassar himself, forcing eye contact with the man who'd violated her so many years earlier.

"In our early hearings, you brought your Bible into the courtroom. And you have spoken of praying for forgiveness," Denhollander told him. "And so, it is on that basis that I appeal to you. If you have read the Bible you carry, you know the definition of sacrificial love portrayed is of God Himself loving so sacrificially that He gave up everything to pay a penalty for the sin He did not commit. By His grace, I, too, choose to love this way.

"You spoke of praying for forgiveness. But, Larry, if you have read the Bible you carry, you know forgiveness does not come from doing good things, as if good deeds can erase what you have done. It comes from repentance, which requires facing and acknowledging the truth about what you have done—in all of its utter depravity and horror without mitigation, without excuse, without acting as if good deeds can erase what you have seen in this courtroom today."

Warning of an eternal judgment that awaits beyond the walls of the mid-Michigan courtroom, Denhollander told Nassar that she was praying for him. She hoped that he would "experience the soul-crushing weight of guilt" that might lead to "true repentance and true forgiveness from God, which you need far more than forgiveness from me."

Then she added: "Though I extend that to you as well."

When Denhollander finished—after going deeper into biblical doctrine, at one point quoting directly from C. S. Lewis on the perversion of God's goodness—the room was hushed. Then the judge saluted Denhollander, calling her "the bravest person I've ever had in my courtroom," and the chamber erupted into a prolonged standing ovation. It was an actual made-for-TV moment: Footage of Denhollander's speech quickly scored millions of YouTube views. She was hailed as a heroine and lavished with recognition, from receiving ESPN's Arthur Ashe Courage Award to being named one of *Time*'s 100 Most Influential People.

Christian outlets took particular satisfaction in promoting her as one of their own. Organizations such as the Christian Broadcasting Network, the Gospel Coalition, and Focus on the Family portrayed her as the exemplar of evangelical womanliness. Several prominent Christian bloggers likened her to a modern-day prophet who had forced a depraved society to confront its sins.

There was just one problem. Denhollander, like the Old Testament prophets of yore, wasn't content to stop at condemning the outside world.

In a little-noticed line from her courtroom speech, Denhollander revealed that her advocacy for sexual abuse survivors had made her and her husband unwelcome at their home church in Louisville. The couple had moved there so that Jacob Denhollander could pursue his PhD at Southern Baptist Theological Seminary, and thought they'd found a home in a local Baptist congregation. But its decision to associate with a network of other churches—Sovereign Grace, which stood accused of brazenly covering up mass cases of sexual abuse—forced the Denhollanders into conflict with the church leadership, and eventually led to their exit.

No sooner had the jail cell slammed shut behind Nassar—who received a 175-year sentence—than Rachael Denhollander was firing a shot across the bow of Sovereign Grace and the evangelical movement as a whole. She made it known that her hunt for predators was just getting started.

"They figured I would be a safe person to parade around. I was a godly woman, a homeschooling graduate, now homeschooling kids of my own, with a husband studying at the most conservative seminary in the country. And I had just extended forgiveness to this pedophile. Like I said, I was the evangelical darling," Denhollander told me. "And so, they made me a household name. They expected that I would become the poster child for meek, submissive femininity. But they never considered what my theology would drive me to do next."

In the four years that followed the Nassar verdict, Denhollander went from Esther to Jezebel in the eyes of many evangelical shot-callers. Turning her attention and considerable legal savvy to the mushrooming sex abuse scandals inside the Church—most notably, within the Southern Baptist Convention—Denhollander took on the mightiest and most entrenched interests in American Christendom. She worked with survivors to unearth evidence that had been expertly buried. She parachuted into megachurches to overhaul broken systems and organize responses aimed at total transparency. She cultivated sources and worked back channels and coordinated investigations that took down some of the biggest names in the evangelical world.

But it wasn't enough. Sitting in the second-floor loft of her favorite café in the spring of 2023, sipping coffee while Jacob toiled on his dissertation at a neighboring table, Rachael Denhollander told me she was realizing the limits of her impact. Even as a renowned advocate and attorney, there was only so much she could uncover, only so much she could do to raise awareness or effect change. The best hope for reforming the Church, she had come to accept, wasn't the law.

"Change happens when the law catches up to public narrative. But what drives public narrative?" Denhollander asked me.

Stupidly, I shrugged. Then she reminded me of the origins of her involvement with the Nassar case. The *Indianapolis Star* piece. Her email to the tip line. The newspaper's dogged reporting that forced the public, and prosecutors in Michigan, to take notice.

"Journalism," Denhollander said.

* * *

TO THIS DAY, JULIE ROYS ISN'T SURE WHY SHE APPLIED FOR THAT JOB AT Moody Radio back in 2007.

Thirteen years earlier, she'd walked away from her journalism career to raise a family. Though nothing quite compared to the thrill of chasing news, Roys loved her life: homeschooling three kids, keeping active in her local Chicagoland church, and running a Christian youth ministry with her husband, a public school teacher. She was content.

Then, one day while listening to Moody Radio, Roys heard an advertisement for the position of part-time talk-show host. She allowed her imagination to wander. Her older two kids were agitating to go to the school where their father taught; Roys and her husband had mused about enrolling their youngest in a local Christian academy. She *did* miss the rush of working in media. Roys sent over her résumé on a whim, landed the job, and within a few years was awarded her own program, *Up for Debate*, which piloted in Chicago and quickly went national across Moody Radio's network of owned and affiliated stations.

The broadcasting enterprise, a subsidiary of Chicago's vastly influential Moody Bible Institute, aimed to manifest the parent organization's motto proclaiming "the word of truth." Having listened to Moody's conservative Christian programming for years, Roys assumed she would be a natural fit. Once on the inside, however, she began to have her doubts. Although Roys was an evangelical and a nominal Republican, she didn't consider herself to be playing for any "team." She had always believed it was her job—as a Christian and as a journalist—to pursue truth without prejudice. Roys wasn't surprised to discover that Moody possessed a governing ideology that was enforced from the top down. Still, the higher she climbed, the more suspicious she became of her organization's conformist culture.

Quickly becoming one of Moody's most popular personalities, Roys would supplement her radio observations by writing commentaries that were distributed through the company's various media platforms. She was encouraged by management—"the ninth floor," where executives had their offices—to stick it to Christianity's adversaries in the culture. She did so regularly. Yet Roys ran into opposition whenever she turned her critical eye toward the Church. That opposition ultimately gave way to censorship: The ninth floor spiked a number of her pieces, explaining that their targets, including Wheaton College and the local megachurch Harvest Bible Chapel, which was pastored by James MacDonald, who hosted a top-rated radio program on the Moody network, were off-limits.

This didn't sit well with Roys. She and her husband had both attended Wheaton as undergrads; if she was willing to criticize the school, then why was Moody so invested in protecting it? The MacDonald episode was even more troubling. Red flags were becoming synonymous with the megachurch pastor. In addition to platforming controversial speakers at his many venues, MacDonald had earned a reputation for an abusive and domineering leadership style. In 2013, Harvest stunned its congregation by excommunicating former elders who'd written a letter raising serious character concerns about their pastor. Around that same time, *World* magazine reported that MacDonald, in addition to Jerry Jenkins—chairman of the board of trustees at Moody Bible Institute and coauthor of the Left Behind book series—had been frequenting casinos to play poker.

Roys was incensed. Not long before the *World* article ran, she had been roped into serving on a committee to revise Moody's standards and disciplinary guidelines. To the confusion of Roys and others, senior management was pushing hard to amend one specific policy: the prohibition on gambling. Now, months later, she knew why. Confronting her boss, Moody's top media executive, Roys extracted a confession: They had rushed to change the gambling rules to insulate MacDonald and Jenkins. "That's when I realized how the sausage gets made," Roys told me. "Moody was running a protection racket."

There was no unlearning what she had learned. Roys tried to keep her head down and focus on her own work, but whispers of her clashes with the ninth floor had begun to spread throughout the Moody empire. Before long, Roys had employees coming to her with tips, complaints, and allegations of wrongdoing. She knew that chasing down these leads—much less publishing her findings—would spell the end of her time at Moody. But she was fast becoming less concerned with her job security than with the broader condition of American Christianity.

Donald Trump was forging a Faustian bargain with evangelical leaders; churches were fracturing around cases of abuse and misconduct; individual pastors and theological figureheads were self-immolating with scandal on what felt like a daily basis. Praying to God and beseeching Him for guidance, Roys felt convicted that a housecleaning was overdue. Moody seemed like a fine place to start.

Having graduated from Northwestern University's prestigious Medill School of Journalism, Roys knew what to do. She set about cultivating sources and procuring evidence, building an investigative case against her employer. The sum of what she documented was enough to bring Moody to its knees: rampant financial mismanagement, profound theological drift in the teaching and curriculum, a culture of fear and intimidation practiced to keep dissenters in line. Most damning was Roys's discovery that Moody had been self-dealing in ways that would make a mobster blush. The Moody Bible Institute had given its then-president a sweetheart half-million-dollar loan to purchase a Chicago condominium—a loan on which he'd made zero payments. Meanwhile, the school had converted two units on the top floor of a campus building into a private residential suite for Jenkins, the board chairman, whose family used it as a second home.

The question for Roys was whether to publish any of this. She loved Moody and cared about its many good, God-fearing employees. Trying to contain the damage at first, she took her findings to the board of trustees. She was brushed aside—and warned, implicitly, to keep quiet about what she knew. Praying more fervently still, she felt God prodding her forward. Whatever harm would be done in the short term—to Moody, and to Roys's own career and relationships in the evangelical world—it could not compare to the consequences of lying, cheating, and stealing in the name of Jesus Christ.

"I knew that I would be blowing up every bridge imaginable. I had just published my first book, I had speaking invitations left and right, I had a lot of moneymaking opportunities. There was no reason to give that up," Roys recalled. "But it just became clear to me that if I stayed silent, that if I didn't speak the truth about these things, then I was selling my soul. And I couldn't do that."

In January 2018, Roys decided to report what she knew. Teeing up her investigation on a backwater blogging domain she'd acquired years earlier—*The Roys Report*—she clicked the button to publish while over international airspace, en route to a family vacation in Mexico, moments before her internet connection cut out. When she landed, there was an email waiting for her. Roys had been fired.

The problem wasn't the reporting itself; Roys had nailed the story. In fact, forty-eight hours after it ran, Moody pushed out three top officials—the school's president, its chief operating officer, and its provost—all but acknowledging the rot she had exposed. No, the problem was that Roys had shamed her own tribe. And the fallout was predictable enough. Those speaking invitations disappeared. So did some longtime friendships. Book sales plateaued and then plummeted. Roys was cast as a villain in evangelical circles, a traitor to the cause of Moody and Christianity itself. She figured that it was time to go back to homeschooling.

But then something happened. Roys, through her blogging site, began to be inundated with unsolicited emails from tipsters. They saw the results she'd gotten at Moody and wondered if she would investigate *their* religious outfit. Roys had zero interest at first—"I needed another story on Christian corruption like I needed a hole in the head"—but the sheer volume of emails, and of evidence, became impossible to ignore.

Wading through her inbox, Roys decided there was one church—one pastor, really—who deserved her attention: James MacDonald.

Over the ensuing year, she published dozens of articles on *The Roys Report* uncovering all manner of transgression at Harvest Bible Chapel. She reported that MacDonald's own elders thought him unfit for ministry; that he'd bullied and mistreated staff; that he'd fattened his own wallet with contributions meant for the church. MacDonald sued Roys in hopes of impeding her work but the suit was dropped and Roys kept on going, not bothering to stop even after MacDonald was fired as a result of her reporting. She revealed how the now ex-pastor's alleged sexual harassment of an employee was well known among other staff; how he'd taken exotic trips on the church's dime and gone to extraordinary lengths to conceal his salary; how he was scheming to start a new ministry despite being thoroughly disgraced by the events at Harvest.

There was no going back to her quiet life as a homeschooling mom.

Tips kept pouring into her inbox; people across the country were reading *The Roys Report* and sending leads for her to chase. She had once
been deeply conflicted over the rightness of investigating her fellow
believers. Not anymore. Both at Moody and at Harvest, Roys saw how
Christian leaders manipulated biblical principles—of unity, harmony,
submission to authority—to crush objections and avoid scrutiny. These
were not just abuses of power; these were abuses of power that carried
the imprimatur of the Almighty. Preparing to stand in judgment one day
before a just and holy God, Roys decided, she was going to err on the
side of justice and holiness.

"It was like a switch got tripped inside of me," Roys said. "I couldn't
turn it off."

TWO THINGS HAPPENED TO RACHAEL DENHOLLANDER AFTER HER
star turn in the Larry Nassar case.

First, she got to know Al Mohler, one of America's foremost evangelical thinkers and president of the Southern Baptist Theological
Seminary in Louisville, where Denhollander's husband was studying.
Mohler had reached out with encouragement during the Nassar trial
in early 2018—even offering extensions for Jacob's academic deadlines,
which the Denhollanders greatly appreciated—and they considered
him an ally. Now, a year later, Mohler needed Rachael's help. His network was besieged by sex scandals; one in particular was afflicting his
school, Southern, where a well-known professor had confessed to sexual contact with a former student. While picking Denhollander's brain
for legal and strategic advice on how to navigate these messes, Mohler
shared with her certain details of the Southern case. That case was
the spark that would soon engulf the Southern Baptist Convention in
controversy: According to a lawsuit later filed by the professor, David
Sills, he was scapegoated by Mohler among others for his alleged sexual
abuse of a former student, Jennifer Lyell, when, according to Sills, the
relationship had been consensual. Sills accused Mohler of wrongly siding with Lyell when Mohler stated publicly that he believed her claims
and that Sills confessed to him, when confronted, things that indicated a
nonconsensual abusive relationship. This put Mohler, Lyell, and others

in the legal crosshairs of Sills, and set the SBC hurtling toward a show-down over sexual misconduct.

Around that same time, Denhollander was approached by the South-ern Baptist Convention—more specifically, by staffers with the Ethics and Religious Liberty Commission—and asked to help design a cutting-edge curriculum program: "Caring Well." The idea was to train pastors to make their churches welcoming and safe environments for survivors of abuse, while also overhauling internal processes to guard against future instances of misconduct. Though Denhollander had never be-longed to an SBC church, she was encouraged that the denomination was making such a public-facing effort. Having signed on to help with the initiative, she was invited to attend the SBC's 2019 annual meeting in Birmingham, Alabama.

That's where Denhollander met Jennifer Lyell.

A vice president with Lifeway Christian Resources, the SBC's pub-lishing and marketing behemoth, Lyell's résumé and reputation were gold. She held an advanced degree from Southern. She handled Life-way's biggest accounts and most complex contracts. She was the highest-placed, highest-paid female executive in the denomination. Then, in the spring of 2019, Lyell unburdened herself of a dark secret.

As alleged in the complaint, Lyell claimed that David Sills violently abused her over a period of many years. Lyell never planned on going public with this information; Sills had long since been pushed out by Southern and she was hoping to move on with her life. But then came the news that Sills had been restored to ministry, in a different denomina-tion, setting off alarms among those who had heard the details of Lyell's allegations. Some of them were bound by the nondisclosure and nondis-paragement agreements signed when Sills departed Southern. But Ly-ell was not. They pressured her to speak out, promising to help protect her from the inevitable backlash. Lyell reluctantly agreed. She wrote a statement of facts summarizing her allegations, then gave it to Baptist Press, the SBC's news agency.

Lyell was blindsided by the betrayal that ensued. Baptist Press, which was governed by the so-called pirates who controlled the SBC Executive Committee, published an article inaccurately claiming that Lyell had confessed to a "morally inappropriate relationship" with Sills.

The story gave the impression of a consensual affair. Everyone who had heard and believed Lyell's allegations was stunned, including Denhollander. She wondered how Baptist Press had gotten the story so wrong.

When Denhollander met Lyell in Birmingham, a couple of months later, it became clear enough. The Executive Committee was run by men who possessed a deep-seated contempt for anything resembling feminism; it loathed the concept of the Caring Well initiative. Despite being furnished with detailed firsthand allegations of Sills's behavior, Baptist Press characterized his relationship with Lyell as a consensual affair. The Executive Committee wasn't going to stand for Lyell, the denomination's most accomplished woman, being turned into an avatar for the #MeToo movement. Its members took a calculated risk: They would paint her as an adulteress, squashing the sordid details of her statement to Baptist Press, and dare her to challenge the official published account of the denomination.

They probably would have gotten away with it—if not for Denhollander.

Talking with Lyell for endless hours in the summer of 2019 and splicing her testimony with what Mohler had relayed from his conversation with Sills, Denhollander smelled an obvious cover-up. She worked with Lyell to nail down the specifics of her case. Soon everyone would know what the Executive Committee had done to her. There was just one hang-up: Lyell didn't want to fight the SBC in public. She had already been bombarded with harassment and threats since the Baptist Press story ran; the last thing she wanted was to invite more. Lyell had been privately pleading with Baptist Press to retract its story and publish her full on-the-record statement. When Denhollander told her that it wasn't going to work—that the only way to get justice was to go public with her claims—Lyell resolved to keep quiet.

"Jen had a broken family, a broken childhood, a broken life, before she found the SBC. The SBC was the only home she ever knew—and they used that against her," Denhollander told me. "Because she loved and trusted the SBC, she decided to let them break the story. Because she loved and trusted the SBC, she wouldn't go to a secular outlet to correct the record. She was still trying to protect them—which is typical trauma response for a survivor. Trying not to be a burden, trying to be obedient, trying to be submissive. All she wanted to do was protect them. And nobody was willing to protect her."

That October, when the ERLC convened its first-ever Caring Well conference in Dallas, Denhollander was invited to be a featured speaker. The plan was for her to join the ERLC's president, Russell Moore, on-stage for a keynote conversation about abuse dynamics in the Church. But Denhollander felt unsettled in the lead-up to the event. Lyell had been spiraling since the Baptist News episode; her mental health had deteriorated to the point of taking a leave from her job with Lifeway, and with the SBC's purposeful distortion of her testimony still concealed, her reputation had suffered permanent injury. Denhollander had worked hard on the Caring Well project, but now it all felt so artificial. How could she stand in front of a room of Southern Baptists and pretend they were making progress when some of those same Southern Baptists were destroying Jennifer Lyell's life?

Sitting in a backstage greenroom, Denhollander made a final appeal to Lyell, who was watching the event from home via livestream. There would never be a better moment—or a bigger venue, Denhollander told Lyell—to share her story. Lyell typed several last-ditch text messages to Executive Committee members, begging for them to issue a public retraction of the Baptist Press article. She watched on her computer screen as one member pulled out his phone, read her message, then put the phone back into his pocket. Lyell texted Denhollander and gave permission for her story to be shared. There was just one condition: She needed to inform Russell Moore before he and Denhollander took the stage together. Lyell thought the world of Moore and didn't want him to be embarrassed at his own event.

Denhollander didn't know Moore. To her, the ERLC president was just another good ol' Southern Baptist boy who was looking out for the institution. But honoring Lyell's wishes—in letter, if not in law—Denhollander waited until she and Moore were approaching the side stage. Moments before they walked out, she notified him that she would be telling Lyell's story.

Moore didn't stop her. In fact, he listened earnestly and probed for details, giving Denhollander every opportunity to shed light on the SBC's appalling treatment of one of its top employees.

"It blew up right then and there. I mean, there were calls and emails flying by the time we walked off the stage," Denhollander remembered. "I think, to this day, that's the real reason that Dr. Moore got run out of the SBC. In that moment, he could have stopped me from telling the truth. And he didn't."

Denhollander had teamed with the SBC to help clean up the Church, not dig for its dirt. Her focus was advocating for survivors; she had never nurtured aspirations of exposing systemic wrongdoing. But now the wrongdoing was front and center for the world to see. And unlike many of her fellow evangelicals, Denhollander didn't want the world to look away. The Church didn't deserve to be spared. It deserved to be scrutinized, humbled, perhaps even humiliated. If there was any hope for the bride of Christ, it would be found in the cycle of crushing guilt and true repentance Denhollander had preached to Nassar. That cycle kicked off, in earnest, when Jennifer Lyell filed suit against the SBC Executive Committee in 2019.

"Jen's case became the linchpin," Denhollander told me, "for pursuing justice in the Southern Baptist Convention."

It wasn't a pretty process. Lyell, shadowed by unceasing online cruelty, lost her job and was diagnosed with post-traumatic stress disorder. The Executive Committee stonewalled requests for records and denied that it had access to any funds to cover Lyell's ongoing medical expenses. Denhollander, who represented Lyell in the case, described her negotiations with Executive Committee members as the most degrading experience of her legal career, rife with taunts alluding to her own infamous abuse experience. ("Now, Rachael, that's just your trauma talking.")

Unpleasant as it was, Denhollander's close encounter with the Executive Committee proved critical in the fights that followed. She studied the choreography of the pirate leaders—which legal firms they contracted with, what messaging tactics they deployed, how they utilized attorney-client privilege as an umbrella to shield *all* internal communications—and began sketching the outlines of a strategy to defeat them. The Executive Committee hoped to be rid of Denhollander when it finally agreed to a monster financial settlement and an official apology to Lyell.

But Denhollander wasn't going anywhere. She had already formed alliances with the most prominent and outspoken abuse survivors in the SBC. She had collaborated with a pair of pastors who were drafting proposals to force an investigation into the Executive Committee. She had also maneuvered to position Guidepost Solutions, a third-party firm she knew and trusted, as an outside partner for the SBC. Having introduced Guidepost to two leading evangelicals who needed probes into their own institutions—Mohler and onetime SBC president J. D. Greear—Denhollander stood back and watched as both men vouched for the integrity of Guidepost at the critical moment when it came time to investigate the Executive Committee.

By the time the bewildered pirates shouted their protestations in Anaheim, it was too late. The yellow ballots were proof of how badly they'd been outsmarted.

"Some of these guys will never take a woman seriously. And I've used that to my advantage," Denhollander told me, a smile curling at the corners of her mouth. "They don't want to feel threatened, so I try hard not to threaten them. You know: business suit, pastel colors, low ponytail, light makeup, collarbone covered, flats not heels—because you *cannot* be taller than any of the men in the room. They need to feel like they're in charge. You know?"

I did know—but then again, I didn't. My own childhood church held to many traditional views and customs, but the treatment of women as second-class Christians was never among them. We had a woman pastor on staff. We had women teaching mixed-gender classes and Bible studies. Every second Sunday in May, my dad handed over the pulpit to my mom, a superb and accomplished speaker in her own right, to deliver the Mother's Day sermon. It was one of the highlights on the church calendar.

This isn't to say there weren't issues with sexism or abuse; in fact, as I would learn later, there were both. But the notion of excluding women from Church leadership seemed backward and decidedly unbiblical. It was Jesus who made the radical (by first-century standards) decision to reveal Himself, after rising from the dead, to groups of women. Not only that, Jesus deputized these women to go and announce to crowds of men—literally, *preach* to them—the world-changing news of His resurrection. (One has to wonder, if these women had complied with the

Jewish norms of the day, which forbade women from instructing men in public spaces, would there even *be* a Church?) Other examples abound: Junia was an apostle, Phoebe was a deacon, and Priscilla was such an important teacher that she is named *ahead* of her husband in the narrative of their mentoring early Church leaders. It's true that Paul wrote in one letter that women should not teach men. It's also true that Paul lauded in *many* letters the numerous women who worked alongside him in various ministry capacities, including teaching, which bolsters the scholarly argument that his instruction was specific to the *one* church he was writing. In short, the biblical case for a blanket ban on women serving in Church leadership is thin and unconvincing—as evidenced by the fact that many of America's most conservative denominations observe no such ban.

The Southern Baptists do things differently. Women are not permitted to teach men in any church setting—even a Sunday School class—or hold positions that impute spiritual authority over men. Hence the other headline coming out of Anaheim in the summer of 2022. The previous year, Rick Warren, the bestselling author and pastor of Saddleback Church in Southern California, had ordained three women on his staff as pastors. The ensuing uproar prompted a motion to eject Saddleback from the SBC. Warren begged his fellow Southern Baptists not to lose the plot. "Are we going to keep bickering over secondary issues, or are we going to keep the main thing the main thing?" Warren asked at the annual meeting.

The effort to disfellowship Saddleback from the SBC stalled. Taken with the other events in Anaheim, it seemed like a triumph for modernity and common sense. Then, the following February, the SBC Executive Committee delivered an abrupt verdict: Saddleback was out.

As I sat with Denhollander a few weeks after the Saddleback ruling, I could read the foreboding written all over her face. If the hard-liners who'd controlled the SBC for half a century were still sufficiently organized and defiant to expel one of its biggest, wealthiest, most established churches, then they certainly had the juice to sabotage these new reforms aimed at stopping sexual abuse. In fact, Denhollander was counting on it.

"Everything we've won," she told me, "could be lost very, very suddenly."

* * *

WHEN RAVI ZACHARIAS DIED IN MAY 2020, THE CHRISTIAN WORLD went into mourning.

The Indian-born Zacharias was an international superstar in the field of apologetics, or the intellectual defense of the Christian faith. He had spent decades zipping between continents, lecturing in palace courts and college cafeterias, big-city sports arenas and small-town sanctuaries. He turned his namesake organization, Ravi Zacharias International Ministries, into a pillar of the modern evangelical movement. Together with his wife and daughter—both of whom sat on the organization's board—they raised tens of millions of dollars while churning out books, videos, and curricula aimed at winning over skeptics for Christ.

Franklin Graham hailed Zacharias as "one of the great Christian apologists of our time." Tim Tebow, the Heisman Trophy–winning quarterback, said Zacharias belonged "in the Hall of Faith." Johnnie Moore, a pastor and top official with the U.S. Commission on International Religious Freedom, called Zacharias "a once-in-a-millennium Christian leader." Louie Giglio, a megachurch pastor in Zacharias's hometown of Atlanta, reacted to his friend's death by saying, "I join the thunderous applause of Heaven." Asked to deliver a eulogy, then–vice president Mike Pence declared, "In Ravi Zacharias, God gave us the greatest Christian apologist of this century."

A year after his death, however, Zacharias was known by another description: "prolific sexual predator."

Zacharias wasn't gone long before allegations started to percolate. Three women who worked at an Atlanta-area spa—co-owned by Zacharias—claimed that he'd sexually abused them. When *Christianity Today* reported these specifics, interviewing the women independently of one another, RZIM vehemently denied the allegations and hired a third-party firm to investigate. That outside probe produced an even darker picture: Zacharias had methodically used his spiritual clout to win the trust of vulnerable women, condition them for financial and emotional dependence, then exploit them for his sexual gratification. Investigators who searched Zacharias's electronic devices found hundreds of contacts for massage therapists in the United States and Asia; they also discovered loads of explicit photos that he'd solicited. Zacharias, multiple women told investigators, described his sexual conquest of their bodies as a "reward" for dedicating his life to God's service. By the time donors filed a class-action lawsuit, arguing that the "prolific sexual predator" had used their funds for evil purposes, there could be no doubting the enormity of the evidence. Ravi Zacharias, a giant of Christianity, had been leading a deviant double life.

Julie Roys never saw it coming. She didn't *want* to see it coming. Like many evangelicals, she considered Zacharias beyond reproach. Back in 2017, when a husband and wife brought disturbing charges against Zacharias—they claimed that he'd manipulated her under the guise of ministry before engaging in sexual conversations and eventually soliciting nude pictures—Roys scoffed at the allegations. When Zacharias sued the couple, eventually silencing them with an NDA, Roys felt righteously aggrieved on his behalf.

"I can still remember texting [his assistant], whom I'd met a few times by that point, saying, 'It's so terrible what they're doing to Ravi,'" Roys told me. She grimaced at the memory of her own naïveté. "Even though I was in the middle of investigating Moody, seeing all this bad behavior with my own eyes, I refused to believe it with Ravi Zacharias."

I could relate. My wife, an Indian immigrant who converted to Christianity as an adult, revered Zacharias. And so did I. We read his books, watched his videos, and attended a live lecture he delivered at Constitution Hall in Washington. Despite some of the disquieting details surrounding that 2017 episode—the sort of disquieting details people in my profession are trained not to ignore—I had the same reaction as Roys: denial.

Roys chuckled when I told her that. Here we were, a couple of veteran hard-boiled journalists, blinded by our biases to what should have been an obvious truth. It was more than bias, though. It was fear. We were *afraid* to see someone like Zacharias fall—not because of what it said about him, but because of what it said about us. Weren't Christians supposed to hold themselves to a higher standard? Why was it that nary a news cycle could pass without fresh allegations of a pastor abusing someone in his flock? If the world's most prominent evangelical was preying on women, what did that suggest about the morals of the rest of us?

Christians are taught never to place their faith in man. Yet the heart, to quote John Calvin, is an idol-making factory. My dad always used to say that humans were designed for worship; whether or not we believe in any higher power, we are predisposed to making gods out of athletes, entertainers, politicians, anyone who can dazzle or inspire or fill us with awe. This predisposition is especially dangerous when it involves figures who claim divine affiliation. Years ago, when Dad learned that an associate pastor was getting handsy with women at the church, he fired him immediately, then gave a full accounting to denominational leaders in hopes of preventing the man from pastoring again. But Dad declined to pursue a formal inquiry, fearing that the findings would become public. He didn't want the congregation to know why the popular, charming pastor was suddenly gone. When there was an outcry from the men's ministry—which that pastor had been leading—Dad felt even firmer in his decision not to disclose the particulars. Lots of the men in that ministry were new Christians, immature and impressionable. What would they think—what would become of their faith—if they learned that their spiritual mentor was groping women for sport?

Dad made the wrong call, I think, but it's obvious why he made it. He wanted to protect the fragile faith of some of his church members; he also wanted to protect the church itself. This approach might be defensible in a vacuum. Yet no vacuum exists. While I don't know whether that associate pastor ever latched on to another church, I do know that pastors just like him resurface at churches every single day. Sometimes their sins are known and confronted; after certain steps they are "restored" to ministry. But many more have no such documentation. They move undetected from one congregation to the next, sexual and spiritual wreckage left in their wake. Roys told me this was "the last straw" at her own longtime church in Wheaton, Illinois. A lay leader from her congregation was found to have abused multiple children at an affiliated church plant, but it wasn't until one family pressed criminal charges—and several more came to Roys with their stories, wanting to go public—that the church finally made its members aware of the situation.

The set-your-watch regularity of evangelical pastors being exposed for victimizing their church members is bad enough. What's worse is that Christianity has become institutionally desensitized to it. The odds are, some faith leader I respect and admire today will reveal themselves to be a fraud and a scoundrel tomorrow. And I won't be able to feign surprise or conjure righteous outrage. Because scandal is now baked into the evangelical experience in ways that distort our standards of leadership. In this sense, numbness is the least of our problems. Plenty of Christians, rather than shaking their head and crossing another spiritual leader off the list, are actively keeping that leader *on* the list. The Pauline criteria for pastoral character no longer apply because, well, we're all just sinners anyway, and can't you see this is an attempt to take down a strong voice for biblical values?

Take John MacArthur. The California pastor, long a leader in the conservative-but-sane lane of modern evangelicalism—someone who spoke passionately about eternal priorities trumping earthly ones— more recently began merging into the fast lane of fringe political advocacy. When Roys broke open the story that MacArthur and his leadership team had fostered a culture of abuse, ignoring the physical mistreatment of women and children in their congregation, people were outraged *at Roys*. A small army of Christian bloggers and influencers descended on her website, pummeling her for having the temerity to report on an objectively horrifying episode: MacArthur had excommunicated a woman from the church for refusing to take back her child-abuser husband (who at the time was threatening to kill her and their kids and who is now incarcerated for aggravated child molestation, corporal injury to a child, and child abuse).

Roys had few allies in the evangelical world. One was Denhollander, who called for an independent investigation into MacArthur's church. Another was *Relevant*, a Christian magazine that covered the "disturbing" facts Roys had uncovered. (The founder and CEO of *Relevant*: Cameron Strang, son of Stephen Strang.) Finally, one of MacArthur's former lieutenants, a well-known and respected elder named Hohn Cho, went on the record with *Christianity Today* detailing MacArthur's "awful pattern" of siding with abusers over victims. The wagon circling that ensued was epic. Prominent evangelicals like Jenna Ellis, the former Trump lawyer who'd admitted in court to lying on his behalf, swore that MacArthur had done nothing wrong, that he was being rail-roaded, that this was a coordinated attack on a courageous Christian man as a means of undermining the entire Church.

I asked Roys why the reporting on MacArthur struck such a nerve.

"He's too big to fail. I mean, he's huge. That's the honest answer: There are too many people making money off John MacArthur," she said. "There are publishers making money off him, conferences making money off him, G3 [his nonprofit ministry group] making money off him. And then Grace to You—his media firm—that's a multi-, multi-, multimillion-dollar company. So, yeah, a pastor like John MacArthur is too big to fail."

She shook her head. "If Jesus were here, I think He'd be overturning tables everywhere," Roys said. *"Everywhere."*

Jesus possessed a uniquely pessimistic view of human nature. Having taken on flesh to redeem a fallen mankind, He saw how people continually tried to justify themselves rather than repenting and seeking renewal in God's grace. He especially saw this among *religious* people. There is a reason why Jesus is harder on the Pharisees than He is on the unbelieving masses. There is a reason why Paul demands we rebuke sinful church leaders "before everyone, so that the others may take warning." Throughout scripture, God demands a greater accountability from those in positions of spiritual influence.

Accountability is unfashionable in today's Church. At the end of 2022, when *Christianity Today* recapped its twenty most-read stories of the year, evangelical author Patrick Miller noticed an interesting trend. Fifteen of those stories focused on scandals that had plagued various pastors and congregations. Scanning the list, "you begin to wonder if CT is making a killing by killing trust in the church," Miller wrote on Twitter. This was a telling complaint, one that echoed throughout my own reporting experiences. Even some of the best, most transparent, most trustworthy pastors I'd met had grumbled about Julie Roys and the journalism she inspired. If we have family disputes, these pastors said, they should be dealt with *in the family.* Broadcasting our dysfunction to unbelievers only undermines our mission to evangelize them.

But if this were the case, then why include Paul's epistles in the New

Testament canon? His writings, after all, were known as "occasional"—letters in response to *occasions* inside of various churches. The occasions were messy: sex scandals, power struggles, personality clashes. Studying these missives centuries later, Church councils surely recognized how depictions of such contemptible conduct might diminish the notion of Christ's transformative power. They could have included Paul's wise admonitions without identifying the squalid happenings within the Church.

But the Bible is a book of brutal candor. Man's sinful nature stars from Genesis through Revelation. No one—not Abraham or Moses, not Peter or even Paul—is spared. The only flawless character is Christ. And that is the entire point.

"This criticism I hear about airing the Church's dirty laundry—give me a break. God couldn't care less about some pastor's reputation. He cares about *His* reputation," Roys told me. "This evangelical-industrial complex—making millions, getting famous, building some 'brand,' restoring wolves to prey on more sheep—it has absolutely nothing to do with Jesus. And we've got to stop pretending it does."

Roys attends a local house church now—"no rock music, no fancy preaching, just study and worship and prayer"—and she said her faith is stronger than it's ever been. Still, she acknowledged the disillusionment that accompanies five years spent examining this "evangelical-industrial complex." Hoping to offer some solution, rather than just diagnosing the problem, she landed on a novel idea. She had always loathed the evangelical conference circuit, what with its consumeristic, exhibit-hall undertones. So, she decided to host a conference of her own. Roys called it "Restore." Rather than focus on rehabilitating pastors, her program would support survivors of abuse. In 2019, on the heels of her reporting on Harvest—and after the pastor of another Chicagoland megachurch, Willow Creek, stepped down amid allegations of misconduct—Roys hosted the first Restore conference at a local college. It attracted some two hundred people from those nearby churches. A few years later, when Roys hosted the second Restore conference, she drew even more attendees. "And they were from forty-four states and two provinces in Canada," she told me.

Roys has been more than vindicated in her pursuit of truth; in March

2023, James MacDonald was arrested in California on charges of felony battery and assault after attacking a fifty-eight-year-old woman during a car-parking dispute. The woman was taken to the hospital with what police described as "serious injuries," while officers on the scene recovered a handgun from inside MacDonald's truck. There's a strange incongruity at work: Roys has received more scrutiny than MacDonald and all the other abusive pastors she's reported on, yet she's the one with the least to answer for.

"I didn't have any grand vision for this. I've never had a grand vision for anything. I've just tried to be obedient," Roys said. "I think God wants us to be tending to the people who have been strewn along the side of the road. There are so many of them, so many casualties of this corruption in the Church. But I'll tell you, these people, they're some of the strongest Christians I've ever known. Because they've held on to their beliefs despite having every reason not to."

Roys kept insisting to me that "God is doing something" in the American Church. Before we parted ways, I asked her what role journalism might play in that something.

"Good question," she replied, grinning. "If there's one thing we've learned, it's that we cannot trust these institutions to police themselves. So, I feel like we don't have a choice. The problem is, I'm reporting on maybe one-third of the leads I've got right now—and they're *good* leads. But I can only cover so much, because we're operating on this bare-bones budget. Meanwhile, these spiritually bankrupt organizations are taking in millions upon millions upon millions—"

She stopped herself.

"I don't want to sound cynical," Roys said. "But somebody said to me once, 'People love building houses; they don't like paying for the housing inspector.' And I think that's right. Maybe that's why all the houses are falling down."

BROADMOOR BAPTIST CHURCH, A PROMINENT SBC MEMBER LOCATED outside Jackson, Mississippi, decided to pay the housing inspector.

In the fall of 2022, a woman approached church leaders, claiming that a former youth pastor had groomed her as a preteen and subsequently abused her over a period of years. Broadmoor's pastor immediately called Denhollander. Mediating between the church and the survivor, Denhollander helped to establish the facts of the case. She confirmed that the alleged abuser, who'd left Broadmoor years earlier to pastor another local SBC church, had paid for the woman's therapy and other medical expenses. She also confirmed that this assistance came only *after* the woman signed an NDA. When witnesses came forward to corroborate the contemporaneous claims made by the woman, Broadmoor decided her allegations were highly credible.

At Denhollander's urging, the church opened a review of its policies and commissioned an outside firm to investigate the incident. Most remarkable was Broadmoor's decision to publish a public statement—even featuring it on the landing page of the church's website—that detailed the allegations, endorsed the credibility of the accuser, emphasized the Christian commitment to truth and transparency, offered resources for survivors to receive counseling, and provided instructions for victims to report their abuse moving forward.

The Jackson *Clarion-Ledger* praised Broadmoor for sharing "a striking amount of detail on an issue that has often been shrouded in secrecy by other faith-groups." The *Tennessean*'s religion reporter, who has documented all manner of devastation inside the SBC, called Broadmoor's response "a model" for the denomination to follow.

"They lost a lot of members at first. But they eventually gained more than they lost. Broadmoor actually grew in membership, and has grown financially, since they released that public statement, because people at other churches saw them do this the right way," Denhollander told me. "And if you ask the pastors at Broadmoor, they'll tell you, they've been hearing nonstop from other SBC pastors ever since. They all saw the response. They want to know how to get this right."

That said, Denhollander doesn't expect most churches, or even many of them, to follow Broadmoor's example. When we talked over coffee in Kentucky, she had just returned from a trip to Atlanta, where she was meeting with fellow task force members in preparation for the 2023 SBC annual meeting. They gamed out scenarios involving Executive Committee–blessed efforts to dismantle the abuser database and strip the task force of its authority. They also talked about the ERLC working with state leaders on legislative reform aimed at criminalizing clergy-congregant sexual relationships, a potential breakthrough in the fight against Church abuse. But much of what Denhollander and her colleagues discussed was whether SBC churches would comply with the new standards around reporting and investigating abuse—or whether they would refuse, forcing a standoff with the denomination.

One of two things is eventually going to happen, Denhollander predicted. Either the SBC will hold the line and show the door to hundreds of churches that refuse to comply with the new guidelines; or so many churches will refuse to comply, effectively calling the denomination's bluff, that the SBC will back down and stop enforcing the rules, which would likely prompt a whole separate clique of churches to leave. Either way, she said, "a massive split" is coming to the country's largest denomination—and maybe that's for the best.

"Unity is a good thing. We are commanded to pursue it. But unity around the wrong thing is sin. And we want so badly to be unified that we get to a point where we excuse and enable sin," Denhollander said. "There is not a path forward, from my perspective, to keep the SBC together in its current form. I think the healthiest thing that can happen—and this is true for a number of different denominations—is to fracture. And maybe, at that point, you can truly have unity."

Denhollander knows the risk of saying this part out loud. She's already viewed as a war profiteer by the far right of the SBC, an opportunistic outsider who "turned her own abuse into a cottage industry," as Denhollander quips, rolling her eyes. The irony is that she's worked harder to fix the denomination than most of its own leaders. Since being asked to help launch Caring Well—and learning of Jennifer Lyell's case—back in 2019, Denhollander has treated the SBC like a full-time job, logging thousands of hours in calls, meetings, flights, paperwork, and so on. Her compensation? Nothing. Denhollander has been formally retained and paid for work at specific churches, such as Broadmoor Baptist. Yet all her work for the SBC, done while homeschooling four kids and working on countless high-profile cases in the secular world, has been pro bono.

That could change at some point. The task force has urged Denhollander to accept payment for her services, an infusion of income she would welcome as the family breadwinner. Yet she cringes at the thought of cashing checks from the SBC. The denomination, as a whole, has brought her family nothing but heartburn. Jacob, her husband, chose to leave Southern seminary after finishing his PhD coursework "because he was having to continually justify his existence on campus because of who his wife is," Rachael told me. The reality is, she added with a sigh, "I have burned every bridge that he might potentially have to cross to teach at any conservative seminary, much less one that's affiliated with the SBC."

She noted that both she and her husband remain "conservative on almost every theological, social, and moral issue." But it hardly matters anymore. Jacob, who is studying Trinitarian theology with a focus on penal substitutionary atonement—an orthodox concentration if ever there was one—eventually transferred to the University of Wales to finish with the dissertation phase of his PhD. Together with his wife, they have marveled at the differences they've seen while interfacing with Christians outside the United States. Recounting one visit to the U.K. in which she was working with local churches on social welfare programs, Rachael told me it was enough to make them muse about leaving the United States altogether.

"It was wild to spend time with Christians whose identity wasn't wrapped up in anything except Christ," she said. "To see what Christianity looks like in a culture where Christians don't filter every idea and conviction through a lens of right versus left—it's sort of shocking, honestly."

Denhollander doesn't know what the future holds for her and her family. What she does know is that God placed her at the center of this madness for a reason. Like Julie Roys with her journalism, Denhollander believes she's been called to use her legal skills and life experiences to advocate for a better, more biblically sound Christianity. She stressed, however, the limits of that calling. If she becomes consumed with saving the SBC, or ending the abuse epidemic in the Church, "I'll wind up burned-out and angry and bitter, because I won't succeed," Denhollander said. The only metric that matters, she added, is whether she's being faithful to what she feels God has asked her to do.

Denhollander told me that her favorite childhood Bible story wasn't about any of the bold female protagonists, but rather the Parable of the

Talents, Jesus's teaching about stewardship and servanthood. In the story, Jesus explains how a master entrusts his servants with various amounts of money, based on their abilities, and expects a certain return according to what they've been given. "Well done, good and faithful servant!" the master says when he sees them making the most of those abilities. "You have been faithful with a few things; I will put you in charge of many things."

"My parents would tell us, growing up, 'Whatever God has for you is the most important thing,'" she said. "That meant if God has a quiet life as a mom for you, that is the most important thing, and don't you ever diminish or underestimate the impact of that. If God has a public platform for you, then be faithful and serve Him. If you're given the responsibility of being a garbage collector, that's great, do it for God's glory. I need to be faithful with what the Lord has asked me to steward—nothing more. And that's what we're trying to teach our kids as well."

Rachael Denhollander has three young daughters. They participate in gymnastics, like she did. They're being raised in a church, like she was. Certainly, she worries about protecting them from the harms of the world. She also worries about preparing them—as Christians—to confront not just the disbelief of the secular world, but the callousness of their own religious movement. For speaking truth about abuse and corruption in the Church, Denhollander has been shunned by many of her fellow believers. Her daughters, and millions of other girls coming of age in the Church, are watching closely. I asked her what she hopes they see.

"Define your identity," Denhollander replied. "If you do that, you will be able to stand up against abuses of your theology *and* speak out against your own community. You will be okay with not having a home, with not fitting in anywhere, because your identity is not tied to anything here."

She thought for a moment. "When you lose sight of your identity, it's easy to lust after power, and to justify the moral compromises necessary to achieve it."

CHAPTER TWENTY-ONE

LYNCHBURG, VIRGINIA

There is nothing concealed that will not be disclosed,
or hidden that will not be made known.

—LUKE 12:2

Nick Olson could no longer justify those moral compromises.

From his earliest memories, Olson's identity had been wrapped up in Liberty University. His parents had met there as undergraduates. His father had prayed to advance Jerry Falwell Sr.'s vision on the mountaintop. He'd grown up romanticizing the school and eventually went there himself, earning a pair of degrees and winning a prized teaching job in the English Department. He had settled down in Lynchburg and started a family. One day, Olson allowed himself to think, his two sons would carry on the flame.

But that identity came at a cost. Belonging to the Liberty family meant believing the story that Liberty told about itself. Sitting on the back patio of his favorite barbecue joint one sunny afternoon in April 2023, Olson told me he didn't believe that story anymore. In truth, he'd stopped believing it a long time ago.

Doug Olson had shielded his son from some of the ugly truths about Liberty. Nick might never have seen it for himself, had he not pursued a career in teaching. As he became close with several of his professors, the younger Olson retraced the same arc of discovery and disillusionment traveled by his father decades earlier. He saw the coercion and intimidation and cruelty. He heard about the methodical suppression of opposing views. He witnessed the ways in which indoctrination—not education, not inquiry, but rather absolute uniformity of opinion—was incentivized from the top down. There was more to Liberty, Olson began to realize, than the feel-good mythology that had been expertly packaged and sold to millions of evangelical families like his. There were, as some of his professors liked to say, "two Liberties." One was a presentable, outward-facing university that trained champions for Christ. The other was an insular, unstable, paranoid family business run by sycophants who weaponized spirituality against any person or idea that might threaten their hold on power.

"Most of the students couldn't see it. They had been brainwashed," Olson told me. "I probably would have gotten brainwashed, too, if certain professors hadn't opened my eyes to it."

When Liberty offered him the teaching position in 2013, Olson struggled to reconcile these competing versions of the school. His idealism about the place had vanished; Olson spoke openly with friends about his darkened view of the institution and questioned whether it would be a healthy workplace. At the same time, he knew the awesome potential of Liberty. Despite its manifest flaws—or perhaps, because of them—he saw a singular opportunity to mold the next generation of Christian leaders and advance the kingdom of God. Things needed to change at Liberty. But the only way to effect that change, Olson convinced himself, was from the inside.

Almost immediately after he arrived on campus in August 2013 for the new faculty orientation, Olson was disabused of his reformist notions. After an opening prayer and some perfunctory welcomes from the provost, a man named Ron Godwin took the stage. One of Jerry Falwell Sr.'s most loyal lieutenants dating back to their days in the Moral Majority, Godwin had held virtually every top executive position at the school, and even served as the de facto caretaker for a period of time after Jerry Falwell Jr.'s sudden succession. But none of the titles on Godwin's résumé truly captured the essence of his role. "Ron was the barking-dog enforcer for the Falwell family," Olson said. "He did all the dirty work for the university."

Even knowing this, Olson told me, he was stunned by Godwin's remarks to Liberty's incoming batch of educators. "Ron gets up and says, 'If you think you're coming here to change things, think again. You need to fall in line with what we're doing here—or leave,'" Olson recalled.

He looked dazed by the memory. "This was the kind of thing I'd only heard about," Olson said. "Now, on my first day as a faculty member, I was seeing it for myself. It was Ron's job to put the fear of God into us. And it worked."

Fear aside, Godwin and his associates had their ways to keep everyone in line. Curricula were streamlined and centralized. Professors were constantly monitored, department by department, for deviations real or perceived. Renegades were promptly fired and bound by nondisclosure agreements. Liberty has never offered tenure to its faculty; professors work on year-to-year contracts that can be terminated at any time. This perpetual state of limbo was very much designed to stifle any freethinking instincts. The message was unmistakable: Get in line, as Godwin warned, or get out.

Professors tolerated this treatment because they loved the Lord and believed they were serving Him. They also loved their students and believed they were making a difference in their lives. Above all, they loved the *idea* of Liberty and believed in what it might yet become. "Everyone could see that Jerry Jr. was building something huge. People wanted to be a part of that future, even if they'd been hurt in the past. And so we just continued to look the other way," Olson said. "Obviously, that was a big mistake."

Olson had gone to work for Liberty just as the boss's life was starting to unravel. Falwell and his wife had met the Miami pool boy a year earlier, the origination of a torrid love triangle that eventually led to the university president's downfall. Olson and his colleagues were unaware of those details at the time, of course, but they could observe the related changes in Falwell's personal comportment. It was an open secret that he was drinking heavily. His lewd comments were becoming the stuff of legend. By the time he joined forces with Trump in 2016—and subsequently ousted Mark DeMoss, the Executive Committee chairman who voiced his objection—everyone could see that Falwell was equal parts emboldened and untouchable.

Professors had never thought of Falwell as hostile; to the extent he came across as standoffish, they chalked it up to his being aloof, awkward, insecure. But now he was increasingly authoritarian in his approach. Falwell had steadily expanded his purview while shrinking his inner circle; he had even pushed out Godwin, the ultimate power-consolidation maneuver. He was meddling ever more in the affairs of students and professors alike, deploying lieutenants to stomp out any trace of dissent. Before long, some employees of the school felt like members of the North Korean military, all but standing and saluting under the watchful eye of the ministers and department heads, never daring to make eye contact with the Dear Leader.

"There had always been warnings—veiled threats, really—to 'remember your place,' stuff like that. But suddenly, we're hearing things from the dean, things that clearly came from above the dean. Like, 'If you see the president in public, don't talk to him. You can say hello, but don't ask any questions. Follow the chain of command,'" Olson said. "It was very bizarre. And it wasn't just about Jerry Jr. We were told not to approach *any* administrators. So, the people in charge are micromanaging every aspect of our teaching, but there's no feedback welcome. We didn't get to offer upward evaluations of anyone. The goal, essentially, was to have zero faculty input in the way Liberty educated its students."

To Olson, there was no divorcing the administration's attitude toward faculty from the pedagogical decisions being made at Liberty. Acceptance rates soared as the school dumbed down its curriculum standards. Time became a quantified and scrutinized commodity; professors were penalized for paper-grading delays that resulted from offering detailed, personalized feedback to their in-person students, and rewarded for taking a standardized, minimum-workload approach to large online classes. Programs focused on business and politics blossomed, while the arts became an afterthought. In 2020, Falwell shocked the faculty by dissolving the school's Philosophy Department.

"Ask yourself why he did that," Olson told me. "It's because philosophy is all about questioning things, challenging things, searching for wisdom and truth in ways that cause people to think for themselves."

It was around this time that Olson began to despair over the future of Liberty. The school was flourishing by every tangible metric: record enrollment, record profits, record endowment. Falwell had built the campus into a marvel and formed a strategic alliance with the president of the United States. Yet this gaining of the world had come at the expense of Liberty's soul. Every *intangible* metric of the school's spiritual health suggested that Liberty was in a state of crisis. Students from that period recalled to me a certain malaise settling in over the campus. Olson and his colleagues, perceiving as much, grieved for their pupils. Some professors began drinking to deal with the devastation. Others contemplated quitting. Olson did both, fantasizing about being free from Liberty, ruing the day he'd accepted that job offer.

Whatever relief accompanied Falwell's ouster was short-lived. By that point Olson—and, he estimated, the great majority of his colleagues—recognized that Liberty's problems ran deeper than any one individual. Soon enough, evidence of this came courtesy of Ron Godwin himself. The longtime university enforcer, still smarting at his own ouster years earlier, reacted to Falwell's demise by writing a lengthy email to the board of trustees that sought to reestablish Jerry Falwell Sr. as the true visionary behind Liberty and diminish his son's role in the school's success. (Olson obtained the email from a source at the university; I have since verified its authenticity.)

To bolster his case, Godwin cited Falwell Sr.'s take-no-prisoners approach to building out Liberty's online learning program, which had become the school's dominant source of revenue. One particular passage stood out:

> While typically the enrollment process for college campuses occurs via a slow-growth relationship, with a counselor developing an affinity with a potential student over many months, Dr. Falwell instead chose to house enrollment in a call center, much like one would find at a for-profit institution. Employees were supervised closely and constantly, and efficiency became a principal goal. For some employees unaccustomed to working in a for-profit environment, accountability and daily productivity standards felt "off"—mechanistic, dehumanizing—and they registered their discomfort by publicly voicing concern that Dr. Falwell's testimony was going to suffer. . . . His answer, though delivered with his characteristic good humor, made his position clear: let him worry about his

testimony, and they should instead worry about being worthy of being retained.

Olson, who'd been reading the email aloud, stopped and looked up.

"Liberty's goal has never been some holistic vision of Christian academics. It's about maximum efficiency, maximum productivity, maximum profit making," he told me. "In that sense, Ron was actually establishing a *continuity* between Jerry Sr. and Jerry Jr. Their visions were the same. How can we make more money? How can we build a bigger institution? How can we gain political power and influence? How can we impose our conservative values on the nation?"

Olson paused. "So, you've got this program that's highly unethical, a terrible work environment, an abusive workplace—but, hey, it serves the mission of training champions for Christ, right?" he scoffed. "The problem is, the mission is lost once you've adopted that mentality. And that's what happened here. Liberty has taken a by-any-means-necessary approach to the ends, because they think those ends glorify God. But the means have distorted those ends so badly."

Olson had agreed to go on the record with me. In doing so, he was not simply stepping outside the cultlike cave of secrecy that had come to envelop the institution he once cherished. He was also throwing away his job; he was risking his future in academia, his family's financial security, and some of his closest relationships. When I asked him why—was blowing the whistle on Liberty worth such personal suffering?—Olson sat in silence for a long time.

"There's this apocalyptic feeling in American Christianity right now," he finally said. "And I've been thinking, maybe that's a good thing. *Apocalypse* means *revelation*. Maybe it's time all these hidden things were revealed."

He was referencing the Book of Luke, chapter twelve, when Jesus promises that the hypocrisy of the religious leaders would soon be exposed.

"There is nothing concealed that will not be disclosed, or hidden that will not be made known," Jesus warned. "What you have said in the dark will be heard in the daylight, and what you have whispered in the ear in the inner rooms will be proclaimed from the roofs."

* * *

OLSON WAS RIGHT ABOUT LIBERTY STUDENTS BEING "BRAINWASHED."
While visiting Lynchburg over the years, I was always struck by the disconnect between the sleaziness of the university and the sincerity of its pupils. Without fail, students were kind, decent, solicitous—everything their school was not. This behavior reflected a serious commitment to Christ. But it also betrayed an underlying ignorance about the place they called home. Questions about controversies or scandals were usually met with a foreign gaze. Like fish born into contaminated waters, these kids were oblivious to the corruption all around them.

There were periodic awakenings on the Liberty campus—a protest here, a petition there—but the student body's disposition generally remained one of wide-eyed witlessness. That started to change toward the end of Trump's presidency. Students organized to register their disapproval of the school's plan to host the Miss Virginia pageant, complete with a swimsuit competition, inside its Center for Music & Worship; of the university remaining open and mandating in-person attendance during the early stages of the COVID-19 pandemic; of Falwell teaming with Charlie Kirk to open a Republican advocacy shop, the ridiculously named Falkirk Center, on campus; and of the racial callousness displayed by Falwell during the summer of 2020, which resulted in several Black student-athletes transferring from the school.

Watching this unfold from his hometown of Johnstown, Pennsylvania, eighteen-year-old Daniel Hostetter was having second thoughts about Liberty. He had, like so many others before him, "fallen in love" with the school during a campus visit. Despite the warnings of his father and his favorite teacher, who worried about Liberty's incessant state of turmoil, he committed to enroll in the fall of 2020. Now, he was reconsidering their advice. Hostetter was a conservative Christian—raised in a Republican home, educated at an evangelical private school—yet there was something deeply unsettling about Liberty's posture toward the culture. His senior year of high school had been marked by a lethal pandemic and escalating racial tensions and the beginnings of an assault on American democracy. On each of these fronts, Liberty had done more to wound than to heal.

It was for this very reason that Hostetter ultimately decided he *needed* to go to Liberty. "I remember being very disillusioned with the direction of Christianity in this country," he told me. "But I also remember thinking, maybe I can help to model a better way."

His first week in Lynchburg was a blur. Falwell resigned the day after Hostetter started class; celebrations and impromptu prayer sessions (often they were one and the same) sprang up around campus as top Liberty officials, while convening public meetings and blasting out public statements, privately jostled for position. That Sunday, Hostetter's first in Lynchburg, he went to Thomas Road Baptist Church and listened to Jonathan Falwell explain why his older brother could no longer lead their father's school. It was surreal, disorienting—a fitting preview of the turbulence to come.

Jerry Prevo, stepping into the role of Liberty's interim president, picked up mostly where Falwell had left off. He spoke unapologetically of an agenda to elect Republican politicians. He attended the White House ceremony at which Trump announced the nomination of Amy Coney Barrett for the U.S. Supreme Court. After Liberty hosted a virtual Convocation in October 2020 featuring two prominent pastors, John Piper and J. D. Greear, during which Piper tacitly condemned Trump's morals and said he'd be voting third-party in the upcoming election, Prevo ordered that the video be scrubbed from the school's website.

Liberty, Hostetter soon realized, was even messier on the inside than it appeared from the outside. The Piper episode was particularly troubling. The 2020 election would be Hostetter's first time voting; after much prayer and reflection, he had decided to support a third-party candidate himself. Now his school was effectively stating its opposition to his ballot preference. Hostetter saw two paths forward: He could run from the repression, keeping quiet about his politics or perhaps even finding a new school to attend; or he could do something about it.

Sensing a unique opportunity to help shape Liberty in the post-Falwell era, Hostetter threw himself into a reconstructionist crusade. He joined an uprising against the Falkirk Center and helped organize "Justice for Janes" to protest the school's systematic mishandling of sexual-abuse allegations. Progress proved halting: Liberty cut ties with Charlie Kirk but kept the offending organization itself, renaming it the

Standing for Freedom Center and renewing its mandate for right-wing agitprop. Hostetter decided he needed to push even harder. He ran for Student Body Government as a sophomore and was elected speaker of the House. When the presidency came open a year later, he went for it.

The campaign took on a harsh tone. Antagonism toward President Joe Biden and his Democratic Party was running high on campus— "Let's Go Brandon" signs and shirts were commonplace—and Hostetter had earned the reputation of a squishy centrist. Seizing on Hostetter's rhetoric around racial reconciliation and justice for abuse survivors, his opponent painted him as an apostate. "People would come up to me and say, 'What are you, woke?'" Hostetter recalled. "All because I refused to expressly run as a Republican."

As he told me this story, in March 2023, Hostetter was campaigning hard for a second term. He had won that first race in nail-biting fashion. Not perceiving a mandate for bold, ambitious objectives, Hostetter spent his first term as student body president sizing up Liberty from the inside. What he saw unnerved him. Senior administrators—"People who've been here since the '70s and have no appetite for structural change," Hostetter told me—were deeply entrenched and ferociously territorial. Policymaking discussions were centralized and cloistered; even as the students' top elected representative, Hostetter was shut out of essential conversations about the school's present and future. At every turn, he saw how politics and self-preservation dictated the big decisions being made at his university.

Hostetter kept these concerns to himself. Rallying the fractured student body around any cause would prove difficult; he certainly didn't have the juice to take on the Liberty administration. Besides, the biggest decision of all was imminent: The presidential search committee had reportedly settled on a permanent replacement for Falwell, a selection that would speak volumes about the school's direction and sense of identity. The search committee had rebuffed Hostetter and his fellow student leaders, making it plain that their opinions and participation were entirely unwelcome. Hostetter tried to sound optimistic. He said they had persisted in sending a letter to the committee, stressing "a pastoral style" and "a gospel-centered approach to life and academics, not a politics-centered approach to everything." He believed that the people who'd gotten so much wrong in the past would actually get this right. He told me he was praying, daily and fervently, that Liberty's new president could turn the page on its past.

But if Hostetter had learned one thing as student body president, it was that Liberty prized its status quo—and punished anyone who challenged it.

Just a few weeks earlier, his favorite professor had abruptly been fired from the School of Divinity. There was no cause given. Hundreds of students signed a petition to reinstate him; when that failed, some of them demanded a meeting with the dean, and then with the provost. This incident, Hostetter told me, represented everything that was wrong with Liberty. There was no transparency. There was no trust. A brilliant teacher—a brilliant *Christian* teacher—had been summarily disposed of, divorced from his students, and cut off from his livelihood. He would be bound and gagged with an NDA, Hostetter said, and his story, his very existence, would be erased from Liberty's memory.

What Hostetter did not know—what Liberty could not have predicted—is that Dr. Aaron Werner would refuse to go quietly.

PAPERS WERE STREWN ACROSS THE KITCHEN TABLE. THERE WAS A CONtract with the terms of Werner's employment with Liberty; the notice of his termination; his appeal to the administration; a denial of the appeal; notes from his recent meeting with a lawyer; and a collection of letters, addressed by his students to the School of Divinity's dean, pleading for their professor's job. In the middle of the table, marked up in his handwriting, was a nondisclosure agreement offering Werner nearly $25,000 in exchange for remaining silent about the university.

His deadline to sign the NDA was three days away. Kathy Werner had been hoping that her husband would agree to the terms, take the money, and leave Liberty in the family's rearview mirror once and for all. She had homeschooled their four daughters, depriving the family of a second income, and it wouldn't be long before the bills started piling up. Tuition funds weighed on the Werners. Their oldest was a freshman in college; her sisters weren't far behind. Taking the hush money would give the family some breathing room as the professor figured out his next move.

And yet Werner could not stomach the idea of letting Liberty off the hook. The termination notice said he'd been fired "with cause," but that cause had never been articulated—not to him, not to his students, not to his friends on the faculty. The only thing he'd been told was that he had "recently" said something problematic in class. Something that warranted his immediate dismissal.

"I've narrowed it down to about eight things," Werner told me, his eyes dancing mischievously. "Bottom line, I wasn't following the example of big J."

He grinned. "Jerry, that is. Not Jesus."

It was probably destined to end this way for Werner. Thirty years earlier, as a Liberty undergrad studying biology, he had resented Falwell Sr. and his imperious style. Werner never would have chosen Liberty on his own. Raised in Maine, the son of a roughneck lobsterman, Werner came to Lynchburg only because his brother, a star athlete, had scored a full ride to the university. Transferring from the University of Maine to run alongside his kid brother on the track team, Werner chafed at Liberty's self-righteous legalism.

"You couldn't have a glass of wine. You couldn't have long hair. You couldn't even wear sandals," Werner recalled. "I remember telling a professor, 'You guys would kick Jesus out of this place.'"

After graduating and meeting his future wife, Werner undertook a zigzagging odyssey of the American evangelical landscape. They taught at a Christian school in Florida, served an evangelical ministry in Indiana, pastored at a church in Arkansas, then landed in Louisville, where Aaron earned both his master of divinity and doctor of philosophy degrees at Southern Seminary. After a few years in California, they tried to put down roots in Georgia. Werner became a dean at Shorter University, a large Southern Baptist affiliate, and emerged as a top candidate to take over as president. But the Werners still felt restless. They had been to so many places, yet their spiritual world felt so small. Aaron and Kathy decided to be missionaries and accepted an assignment in Vietnam. When that fell through—and as they debated alternative countries for their young family of six—the Werners fielded an unexpected request: What if they planted a church *here*, in the United States, right in Aaron's hometown in Maine?

His family and friends were not exactly church types. Aaron had earned a PhD in apologetics specifically for the purpose of converting his father—a crabby old New Englander known as "the Skippah"—but the hot-shot academic had failed. Naturally, it was an old drinking buddy who eventually reached Werner's dad with the gospel and convinced him to attend church. Knowing that his father's new faith was shallow, Werner jumped at the chance to help nurture it. He moved the family back to Maine, and for the next seven years worked as a bi-vocational pastor, raising up a congregation of two hundred while lobstering with his dad to pay the bills. Werner finally felt content. When a phone call came from Liberty University, he laughed it off.

The more Werner thought about returning to Lynchburg, however, the less crazy it seemed. Having spent the past two decades as an itinerant evangelical—pastoring, teaching, planting—he had seen the very worst of the Church. His brother-in-law, once a popular pastor, was outed after carrying on sexual relationships with numerous men while married to a woman. His direct supervisor at seminary, David Sills, was mired in scandal over his relationship with Jennifer Lyell. One of his favorite pastors, Southern Baptist celebrity Johnny Hunt, would soon admit to sexual misconduct (and be accused of sexual assault, which he denied) stemming from an incident with a fellow pastor's wife. Still, to Werner, nothing embodied the drift of American evangelicalism quite like Liberty University. It was for this reason—like Nick Olson and Daniel Hostetter and so many others—that Werner felt God calling him to Lynchburg.

The initial offer was to become dean of the School of Divinity. Werner wanted nothing to do with such a high-profile posting; he suspected that an old acquaintance, Harvey Gainey, the longtime Liberty trustee who succeeded Mark DeMoss as Executive Committee chairman, wanted him in that job to help contain the excesses of Jerry Falwell Jr. Werner informed Gainey that he wasn't interested in bureaucratic responsibilities or babysitting duties. If he came to Liberty, it would be to teach. In summer 2019, as Werner weighed his decision, twelve professors were purged from the School of Divinity. It made waves beyond Lynchburg: Despite record profits, Liberty was axing a dozen educators from what was once its most prominent department. Werner took this as a dreadful omen. Yet he also took it as a challenge: Falwell was now brazenly dismantling what little remained of Liberty's theological heritage, and nobody was doing anything about it.

Werner took the job, in late 2019, on the condition that he would teach classes in the honors program. If Falwell's goal was to empty the school of its intellectualism, making Liberty into an assembly line that churned out lawyers and businessmen and political activists, then Werner would create his own little fiefdom, a refuge of erudition and self-examination and critical thinking. "I could sense that God wanted me to help turn this honors program into something really special. Something that could be distinct from the rest of the university," Werner recalled.

The seven hundred or so students in the honors program were even brighter than Werner had expected. Many had chosen Liberty over the Ivy League; the average SAT score of his students, Werner told me, was higher than those at Harvard. These students were training for careers in every vocation imaginable, from medicine to ministry. Their futures were limitless. Werner spotted just one dilemma. "Lots of these kids came to Liberty from white conservative evangelical households," the professor said, "and they had never challenged their own assumptions. And I mean *never*."

Werner got to work changing that. In each of the courses he taught—evangelism, theology, New Testament—the professor came equipped with a PowerPoint deck, hundreds of slides long, that he used to provoke discussion and debate. Pairing certain slides with the week's readings or lectures, Werner would dare his students to interrogate their own beliefs about the world. He showed a meme image of Jesus holding an assault rifle to question the Church's commitment to nonviolence. He displayed quotes from Jerry Falwell Sr. on a range of topics—race, education, warfare, even prayer—to highlight the spiritual inconsistencies of their school's founder. He shared images of Bernie Sanders, the socialist turned Democratic presidential candidate, whom Falwell Jr. had hosted at Convocation as a publicity stunt, to examine the relationship between Christianity and economic systems. He presented a passage from C. S. Lewis's *The Screwtape Letters*, in which a senior devil advises his demon apprentice that patriotism is a most seductive substitute religion, to ask students about their true loyalties.

The only thing off-limits, the only person above reproach, was Christ.

Pressing his pupils to investigate the claims of any mortal man, Werner demanded that they start with their professor. He told the students that he was continually finding flaws with his own arguments and conclusions; surely, they could find some, too. This invitation—to open, searching, potentially subversive inquiry—was entirely alien to most of these students. And they revered Dr. Werner for it. The nonconformist approach made him a sensation on campus.

It also made him a liability.

Near the end of his first semester teaching, Werner was asked to lead the faculty devotional. If this was a trap—the buzz about his classes had put him on the administration's radar, and now the new professor was being asked to present to his colleagues—Werner didn't bother avoiding it. Armed with a few of his favorite slides, Werner dedicated the session to probing the ties between nationalism and American Christianity. The timing was purposeful: Trump and Biden were heading for a showdown that November and the Liberty campus was all but painted red. As his presentation wound down, Werner put up a final slide. It was an image of Jesus on Palm Sunday—in the saddle of a donkey, arriving triumphantly in Jerusalem, the gathered crowd singing hosannahs to their promised savior—wearing a red baseball cap. It read: MAKE ISRAEL GREAT AGAIN. The earliest followers of Jesus believed that He was delivering them a state superpower, Werner reminded his colleagues. American Christians ought to guard against similar fantasies.

He left that assembly a marked man. Werner wasn't dumb; he knew the bull's-eye he'd placed on his own back. But he didn't especially care. He had come to Liberty with a mission to edify these young Christians, to elevate their thinking and expose them to a world bigger than Lynchburg. Werner plowed ahead. He stepped on toes and slaughtered sacred cows, all but daring someone to stop him. "The bolder I became, the more the students loved it," Werner told me. "And the more the students loved it, the more fearful the administration became."

Werner's self-assurance owed in part to the fact that Gainey, the Executive Committee chairman, had personally recruited him to Lynchburg. When Gainey died unexpectedly in late 2021, just a few semesters into Werner's career at Liberty, the clock began to tick. It wasn't lost on Troy Temple, the dean of the Divinity School, that Werner had been offered the position that Temple himself now held. Temple—and, for that matter, much of the school's leadership—could see the risk Werner represented. The professor's popularity now extended well beyond his own department; this ideological rebellion he was fomenting in one small corner of campus might soon spread.

Kathy Werner could see what was coming. She warned her husband to button things up, to keep his head down for a while and not make any noise. He had extra incentive to do so: Reluctantly, Werner had allowed his oldest daughter, Kayla, a star athlete who'd scored a 1570 on her SAT, to enroll at Liberty. ("She wanted to be close to me, but I shouldn't have let her come here," he sighed.) Now, feeling this added family pressure, Werner tried to tone down the provocation. But he couldn't help himself. The year following Gainey's death was marked by clashes with Temple, run-ins with the administration—and such swelling demand from students that Werner taught five courses. Ultimately, the long wait lists and stellar reviews and he-changed-my-life testimonials couldn't save the professor. In January 2023, without any warning, he was terminated. Werner was promptly locked out of his office; security escorted him away from campus, not allowing him to collect any belongings or say goodbye to students or even see his own daughter. "It was pretty malicious," he recalled. "If you're going to fire me, fire me in a Christian way, you know?"

The outcry from students was overwhelming. Werner was inundated with phone calls and voicemails, emails and text messages. Some five hundred students signed the petition for his reinstatement. Several of them met with Temple, then demanded an audience with the provost, Scott Hicks, Liberty's top academic official. Audio recordings of both meetings—stealthily captured by one of the students—reveal the paternalistic wielding of spiritualized power that permeates Liberty as an institution. Temple told the students three times that "God works through authority"—in this case, him—and that they needed to trust that authority, hinting at the existence of a pattern of troubling behavior by Werner that he wasn't permitted to itemize. Hicks contradicted this sentiment, sticking to the story that Werner had been fired for a specific recent infraction, but stressed the underlying point about deferring to authority. After making several factual misstatements about the process of Werner's appeal, regarding what details could and could not be disclosed, Hicks told the students—the honors students—that education isn't "a popularity contest."

Werner had kept a sense of humor in recounting to me this entire saga. But now his demeanor shifted. Maybe it was because his daughter sat on the nearby couch, studying; maybe he was thinking about all the parents who had sacrificed to send their kids to Liberty, who had entrusted them to the Falwells and their lackeys, who had believed they would be trained as champions for Christ. Whatever the inspiration, Werner could no longer suppress his chagrin. He knew too many Liberty graduates who had drifted from their faith, or abandoned it altogether, after leaving Lynchburg. However naïve they might have been while in school, the eyes of many an alumnus were soon opened. The painful realization they would reach wasn't simply that Liberty was no better—no holier, no more Christlike—than what they encountered in secular spaces. It was that Liberty was *worse* than the secular world.

"Remember what Paul says to the Corinthians: 'You guys are doing stuff that even the pagans don't do!'" Werner said, paraphrasing the apostle's rebuke of the church in ancient Greece.

Werner was a traveled, cultured man. He had seen a lot of things. But nothing quite compared to what he claimed was going on at Liberty. There was his friend in the registrar's office who discovered the school was admitting students into its online graduate program who had phony undergraduate degrees—and was fired for refusing to cover it up. There was the gay student who was kicked out of school while his boyfriend, a football player, was allowed to stay. There was the administrator who admitted to him that he'd pushed a faulty textbook for years, one that is required reading for Liberty's entire student body, because of a massive kickback from the publisher. Summarizing it all—the enforcers and cronies, the lawsuits and payoffs, the shameless self-dealing and shady real estate transactions—Werner threw up his hands. "You tell me," he said. "Kind of sounds criminal, doesn't it?"

Kathy Werner had heard enough. We had been sitting for several hours around their kitchen table, and the longer we talked, the less interested she seemed in her husband signing the NDA. She was still worried about her family and their livelihood. But she was also concerned about the truth. Despite being married to a professor, Kathy had never appreciated the extent of Liberty's deception until her own daughter was enrolled there. Prospective students and their parents deserved to know what they were getting themselves into.

"Just to be clear, this is not about hurting anyone," Kathy said. "I don't want to hurt Liberty."

"Martin Luther didn't want to hurt the Catholic Church," her husband responded. "He wanted to purify it."

They both agreed: Liberty needed purifying.

"I think we need to be honest about the Falwells," Werner told me. "Jerry Sr. was always a bit of a scoundrel. And Jerry Jr. perfected the art of using fear and hatred as a growth strategy. Christianity happens to be the thing they used to build a multibillion-dollar institution. It could have been anything else; it could have been moonshine. But they chose Christianity. And it's gained them a lot of power and a lot of money, the two things these people truly worship."

Werner was quick to issue a caveat. He didn't believe the other Falwell son, Jonathan, was complicit in the family's sins. In fact, he was encouraged to know that Jonathan, the lead pastor of Thomas Road, was reportedly leading the search for a new university president. Werner was watching closely, just like everyone else, waiting for the announcement of Liberty's new leader. He was praying for a modern-day reformation.

"They have a chance," Werner told me, "to finally get this right."

MOST PASTORS, IF THEY SERVE A CHURCH LONG ENOUGH, WIND UP WITH a commemorative plaque somewhere in the building. Others might even have a gymnasium or office wing named after them. A select few will prove so impactful as to be honored with the title "pastor emeritus."

At Thomas Road, the shrine to Jerry Falwell Sr. fills an entire corridor of the church.

Stretching several hundred feet of pale, mint-shaded walls, the panoramic spectacle commemorates 50 YEARS OF MIRACLES. It was unlike anything I'd ever seen inside a Protestant house of worship. Clear floating cases, arranged into sections by date and theme, displayed the red tie he wore and the blue pen he wrote with; his vinyl-record sermon recordings and his *God Save America* musical CDs; five of the magazine covers he graced and fourteen books he authored; promotional pamphlets he hawked and fundamentalist periodicals he appeared in; some *Old-Time Gospel Hour* videotapes and a Hollywood clapboard bearing his name.

All this was a tribute to Falwell *himself*. The celebration of Thomas Road unfolded on alternating, beige-colored banners nearby, each of them commemorating one decade of the church's existence (1980–1989: A DECADE OF DESTINY). Of course, separate paeans to Falwell (A FAITHFUL SERVANT) and his children (A GODLY FAMILY) featured in these presentations as well, spanning his overlapping careers with Thomas Road, Liberty University, and the Moral Majority. The final section, documenting his death in 2007, was headlined with a quote from Ron Godwin: "A Giant Has Fallen." Just beneath that, the exhibition concluded—"The Legacy Continues"—with a photo of Jerry Falwell Jr. and his brother, Jonathan.

It had been nearly three years since Jerry Jr. was defenestrated. And yet there he was, on display inside Thomas Road Baptist Church, still identified as the leader of Liberty University. Maybe his brother didn't have the heart to scrub the caption or order an updated placard; maybe he was too busy with his booming church to worry about visiting gawkers doing a double take at the photo and revisiting the humiliation foisted upon the entire Falwell clan. There was no way of knowing: Despite my attempts to reach him—by email, by phone, even by visiting his church office—the youngest Falwell never made himself available for an interview.

Getting a read on Jonathan proved elusive. In speaking with a few dozen people who know him, everyone at least agreed that he was, unlike his brother, sincere about living out his faith. There was little consensus beyond that. Some of his friends, contemporaries, and congregants saw a squeaky-clean pastor who kept his distance from Liberty and was thus ignorant of much of the mischief there; others described Jonathan as the consummate insider, someone who had the university wired yet stayed strategically detached from its internecine jockeying, clinging to a plausible deniability that might insulate the pulpit from politics in a way his father never had.

Jonathan was certainly well connected at Liberty; for years, he had been the school's senior vice president of spiritual development. Yet it was widely understood that he and his older brother did not get along. That personal tension—and Jerry Jr.'s rapid consolidation of power at the school—seemingly pushed Jonathan further and further toward the periphery. By the time of his brother's resignation in August 2020, the Thomas Road pastor was scarcely ever seen around campus.

Jonathan now occupied center stage at Liberty. He was something of a tragic figure, a man burdened with the weight of restoring both the family's name and the university's reputation. Everyone affiliated with the school was studying him, parsing his sermons for clues about *his* vision for Liberty. One Sunday in the spring of 2023, I came to Thomas Road to listen for myself.

Inside the prodigious sanctuary, under an embankment of soft neon lights, Falwell continued a weeks-long series on Jesus's Sermon on the Mount. He had reached chapter seven, a crucial passage in which Jesus, having just explained how we are to live—by humbling ourselves, by shunning worldly possessions, by loving our enemies—suddenly turns to the subject of judgment.

Invoking Jesus's words about the wide road that leads to destruction and the "narrow gate" that leads to eternal life, Falwell issued a warning about which direction we are headed—and, more pointedly, who we are following.

In America today, Falwell said, "truth is being redefined." There are "ravenous wolves" seeking to devour God's sheep by watering down biblical standards and making the narrow gate appear wider than it really is. If Christians stick to God's truth, the pastor continued, they will be portrayed as extremists and bigots. They will be ostracized by society and relegated to the fringes. "I don't have any doubt in my mind," Falwell said, "there will be a time when the government tries to come into churches like this one and say, 'You can't preach that anymore.'"

He seemed to be careening toward a culture-war homily, pitting the pious true believers at churches like Thomas Road against the sinister secular-progressives in the culture at large. At this juncture in the sermon, based on my travels, the pastor would issue a call to political (and perhaps literal) arms, bracing his flock for a clash between the partisan forces of good and evil.

But then Falwell pivoted. He said that Christianity had always been under attack; that there was nothing new about this twisting of truth. The best defense against ravenous wolves, Falwell suggested, is a Good Shepherd. The pastor's message contained no real ambiguity: Rather than seeking out external conflict, Christians must focus on internal sanctification, meditating on the truth of Christ, keeping our eyes fixed on that narrow gate and nothing else.

Falwell then went a step further. The wolves Jesus described don't simply roam outside the church walls. In fact, Falwell reminded us, Jesus warned that one day many of His so-called disciples—people who'd been duplicitous, who'd practiced a religion based on rules and rituals but had no relationship with Him—would show up to heaven expecting obvious admission. "And then I will declare to them, 'I never knew you. Depart from me, you who practice lawlessness!'" Jesus thundered. Falwell told the people at Thomas Road that Jesus's words should frighten them. Some of the people in this sanctuary—who came every Sunday, who gave their money to the church, who threw themselves into related causes—were estranged from Jesus.

It was a deft, delicate threading of the oratorical needle. Falwell had identified the cultural threats to Christianity while holding Christianity itself accountable. He had diagnosed a war on truth and prescribed truth as the only solution. He had predicted an assault on the Church without giving a corresponding battle cry.

Daniel Hostetter didn't think Liberty's search committee would read the letter he'd written them, articulating what he and other student leaders were looking for in their next president. But it sure sounded like Jonathan Falwell had. This sermon had captured almost precisely the conservative, Christ-centered, evangelical-but-not-antagonistic approach Hostetter hoped for. Walking out of Thomas Road, I halfway wondered if Falwell would pull a Dick Cheney, concluding the search process by choosing himself.

That hunch proved halfway right.

A few weeks after my visit to Thomas Road, Liberty announced *two* leadership appointments. Whereas Jerry Falwell Jr. had held the dual titles of president and chancellor, those duties would now be split. His younger brother, Jonathan, would assume the role of chancellor. The new president would be Dondi Costin, a retired Air Force general who had most recently served as president of Charleston Southern University.

The response was tremendously positive. Just about everyone I spoke with about these appointments —faculty, students, alumni, employees— was pleased with the promotion of Jonathan Falwell, and especially thrilled about the selection of Costin. For a half century, Liberty had operated as a family business, free to flout attempts at oversight or the enforcement of industry standards. The school needed an outsider. Although Costin had earned a pair of master's degrees from Liberty early in his military career—the Executive Committee was never going to approve someone who had *no* ties to the school—he was as close to an outsider as anyone could hope. Hostetter was positively giddy at the news. Even Aaron Werner—who refused to sign Liberty's NDA— was encouraged, telling me it "seems like a step in the right direction."

There was but one angry critic: Jerry Falwell Jr.

"Based on these hires, they're choosing piety over competence. And it's just pitiful," Jerry Jr. told me. "It's exactly what my dad didn't want to see happen."

We were speaking by phone, soon after the appointments had been announced, but before Costin and Jonathan Falwell took office. Jerry Jr. was in a bad place. He had been banned from campus—the place where his father is buried. He was locked in a vicious legal dispute with Liberty, seeking $8.5 million in withheld retirement payments after the school sued *him* for $10 million. ("My dad turned over in his grave," Jerry Jr. said of the university's action against him. "I'm sure of it.") He was no longer of any use to his friend Donald J. Trump, who was fighting to keep evangelicals in the fold after recently being indicted on thirty-four felony counts and separately being found liable for sexual abuse. Falwell's longtime associates had cut him off; people he considered friends had turned on him, his wife, and their children.

The appointment of his younger brother proved especially stinging. Not long after Liberty announced its new leadership team, Jonathan and Costin joined Troy Temple, the divinity dean, to shoot a video for the school's Facebook page. With cameras rolling, Jonathan extolled the virtues of the man who'd replaced his brother, slapping Costin on the back and telling of his moral rectitude. When the incoming president offered paeans to "Dr. Falwell's original vision," Jonathan nodded. "Dondi is actually a *picture* of that original vision," he bragged to Temple. "You can't find scandals, you can't find issues. Why? Because he's walked with character, he's walked with integrity." As if the implication wasn't clear enough, Jonathan pointed out Costin's loyal relationship with his loving wife, calling them "great role models for our students."

"It's a direct slap at me," Jerry Jr. told me the day after the video posted. "They've all tried to paint this picture like I was some kind of reprobate, and it's all based on lies so they can take power and take control. If you watch that video, you will see right away there is no academic competence whatsoever; no knowledge of how to run a major institution of higher learning."

He was especially irked by Jonathan's suggestion that Liberty's spiritual life had suffered in recent years. "Guess who was in charge of the spiritual life of the school since 2010? *My brother*," Jerry Jr. said, lingering on the two words, his syrupy drawl now dripping with disdain. "If he really thought things were going bad spiritually, he could have said something. I couldn't have done a thing about it because the board appointed him. But he never did. And yet, there he sits. They made him chancellor."

Changing the inflection of his voice to imitate Jonathan—uptight, performed, preacherlike—Jerry Jr. mimicked: "Our founder had a mission for Liberty, and that was to train champions for Christ, and that's what we're gonna do."

Jerry Jr. told me he was spoiling for a fight—with his brother, with Costin, with anyone at Liberty who would try to erase his legacy and dilute the real vision of his father. He told me the school was building a new $35 million facility, the Jerry Falwell Center, that would make the altar at Thomas Road look modest by comparison. It was planned as the ultimate tribute to Liberty's founder; there would even be a hologram of Falwell Sr. preaching.

"I'm going to do everything I can to prevent them from being able to open it," Jerry Jr. told me. "Because I actually own my father's name, and it happens to be my name, too."

He paused. "Also, his vision for Liberty was nothing like theirs."

THE ARENA WAS DARK SAVE FOR THE RADIANT BEAMS OF RED AND white that swept across center stage, giving a rock-concert vibe to a Friday-morning chapel service. Thousands of students packed into the Vines Center, a gorgeous facility in the center of Liberty's bustling campus, arms raised and eyes closed as they sang praise to the Lord. "For if my God is for me / Then what have I to fear / And I will not deny Him / The glory that is His."

In fact, these Christians had plenty to fear, according to the day's special Convocation speaker: Ron DeSantis.

The Florida governor was more than a month out from the formal launch of his 2024 presidential campaign but had scheduled a mid-April swing through Lynchburg to flex some spiritual muscle. His timing was impeccable: Less than twenty-four hours before arriving at Liberty, DeSantis had signed a so-called heartbeat bill in Florida, effectively banning all abortions after six weeks of gestation. Trump had alienated key pro-life allies after blaming them for the Republican Party's woeful performance in the 2022 election. If abortion was indeed Trump's great vulnerability, then DeSantis was now uniquely positioned to take advantage.

When the arena ceased to pulsate from guitar blasts, Jonathan Falwell jogged up the steps and onto the main stage. Liberty had come full circle—sort of. In the very place where his brother had promoted Trump ahead of the 2016 Republican primary, Jonathan now stood pushing DeSantis, widely expected to be Trump's chief challenger, as a holier alternative. Touting the newly signed heartbeat bill, Falwell told the students that DeSantis "recognizes and knows that life is a gift from God!" The school's incoming chancellor looked at DeSantis. "We thank you today for coming to help inspire our students to become champions for Christ," Falwell said.

It was the dream introduction for a presidential contender. DeSantis swaggered toward the platform like a prizefighter making his way to the ring for a heavyweight bout, weaving through rows of screaming fans, a spotlight tracking him every step of the way. "Greetings from the free state of Florida!" he bellowed. The standing ovation lasted more than thirty seconds. And then, as though he'd forgotten which Falwell had invited him, DeSantis delivered a speech that had nothing to do with training champions for Christ.

In his half-hour-long address to America's most influential Christian college, Florida's governor made zero mention of Jesus. Instead, he boasted of bloody political crusades: how he'd shunned the advice of his party's establishment, rejected any semblance of compromise with Democrats, pummeled the liberal media, and used the power of the state to punish partisan enemies. Not that his audience seemed to mind. DeSantis won applause for touting his enormous margin of victory in 2022, and the cheers grew louder still when he announced, "There is not a single Democrat that's elected to statewide office in Florida!"

Each time DeSantis appeared poised to transition into religious doctrine, he doubled down on political pugilism. He bashed "leftist politicians" who endanger our way of life. He spoke of "crime skyrocketing" and "medical authoritarianism." He warned that "cultural Marxism" and "the woke agenda" would destroy America unless we fought back. When DeSantis began describing a "war on truth," it seemed that his moment of rhetorical transition had arrived. But it hadn't. The "truth" he spoke of wasn't the gospel of Jesus Christ; it was right-wing conservativism, inherited from the founding fathers, who if alive today, he intimated, would be leading the charge against Disney World.

Finally, twenty minutes into his speech, DeSantis declared that our constitutional freedoms are "a gift from Almighty God." He told the Liberty students it was time for "a revival." Of their faith? Of their commitment to following Christ's example? No. Rather, DeSantis was calling for an *American* revival, a return to the Revolutionary-era struggle against big government.

The only thing more jarring than the lazy, lowest-common-denominator substance of DeSantis's speech was the reception it earned. Many students stood and cheered throughout. When DeSantis finished, their raucous ovation gave way to a thumping chant: "U-S-A! U-S-A! U-S-A!"

Not everyone was so enthralled. As the lights came on and the crowds emptied out, I plopped down in a seat at the top of the arena. An old friend came over and joined me: Daniel Hostetter.

The student body president wore a VIP badge pinned to a dark gray suit. Hoping to find a palatable Republican alternative to Trump ahead of 2024, Hostetter had been excited about today's Convocation. He had met DeSantis beforehand, chatted with him a bit, watched his speech from the front row. And now he looked utterly dejected.

"Some of us are just tired of being used as political props," Hostetter said, citing text messages from friends who'd been disgusted with the tone of the event. "We were hoping this would be more than another campaign rally. I mean, if you want to use biblical language to speak to political issues, fine. But at some point, you have to actually speak *to* the Bible. Right?"

The pained expression on Hostetter's face suggested that this was a rhetorical question. He knew the answer, and it hurt. Evangelicals by and large no longer seemed to care whether their preferred candidate had a biblical worldview, much less a command of scripture. Even at a place like Liberty—*especially* at a place like Liberty—politicians saw the pointlessness in talking about servanthood, about humility, about unity and peace and love for thy neighbor. The market for such a message had long since disappeared. The demand was for domination, and Republicans like Trump and DeSantis were happy to supply it. Their appeal to evangelicals had everything to do with acting like champions and nothing to do with acting like Christ.

In the weeks leading up to DeSantis's visit, Hostetter had sensed that something was different about Liberty. The appointments of Costin and Jonathan Falwell hinted at a distinct new identity for the school. He had just cruised to reelection in the race for student body president, defying the attacks on his supposed wokeness that had proved so resonant in the previous campaign. Meanwhile, the revival at Asbury University—where his younger sister attended—had roused Liberty's students in ways that Hostetter had never seen. Sure, there were still some hard-liners on campus, guys who wore MAGA hats to class and flew "Let's Go Brandon" flags from their dorm rooms. But they seemed to be shrinking into an ever-smaller minority. For the first time since he'd arrived at Liberty, Hostetter believed that the school was turning a corner.

"And yet . . . ," he told me, sweeping his outstretched palm across the emptying arena before us.

Hostetter would soon have a choice to make. He could spend his second term as student body president laboring at the margins toward incremental gains. Or he could use the capital he now had—capital he'd lacked during his first term—to advocate for serious reform. Persuasion and collaboration hadn't gotten him very far in dealing with the entrenched interests at Liberty. However optimistic he felt about a long-term directional shift under Costin and Jonathan Falwell, if more immediate change was going to come, it would have to come from the students. It would have to come from him.

There was so much work to do. Hostetter wanted permanent student representation on the board of trustees. He wanted tenure for professors and transparency in the hiring and firing processes. He wanted certain prohibitions lifted—off-campus drinking for students over twenty-one, for instance—and a comprehensive review of the school's policies around sexual assault. He wanted to dramatically cut funding to the Standing for Freedom Center, which uses students' tuition money to bankroll the extrabiblical musings of professional provocateurs such as William Wolfe.

The most urgent item on his to-do list, Hostetter told me, was also the most symbolic.

"This new shrine they're building to Jerry Falwell Sr.—and that's the only word to describe it, honestly—it's bordering on idolatry," he told me. "I think more and more students realize we have to do something about it."

The arena was now still and completely silent. Hostetter and I were the last two people in sight. He looked all around us, taking in the scene, looking wistful. He recalled the first time he'd visited the Liberty campus and heard about the founder's famous mountaintop vision in 1976.

"This place is bigger than one man. I'm worried we're glorifying—" He stopped himself.

"Our goal is to glorify the Lord," Hostetter said. "Isn't it?"

* * *

WHEN I SAT DOWN WITH NICK OLSON A FEW HOURS LATER, AT THAT roadside barbecue joint on the outskirts of Lynchburg, he was thinking about Jonathan Falwell.

Like so many people at Liberty, Olson had been pleased to see the youngest Falwell sibling appointed chancellor of the university. This wasn't because he thought Jonathan to be blameless; in fact, one of Olson's faculty mentors, a longtime Thomas Road member who was close to the pastor, had warned him that Jonathan knew *exactly* how bad things had become at Liberty. He was every bit as complicit in the school's corruption as his older brother, Olson's mentor insisted, because he was the one person with the standing to expose all the wrongdoing—and he chose not to.

Now, Olson told me, Jonathan was being given a second chance.

"To truly fix this place, someone has to step up. Someone has to be willing to tell the truth, to cross some powerful people, to lose some powerful friends and make some powerful enemies," Olson told me. "Now ask yourself: Who at Liberty is in a position to do that? Jonathan. That's it. There's nobody else. This is still a family business, and he's the one with the family name."

I asked Olson, if he were advising Jonathan on a plan to clean up Liberty, where he would suggest the new chancellor should start.

"The Standing for Freedom Center," Olson replied. "We've got brilliant students here, brilliant faculty members, people who've dedicated their lives to exploring the relationship between faith and education. But it's the Freedom Center—*the Freedom Center*—that speaks for our university. Think about how insulting that is. And then ask yourself: *Why?* Why do we hire these people? Why do we pay them to say and write outrageous things? Why do we promote them as the representatives of an institution of higher learning?"

The answer was obvious enough. Liberty has been guarding against "liberal drift" since the moment of its inception. Jerry Falwell Sr. would regularly cite the cautionary tale of certain Ivy League schools, established by conservative Christians, that had devolved into havens of secular progressive thinking. This explains why alcohol continues to be prohibited on campus; why the school newspaper is still censored by administrators; why Republican politics remain a focal point of the university's mission. Liberty has always taken extraordinary measures to avoid any hint of backsliding. Given both the intensifying external scrutiny and rising internal restlessness of students and professors alike, it was only fitting that Liberty would overcompensate by making the Freedom Center, with its cartoonishly far-right politics, the voice of the university.

Olson told me about an old expression, one that began as an inside joke among Falwell Sr.'s close friends and later morphed into an unofficial school motto: "Politically incorrect since 1971." The irony, Olson noted, is that dissension has never been tolerated at Liberty University. Rebellion against the status quo is acceptable only if rebelling in the approved direction. Falwell Sr. may have reveled in provoking the thought police of his time, but his school had become its own totalitarian regime. "You can say anything you want to disparage Democrats and 'own the libs,'" Olson told me, "but the moment you step out of line with respect to conservative Republican politics, they'll come after you."

We had been talking for hours. Now, just as the sun dropped below the Blue Ridge Mountains, storm clouds moved in over Lynchburg. The skies opened up a few minutes later. Fleeing from the back patio of the restaurant, Olson invited me to his nearby home, where we could finish the conversation over a glass of wine. His wife, Eliza, joined us in the living room.

Eliza Olson had watched her husband suffer under the stress of his association with Liberty. She had listened to his anguished conversations with colleagues and read his tortured private writings. She had spent the past month in prayer with him as they debated whether he should speak with me on the record about Liberty. When the decision was made, Eliza had one condition: Nick needed to force Liberty's hand. Whereas he seemed more comfortable resigning from the school before his interviews with me were published, she insisted that he stay on the job, giving his words maximum impact and daring the new leadership to deal with him straightforwardly—not as some disgruntled ex-employee taking shots at Liberty, but as a legacy student and current professor trying to save it.

"They've always been able to do their dirty work in private," Eliza told Nick. "Make them deal with this in public."

Nick agreed to her terms. Yet he was under no illusion about how this would end. He knew that Costin and Jonathan Falwell wouldn't want to risk opening the floodgates by tolerating one professor's public criticisms; he knew that he wasn't long for Liberty University. There was a time, early in our conversations, when this reality weighed on him. He had sounded forsaken and self-pitying. But now he was past that. Nick didn't feel sorry for himself anymore; he mostly felt sorry for his father. Doug Olson had been the one who initiated Nick, when he was just a child, into the folklore of Jerry Falwell's vision on the mountaintop. Doug had seen his own share of ugliness at Liberty. Yet he still believed, fifty years later, that Falwell's founding vision for Liberty was pure.

Nick Olson did not.

"Jerry Jr. found his whole identity in building this amazing physical campus, in establishing Liberty as this ruthless force for Republican causes, because he thought that was the fulfillment of his father's vision. And it's heartbreaking," Nick told me. "It's heartbreaking because it *was* the fulfillment of his father's vision."

That "original vision" Costin and Jonathan Falwell spoke of—to train champions for Christ, to shine God's light in the culture, to share His love with the world—was little more than a convenient counterfactual, Olson said, a story people have told themselves because the real history is so lamentable. I asked Olson to indulge a theoretical exercise. Suppose that so-called original vision was truly what Falwell Sr. wanted; suppose it was truly the standard he hoped future generations would use to gauge the school's success. Using that measure, I asked him, had Liberty University failed?

He sat quietly for a long time. "Yes," he finally murmured. "Catastrophically."

Olson winced when he said this. He had learned under faithful Christians at Liberty. He had studied alongside faithful Christians at Liberty. He had educated faithful Christians at Liberty. These people, he stressed, are a credit to the school. But individual triumphs do not offset institutional tragedy. If a megachurch pastor is exposed for misconduct—if he and his staff are proven to be liars, bullies, scoundrels, enablers of abuse—then what good is the testimony of thousands of people who insist that the pastor brought them closer to Christ? One must take a comically small view of God to believe that these people could not have drawn closer to Christ while attending another church—one *not* guilty of systemic misbehavior. After all, was it the pastor who had brought them closer to Christ or was it the work of the Holy Spirit? Does Jesus need the help of our broken institutions or do our broken institutions need the help of Jesus?

"If Liberty was even in the ballpark of that original vision, then you and I wouldn't be sitting here talking right now," he told me. "I believe God has a different vision for us moving forward—not just for Liberty, but for the entire American Church. And we need to be willing to step out in faith to pursue it."

This was the first time, in our many hours of conversations, that Olson had broadened his gaze beyond Liberty University. I asked him what this different vision for the American Church might look like.

"I think the first step is reimagining the Christian worldview. And that means replacing our dominant metaphor—culture war—with something different," he answered. "That's been the running theme for evangelicals: we're always embattled, always fighting back. But what if we laid down our defense mechanisms? What if we reframed our relationship to creation, to our neighbors, to our enemies, in ways that are more closely aligned to the Sermon on the Mount? What if we were willing to lay down our power and our status to love others, even if that comes at cost to ourselves?"

Olson was describing the biblical concept of God's power being made perfect in human weakness. Laying down our status and loving others sounds to many American Christians like a recipe for leaving the Church vulnerable. But in fact, nothing could make it stronger. When Paul wrote to fellow believers, saying that he delighted in insults and beatings and persecution, the apostle wasn't being a masochist. He was boasting—when translated from the Greek, he was seeking glory—in the one way that God permits. He was celebrating the knowledge of God.

To know God, Olson said, is to forget what we *think* we know about everything else.

"We were created as finite, limited beings. We are called to seek. We are called to humble ourselves and learn and grow," he told me. "Here, in an academic setting, I don't see that humility. I don't see a lot of humility in the way that Christians relate to the world around us. And that's strange. Because the best teacher is the one who modeled humility. The best teacher is the one who said, 'Knock and the door will be opened to you.'"

When Olson said this, my mind flashed to a mid-nineteenth-century painting, *The Light of the World*, by William Holman Hunt. It had been my father's favorite; after he died, I acquired a framed copy for my home office. The artwork depicts Jesus—a majestic cloak draped over His dirty garments, a golden crown placed over top of that excruciating coronet of thorns—standing outside a door. He is knocking. The door, as my dad pointed out to me when I was a little boy, has no handle on the outside. Jesus cannot open it. He needs to be let in. This is the nature of Christ's relationship to man: He stands at the door and knocks, waiting patiently for us to accept Him.

Accepting Jesus is not the end of a believer's journey; it is the beginning. Once the door to our heart is opened, and Christ is welcomed inside, He tells us that it's our turn to start knocking.

EPILOGUE

I slipped into the building through a side entrance, five minutes after the worship service began, and snuck upstairs into the balcony. Satisfied at having gone undetected, I found a corner seat. All at once, a thousand sights and sounds and smells came rushing back to me: the rose-colored carpeting and matching pew upholstery; the towering, triangular beams of oak and cedar; the wall of exposed brick outlining three stained-glass windows, each one shot through with sunlight, the glow of the red-and-orange cross in the middle pane warming all who held its gaze.

It was four summers earlier that I stood in the pulpit of this sanctuary, where my father had preached for a quarter of a century, where I'd honored his life and scolded the people who'd used the occasion of his funeral to pick a political fight. I hadn't been back to Cornerstone since. After moving home to Michigan, my wife and I found a different church for our family—a church where we could blend in, build a community of our own, avoid the internecine wrangling that had consumed Cornerstone. And yet, scanning my surroundings this summer morning, I was awash in nostalgia. So much of my life had been shaped by this place, and so much of this place remained the same. I spotted my mother, in her usual place by the west side of the stage, singing and raising her open palms skyward. My childhood Sunday School teachers, now senior citizens, patrolled the aisleways and ushered guests to their seats. Just outside the sanctuary, no more than fifty feet down the main hallway, my initials were still carved in the brickwork.

The only thing unrecognizable about Cornerstone was its senior pastor.

I had walked into the church fairly expecting to see my father up front, baggy sport coat unbuttoned, his specter pacing the stage while unpacking the four points of his latest homiletic. What I encountered instead was every bit as fantastical. The preacher who now stood before Cornerstone was not only not my father; it was a very different Chris Winans from the version I'd once known.

He had nearly been run out of the church after succeeding my dad. He had almost quit, a couple of years later, in the face of the continued turmoil over COVID closures and racial-justice activism and Donald Trump's defeat. Winans survived these ordeals but was badly wounded. The anxiety disorder he'd developed might never fully recede. He could hear the whispers about him, about the church, about the long-term viability of both. As he surveyed the damage in early 2021, watching "an exodus" of members from Cornerstone, Winans was a man thoroughly paralyzed by his predicament. There was no obvious path forward: He could launch a frontal assault on the extremism that had infiltrated his church, challenging congregants in a manner that would surely trigger even more defections; or he could keep quiet, pretending that everything was fine at Cornerstone, all but guaranteeing that things would get much worse.

Winans was not by nature confrontational. Still, the pastor told me, he could not in good conscience perpetuate the toxic status quo at Cornerstone. Desperate to bypass this lose-lose binary, he prayed for a way to confront the problems at the church without alienating more of its people. After struggling for some time in this regard, Winans finally had something of a breakthrough. The strategy he settled on—which he described to me as "pull, don't push"—was something of an elaborate Jedi mind trick. Winans wanted to bring his congregants along, to compel them to second-guess their extrabiblical desires, but make them think it was their own conviction. He would preach on godly character, then play dumb when someone approached him afterward to admit they were rethinking their allegiance to certain politicians or pop-culture personalities; he would preach on the spiritual principle of discernment, then offer a bemused shrug when someone confessed to him that they were beginning to doubt conspiracy theories or question the information they'd been imbibing on social media.

The situation at Cornerstone began to stabilize. New families joined the congregation—a trickle, at first, and then a wave. Before long, the church had regained all the members it once lost. By the time of my visit, in July 2023, the sanctuary was as full as I had ever seen it. Winans had remarked to me, over breakfast earlier that summer, about the massive turnover at Cornerstone since my dad's death. He shared with me how, several times recently, he'd been explaining to someone how "Pastor Alberta would always say . . ." only to be interrupted, "Pastor who?"

The anecdote stung at first. *Dad gave every ounce of himself to Cornerstone,* I thought, *and now half its members don't know his name.* But the sensation was short-lived. Though Dad had plenty of flaws, self-glorification wasn't one of them. He wouldn't want a gym named after him or a shrine dedicated to his memory. All he wanted was to enter into the presence of the Lord and hear the words, "Well done, good and faithful servant." Cornerstone never belonged to my dad. It belongs to Jesus Christ, the chief cornerstone, who promised that He would build the Church and that the gates of hell would not prevail against it. Dad had been a faithful instrument of God's grand construction project. Now it was Chris Winans's turn.

I hardly recognized him in the pulpit. Having spent the previous few years getting to know Winans—comparing notes on the situation at Cornerstone, talking through some of the darkest days of his life and career—I considered him a friend. But he wasn't *my pastor.* To the extent I kept tabs on his preaching, it was via occasional YouTube clips. Sitting in the sanctuary that July morning, I could scarcely believe Winans's transformation. Gone was the timid young preacher who'd struggled to escape his predecessor's shadow; in his place was a seasoned, assertive, intellectually imposing leader. Winans had salvaged his job by refining the "pull, don't push" formula at Cornerstone. But even those days were history. Winans wasn't content to pull people along anymore. He was now pushing, and pushing hard.

This was a special Sunday at Cornerstone. The church was breaking ground on a new wing and announcing a major new initiative, "Shine," which would emphasize witnessing to unbelievers by reflecting God's light and love into the community. This was no empty gesture: Cornerstone was fundamentally reorienting its approach to the surrounding

area and to the culture at large. Winans believed evangelicals in congregations like his had created needless barriers to entry; that they had
allowed tribal litmus tests to supersede biblical mandates, squander-
ing key opportunities to introduce Christ to people who needed Him
the most. It was time for that to change. Nearly six years into the job,
Winans was finally putting his imprint on the church.

At Cornerstone, tradition calls for the congregation to stand and
recite a long scripture passage to preface the day's sermon. Winans re-
quested instead that we remain seated. Today's sermon, he explained,
hinged on a single verse.

My body went numb when the words flashed onto the overhead
screens. It was from the Book of Second Corinthians. Chapter four.
Verse eighteen. It was my favorite verse—the first one I'd memorized as
a child, the one I'd meditated on every day since, the one I'd read during
my father's eulogy.

To understand this single verse, Winans explained, was to understand "the purpose of the Church."

WHAT *IS* THE PURPOSE OF THE CHURCH?

For most of my life, I thought the answer was simple. The purpose
of the Church is to make disciples of all the nations—first by sharing
the gospel, then by baptizing unbelievers into faith, and ultimately by
training followers of Jesus to become more and more like Him. This
work is inherently self-perpetuating. Witnessing to the world is not
enough. Converting unbelievers is not enough. Christians are called to
help God's family grow both quantitatively *and* qualitatively. This is the
enduring purpose of the Church: to mold fallen mortals into citizens of a
kingdom they have inherited, through the saving power of Jesus Christ,
to the everlasting glory of God, so that they might go and make disciples
of their own.

What I struggled for so long to accept—what I finally was forced to
confront during the four years I spent reporting this book—is that not
everyone shares this vision for the Church.

To some evangelicals, the purpose of the Church is to "own the libs"
with an aggressive, identitarian conservatism. They might cloak their

ambitions with biblical language—like Ralph Reed at his Faith and Freedom conferences or Charlie Kirk at his flag-waving sanctuary symposiums—but that facade isn't sustainable. The 2023 edition of Reed's event abandoned any pretense of spirituality; one speaker, who earned applause for introducing himself as a "straight white Christian," said that all of America's problems could be solved by men reasserting "an alpha male mindset." Kirk, for his part, kept up his evangelizing by prescribing the death penalty for Joe Biden and calling for "an amazing patriot" to bail out the deranged man who had brutally attacked and nearly killed the husband of Nancy Pelosi.

Kirk is not a pastor or religious leader. So why is he enlisted—time and again—by the hard-line "pirates" of the Southern Baptist Convention? Because they share a common goal: preventing progressive ideas from infiltrating the strongholds of traditional social conservatism. At the SBC's 2023 annual meeting, just as Rachael Denhollander predicted, the pirates launched an all-out attack on the newly adopted reforms targeting sexual abuse inside SBC churches. Their chosen candidate, Pastor Mike Stone, campaigned for president this time on a promise to remove Denhollander from the task force, abolish the category of "credibly accused" abusers from the database, and return most authority to the local congregations, essentially freeing them from the pesky standards that would necessitate reporting cases of misconduct. The rationale goes deeper than surface-level fights against feminism. Many right-wing pastors simply cannot stomach the notion of their churches being accountable to secular actors—legal bodies, law enforcement agencies, media outlets—because their vision for Christianity is one of absolute supremacy. The Church, in their view, answers to no one but God; they are the authority to which *the rest of culture* must answer. (Stone lost his campaign, and SBC president Bart Barber is pushing ahead to codify the efforts of Denhollander's task force.)

This effort to assert dominance over the culture is but a precondition for dominating the country itself.

In February 2023, a landmark national survey conducted by the Public Religion Research Institute and Brookings Institution found that roughly two-thirds of white evangelicals either explicitly supported the notion of Christian nationalism or were sympathetic to it. The share of white evangelicals who expressed support for certain ideas—that the government should declare Christianity the state religion; that being Christian is an important part of being an American; that God has called on Christians to exercise dominion over all areas of society—dwarfed that of white mainline Protestants, white Catholics, and Protestants of color. The research established a clear link between Christian nationalist ideology and racism, xenophobia, misogyny, authoritarian and anti-democratic sentiments, and an appetite for political violence. The most remarkable finding: Nearly 90 percent of white adherents to Christian nationalism agreed that "God intended America to be a new promised land" run by "European Christians." The broader sample of respondents rejected that statement by a two-to-one margin.

Hoping to capitalize on the passions of their base, Texas Republicans introduced a bill in early 2023 that would require public school classrooms throughout the state to display the Ten Commandments "in a size and typeface that is legible to a person with average vision from anywhere in the classroom." This was part of a coordinated legislative effort to Christianize civics in the state. Texas had already enacted a law requiring classrooms to display donated "In God We Trust" placards (one local district made headlines by banning Arabic versions while accepting those written in English). At the same time, Republicans were pushing to replace public school counselors with religious chaplains. When it came time to muscle the Ten Commandments bill through the Senate, the bill's sponsor called on—who else?—the "esteemed" pseudo-historian David Barton to testify. Barton did his part: The bill cleared the Senate on a party-line vote. Its failure in the House coincided with an ironic twist of timing: Weeks before the bill died, Bryan Slaton, a Republican representative and former SBC youth pastor who branded himself a champion for family values—criminalizing abortion, warring with LGBTQ "groomers," and, yes, promoting the Ten Commandments in public spaces—was expelled by the House after an investigation found that he'd cheated on his wife with a nineteen-year-old aide who "could not effectively consent to intercourse" after he'd plied her with copious amounts of liquor.

Champions of Christian nationalism would have you believe that these efforts to rule the country are inherently theological; that they are in service of a broader effort to reclaim America for God. This is a lie. Christian nationalism is a contradiction in terms: Paul told the Galatians, "There is neither Jew nor Gentile, neither slave nor free, nor is there male and female, for you are all one in Christ Jesus. If you belong to Christ, then you are Abraham's seed, and heirs according to the promise." This assurance—that anyone who accepts Christ becomes a part of the Abrahamic family, residents of the promised New Jerusalem—transcends all known racial, ethnic, and national identities. This is why Paul wrote so explicitly to the people in Philippi, a Roman colony full of soldiers and state officials, imploring the Christians there to pledge allegiance to Christ alone. "Their destiny is destruction, their god is their stomach, and their glory is in their shame. Their mind is set on earthly things," Paul warned of those who would reject his plea. "But our citizenship is in heaven."

There is nothing here to reclaim. This country—a drop in the bucket, like all the nations—was never God's to begin with, because "God does not show favoritism," as Peter said, "but accepts from every nation the one who fears him and does what is right." Attempts to devise some divine conception of the United States often end up demonstrating exactly the opposite. Take, for example, an Independence Day 2023 tweet from Josh Hawley, the disgraced Missouri senator whose lies and deceptive parliamentary maneuverings helped set in motion the violence of January 6. Celebrating the holiday with a "quote" from Patrick Henry, the senator tweeted: "It cannot be emphasized too strongly or too often that this great nation was founded, not by religionists, but by Christians; not on religions, but on the Gospel of Jesus Christ." It might have been humiliating enough for Hawley to learn that the founding father never spoke or wrote these words; what should have been downright mortifying was to realize, as the historian Seth Cotlar documented, that these words actually originated in a notoriously antisemitic and white-nationalist publication, the *Virginian*, 150 years after Henry's death.

Hawley never bothered to apologize for the error. And why would he? The way many of his constituents see it, secular progressives, in their quest to destroy America's Christian heritage, stopped playing by the rules a long time ago. Fire must be fought with fire. Standards must be suspended. A winner-takes-all mentality must be embraced. When the conservative activist (and future Trump administration official) Michael Anton wrote his 2016 essay, "The Flight 93 Election," he argued that leftists had hijacked America; the only chance for its survival was if conservatives rushed the cockpit, knowing full well that they might just crash the plane themselves. Notably absent from that essay was any reference to Christ, or to Christianity, or even to God. And yet the argument Anton makes—that imminent destruction justifies the unthinkable acts that may themselves lead to imminent destruction—has come to define the modern religious right.

"I think there are two virtues: loyalty and confidentiality," Mike Huckabee, the Baptist preacher turned governor and two-time presidential candidate, said on Newsmax in the spring of 2023. "Be loyal to the people who helped you and learn how to keep your mouth shut."

Naturally, in this context, Huckabee was discussing Donald Trump. The former president had just held at a campaign rally in Waco, Texas—not coincidentally, the site of a deadly showdown with the federal government—after announcing that he was about to be arrested for the first of a string of criminal indictments. There was a time when Huckabee, who once authored a book, *Character IS the Issue: How People with Integrity Can Revolutionize America*, believed, well, that people with integrity can revolutionize America. Not anymore. The same night as his mafioso soliloquy on Newsmax, Huckabee announced on his own Trinity Broadcasting Network program that he was endorsing Trump for president in 2024. Not because he was a righteous leader, much less a religious one—the former president couldn't find John 3:16 if he tried, Huckabee quipped—but because he fought with the same ferocity as his enemies. It was this impious man, Huckabee said, who on behalf of Christians endured "never-ending persecutions and prosecutions of the demonic deep state."

Huckabee at least had the decency to hedge on Trump's holiness before depicting him as a sacrificial lamb for the modern Church. The same couldn't be said for his contemporaries.

"President Trump is joining some of the most incredible people in history, being arrested today," Georgia congresswoman Marjorie Taylor Greene declared on Right Side Broadcasting, live from New York, on the morning of Trump's arraignment. After mentioning Nelson

Mandela, she cried out: "Jesus! Jesus was arrested and murdered by the Roman government."

"President Trump will be arrested during Lent—a time of suffering and purification for the followers of Jesus Christ," tweeted Joseph D. McBride, the attorney who gained prominence for his defense of several January 6 rioters. "As Christ was crucified, and then rose again on the 3rd day, so too will @realDonaldTrump."

The response from Trump's evangelical allies was every bit as predictable. Paula White beseeched Christians to pray for Trump, saying Americans should be "appalled by the weaponization of the judicial system." Franklin Graham denounced the "politicized" effort to hold Trump accountable for his actions, calling it "a shameful day for America." (Around that time, Graham also praised Taylor Greene's "common sense" approach, adding, "It will be interesting to see how God uses her.") Robert Jeffress, who had delivered the invocation at Trump's Waco rally, reacted to news of the second indictment by traveling to the former president's club in Bedminster, New Jersey, a show of solidarity as the walls began to close in. In reaction to the third indictment later that summer—which quoted Trump disparaging his then–vice president, Mike Pence, for being "too honest" after he refused to sabotage the Constitution to keep them in office—Richard Land, the former president of the Ethics and Religious Liberty Commission, accused the Justice Department of waging "jihad" against Trump.

By this point the religious right had closed ranks around its champion. A *New York Times*/Siena poll of the Republican primary showed that 76 percent of white evangelicals believed Trump had not committed any serious crime; according to a Marist survey, 81 percent of white evangelicals held a favorable impression of Trump, and 67 percent said they planned to vote for him in the upcoming Republican presidential primary. The exhaustion voters had expressed earlier in the year, when a majority of evangelicals signaled their preference to find a new Republican standard-bearer, had since vanished. The greater Trump's criminal difficulties—he faced charges for falsifying business records related to the hush money paid to his porn-star paramour, illegally taking national-security secrets to his Florida home (and obstructing justice in the ensuing investigation), and attempting to overthrow the

2020 election, all while fighting a civil case for rape and defamation—the greater his support from evangelical Christians.

When a fourth indictment landed in August 2023—charging Trump and eighteen codefendants with criminal racketeering, part of a coordinated conspiracy to overturn the election results—the most telling response belonged to Jenna Ellis. The former Trump lawyer had spun a documented web of deceptions; she was even censured by a judge after admitting to a propagating a dangerous series of falsehoods. For an outspoken evangelical Christian, this might have been a moment to model humility and repentance. Instead, Ellis took to Twitter promoting her legal defense fund—Trump wouldn't assist with her fees, on account that she'd endorsed DeSantis for president—and captioned her mugshot photo with scripture, performative piety in the face of supposed persecution. I was reminded of the words Ellis wrote in a 2016 Facebook post, back when she opposed Trump, that slammed the candidate and his supporters for their aversion to honesty. "And this is the cumulative reason why this nation is in such terrible shape," Ellis wrote. "We don't have truth seekers; we have narcissists."

Whether or not Trump would go on to represent the Republican Party in November 2024—whether or not Trump would win a rematch with Biden and move back into the White House—his legacy in the sweep of western Christendom was already secure. More than any figure in American history, the forty-fifth president transformed *evangelical* from spiritual signifier into political punch line, exposing the selective morality and ethical inconsistency and rank hypocrisy that had for so long lurked in the subconscious of the movement. To be fair, this slow-motion reputational collapse predated Trump; he did not author the cultural insecurities of the Church. But he did identify them, and prey upon them, in ways that have accelerated the unraveling of institutional Christianity in the United States.

Since 1944, the Gallup polling organization has asked Americans whether they believe in God. That number remained north of 90 percent for much of the past century; as recently as 2016, a full 89 percent of Americans responded in the affirmative. In 2022, that number reached an all-time low of 81 percent. That same year, the General Social Survey poll, which has analyzed religious trends since 1972, published the semicentennial anniversary of its research. The conclusions were breathtaking: Fifty years ago, only 9 percent of Americans said they "never" attended worship services, but by 2022 that number had reached 33 percent. These and other findings are consistent with years of social science that demonstrate the historic pace at which Americans are abandoning religion. In 2007, the percentage of Americans who claimed no faith affiliation—commonly called the "nones"—was estimated at 16 percent; by 2021, according to the Pew Research Center, it was 30 percent. If that trajectory holds, people who claim no religious affiliation will represent a majority of the American population within two generations. Meanwhile, reflexive distrust of the Church, long a phenomenon on the left, is newly ascendant on the right. An August 2023 poll from CBS News and YouGov found that only 44 percent of Republican primary voters trust what religious leaders tell them is the truth; among the Trump supporters who were polled, that number was just 42 percent, compared to 71 percent of those same respondents who said they trusted *Trump* to tell them the truth.

From a purely organizational standpoint, Christianity is in disarray. Pastors are becoming an endangered species: According to Barna Research, one-third of pastors were under the age of forty in the 1990s, whereas today that number is 16 percent. Denominations are imploding in real time. The United Methodist Church has effectively split into two new entities, forcing thousands of individual congregations to permanently fracture over social and theological disagreements. The Southern Baptist Convention has continued to bleed its affiliate churches—in some cases because congregants perceive the denomination to be too aggressive in policing racism, misogyny, and sexual assault, and in other cases, because they perceive it to be not aggressive enough. The Presbyterian Church of America (PCA), one of the nation's largest denominations, voted recently to leave the National Association of Evangelicals. My home denomination, the Evangelical Presbyterian Church—further to the right, theologically and otherwise, than the PCA—has begun discussing whether to jettison *Evangelical* from its title.

That won't happen anytime soon. Too many older Christians have their identity wrapped up in the label to let it go, no matter how damaging the connotations. And make no mistake: The damage is significant.

In March 2023, the Pew Research Center published a major survey on the perceptions of faith traditions in America. The findings helped to quantify what was already apparent: Evangelicals are the most disliked group. This does not reflect some sweeping anti-Christian bias. The perception of Catholics and mainline Protestants was, among secular respondents, still a net positive, while those same respondents registered overwhelmingly negative feelings toward evangelicals. (On the bright side, evangelicals still held positive views of themselves; as the *Christianity Today* headline reassured: "Evangelicals Are the Most Beloved US Faith Group among Evangelicals.")

At an individual level, many Christians have already commenced a rebranding exercise. Just like those erstwhile fundamentalists who switched to embrace evangelicalism fifty years ago—fearful that their tradition had become culturally irrelevant—today's evangelicals are searching for a new designation. A body of recent polling has shown a surge in the number of Christians who self-identify as mainline Protestants—and a corollary drop in those who call themselves evangelicals. (Some go by "ex-vangelical.") This represents a sea change in religious subculture. Evangelicalism has been ascendant since the founding of the nation. Now more white Protestants are identifying with the mainline tradition than with the evangelical Church.

Why?

Speaking only for myself, the answer is obvious: *Evangelical* has become an impediment to *evangelizing*. The people to whom we are witnessing—our friends, neighbors, coworkers—are completely and categorically repelled by that word. They sense that it has nothing to do with the teachings of Christ and everything to do with social and political power. That perception must inform our reality. We are called to be followers of Jesus; we are called to make disciples of all the nations. If we allow a word to get in the way of that great commission—a man-made construct, a marker of tribal belonging more than theological conviction—then we will answer to God for our pride.

SEVERAL DECADES AGO, PASTOR WINANS TOLD US, A PHILOSOPHER named James Carse offered a novel take on the academic debate surrounding game theory. Unlike the mathematicians and military strategists who'd adapted this discipline to their own fields, Carse was interested in understanding sociology and existentialism. In his 1986 book, *Finite and Infinite Games*, Carse argued that man's approach to the world around him typically fits one of these two categories.

Finite games are defined by several criteria: known players, fixed rules, and a zero-sum objective. Think of a baseball game. Spectators cannot enter from the stands and begin pitching for the home team, nor can the pitcher move the mound to third base. The objective—in baseball, as in all finite games—is to defeat an opponent, and every game concludes with a winner and a loser.

Infinite games, on the other hand, are defined by the opposite criteria. There are known *and* unknown players. The rules are flexible and can change. The objective is to constantly improve, to be better than one's own self, because the game has no conclusion. Education is an obvious example: There is no winning at education; only learning, growing, maturing.

"I want to suggest to you this morning that the Church is an infinite game," Winans said. "But the believer will be tempted to approach the Church in a finite way."

Echoing the vivid contrast Paul offered up in his second letter to the Corinthians, the pastor asked his congregation to consider the purpose of the Church in the context of three questions relating to the finite and the infinite.

First: Who are the players?

Some Christians operate as though the players are known, Winans said, hence the segregated framing of believers versus unbelievers, Republicans versus Democrats, and so on. This is nothing new. Winans reminded us that Jonah wound up in the belly of the whale because he refused God's command to go and preach to the violent, godless, wicked people of Nineveh. They were *not* known players; they had no place in Jonah's finite view of God's kingdom. Only after he repented, traveled to Nineveh, and won many souls there could Jonah comprehend the infinite nature of God's design. It was the same story in the first century, Winans added, when Jesus was chastised by religious elites— and second-guessed by his own disciples—for engaging with sinners, ethnic enemies, people who were supposedly unwelcome to the game. What the critics didn't understand is that while Jesus was offering an exclusive path to salvation, the offer itself was not exclusionary. To this day, consciously or subconsciously, Christians possess a limited view of God's kingdom. We tend to think of the Church as a castle with high walls, Winans explained, when Jesus made clear that He was building a hospital to make sick people well. "We dare not think that we know who the right and wrong people are," the pastor said, his voice stern. "The gospel goes out to *everyone*."

Second: What are the rules?

One reason many Christians are reluctant to engage with these unknown players, Winans said, is because they are rigid in their ways. The modern evangelical movement has assumed that Christians ought to talk a certain way, keep certain company, and observe certain boundaries if they are to properly witness for Christ. But the New Testament model demands just the opposite. Jesus's disciples spoke of the need to adapt to their environments and meet people where they were at, instead of forcing every prospective convert into the same box. Winans reminded us how Peter invoked the Jewish prophets and traditions when preaching to the Jews at Pentecost, while Paul appealed to Greek cultural customs when evangelizing the Athenians. Their message stayed the same—and to be clear, Winans emphasized, our message *always* stays the same—but their methods were constantly evolving. If Christians are to make disciples in a changing world, we must be willing to break from the strictures that have stifled the Church's outreach to the unknown players. "We are increasingly in a post-Christian culture," Winans said. "We need to be flexible in order to effectively embody and proclaim the gospel to the culture that we exist in today."

Third: Why are we playing?

In a finite game, the Church's objective would be to defeat a competitor. Except that Christians believe that the battle is already won: Unlike Adam, who gave in to the devil's temptation and doomed mankind to an existence of sin and death, Jesus resisted Satan in the wilderness, conquered the grave, and in so doing extended redemption and eternal life for all of Adam's descendants. Because of this, the objective of the

Church is infinite: to shed our earthly selves, to become sanctified, to transform more into the likeness of Christ. "We don't *win* at holiness," Winans said. Instead, "We strive to become more mature and become better than ourselves."

The pastor had preached a fine sermon—innovative, unambiguous, well executed. He could have stopped there. But Winans chose not to.

Expanding on that final point, Winans asked us to compare two theoretical versions of the Church. In the infinite version, he explained, "the goal of the Church is to be a faithful presence for Jesus in the culture." In the finite version, "the goal is to win the culture wars." When Winans said this, I glanced around the pews nervously, uncertain if he was planning to take this to the place where I suspected he was headed. Sure enough.

"Let's think of this through the lens of an issue—an issue that's near and dear to many people in this congregation. The issue of abortion," Winans said. He affirmed his own view: that life begins at conception, that God knows souls before they are knit together in their mothers' wombs, that human life is made in His own divine image. Several people shouted, "Amen!" And then the crowd fell silent. Too many evangelicals have taken a finite approach to abortion, the pastor said, trying to "win through the electing of particular political people so they can write certain kinds of civic laws." Winans conceded that there are political and legal implications to the question of abortion. "But we're talking about the nature of the *Church*," he said. "The issue of abortion is not primarily legal or political. The issue of abortion is spiritual."

There is a reason the culture wars become a quagmire for Christians. Even if they elect the right politicians and pass the right laws—and the meaning of "right" looks very different to believers in Brighton, Winans said, than it does to the brothers and sisters at their affiliated church in nearby Flint—they are *still* not winning, because they are playing the wrong game.

I was stunned. In the space of a few minutes, the senior pastor of Cornerstone Evangelical Presbyterian Church had dismantled the finite worldview that beckons to his congregants—his wealthy, white, conservative Republican congregants—and challenged them to embrace the infinite.

My heart responded with delight. But my head registered disappointment—not in Winans, or in his sermon, but at the thought of all the people who would never hear it.

To be clear, there are still thousands of healthy, vibrant churches across this country, places that have their gospel priorities straight and lean into the tradition of discipling with hard truths. And yet, from everything I have seen, most Christians in America have no interest in being provoked this way from the pulpit. They have become captive to a cultural religion; they have self-selected into theological milieus that either reaffirm their existing dogmas or leave them undefiled. In Brighton alone, countless numbers of congregants had quit churches like Cornerstone and defected to a God-and-country roadside jamboree called FloodGate. (A few weeks after my visit to Cornerstone, FloodGate hosted an event—admission was $99 plus fees—featuring, among other headliners, a tomahawk-toting "Patriot Streetfighter" named Scott McKay, as well as Patrick Byrne, the former Overstock CEO who traffics in gratuitous f-bombs and conspiracies about the feds trying to eliminate him.) I grieved for the people over there, just down the road that very morning, consumed with the finite concerns of this fallen world.

More immediately, however, I worried about the people *here.* I could sense an uneasiness in the crowd at Cornerstone. Winans clearly felt emboldened by the makeover of his congregation—by how healthy the church was compared with a few years earlier—yet so many hazards remained. This was still Brighton. This was still *America.* Another election was coming, and inevitably Winans would at some point alienate portions of his flock with a message that calls for aiding and abetting the political enemy. Some of the folks around me were already uncomfortable; certain visibly perturbed members would no doubt go home grumbling about that woke lefty, Pastor Winans, and pining for the days of Pastor Alberta, who never would have preached that sermon. (Indeed, one member confronted Winans afterward, demanding to know why he'd given people permission to vote for Democrats.)

My father's death had ushered me into an age of gnawing unknowns. How would he have handled the hostility around COVID-19 shutdowns and the election of 2020? What would he think of me writing a book about the crack-up of the Church? Why did I have to wait until he was gone to pursue a master's degree at seminary—and where would he have encouraged me to apply? Each and every day I had wrestled with a ghost. The only thing harder than heeding the example of a good and godly man was to question whether it might yet be improved upon.

Praying silently that Sunday morning, alone in the balcony of my childhood church, I was overcome with a sense of assurance. My anxieties could rest. God, as a wise preacher once said, doesn't bite His fingernails. Those malcontents were right: Dad never would have preached that sermon. He wasn't *capable* of preaching that sermon. Which is exactly why he chose Chris Winans to be his successor: Dad understood that while his own ministry was finite, the work of Cornerstone was infinite. He had grown this congregation from several hundred people to several thousand. Now came a different season of growth. And when it was time for Winans to move on—after a quarter century of his own, I hoped—the church would grow anew.

"Lord, I pray that we would not fall into the trap of thinking we know who the right or the wrong people are; that we would extend the mercy and grace, the forgiveness and the message of Jesus, to everyone," Winans said, bowing his head. "And, Lord, may we be on mission to be a faithful presence, to communicate the gospel, that all who hear may turn and be healed."

The congregation stood for a benediction. Returning to his prefatory passage, Winans recited the apostle Paul's words from the Second Book of Corinthians, chapter four, verse eighteen.

"So we fix our eyes not on what is seen, but on what is unseen, since what is seen is temporary, but what is unseen is eternal."

Amen.

ACKNOWLEDGMENTS

For much of my life I have struggled to fathom the dimensions of God's mercy. How could it be that the maker of heaven and earth, the Alpha and the Omega, the ruler of the cosmos, thinks me significant enough to even pay attention—much less to lavish me with unconditional love? The answer, I've come to appreciate more fully, is revealed not in the codes of a religion but in the context of a relationship. The way I treasure and adore my sons—and the way my dad treasured and adored me—is how the heavenly Father treasures and adores us. He is generous beyond measure and gracious beyond comprehension, the original archetype of parental love. Yet the bond is not strictly paternalistic. God also gifted the world a Son. In so doing, He provided us the ultimate big brother: one who sets the example we must emulate, one who always has our back and never abandons us. It is only because of this relationship—with God the Father, with Jesus Christ His only Son, and with the Holy Spirit imparted through faith and repentance—that I am able to communicate, however imperfectly, the perfection of the gospel. I have endeavored to honor God with this book. If anything in these pages fails to do so, I pray that He brings it to nothing, and that He carries to completion the good work He has begun. Thank you, Jesus. I love you.

Some time ago, an astute friend asked if I'd ever considered what my life might look like had my father not converted to Christianity before I was born. He was probing the broader implications of a counterfactual childhood: How different might I be had I grown up in New York City, the son of a financier, instead of in small-town Michigan as a pastor's kid? What I heard, however, was a narrower question, one that haunts me to this day: Would I have become a Christian *on my own*? I want to believe the answer is yes; I want to believe that God would have opened my eyes to His truth. But I fear the answer is no; I fear the arrogance and pride I have in such abundance would have hardened my heart. Not a day goes by, then, that I don't thank God for my father—for his faith, for his conviction, for his integrity, for his bravery, and for his love. My dad was a flawed dude. He made his share of mistakes. But he taught me how to be a good husband, a good father, and a good neighbor. Most important, he showed me how to live for Christ. Thanks for everything, Pop. I love you. And I miss you.

We are assured in scripture, time and again, that all of humanity is broken; that every person sins and consistently falls short of God's standard. I've had but one reason to ever doubt this doctrine: my mother. Simply put, I have never encountered anyone who embodies love, joy, peace, patience, kindness, goodness, faithfulness, gentleness, and self-control in the way that Donna Rae Alberta does. I have been blessed to know and learn from some truly extraordinary Christians. But the very first blessing—the very first person from whom I learned about Christ—was my mother. No words can articulate what she means to me, what she means to my wife and sons, and what she has meant to this story. Thank you, Mom. I'll love you forever.

One of the Old Testament's most poignant passages is found in the Book of Ruth: "Where you go I will go, and where you stay I will stay. Your people will be my people and your God my God." This verse is sometimes invoked to celebrate nuptial loyalty, but in fact Ruth spoke these words to her mother-in-law, Naomi. In this older woman's moment of deep uncertainty and vulnerability, Ruth promises that she will not be forsaken. This is more than a devotion born out of familial duty; it is a love styled after God's own. My wife has demonstrated this love in ways that defy explanation. Not only did she propose moving to Michigan after my father died, channeling her inner Ruth, but she charged into the work of building us a community, COVID-19 be damned, finding a church and a Christian school for her family while stepping up to provide every form of support my mother could possibly need. She also gamely signed onto her husband writing a book that would continually take him away from home, leaving her unaided to manage three rambunctious boys, a full-time job, a psychotic dog, and a childcare dilemma that proved impossible to resolve. I am awestruck. And I find myself falling more in love with her every day. She is the very manifestation of Proverbs 31: "Her children arise and call her blessed; her husband also, and he praises her: 'Many women do noble things, but you surpass them all.'" Sweta, you are my rock. You are my best friend. You are the headline of my heart. I love you.

I do not deserve my three sons. They are pure and compassionate and kindhearted in ways that make me wake up every day wanting to be a better man. The patience they have shown their father throughout this process—all the weekends he was traveling, all the long days he spent secluded in his office—reveals a maturity of character that makes me, if even possible, all the prouder of them. Still, it has come at a cost. I know that those countless hours we could have spent together are ones we will never get back. I can only hope that one day these boys will understand the sacrifices that were made and why they were necessary. Abraham, Lewis, Brooks: You guys are the light of my life. Thank you for bringing me such happiness. Always remember who you are and whose you are. And never forget that while I constantly strive to model the very best behavior for you, the true standard is set by Jesus. My prayer is that you will follow Him and Him alone. I love you, Abraham. I love you, Lewis. I love you, Brooks.

What can I say about my three big brothers, except that they were no help with this book whatsoever? Just kidding. (Well, I mean, they *weren't*; but I *can* say other things about them.) One thing our father never had was a stable home life; he had no meaningful relationship with his brothers, something that always gnawed at him. I feel fortunate to have brothers who know the enduring importance of family and who love my children as their own. I feel all the more fortunate to have a brother-in-law who personifies honor and decency. Chris, J.J., Brian, Rudy: If you guys have defied the odds and read this far, know that you have my love and my respect.

I'm fortunate to have some great friends who have kept me company (and kept me sane) throughout this process. No need to name names; you guys know who you are. Thanks for being a part of our extended family.

Now that I've checked off the loved ones—without even mentioning my wife's parents, or my sisters-in-law, or my nieces and nephews, or my aunts and uncles and cousins, all of whom mean a great deal to me— it's time to salute the people who really made this book happen.

I first need to thank Jonathan Jao, my editor, partner, and friend, who understood my ambition with this book and encouraged me to hold nothing back. I'm immensely grateful to Matt Latimer and Keith Urbahn, my agents at Javelin, for first recommending Jonathan to me all those years ago and for continuing to support our efforts here. I owe a special debt to my Catholic comrade and dear friend, Jim O'Sullivan, who not only provided invaluable feedback at every stage of writing but inspired me with his faith and courage in the face of tragedy. Additionally, I cannot overstate the excellence of my fact-checkers—and *Atlantic* colleagues—Jack Segelstein and Sam Fentress, who were characteristically relentless in catching mistakes, throwing up red flags, and generally saving me from embarrassment. Speaking of which, I must acknowledge Bill Adams for his exacting legal guidance. I'm also thankful for the hard work done by so many others at HarperCollins: David Howe and David Koral for their steady hand and considerable patience in getting this through production; Theresa Dooley and Tina Andreadis for their help with all things marketing and promotion; and Sean Desmond, who swooped in during crunch time and offered calming counsel when it was much needed.

This project would not have been possible without the support of my world-class colleagues at *The Atlantic*. I'm particularly appreciative of Jeff Goldberg, who pushed me to do the reading and research necessary to better ground my own reporting, and Denise Wills, who labored alongside me in shaping the magazine story that formed the thematic backbone of this book. Jeff and Denise gave me a dream job; they also provided encouragement and empathy at critical junctures. I'm lucky to call them both my friends. I'm also lucky to work every day with the likes of Adrienne LaFrance, Yoni Appelbaum, Amy Weiss-Meyer, Margy Slattery, Andrew Aoyama, Yvonne Rolzhausen, Janicy Wolly, Anna Bross, and too many others to name here.

I was advised, because the acknowledgments in my first book were so, ahem, *comprehensive*, that I need not again thank every single human being I've ever worked with or learned from. For brevity's sake, I've taken that advice. I just want all my erstwhile colleagues—from the *Wall Street Journal* to *The Hotline*, *National Journal* to *National Review*, *Politico* to *Politico Magazine*—to know how much they mean to me.

On January 10, 2023, I lost a close friend and cherished collaborator: Blake Hounshell. Man, what I would have given for a chat with Blake as the deadlines came crashing down around me this summer and fall. We would have compared notes about our mental health. We would have swapped funny stories about our kids. He would have made a breezy suggestion that revolutionized a rough passage of my writing, and I would have told him that I owe him a beer. The world of journalism—and the world as I know it, period—will never be quite the same without Blake. I take comfort in the knowledge that his light shines on through his wife, Sandy, and their beautiful children, David and Astrid. I pray for them to continually know a peace that surpasses all understanding. And I pray that everyone reading this, especially those who are struggling, remembers that they have inherent, immeasurable worth in the eyes of their creator. Rest in peace, Blake.

I have been blessed during this journey to come into contact with some wonderful, godly people who have sustained me with their prayers. Here again there are too many of them to list (and, frankly, given the brain fog that accompanies this phase of the process, I would almost certainly omit an important name!). But I do want to recognize two people who have meant a great deal to me. The first is someone I've never met: Fr. Mike Schmitz, who, our doctrinal disagreements notwithstanding, provided wisdom, humor, and sharp assessments with his *Bible in a Year* podcast. What a gift, indeed.

The second is someone who has become like a brother: Tyson Lemke. Finding a church home isn't easy for a guy with my institutional baggage; finding a pastor to trust, to take instruction from, to be shepherded by, is that much harder. God truly does work all things for good. I had no idea, when we walked into Grace Bible Church for the first time, that Tyson's parents had attended Cornerstone when he was in college, or that he'd listened to my dad's sermon tapes while he was in seminary and considered him a preaching mentor from afar. All I knew was that Grace felt strangely familiar, like we'd been there before, like it was our home. And now it is. More than any one person whose counsel I sought while writing, he supplied the perspective, the pushback, and the reassurance necessary to finish this book and finish it well. Thank you, Pastor Ty, for everything you've done for me—and for all you continue to do for the Kingdom.

Last but not least—in fact, we are in first place as I write these very words, coming off a season-opening win against the defending champion Kansas City Chiefs—is my first true love, the Detroit Lions. The last time I "thanked" the Lions was in the fall of 2018, when their putrid performances freed more of my Sunday afternoons for the completion of *American Carnage.* This time around, having spent portions of the summer covering training camp and writing about this team's significance to generations of my family, I want to thank Dan Campbell and Brad Holmes for building a contender and restoring this fan's hope. *Forward down the field!*

NOTES

CHAPTER ONE

Hernandez, Noe. "From Clubs to Christ: One Local Pastor's Journey of Faith." *Livingston Daily*, April 10, 2016, https://www.livingstondaily.com/story/news/local /community/brighton-township/2016/04/10/clubs-christ-one-local-pastors -journey-faith/82664118/.

LeBlanc, Beth. "Whitmer Bans Large Gatherings, Including at Churches and Casinos, to Fight Spread of Virus." *Detroit News*, March 13, 2020, https://www.detroitnews .com/story/news/local/michigan/2020/03/13/whitmer-bans-gatherings-larger -than-250-people-prevent-spread-covid-19/5042130002/.

Washington, George. "From George Washington to the United Baptist Churches of Virginia, May 1789." National Archives, https://founders.archives.gov/documents /Washington/05-02-02-0309.

CHAPTER TWO

Johnson, Mark. "Slow and Steady Wins the Race at Goodwill Church, Montgomery, NY." Church Production, https://www.churchproduction.com/education/slow _and_steady_wins_the_race_at_goodwill_church_montgomery_ny/.

Vindman, Yevgeny. "Russia's Butchers of Bucha Aren't True Soldiers. They Are Barbarians Murdering Civilians." *USA Today*, April 9, 2022, https://www.usatoday .com/story/opinion/columnists/2022/04/09/russias-war-crimes-spill-blood -innocent-ukrainians/7262765001/?gnt-cfr=1.

Warburton, Moira. "U.S. Senate Unanimously Condemns Putin as War Criminal." Reuters, March 15, 2022, https://www.reuters.com/world/us/us-senate-unanimously -condemns-putin-war-criminal-2022-03-15/.

Winsor, Morgan, et al. "Cuomo Extends New York Statewide Stay-At-Home Order until June 13." ABC News, May 14, 2020, https://abcnews.go.com/Health/coronavirus -updates-police-arrest-woman-selling-approved-covid/story?id=70675027.

CHAPTER THREE

Ambrosino, Brandon. "'Someone's Gotta Tell the Freakin' Truth': Jerry Falwell's Aides Break Their Silence." *Politico*, September 9, 2019, https://www.politico .com/magazine/story/2019/09/09/jerry-falwell-liberty-university-loans-227 914/.

Bailey, Sarah Pulliam. "Jerry Falwell Jr.: 'If More Good People Had Concealed-Carry Permits, Then We Could End Those' Islamist Terrorists." *Washington Post*, December 5, 2015, https://www.washingtonpost.com/news/acts-of-faith/wp /2015/12/05/liberty-university-president-if-more-good-people-had-concealed -guns-we-could-end-those-muslims/.

Ballmer, Randall. "The Real Origins of the Religious Right." *Politico*, May 27, 2014,

https://www.politico.com/magazine/story/2014/05/religious-right-real
-origins-107133/.

Bedard, Paul. "Falwell Says *Fatal Attraction* Threat Led to Depression." *Washington Examiner*, August 23, 2020, https://www.washingtonexaminer.com/washington
-secrets/exclusive-falwell-says-fatal-attraction-threat-led-to-depression.

Collins, Eliza. "Christian Leaders Balk at Falwell's Trump Endorsement." *Politico*, January 26, 2016, https://www.politico.com/story/2016/01/jerry-falwell-jr
-endorses-trump-218238.

Dreyfus, Hannah. "'The Liberty Way': How Liberty University Discourages and Dismisses Students' Reports of Sexual Assaults." *ProPublica*, October 24, 2021, https://www.propublica.org/article/the-liberty-way-how-liberty-university
-discourages-and-dismisses-students-reports-of-sexual-assaults.

"Evangelical Scholars Endorse Birth Control." *Christianity Today*, September 27, 1968, https://www.christianitytoday.com/ct/1968/september-27/evangelical-scholars
-endorse-birth-control.html.

"An Interview with the Lone Ranger of American Fundamentalism." *Christianity Today*, September 4, 1981, https://www.christianitytoday.com/ct/1981/september-4
/interview-with-lone-ranger-of-american-fundamentalism.html.

Kennedy, John W. "Jerry Falwell's Uncertain Legacy." *Christianity Today*, December 9, 1996, https://www.christianitytoday.com/ct/1996/december9/jerry-falwell
-uncertain-legacy.html.

Legg, Kathryn. "Equal in His Sight: An Examination of the Evolving Opinions on Race in the Life of Jerry Falwell, Sr." Liberty University, Fall 2019, https://
digitalcommons.liberty.edu/cgi/viewcontent.cgi?article=2002&context=honors.

Lindsey, Sue. "Jerry Falwell Marks 50 Years at Thomas Road Pulpit." *Washington Post*, July 1, 2006, https://www.washingtonpost.com/archive/local/2006/07/01/jerry
-falwell-marks-50-years-at-thomas-road-pulpit-span-classbankheadcontroversial
-pastors-church-has-grown-from-35-to-24000span/1b1df8a7-cb75-459c-8a29
-288c2776c99e/.

Miller, Emily McFarlan. "Liberty University Board Member Resigns over Trump Endorsement." Religion News Service, May 5, 2016, https://religionnews.com
/2016/05/05/mark-demoes-liberty-board-trump-evangelicals/.

———. "Student-Led Petition Calls for Liberty University to Close Falkirk Center, Its Political Think Tank." Religion News Service, December 30, 2020, https://religion
news.com/2020/12/30/student-led-petition-calls-for-liberty-university-to-close
-falkirk-center-its-political-think-tank/.

"Poll Finds 34% Share 'Born Again' Feeling." *New York Times*, September 26, 1976, https://www.nytimes.com/1976/09/26/archives/poll-finds-34-share-born-again
-feeling-gallup-survey-shows-that-58.html.

Roach, David. "How Southern Baptists Became Pro-Life." *Baptist Press*, January 16, 2015, https://www.baptistpress.com/resource-library/news/how-southern
-baptists-became-pro-life/.

Roston, Aram. "Business Partner of Falwells Says Affair with Evangelical Power Couple Spanned Seven Years." Reuters, August 24, 2020, https://www.reuters.com
/investigates/special-report/usa-falwell-relationship/.

Roys, Julie. "Former Liberty University Chairman Hints He Was Demoted For Speaking Out About Trump." *Roys Report*, November 15, 2021, https://julieroys
.com/chairman-liberty-university-demoted-speaking-out-trump/.

Rucker, Philip. "Jerry Falwell Jr.'s Trump Endorsement Draws Objections from His Late Father's Confidant." *Washington Post*, March 1, 2016, https://www.washingtonpost
.com/news/post-politics/wp/2016/03/01/jerry-falwell-jr-s-trump-endorsement
-draws-objections-from-his-late-fathers-confidant/.

Scheer, Robert. "Playboy Interview: Jimmy Carter." *Playboy*, November 1, 1976, https://www.playboy.com/read/playboy-interview-jimmy-carter.

Sherman, Gabriel. "Inside Jerry Falwell Jr.'s Unlikely Rise and Precipitous Fall at Liberty University." *Vanity Fair*, January 24, 2022, https://www.vanityfair.com/news/2022/01/inside-jerry-falwell-jr-unlikely-rise-and-precipitous-fall.

"Southern Baptists Approve Abortion in Certain Cases." *New York Times*, June 3, 1971, https://www.nytimes.com/1971/06/03/archives/southern-baptists-approve-abortion-in-certain-cases.html.

CHAPTER FOUR

Campbell, Kay. "Russell Moore Chosen as President of Southern Baptists' Ethics and Religious Liberty Commission." al.com, March 27, 2013, https://www.al.com/living/2013/03/russell_moore_ethics_religious.html.

"How U.S. Religious Composition Has Changed in Recent Decades." Pew Research Center, September 13, 2022, https://www.pewresearch.org/religion/2022/09/13/how-u-s-religious-composition-has-changed-in-recent-decades/.

Kilgore, Ed. "Is Anyone Listening to Russell Moore in Iowa?" *Washington Monthly*, November 20, 2015, https://washingtonmonthly.com/2015/11/20/is-anyone-listening-to-russell-moore-in-iowa/.

Moody, Chris. "The Survival of a Southern Baptist Who Dared to Oppose Trump." CNN Politics, July 2017, https://www.cnn.com/interactive/2017/politics/state/russell-moore-donald-trump-southern-baptists/.

"Russell Moore to ERLC Trustees: They Want Me to Live in Psychological Terror." Religion News Service, June 2, 2021, https://religionnews.com/2021/06/02/russell-moore-to-erlc-trustees-they-want-me-to-live-in-psychological-terror/.

Smietana, Bob. "Beth Moore Says She's No Longer Southern Baptist." *Christianity Today*, March 9, 2021, https://www.christianitytoday.com/news/2021/march/beth-moore-leave-southern-baptist-sbc-lifeway-abuse-trump.html.

———. "SBC Calls Never-Trumper Russell Moore's Agency a 'Significant Distraction.'" Religion News Service, February 1, 2021, https://religionnews.com/2021/02/01/report-calls-agency-led-by-never-trumper-russell-moore-a-significant-distraction-for-southern-baptists/.

CHAPTER FIVE

Gryboski, Michael. "Texas Megachurch Pastor Says Obama Will 'Pave Way' for Antichrist." *Christian Post*, November 8, 2012, https://www.christianpost.com/news/texas-megachurch-pastor-says-obama-will-pave-way-for-antichrist.html.

Jones, Robert P., and Daniel Cox. "Clinton Maintains Double-Digit Lead (51% vs. 36%) over Trump." PRRI, October 19, 2016. http://www.prri.org/research/prri-brookings-oct-19-poll-politics-election-clinton-double-digit-lead-trump/.

Mooney, Michael J. "Trump's Apostle." *Texas Monthly*, August 2019, https://www.texasmonthly.com/news-politics/donald-trump-defender-dallas-pastor-robert-jeffress/.

Newport, Frank. "Why Are Americans Losing Confidence in Organized Religion?" Gallup, July 16, 2019, https://news.gallup.com/opinion/polling-matters/260738/why-americans-losing-confidence-organized-religion.aspx.

"Pastor Robert Jeffress Explains His Support for Trump." NPR, October 16, 2016, https://www.npr.org/2016/10/16/498171498/pastor-robert-jeffress-explains-his-support-for-trump.

Priest, Jessica, and Jeremy Schwartz. "Churches Are Breaking the Law and Endorsing in Elections, Experts Say. The IRS Looks the Other Way." *Texas Tribune*, October 30, 2022, https://www.texastribune.org/2022/10/30/johnson-amendment-elections-irs/.

——. "These 20 Churches Supported Political Candidates. Experts Say They Violated Federal Law. " *Texas Tribune*, November 7, 2022, https://www.texastribune.org/2022 /11/07/churches-list-violations-johnson-amendment/.

Priest, Jessica, et al. " Texas Churches Violated Tax Law Ahead of Tuesday's Election, Experts Say." *Texas Tribune*, November 6, 2022, https://www.texastribune.org /2022/11/06/texas-churches-johnson-amendment-election/.

Vazquez, Maegan. "Trump Circulates Quote Invoking 'Civil War-like Fracture' If He's Removed from Office." CNN Politics, September 30, 2019, https://www.cnn .com/2019/09/30/politics/donald-trump-civil-war-impeachment/index.html.

Weiner, Rachel. "Robert Jeffress Endorses Rick Perry, Says Mormonism Is a 'Cult.'" *Washington Post*, October 7, 2011, https://www.washingtonpost.com/blogs /the-fix/post/values-voters-summit-liveblog/2011/10/07/gIQAMo77SL_blog .html.

CHAPTER SIX

"America's Changing Religious Landscape." Pew Research Center, May 12, 2015, https:// www.pewresearch.org/religion/2015/05/12/americas-changing-religious-landscape/.

Bechtel, Paul M. *Wheaton College: A Heritage Remembered, 1860–1984*. Wheaton, Ill: H. Shaw Publishers, 1984.

"Community Covenant." Wheaton College, https://www.wheaton.edu/about-wheaton /community-covenant/.

"Religious Affiliation in Australia." Australian Bureau of Statistics, July 4, 2022, https://www.abs.gov.au/articles/religious-affiliation-australia.

Riley, Jennifer. "Wheaton College Alumni Group Says Being Gay Is Not a Sin." *Christian Post*, May 5, 2011, https://www.christianpost.com/news/wheaton-college-alumni -group-says-being-gay-is-not-a-sin.html.

Turnbull, Tiffany. "Australia Census: Five Ways the Country Is Changing." BBC News, June 28, 2022, https://www.bbc.com/news/world-australia-61961744.

Wolfe, Alan. "The Opening of the Evangelical Mind." *The Atlantic*, October 2000, https://www.theatlantic.com/magazine/archive/2000/10/the-opening-of-the -evangelical-mind/378388/.

CHAPTER SEVEN

Epps, Garrett. "Genuine Christian Scholars Smack Down an Unruly Colleague." *The Atlantic*, August 10, 2012, https://www.theatlantic.com/national/archive/2012 /08/genuine-christian-scholars-smack-down-an-unruly-colleague/260 994/.

HarperCollins Publishers. "Thomas Nelson: A History of Growth and Transformation." https://200.hc.com/stories/thomas-nelson-growth/.

Oak Pointe Church. "Conversations Series Follow-Up: A Letter from Pastor Bob." July 11, 2020, https://www.oakpointe.org/conversations-series-follow-up-a-letter -from-pastor-bob/.

CHAPTER EIGHT

Antle, W. James, III. "'Jesus Isn't Running': Trump on Track to Secure Vital Evangelical Vote Despite Personal Flaws." *Washington Examiner*, May 10, 2020, https://www .washingtonexaminer.com/news/jesus-isnt-running-trump-on-track-to-secure -vital-evangelical-vote-despite-personal-flaws.

Brody, David. "Why Evangelicals Should Care About a Man Named Chad Connelly." CBN News, November 3, 2017, https://www1.cbn.com/thebrodyfile /archive/2017/11/03/why-evangelicals-should-care-about-a-man-named-chad -connelly.

Jones, Jeffrey M. "Belief in God in U.S. Dips to 81%, a New Low." Gallup, June 17, 2022, https://news.gallup.com/poll/393737/belief-god-dips-new-low.aspx.

———. "U.S. LGBT Identification Steady at 7.2%." Gallup, February 22, 2023, https://news.gallup.com/poll/470708/lgbt-identification-steady.aspx.

Mastrangelo, Alana. "Over 500 Pastors, Faith Leaders Gather in San Diego for Turning Point USA Faith Summit: Only Pulpits Have Power to Change America." *Breitbart*, August 17, 2022, https://www.breitbart.com/politics/2022/08/17/over-500-pastors-faith-leaders-gather-san-diego-turning-point-usa-faith-summit-only-pulpits-have-power-change-america/.

CHAPTER NINE

Barrett, Laurence I. " Fighting for God and the Right Wing: Ralph Reed." *Time*, September 13, 1993, https://web.archive.org/web/20121106061843/http://www.time.com/time/magazine/article/0,9171,979189-4,00.html.

Day, Sherri. "Questions Tarnish Rise of an Evangelist." *St. Petersburg Times*, July 15, 2007, https://web.archive.org/web/20070920131436/http://www.sptimes.com/2007/07/15/Hillsborough/Questions_tarnish_ris.shtml.

Flynn, Sean. "The Sins of Ralph Reed." *GQ*, July 11, 2006, https://www.gq.com/story/ralph-reed-gop-lobbyist-jack-abramoff.

Kertscher, Tom. "Sorting Out Police Encounters Highlighted in Ad Attacking US Senate Candidate Herschel Walker." *PolitiFact*, April 4, 2022, https://www.politifact.com/article/2022/apr/04/sorting-out-police-encounters-highlighted-ad-attac/.

Slavin, Barbara. "He Changed the Face of the Christian Coalition. Now He'd like to Give Government the Same Treatment." *Los Angeles Times*, May 1, 1995, https://www.latimes.com/archives/la-xpm-1995-05-01-ls-61050-story.html.

Sollenberger, Roger. "'Pro-Life' Herschel Walker Paid for Girlfriend's Abortion." *Daily Beast*, October 3, 2022, https://www.thedailybeast.com/pro-life-herschel-walker-paid-for-girlfriends-abortion-georgia-senate.

Zauzmer, Julie. "Paula White, Prosperity Preacher Once Investigated by Senate, Is a Controversial Pick for Inauguration Prayer." *Washington Post*, December 29, 2016, https://www.washingtonpost.com/news/acts-of-faith/wp/2016/12/29/paula-white-prosperity-preacher-once-investigated-by-senate-is-a-controversial-pick-for-inauguration-prayer/.

CHAPTER TEN

Badejo, Anita. "Ralph Reed Is Helping One Gambling Interest Fight Another—Again." *BuzzFeed*, July 16, 2014, https://www.buzzfeednews.com/article/anitabadejo/ralph-reeds-coalition-stop-internet-gambling.

Bat, John. " Hanna Becomes First GOP Congressman to Say He's Voting for Clinton." CBS News, August 2, 2016, https://www.cbsnews.com/news/republican-rep-richard-hanna-says-hell-vote-for-clinton-over-trump/.

Eberly, Don. "Fighting the Wrong Battle." *Christianity Today*, September 6, 1999, https://www.christianitytoday.com/ct/1999/september6/9ta052.html.

Epstein, Reid J. "Adam Kinzberg's Lonely Mission." *New York Times*, February 15, 2021, https://www.nytimes.com/2021/02/15/us/politics/adam-kinzinger-republicans-trump.html.

Gibney, Alex. "The Deceptions of Ralph Reed." *The Atlantic*, September 26, 2010, https://www.theatlantic.com/politics/archive/2010/09/the-deceptions-of-ralph-reed/63568/.

Peters, Jeremy. *Insurgency: How Republicans Lost Their Party and Got Everything They Ever Wanted*. New York: Crown, 2022.

Thomas, Cal. *Blinded by Might*. Nashville, TN: Zondervan Publishing House, 1998.

Yourish, Karen, et al. " The 147 Republicans Who Voted to Overturn Election Results."
New York Times, January 7, 2021, https://www.nytimes.com/interactive
/2021/01/07/us/elections/electoral-college-biden-objectors.html.

CHAPTER ELEVEN

Crump, James. "Pastor Greg Locke's Speech against 'Pedophiles in Hollywood' Viewed
over 1.5M Times." *Newsweek*, June 28, 2021, https://www.newsweek.com/pastor
-greg-locke-pedophiles-washington-dc-tom-hanks-oprah-1604725.

Humbles, Andy. "Roger Stone and Pastor Greg Locke Deliver Energetic Church Service
in Mt. Juliet." *Tennessean*, August 30, 2020, https://www.tennessean.com/story
/news/2020/08/30/roger-stone-appearance-mt-juliet-church-god-spared-my-life
-purpose/3433049001/.

Schmitt, Brad. "Target-Blasting Pastor Greg Locke Channels Anger in a New Way."
Tennessean, May 2, 2016, https://www.tennessean.com/story/news/2016/05/01
/target-blasting-pastor-greg-locke-channels-anger-new-way/83615088/.

CHAPTER TWELVE

de Carbonnel, Alissa. "Putin Signs Ban on U.S. Adoptions of Russian Children." Reuters,
December 28, 2012, https://www.reuters.com/article/us-russia-usa-adoptions
-putin/putin-signs-ban-on-u-s-adoptions-of-russian-children-idUSBRE8BQ06
K20121228.

Dhumieres, Marie. "Suffering Goes On for 330,000 Refugees of the Yugoslav War."
Independent, April 5, 2012, https://www.independent.co.uk/news/world/europe
/suffering-goes-on-for-330-000-refugees-of-the-yugoslav-war-7622108.html.

Kozelsky, Mara. "Don't Underestimate Importance of Religion for Understanding
Russia's Actions in Crimea." *Washington Post*, March 3, 2014, https://www.washington
post.com/news/monkey-cage/wp/2014/03/13/dont-underestimate-importance
-of-religion-for-understanding-russias-actions-in-crimea/.

McPherson, Hope. "Wartime Blessings." *Response*, Spring 2008, https://spu.edu/depts
/uc/response/spring2k8/features/wartime-blessings.asp.

"Meet the Russian Orthodox Army, Ukrainian Separatists' Shock Troops." NBC News,
May 16, 2014, https://www.nbcnews.com/storyline/ukraine-crisis/meet-russian
-orthodox-army-ukrainian-separatists-shock-troops-n107426.

"Russia Turns to Trucks and Big Wages to Woo Volunteer Soldiers." Al Jazeera,
September 18, 2022, https://www.aljazeera.com/news/2022/9/18/russia-turns-to
-trucks-and-big-wages-to-woo-volunteer-soldiers.

Van Brugen, Isabel. "Putin's Top Priest Tells Russians Not to Fear Death Amid
Mobilization." *Newsweek*, September 23, 2022, https://www.newsweek.com/russia
-priest-patriarch-kirill-mobilization-putin-death-ukraine-1745616.

Varadarajan, Tunku. "The Patriarch Behind Vladimir Putin." *Wall Street Journal*,
December 29, 2022, https://www.wsj.com/articles/vladimir-putin-the-patriarchs
-altar-boy-kirill-russia-ukraine-war-invasion-theology-orthodox-church-11672
345937.

CHAPTER THIRTEEN

"Critical Issue Poll: American Attitudes on Race, Ethnicity, and Religion." University of
Maryland, May 2016, https://criticalissues.umd.edu/sites/criticalissues.umd.edu
/files/American%20Attitudes%20on%20Race%2CEthnicity%2CReligion.pdf.

Dickinson, Tim. "Caught on Tape: Doug Mastriano Prayed for MAGA to 'Seize the
Power' Ahead of Jan. 6." *Rolling Stone*, September 9, 2022, https://www.rollingstone
.com/politics/politics-features/doug-mastriano-donald-trump-christian-right
-1234589455/.

Notes 459

Folmar, Chloe. "Boebert: Jesus Didn't Have Enough AR-15s to 'Keep His Government from Killing Him.'" *The Hill*, June 17, 2022, https://thehill.com/homenews/house/3528049-boebert-jesus-didnt-have-enough-ar-15s-to-keep-his-government-from-killing-him/.

Hillyard, Vaughn. "How an Obama-Backing Arizona News Anchor Became Trump's Pick for Governor." NBC News, July 21, 2022, https://www.nbcnews.com/politics/2022-election/obama-backing-arizona-news-anchor-became-trumps-pick-governor-rcna38985.

Liston, Broward. "Interview: Missionary work in Iraq." *Time*, April 15, 2003, https://content.time.com/time/world/article/0,8599,443800,00.html.

Meyer, Katie, et al. "Mastriano Campaign Spent Thousands on Buses Ahead of D.C. Insurrection." *WHYY*, January 12, 2021, https://whyy.org/articles/mastriano-campaign-spent-thousands-on-buses-ahead-of-d-c-insurrection/.

Mohler, R. Albert, Jr. "Donald Trump Has Created an Excruciating Moment for Evangelicals." *Washington Post*, October 9, 2016, https://www.washingtonpost.com/news/acts-of-faith/wp/2016/10/09/donald-trump-has-created-an-excruciating-moment-for-evangelicals/.

———. "Briefing 1.13.21." AlbertMohler.com, January 13, 2021, https://albertmohler.com/2021/01/13/briefing-1-13-21.

"National Conservatism: A Statement of Principles." 2022: https://nationalconservatism.org/national-conservatism-a-statement-of-principles/.

Thakker, Prem. "Lauren Boebert Says She Prays That Joe Biden's 'Days Be Few' in Texas Sermon." *New Republic*, February 7, 2023, https://newrepublic.com/post/170439/lauren-boebert-prays-joe-biden-days-few.

Yang, Maya. "Boebert Tells Republican Dinner Guests They're Part of 'Second Coming of Jesus.'" *Guardian*, October 20, 2022, https://www.theguardian.com/us-news/2022/oct/20/lauren-boebert-republican-dinner-jesus-second-coming.

CHAPTER FOURTEEN

"Evangelical: Trump Has Changed, Accepted God." CNN, March 28, 2018, https://www.cnn.com/videos/politics/2018/03/28/stephen-strang-trump-evangelicals-interview-newday.cnn.

Gellman, Barton. "What Happened to Michael Flynn?" *The Atlantic*, July 8, 2022, https://www.theatlantic.com/ideas/archive/2022/07/michael-flynn-conspiracy-theories-january-6-trump/661439/.

Kestenbaum, Sam. "Life After Proclaiming a Trump Re-election as Divinely Ordained." *New York Times*, September 19, 2021, https://www.nytimes.com/2021/09/19/business/trump-election-prophecy-charisma-media.html.

Tercek, Katie, and Jill Lyman. "Owensboro Pastor among Protesters at Capitol Hill." WFIE 14 News, January 7, 2021, https://www.14news.com/2021/01/07/owensboro-pastor-among-protestors-capitol-hill/.

Time Staff. "Influential Evangelicals: Stephen Strang." *Time*, February 7, 2005, https://content.time.com/time/specials/packages/article/0,28804,1993235_1993243_1993319,00.html.

"25 Years Reporting 'What God Is Doing.'" *Sun Sentinel*, August 17, 2000, https://www.sun-sentinel.com/2000/08/17/25-years-reporting-what-god-is-doing/.

CHAPTER FIFTEEN

Helgeson, Baird, and Michelle Bearden. "Donald Trump's Newest Adviser Got Her Start in Tampa." *Tampa Bay Times*, November 3, 2019, https://www.tampabay.com/news/tampa/2019/11/03/donald-trumps-newest-adviser-got-her-start-in-tampa-preaching-the-prosperity-gospel/.

"Loyal Texas Trump Voters Want Biden to Be Less Divisive." CNN, January 23, 2021, https://www.cnn.com/videos/politics/2021/01/23/texas-trump-voters-joe-biden -presidency-unify-tuchman-pkg-ac360-vpx.cnn.

CHAPTER SIXTEEN

"Ahead of Anniversary of 1/6 Insurrection, Republicans Remain Entangled in the Big Lie, QAnon, and Temptations toward Political Violence." PRRI, January 4, 2021, https://www.prri.org/spotlight/anniversary-of-jan-6-insurrection/.

"Americans Feel More Positive Than Negative About Jews, Mainline Protestants, Catholics." Pew Research Center, March 15, 2023, https://www.pewresearch.org /religion/2023/03/15/americans-feel-more-positive-than-negative-about-jews -mainline-protestants-catholics/.

"Born-Alive Amendment Fails Again in the Senate." *National Catholic Register*, February 5, 2021, https://www.ncregister.com/cna/born-alive-amendment-fails -again-in-the-senate.

Brenan, Megan. "Dissatisfaction with Abortion Policy Hits High." Gallup, February 10, 2023, https://news.gallup.com/poll/470279/dissatisfaction-abortion-policy-hits -high.aspx.

Choi, Annette. "Children and teens are more likely to die by guns than anything else." CNN, March 29, 2023, https://www.cnn.com/2023/03/29/health/us-children-gun- deaths-dg/index.html.

Drucker, David M. "Walker Likens Warnock to Satan in contentious Georgia Senate Race." *Washington Examiner*, November 6, 2022, https://www.washingtonexaminer .com/news/campaigns/walker-likens-warnock-satan-georgia-race-senate-majority.

Edsall, Thomas B. "Reed Attacks Clinton on Family Faith." *Washington Post*, September 14, 1996, https://www.washingtonpost.com/archive/politics/1996/09/14 /reed-attacks-clinton-on-family-faith/60475bc2-49de-4918-b506-bb123ec3a17d/.

Fowler, Stephen. "Second Woman Says GA Republican Senate Candidate Herschel Walker Paid for Abortion." NPR, October 26, 2022, https://www.npr.org /2022/10/26/1131751304/second-woman-says-ga-republican-senate-candidate -herschel-walker-paid-for-aborti.

"Georgia Senate—Exit Polls." CNN, November 2022, https://www.cnn.com/election /2022/exit-polls/georgia/senate/0.

Goodstein, Laurie. "The Testing of a President: Conservatives' Christian Coalition Moans Lack of Anger at Clinton." *New York Times*, September 20, 1998, https:// www.nytimes.com/1998/09/20/us/testing-president-conservatives-christian -coalition-moans-lack-anger-clinton.html.

Kaylor, Brian. "Baptist Megachurch Pastor Leads Prayer Event for Herschel Walker after Abortion Allegation." *Word and Way*, October 4, 2022, https://wordandway .org/2022/10/04/baptist-megachurch-pastor-leads-prayer-event-for-herschel -walker-after-abortion-allegation/.

Kerr, Andrew. "Warnock's Church Drops Eviction Case against Vietnam War Vet following Free Beacon Report." *Washington Free Beacon*, November 28, 2022, https://freebeacon.com/democrats/warnocks-church-drops-eviction-case-against -vietnam-war-vet-following-free-beacon-report/.

Kertscher, Tom. "Fact-Checking Herschel Walker Attack Ad about Raphael Warnock." *PolitiFact*, September 8, 2022, https://www.politifact.com/article/2022/sep/08/fact -checking-herschel-walker-attack-ad-about-raph/.

King, Maya. "Herschel Walker Acknowledges Two More Children He Hadn't Mentioned." *New York Times*, June 16, 2022, https://www.nytimes.com/2022 /06/16/us/politics/herschel-walker-children.html.

Mitchell, Alison, and Eric Schmitt. "G.O.P. Scramble Over Blame for Poor Showing in

Polls." *New York Times,* November 5, 1998, https://www.nytimes.com/1998/11/05 /us/1998-elections-congress-overview-gop-scramble-over-blame-for-poor -showing-polls.html.

"Presidential Approval Ratings—Bill Clinton." Gallup, n.d., https://news.gallup.com /poll/116584/presidential-approval-ratings-bill-clinton.aspx.

"Religious Identities and the Race Against the Virus: Successes and Opportunities for Engaging Faith Communities on COVID-19 Vaccination." PRRI, July 28, 2021, https://www.prri.org/research/religious-vaccines-covid-vaccination

"Republicans Turn More Negative Toward Refugees as Number Admitted to U.S. Plummets." Pew Research Center, May 24, 2018, https://www.pewresearch.org /short-reads/2018/05/24/republicans-turn-more-negative-toward-refugees-as -number-admitted-to-u-s-plummets/.

Saad, Lydia. "Broader Support for Abortion Rights Continues Post-Dobbs." Gallup, June 14, 2023, https://news.gallup.com/poll/506759/broader-support-abortion -rights-continues-post-dobbs.aspx.

Shepherd, Brittany. "Christian Walker Says Father Herschel Walker's Campaign 'Has Been a Lie.'" ABC News, October 4, 2022, https://abcnews.go.com/Politics /christian-walker-father-herschel-walkers-campaign-lie/story?id=90973801.

Sollenberger, Roger. "Herschel Walker, Critic of Absentee Dads, Admits to Yet Another Secret Son." *Daily Beast,* June 16, 2022, https://www.thedailybeast.com/herschel -walker-critic-of-absentee-dads-admits-to-yet-another-secret-son.

——. "Pro-Life Herschel Walker Paid for Girlfriend's Abortion." *Daily Beast,* October 3, 2022, https://www.thedailybeast.com/pro-life-herschel-walker-paid-for- girlfriends-abortion-georgia-senate.

——. "She Had an Abortion with Herschel Walker. She Also Had a Child with Him." *Daily Beast,* October 5, 2022, https://www.thedailybeast.com/she-had-an-abortion -with-herschel-walker-she-also-had-a-child-with-him.

Stern, Ray. "Kari Lake 'Excited' over Election Trial but Katie Hobbs Won't Have to Testify." *Arizona Republic,* December 20, 2022, https://www.azcentral.com/story /news/politics/elections/2022/12/20/katie-hobbs-wont-have-to-testify-in-kari -lake-election-trial/69744675007/.

Wagner, John. "Walker Concedes Giving Check to Ex-Partner, Denies Knowing It Was for Abortion." *Washington Post,* October 17, 2022, https://www.washingtonpost .com/politics/2022/10/17/walker-georgia-senate-abortion/.

CHAPTER SEVENTEEN

Baily, Sarah Pulliam. "Is Eric Metaxas the Next Chuck Colson?" Religion News Service, July 29, 2013, https://religionnews.com/2013/07/29/is-eric-metaxas-the-next -chuck-colson/.

Barnett, Victoria J. "Review of Eric Metaxas, 'Bonhoeffer: Pastor, Martyr, Prophet, Spy; A Righteous Gentile vs. the Third Reich.'" *ACCH Quarterly* 15, no. 3 (September 2010), https://contemporarychurchhistory.org/2010/09/review-of-eric-metaxas -bonhoeffer-pastor-martyr-prophet-spy-a-righteous-gentile-vs-the-third-reich/.

Bland, Karina. "A Pastor's Survival Story Is Also a COVID-19 Controversy. Should We Look Again, or Look Away?" *Arizona Republic,* January 2, 2021, https://www .azcentral.com/story/news/local/karinabland/2021/01/02/pastor-luke-barnett -survival-story-also-covid-19-controversy/4096027001/.

Bump, Philip. "The Inevitable, Grotesque Effort to Blame Vaccines for Damar Hamlin's Collapse." *Washington Post,* January 3, 2023, https://www.washingtonpost.com /politics/2023/01/03/damar-hamlin-charlie-kirk-vaccines-coronavirus/.

Cox, Ashley. "DeSantis Points to Looming Culture Wars with Florida 'on the Front Lines in the Battle for Freedom.'" CBS News, March 7, 2023, https://www.cbsnews

.com/tampa/news/desantis-points-to-looming-culture-wars-with-florida-on-the
-front-lines-in-the-battle-for-freedom/.

Fea, John. "Eric Metaxas Believes Rick Warren, Tim Keller, and Andy Stanley Are
'Hitler's Favorite Kind of Pastors.'" *Current*, October 31, 2022, https://currentpub
.com/2022/10/31/eric-metaxas-believes-rick-warren-tim-keller-and-andy-stanley
-are-hitlers-favorite-kind-of-pastors/.

Glader, Paul. "Exclusive: Author Eric Metaxas Admits Punching Protestor in DC and
Offers More Context." *Religion Unplugged*, September 3, 2020, https://religion
unplugged.com/news/2020/9/3/exclusive-author-eric-metaxas-admits-punching
-protestor-in-dc-and-offers-more-context.

Green, Emma. "Eric Metaxas Believes America Is Creeping Toward Nazi Germany." *The
Atlantic*, February 14, 2021, https://www.theatlantic.com/politics/archive/2021/02
/eric-metaxas-2020-election-trump/617999/.

Kitchener, Caroline, et al. "Trump Would Act 'like a Little Elementary Schoolchild,'
Former Spiritual Adviser Says." *Washington Post*, November 17, 2022, https://www
.washingtonpost.com/politics/2022/11/17/trump-spiritual-adviser-criticism
-child/.

Looper, Joel. "Bonhoeffer Co-Opted." *Los Angeles Review of Books*, September 10, 2014,
https://lareviewofbooks.org/article/bonhoeffer-co-opted/.

Olson, Emily. "How (and Why) Gov. Ron Desantis Took Control over Disney World's
Special District." NPR, February 28, 2023, https://www.npr.org/2023/02/28
/1160018771/disney-world-desantis-special-district.

Orr, Gabby, et al. "Former President Donald Trump Announces a White House Bid for
2024." CNN, November 16, 2022, https://www.cnn.com/2022/11/15/politics/trump
-2024-presidential-bid/index.html.

Piper, Everett. "It's Time for the GOP to Say It: Donald Trump Is Hurting Our Party."
Washington Times, November 13, 2022, https://www.washingtontimes.com/news
/2022/nov/13/its-time-for-gop-to-say-it-donald-trump-is-hurting/.

Ruelas, Richard, and BrieAnna J. Frank. "Inside One of Charlie Kirk's Freedom Night
in America Events at Dream City Church." *Arizona Republic*, June 2, 2022, https://
www.azcentral.com/in-depth/news/politics/arizona/2022/06/02/charlie-kirk
-freedom-night-america-dream-city-church/7434768001/.

Shimron, Yonat. "Evangelical Influencers Criticize Candidate Trump." *Baptist
Standard*/Religion News Service, December 1, 2022, https://www.baptiststandard
.com/news/nation/evangelical-influencers-criticize-candidate-trump/.

Smietana, Bob. "Eric Metaxas, Christian Radio Host, Tells Trump, 'Jesus Is with Us in
This Fight.'" Religion News Service, November 30, 2020, https://religionnews
.com/2020/11/30/eric-metaxas-christian-radio-host-offers-to-lay-down-his-life
-for-trump-election-triumph/.

———. "How Eric Metaxas Went from Trump Despiser to True Believer." Religion
News Service, December 3, 2020, https://religionnews.com/2020/12/03
/metaxas-jesus-trump-stolen-election-christian-nationalism-rod-dreher-sidney
-powell/.

Ward, Jon. "Author Eric Metaxas: Evangelical Intellectual Who Chose Trump, and He's
Sticking With Him." Yahoo! News, February 23, 2018, https://www.yahoo.com/news
/author-eric-metaxas-evangelical-intellectual-chose-trump-hes-sticking-10001
2875.html.

Wehner, Peter. "Are Trump's Critics Demonically Possessed?" *The Atlantic*,
November 25, 2019, https://www.theatlantic.com/ideas/archive/2019/11/to-trumps
-evangelicals-everyone-else-is-a-sinner/602569/.

———. "The Gospel of Donald Trump Jr." *The Atlantic*, December 26, 2021, https://www
.theatlantic.com/ideas/archive/2021/12/gospel-donald-trump-jr/621122/.

CHAPTER EIGHTEEN

Bailey, Sarah Pulliam, and Michelle Boorstein. "Russell Moore's Departure from the Southern Baptist Convention's Leadership Prompts Questions over Its Future." *Washington Post*, May 19, 2021, https://www.washingtonpost.com/religion /2021/05/19/russell-moore-leaves-southern-baptist-convention-evangelical -future/.

Chang, Curtis. "I'm a Former Pastor, and I Don't Believe in 'Religious Exemptions' to Vaccine Mandates." *New York Times*, September 6, 2021, https://www.nytimes .com/2021/09/06/opinion/religious-exemptions-vaccine-mandates.html.

Chang, Curtis, and Kris Carter. "Our Fellow Evangelicals Need to Get Vaccinated." *New York Times*, May 14, 2021, https://www.nytimes.com/2021/05/14/opinion/evangel ical-christians-vaccine.html.

Dalrymple, Timothy. "Christianity Today Names Russell Moore Editor in Chief." *Christianity Today*, August 4, 2022, https://www.christianitytoday.com/ct/2022 /august-web-only/russell-moore-editor-chief-christianity-today-joy-allmond .html.

French, David. "The Price I've Paid for Opposing Donald Trump." *National Review*, October 21, 2016, https://www.nationalreview.com/2016/10/donald-trump-alt -right-internet-abuse-never-trump-movement/.

Guzman, Andrea. "This Former Pastor Is Changing Evangelicals' Minds on Covid Vaccines." *Mother Jones*, August 17, 2021, https://www.motherjones.com /politics/2021/08/this-former-pastor-is-changing-evangelicals-minds-on-covid -vaccines/.

Moore, Russell. "This Is the Southern Baptist Apocalypse." *Christianity Today*, May 22, 2022, https://www.christianitytoday.com/ct/2022/may-web-only/southern -baptist-abuse-apocalypse-russell-moore.html.

Ramirez, Nikki McCann. "Tucker Carlson on Trump: 'I Hate Him Passionately.'" *Rolling Stone*, March 7, 2023, https://www.rollingstone.com/politics/politics-news /tucker-carlson-trump-hate-him-passionately-dominion-lawsuit-1234692527/.

"Russell Moore to Join Christianity Today to Lead New Public Theology Project." *Christianity Today*, May 18, 2021, https://www.christianitytoday.com/ct/2021/may -web-only/russell-moore-to-join-christianity-today.html.

Shimron, Yonat. "A Q&A with Evangelical Writer David French on Christian Nationalism." *Washington Post*, February 5, 2021, https://www.washingtonpost .com/religion/david-french-christian-nationalism/2021/02/05/734865a8-6723 -11eb-8c64-9595888caa15_story.html.

Smietana, Bob. "NRB Spokesman Dan Darling Fired after Pro-Vaccine Statements on 'Morning Joe.'" Religion News Service, August 27, 2021, https://religionnews .com/2021/08/27/nrb-spokesman-dan-darling-fired-after-pro-vaccine-statements -on-morning-joe-evangelical-covid-hesitancy/.

CHAPTER NINETEEN

Bharath, Deepa, and Peter Smith. "Saddleback Church Doubles Down on Support for Female Pastors." Associated Press, March 1, 2023, https://apnews.com/article/southern -baptists-saddleback-church-women-pastors-7b2bf53ddb413809b9ca18d87b630fd7.

Burgess, Katherine, and Liam Adams. "Southern Baptists Reelect Bart Barber as President in Win for Mainstream Conservatives." *Tennessean*, June 13, 2023, https://www.tennessean.com/story/news/religion/2023/06/13/southern -baptists-reelect-texas-pastor-bart-barber-president-of-the-southern-baptist -convention/70290892007/.

Downen, Robert. "Houston GOP Activist Knew for Years of Child Sex Abuse Claims against Southern Baptist Leader, Law Partner." *Texas Tribune*, March 27, 2023,

https://www.texastribune.org/2023/03/27/houston-jared-woodfill-gop-paul
-pressler-southern-baptist.

———. "Southern Baptist Group Hosts Right-Wing Leader Charlie Kirk, Decries Crt
Ahead of Sex Abuse Meeting." *Houston Chronicle*, June 14, 2022, https://www
.houstonchronicle.com/news/houston-texas/religion/article/Southern-Baptist
-group-hosts-right-wing-leader-17240960.php.

———. "Texas Supreme Court Rules against Southern Baptist Leader Accused of Rape, a
Win for Survivors." *Houston Chronicle*, April 12, 2022, https://www.houston
chronicle.com/news/houston-texas/houston/article/Texas-Supreme-Court
-rules-against-Southern-17076007.php.

Downen, Robert, and John Tedesco. "'The Hunter Is Now the Hunted': Southern Baptist
Persecution of Sexual Abuse Survivors Has Been Relentless." *Houston Chronicle*,
June 15, 2022, https://www.houstonchronicle.com/news/investigations/article
/The-hunter-is-now-the-hunted-Southern-17244550.php.

Foust, Michael. "25 Years Ago, Conservative Resurgence Got Its Start." *Baptist Press*,
June 15, 2004, https://www.baptistpress.com/resource-library/news/25-years-ago
-conservative-resurgence-got-its-start/.

Meyer, Holly, et al. "Tuesday Updates: Southern Baptists Elect Alabama Pastor Ed
Litton as New SBC President." *Tennessean*, June 15, 2021, https://www.tennessean
.com/story/news/religion/2021/06/15/southern-baptist-convention-updates
-nashville-2021-new-leader-vote/7637494002/.

O'Donnell, Paul, and Bob Smietana. "Leaked Russell Moore letter blasts SBC
conservatives, sheds light on his resignation." Religion News Service, June 2, 2021,
https://religionnews.com/2021/06/02/leaked-russell-moore-letter-blasts-sbc
-conservatives-sheds-light-on-his-resignation/.

Roach, David. "ARITF Granted Additional Year to Fight Sexual Abuse." *Baptist Press*,
June 14, 2023, https://www.baptistpress.com/resource-library/news/aritf-granted
-additional-year-to-fight-sexual-abuse/.

Schroeder, George. "Litton Names Task Force to Oversee Sex Abuse Review." *Baptist
Standard*, July 9, 2021, https://www.baptiststandard.com/news/baptists/litton
-names-task-force-to-oversee-sex-abuse-review/.

Smietana, Bob. "Mike Stone Sues Russell Moore, Saying Moore Cost Him SBC
Presidency." *Washington Post*, October 29, 2021, https://www.washingtonpost.com
/religion/2021/10/29/mike-stone-lawsuit-russell-moore/.

———. "SBC President Ed Litton Won't Run Again, Saying He Will Instead Focus on
Racial Reconciliation." *Washington Post*, March 4, 2022, https://www.washington
post.com/religion/2022/03/04/southern-baptist-litton/.

———. "Southern Baptists to Hire Guidepost Solutions to Run Abuser Database."
Washington Post, February 22, 2023, https://www.washingtonpost.com/religion
/2023/02/22/southern-baptists-sexual-abuse-database-guidepost/.

———. "Tom Ascol, Would-Be SBC President, Worries Churches Have Lost Hold of the
Bible." Religion News Service, June 10, 2022, https://religionnews.com/2022/06/10
/tom-ascol-would-sbc-president-worries-churches-have-lost-hold-of-the-bible/.

Wingfield, Mark. "New Court Documents Show First Baptist Houston Leaders Knew of
Allegations against Pressler in 2004." *Baptist News Global*, March 28, 2023, https://
baptistnews.com/article/new-court-documents-show-first-baptist-houston-leaders
-knew-of-allegations-against-pressler-in-2004/.

———. "SBC Task Force Says Ministry Check Website for Sexual Abuse Will Require
Cooperation." *Baptist News Global*, February 28, 2023, https://baptistnews.com
/article/sbc-task-force-says-ministry-check-website-for-sexual-abuse-will
-require-cooperation/.

CHAPTER TWENTY

Adams, Liam. "'Ignored, Disbelieved': Southern Baptist Convention Sexual Abuse Report Details Cover Up, Decades of Inaction." *Courier-Journal*, May 22, 2022, https://www.courier-journal.com/story/news/nation/2022/05/22/southern -baptist-convention-sexual-abuse-report-victims/9886656002/.

Associated Press. "Southern Baptists Boot Saddleback Church for Having a Female Pastor." NBC News, February 21, 2023, https://www.nbcnews.com/news/us-news /southern-baptists-boot-saddleback-church-woman-pastor-rcna71714.

"Book: What Is a Girl Worth?" NPR, September 15, 2019, https://www.npr.org/2019 /09/15/761046403/book-what-is-a-girl-worth.

Burgess, Katherine. "'Our Family Is Sick': Abuse Survivors Call on Southern Baptists to Move beyond Words to Action." *Commercial Appeal*, June 10, 2019, https://www .commercialappeal.com/story/news/2019/06/10/southern-baptist-convention -beth-moore-rachael-denhollander-russell-moore-susan-codone-sexual-abuse /1414911001/.

Denhollander, Rachael. "Rachael Denhollander: The Price I Paid for Taking On Larry Nassar." *New York Times*, January 26, 2018, https://www.nytimes.com/2018/01/26 /opinion/sunday/larry-nassar-rachael-denhollander.html.

Devine, Daniel James. "Not Bluffing." *World News Group*, October 18, 2013, https://wng .org/articles/not-bluffing-1620624477.

Evans, Tim, et al. "Former USA Gymnastics Doctor Accused of Abuse." *IndyStar*, September 12, 2016, https://www.indystar.com/story/news/2016/09/12/former -usa-gymnastics-doctor-accused-abuse/89995734/.

Guidepost Solutions. "Report: The Southern Baptist Convention Executive Committee's Response to Sexual Abuse Allegations and an Audit of the Procedures and Actions of the Credentials Committee," May 15, 2022, https://static1.square space.com/static/6108172d83d55d3c9db4dd67/t/628a9326312a4216a3c0679d /1653248810253/Guidepost+Solutions+Independent+Investigation+Report.pdf.

Jenkins, Jack. "At Caring Well Conference, SBC Leaders Hear Criticism of Abuse Response." Religion News Service, October 5, 2019, https://religionnews.com /2019/10/05/at-caring-well-conference-sbc-leaders-hear-criticism-of-abuse -response/.

Kwiatkowski, Marisa, et al. "A Blind Eye to Sex Abuse: How USA Gymnastics Failed to Report Cases." *IndyStar*, June 24, 2020, https://www.indystar.com/story/news /investigations/2016/08/04/usa-gymnastics-sex-abuse-protected-coaches /85829732/.

Mack, Julie. "Rachael Denhollander, Nassar's First Public Accuser: 'You Chose to Pursue Wickedness.'" *MLive*, January 24, 2018, https://www.mlive.com/news /2018/01/nassar_rachael_denhollander.html.

Parke, Caleb. "Ravi Zacharias Tributes Pour in from Pence, Christian Leaders." Fox News, May 20, 2020, https://www.foxnews.com/faith-values/ravi-zacharias-passed -away-christian-tribute.

Roys, Julie. "John MacArthur Covered Up Pastor's Sexual Abuse, Witnesses Say." *Roys Report*, April 19, 2022, https://julieroys.com/john-macarthur-covered-up-pastor -sexual-abuse-witnesses-say/.

——. "John MacArthur's Church Supported Convicted Abuser and Pedophile." *Roys Report*, March 17, 2022, https://julieroys.com/john-macarthur-church-supported -convicted-abuser-pedophile/.

——. "John MacArthur Shamed, Excommunicated Mother for Refusing to Take Back Child Abuser." *Roys Report*, March 8, 2022, https://julieroys.com/macarthur -shamed-excommunicated-mother-take-back-child-abuser/.

———. "John MacArthur Warned Moody Years Ago about James MacDonald, Emails Reveal." *Roys Report*, February 20, 2020, https://julieroys.com/john-macarthur-warned-moody-years-ago-about-james-macdonald-emails-reveal/.

———. "Why I Blew the Whistle on Moody." *Roys Report*, March 21, 2018, https://julieroys.com/blew-whistle-moody/.

Sells, Heather. "Rachael Denhollander: Predators Are Always Watching—Here's What to Do." CBN News, October 7, 2019, https://www2.cbn.com/news/us/rachael-denhollander-predators-are-always-watching-heres-what-do.

Shellnut, Kate. "Moody Bible President and COO Both Resign, Provost Retires." *Christianity Today*, January 10, 2018, https://www.christianitytoday.com/news/2018/january/moody-bible-president-paul-nyquist-resigns-julie-roys-fired.html.

Shellnut, Kate, and Sarah Eekhoff Zylstra. "Ravi Zacharias Responds to Sexting Allegations, Credentials Critique." *Christianity Today*, December 3, 2017, https://www.christianitytoday.com/news/2017/december/ravi-zacharias-sexting-extortion-lawsuit-doctorate-bio-rzim.html.

Showalter, Brandon. "Moody Bible Fires Radio Host Julie Roys; Tension Builds Amid Faculty Cuts, 'Self-Dealing' Allegations." *Christian Post*, January 9, 2018, https://www.christianpost.com/news/moody-bible-fires-radio-host-julie-roys-tension-builds-amid-faculty-cuts-self-dealing-allegations.html.

Silliman, Daniel. "Ravi Zacharias's Ministry Investigates Claims of Sexual Misconduct at Spas." *Christianity Today*, September 29, 2020, https://www.christianitytoday.com/news/2020/september/ravi-zacharias-sexual-harassment-rzim-spa-massage-investiga.html.

———. "RZIM Spent Nearly $1M Suing Ravi Zacharias Abuse Victim." *Christianity Today*, February 23, 2022, https://www.christianitytoday.com/news/2022/february/rzim-board-donor-money-guidepost-report-ravi.html.

Silliman, Daniel, and Kate Shellnut. "Ravi Zacharias Hid Hundreds of Pictures of Women, Abuse During Massages, and a Rape Allegation." *Christianity Today*, February 11, 2021, https://www.christianitytoday.com/news/2021/february/ravi-zacharias-rzim-investigation-sexual-abuse-sexting-rape.html.

Smietana, Bob. "Class-Action Lawsuit Claims RZIM Misled Donors, Covered Up Ravi Zacharias Abuse." Religion News Service, August 5, 2021, https://religionnews.com/2021/08/05/class-action-lawsuit-claims-rzim-misled-donors-covered-up-ravi-zacharias-abuse/.

Smietana, Bob, and Emily McFarlan Miller. "James MacDonald Fired as Harvest Bible Chapel Pastor." Religion News Service, February 13, 2019, https://religionnews.com/2019/02/13/james-macdonald-fired-as-pastor-harvest-bible-chapel-by-church-elders/.

Sun, Eryn. "TD Jakes Linked to James MacDonald's Resignation from Gospel Coalition." *Christian Post*, January 25, 2012, https://www.christianpost.com/news/t-d-jakes-connection-to-james-macdonalds-resignation-from-the-gospel-coalition.html.

Wolfson, Andrew. "Report: Southern Baptist Executive Smeared Louisville Victim Advocate in 'Satanic Scheme.'" *Courier-Journal*, May 24, 2022, https://www.courier-journal.com/story/news/2022/05/24/southern-baptist-lawyer-accused-kentucky-victim-advocate-satanic-scheme/9897196002/.

CHAPTER TWENTY-ONE

Ambrosino, Brandon. "'Someone's Gotta Tell the Freakin' Truth': Jerry Falwell's Aides Break Their Silence." *Politico*, September 9, 2019, https://www.politico.com/magazine/story/2019/09/09/jerry-falwell-liberty-university-loans-227914/.

Anne, Ashley. "Miss Virginia Pageant to Nix Swimsuit Competition Next Year." WDBJ7,

June 18, 2018, https://www.wdbj7.com/content/news/Miss-Virginia-pageant-to
-nix-swimsuit-competition-next-year-485867811.html.

Bromwich, Jonah E., et al. "From President to Defendant: Trump Pleads Not
Guilty to 34 Felonies." *New York Times*, April 4, 2023, https://www.nytimes.
com/2023/04/04/nyregion/trump-arraignment-felony-charges.html.

Bumbaca, Chris. "Liberty Basketball Player Asia Todd Transfers Due to 'Racial
Insensitivity' from Leadership." *USA Today*, June 11, 2020, https://www.usatoday
.com/story/sports/ncaaw/2020/06/11/liberty-university-basketball-asia-todd
-transfers-racial-insensitivity-jerry-falwell/5342672002/.

Gleeson, Scott. "Two Liberty Football Players to Transfer, Citing 'Racial Insensitivity'
and 'Cultural' Incompetence." *USA Today*, June 22, 2020, https://www.usatoday
.com/story/sports/ncaaf/2020/06/22/liberty-football-players-tayvion-land-and
-tre-clark-transfer/3236318001/.

Ortiz, Erik. "Jerry Falwell Jr. Resigns as Liberty University President after Accusations
That He Participated in a Partner's Affair with His Wife." NBC News, August 24,
2020, https://www.nbcnews.com/news/us-news/jerry-falwell-jr-resigns-president
-liberty-university-reports-say-n1237886.

Rankin, Sarah. "Liberty Sues Jerry Falwell Jr., Seeking Millions in Damages."
Associated Press, April 16, 2021, https://apnews.com/article/jerry-falwell-lawsuits
-virginia-lynchburg-3b9c8e0c3bf525c79fbd54dc95889c86.

Seltzer, Rick. "Cuts at Liberty Hit Divinity." *Inside Higher Ed*, June 16, 2019, https://
www.insidehighered.com/news/2019/06/17/liberty-university-cuts-divinity
-faculty.

Severns, Maggie, et al. "'They All Got Careless': How Falwell Kept His Grip on Liberty
Amid Sexual 'Games,' Self-Dealing." *Politico*, November 1, 2020, https://www
.politico.com/news/magazine/2020/11/01/jerry-falwell-liberty-university-becki
-self-dealing-sex-430207.

Shellnut, Kate. "As Students Rally for Victims, Liberty Board Approves Title IX
Review." *Christianity Today*, November 5, 2021, https://www.christianitytoday.com
/news/2021/november/liberty-university-rally-justice-for-janes-abuse-victims
.html.

———. "John Piper's Liberty Convocation Pulled After Election Post." *Christianity Today*,
November 3, 2020, https://www.christianitytoday.com/news/2020/november/john
-piper-liberty-university-convocation-election-trump-jd.html.

Smietana, Bob. "David Sills, Former Seminary Professor Named in Guidepost Report,
Sues SBC." *Washington Post*, May 15, 2023, https://www.washingtonpost.com
/religion/2023/05/15/david-sills-former-seminary-professor-named-guidepost
-report-sues-sbc/.

———. "Former Southern Seminary Prof Sues SBC Leaders for Labeling Him an Abuser."
Christianity Today, November 29, 2022, https://www.christianitytoday.com/news
/2022/november/sbts-david-sills-sue-sbc-guidepost-abuse-investigation.html.

Stratford, Michael, and Brandon Ambrosino. "Liberty U President Says on Tape That
'Getting People Elected' Is His Goal." *Politico*, October 27, 2021, https://www
.politico.com/news/2021/10/27/liberty-university-jerry-prevo-influence-517303.

Young, Will E. "Inside Liberty University's 'Culture of Fear.'" *Washington Post*, July 24,
2019, https://www.washingtonpost.com/outlook/2019/07/24/inside-liberty
-universitys-culture-fear-how-jerry-falwell-jr-silences-students-professors-who
-reject-his-pro-trump-politics/.

EPILOGUE

"A Christian Nation? Understanding the Threat of Christian Nationalism to American
Democracy and Culture." PRRI, February 2023, https://www.prri.org/research/a

-christian-nation-understanding-the-threat-of-christian-nationalism-to-american
-democracy-and-culture/.

"April Omnibus 2023." Echelon Insights, April 2023, https://echelonin.wpengine
powered.com/wp-content/uploads/April-2023-Omnibus-Crosstabs-EXTERNAL
.pdf.

Belz, Emily. "Presbyterian Church in America Leaves National Association of
Evangelicals." *Christianity Today*, June 23, 2022, https://www.christianitytoday
.com/news/2022/june/presbyterian-church-leaves-nae.html.

Burge, Ryan [@ryanburge]. "Big data in the religion data world . . .", May 17, 2023,
https://twitter.com/ryanburge/status/1658896455417962498.

"Competing Visions of America: An Evolving Identity or a Culture Under Attack?"
PRRI, November 1, 2021, https://www.prri.org/research/competing-visions-of
-america-an-evolving-identity-or-a-culture-under-attack/.

"Dismissing Trump's E. Jean Carroll Verdict Has 'Devastating Implications,' Says
Russell Moore." *Meet the Press*, May 14, 2023, https://www.nbc.com/meet
-the-press/video/dismissing-trumps-e-jean-carroll-verdict-has-devastating
-implications-says-russell-moore/NBCN334021739.

Downen, Robert. "Bill Requiring Ten Commandments in Texas Classrooms Fails in
House after Missing Crucial Deadline." *Texas Tribune*, May 24, 2023, https://www
.texastribune.org/2023/05/24/texas-legislature-ten-commandments-bill/.

———. "Conservative Christians Want More Religion in Public Life. Texas Lawmakers
Are Listening." *Texas Tribune*, May 4, 2023, https://www.texastribune.org/2023
/05/04/texas-legislature-church-state-separation/.

———. "Texas House Expels Bryan Slaton, First Member Ousted since 1927." *Texas
Tribune*, May 9, 2023, https://www.texastribune.org/2023/05/09/bryan-slaton
-expel-house-vote/.

Earls, Aaron. "Fear Prevalent in Pews, According to Protestant Pastors." *Lifeway
Research*, August 8, 2023, https://research.lifeway.com/2023/08/08/fear-prevalent
-in-pews-according-to-protestant-pastors/.

Gage, Brandon. "'Mafia Behavior': Mike Huckabee Skewered for Demanding Loyalty to
Trump." *Raw Story*, March 27, 2023, https://www.rawstory.com/mafia-behavior
-mike-huckabee-skewered-for-demanding-loyalty-to-trump/.

Jenkins, Jack. "Josh Hawley Tweets Fake Quote about U.S. Founding, Sparking
Allegations of Christian Nationalism." Religion News Service, July 6, 2023, https://
religionnews-com.webpkgcache.com/doc/-/s/religionnews.com/2023/07/06
/josh-hawley-tweets-fake-quote-about-u-s-founding-doubles-down-on-christian
-nationalism/.

———. "Survey: White Mainline Protestants Outnumber White Evangelicals, While
'Nones' Shrink." Religion News Service, July 8, 2021, https://religionnews.com
/2021/07/08/survey-white-mainline-protestants-outnumber-white-evangelicals/.

Jones, Jeffrey M. "Belief in God in U.S. Dips to 81%, a New Low." Gallup, June 17, 2022,
https://news.gallup.com/poll/393737/belief-god-dips-new-low.aspx.

"Modeling the Future of Religion in America." Pew Research Center, September 13,
2022, https://www.pewresearch.org/religion/2022/09/13/modeling-the-future-of
-religion-in-america/.

"National: DeSantis, Trump are Main Focus of GOP Voters for 2024." Monmouth
University Poll, February 9, 2023, https://monmouth.edu/polling-institute
/documents/monmouthpoll_us_020923.pdf/.

Roach, David. "1 in 4 Pastors Plan to Retire before 2030." *Christianity Today*, April 28,
2023, https://www.christianitytoday.com/news/2023/april/pastor-succession
-church-next-generation-leader-barna-surve.html.

Smith, Gregory A. "About Three-in-Ten U.S. Adults Are Now Religiously Unaffiliated."

Pew Research Center, December 14, 2021, https://www.pewresearch.org
/religion/2021/12/14/about-three-in-ten-u-s-adults-are-now-religiously
-unaffiliated/.

Tevington, Patricia. "Americans Feel More Positive than Negative about Jews,
Mainline Protestants, Catholics." Pew Research Center, March 15, 2023, https://
www.pewresearch.org/religion/2023/03/15/americans-feel-more-positive-than
-negative-about-jews-mainline-protestants-catholics/.

"Texas Representative Bryan Slaton." TrackBill, https://trackbill.com/legislator/texas
-representative-bryan-slaton/760-20517/.

INDEX

ABOUT THE AUTHOR

TIM ALBERTA is a staff writer for *The Atlantic* and the former chief political correspondent for *Politico*, and has written for dozens of other publications, including the *Wall Street Journal, Sports Illustrated,* and *Vanity Fair.* He is the author of the *New York Times* bestseller *American Carnage: On the Front Lines of the Republican Civil War and the Rise of President Trump.* He co-moderated the final Democratic presidential debate of 2019 and frequently appears as a commentator on television programs in the United States and around the world. He lives in Michigan with his wife and three sons.